THE LION FROM THE NORTH

Volume 2 – The Swedish Army during the
Thirty Years War, 1632-48

Michael Fredholm von Essen

'This is the Century of the Soldier', Fulvio Testi, Poet, 1641

Helion & Company

Helion & Company Limited
Unit 8 Amherst Business Centre
Budbrooke Road
Warwick
CV34 5WE
England
Tel. 01926 499 619
Email: info@helion.co.uk
Website: www.helion.co.uk
Twitter: @helionbooks
blog.helion.co.uk

Published by Helion & Company 2020
Designed and typeset by Mach 3 Solutions Ltd (www.mach3solutions.co.uk)
Cover designed by Paul Hewitt, Battlefield Design (www.battlefield-design.co.uk)

Text © Michael Fredholm von Essen 2020
Illustrations © as individually credited
Colour artwork by Sergey Shamenkov © Helion & Company 2020
Maps drawn by Alan Turton © Helion & Company 2020

Every reasonable effort has been made to trace copyright holders and to obtain their
permission for the use of copyright material. The author and publisher apologize for
any errors or omissions in this work and would be grateful if notified of any corrections
that should be incorporated in future reprints or editions of this book.

ISBN 978-1-913118-83-9

British Library Cataloguing-in-Publication Data.
A catalogue record for this book is available from the British Library.

For details of other military history titles published by Helion & Company Limited
contact the above address or visit our website: http://www.helion.co.uk.

We always welcome receiving book proposals from prospective authors.

Contents

Chronology

All dates are N.S. *Significant world events with a major impact upon Sweden but no Swedish involvement are marked in italics.*

1632   16 Nov.   Battle of Lützen, death of Gustavus Adolphus; Bernard of Saxe-Weimar and Dodo von Innhausen und zu Knyphausen save the Swedish main field army; Imperial commander-in-chief Albrecht von Wallenstein retreats to Bohemia; Christina succeeds as Queen of Sweden

1633   6 Jan.   Bernard and Knyphausen take Zwickau, which concludes the removal of Imperial troops from Saxony

21 Jan.   Axel Oxenstierna formally appointed the senior representative of the Swedish Crown in Germany and commander-in-chief of the Swedish armies there

14 Mar.   A joint Hessian–Swedish army under Peter Melander von Holzapfel and Lars Kagg lays siege to Hameln

18 Mar.   Oxenstierna opens a meeting at Heilbronn, with the intention to unite the Protestant party in Germany

19 Apr.   Franco-Swedish treaty renewed (the treaty, an agreement between two kings, had temporarily lapsed with the death of Gustavus Adolphus)

20 Apr.   Swedes under Lennart Torstensson storm Landsberg-am-Lech

23 Apr.   Formation of Heilbronn League with Oxenstierna as Director-General

30 Apr.   Swedish army colonels mutiny at Donauwörth, forming an association and refusing to carry out any duties until arrears have been paid; the disturbances continue for several weeks

3 June   The Swedish army of the Rhine under Christian, Count Palatine of Birkenfeld-Bischweiler, takes Heidelberg, from which the defenders move to Hagenau on the Spanish supply line

8 July   A joint Swedish–Hessian army under Knyphausen, Holzapfel, and Kagg defeats an Imperial–League army under Jost Maximilian von Bronckhorst-Gronsfeld and Jean de Merode at Hessisch-Oldendorf

	12 July	Hameln surrenders to George, Duke of Brunswick-Lüneburg, and the joint Swedish–Hessian army
	15 July	The Swedish Alsace army under Otto Louis of Salm-Kyrburg-Mörchingen take Rheinfelden
	10 Aug.	The Swedish army of the Rhine under Christian, Count Palatine of Birkenfeld-Bischweiler, defeats Charles IV, Duke of Lorraine, at Pfaffenhofen, Alsace
	12 Sep.	Osnabrück surrenders to Knyphausen
	19 Sep.	Gómez Suárez de Figueroa y Córdoba, Duke of Feria and commander of a Spanish army from Milan, joins forces with a Catholic League army under Field Marshal Johann von Aldringen at Lake Constance, in an attempt to reopen the route to the Spanish Netherlands
	11 Oct.	Rudolf von Morzin defeats Swedes, under Heinrich Matthias von Thurn and Jacob Duwall, at Steinau-an-der-Oder, Silesia; Wallenstein then advances into Saxony and sends raiding parties into Pomerania, threatening the Swedish lines of communication
	16 Oct.	Feria retakes Rheinfelden
	15 Nov.	Bernard of Saxe-Weimar and Lars Kagg take Ratisbon (Regensburg); Kagg appointed commandant of the town
	Nov.–Dec.	Gustav Horn's Swedish Swabia army blocks Feria's and Aldringen's access to the Rhine; harassed by Horn's men and under pressure because of the fall of Regensburg, Feria and Aldringen instead move into Bavaria, where they go into winter quarters and Feria dies of typhoid
1634	13 Jan.	Philippsburg, an important stronghold on the Rhine coveted by France, surrenders to the Swedish Alsace army under Otto Louis of Salm-Kyrburg-Mörchingen
	1 Feb.	Johan Banér receives independent command of and orders to reconstitute the Swedish field army in the north-east, in the Upper Saxon Circle
	25 Feb.	*Wallenstein assassinated; Matthias Gallas assumes command of the Imperial army*
	4 Apr.	Alexander Leslie takes Landsberg with a Swedish expeditionary force from Pomerania
	22 Apr.	George William of Brandenburg insists on a resolution to the issue of ownership of Pomerania before committing to the Heilbronn League
	2 May	*Archduke Ferdinand of Austria, the Emperor's son, designated commander-in-chief of the Imperial army*
	22 May	Banér lays siege to Frankfurt-an-der-Oder, which had fallen to Imperial troops in the previous year following the defeat at Steinau-an-der-Oder
	2 June	Banér takes Frankfurt-an-der-Oder

	3 June	Archduke Ferdinand and Gallas lay siege to Regensburg, defended by Kagg
	12 July	Horn and Bernard join forces at Aichach near Augsburg; Banér occupies Friedland, Bohemia, having failed to agree on strategy with the Saxon general Hans Georg von Arnim
	21 July	Banér takes Leitmeritz, Bohemia, in the process disturbing the peace negotiations there between Saxon and Imperial representatives (who fled during the night and continued negotiations in Pirna)
	22 July	Horn and Bernard take Landshut; death of Catholic League commander Johann von Aldringen
	23 July	Banér crosses the River Elbe, at the confluence with the Moldau; Arnim follows Banér with the Saxon army, after which they agree on a joint operation against Prague
	26 July	Banér and Arnim reach Prague; however, Prague is too strongly defended; out of gunpowder, Kagg surrenders Regensburg
	16 Aug.	Archduke Ferdinand and Gallas take Donauwörth
	18 Aug.	Archduke Ferdinand and Gallas lay siege to Nördlingen
	2 Sep.	A Spanish army from Italy under the Cardinal-Infante Ferdinand joins the Imperial and Catholic League army of Archduke Ferdinand and Gallas at Nördlingen
	6 Sep.	The two Ferdinands defeat Horn and Bernard at Nördlingen; Horn falls into captivity
	22 Sep.	Learning of the defeat at Nördlingen, Banér leaves Bohemia, moves into Thuringia; the Brandenburgian regiments abandon him, instead joining the Saxon army
	13 Oct.	Banér enters Weimar, Thuringia, then goes into winter quarters in Erfurt
	Nov.– Dec.	Heilbronn League gradually collapses; Banér de facto overall commander of Swedish military forces in Germany
	24 Dec.	William of Saxe-Weimar formally withdraws from his position as Swedish lieutenant general
1635	12 Mar.	Bernard appointed commander-in-chief in Germany on behalf of both the increasingly irrelevant Heilbronn League and the King of France
	23 Apr.	Conspiracy to assassinate Banér exposed, but instigator remains unknown
	30 Apr.	Treaty of Compiègne between Sweden and France negotiated by Oxenstierna and Cardinal Richelieu, who is concerned about the Spanish successes in Germany and the escalating conflict between France and Spain; Oxenstierna delays ratification of the Treaty so as to force France to break with the Emperor

	19 May	*France declares war on Spain*
	30 May	*Peace of Prague between John George of Saxony and the Emperor; soon Maximilian of Bavaria agrees to same terms, dissolves the Catholic League, and places his troops under Imperial command*
	1 Aug.	Banér musters the remaining Swedish army field units in Germany near Magdeburg
	4 Aug.	Instigated by Saxon letters, Banér's army at Magdeburg mutinies, refusing to carry out any duties until arrears have been paid; Oxenstierna de facto taken hostage in the army camp near Magdeburg
	6 Aug.	*William of Saxe-Weimar agrees to the terms of the Peace of Prague*
	31 Aug.	*George of Brunswick-Lüneburg agrees to the terms of the Peace of Prague; he formally withdraws from his position as a Swedish general*
	6 Sep.	*George William of Brandenburg agrees to the terms of the Peace of Prague*
	12 Sep.	Swedish–Commonwealth truce renewed for 26 years at Stuhmsdorf; Sweden returns the Prussian ports acquired in the 1629 Truce of Altmark; some Swedish units in Prussia are redeployed to Sweden but most are sent in support of Banér in Germany
	18 Sep.	*France declares war on the Empire*
	22 Sep.	Imperials lay siege to Hanau, held by a Swedish garrison under Jacob Ramsay
	29 Sep.	Oxenstierna escorted out of reach of the mutineers
	8 Oct.	Having restored order, Banér leads his army out of camp
	16 Oct.	John George of Saxony declares war against the Swedes and orders his recently appointed lieutenant general, Wolf Heinrich von Baudissin, to push the Swedes out of Germany
	24 Oct.	Torstensson and Kagg bring a first batch of reinforcements from Prussia to Wollin, Pomerania
	27 Oct.	France hires Bernard of Saxe-Weimar
	1 Nov.	Swedes under Patrick Ruthven defeat Baudissin's Saxon army at Dömitz, Mecklenburg
	12 Nov.	Knyphausen, no longer in favour with Oxenstierna, appointed commander in the Westphalian Circle, where four regiments remain loyal to the Swedish Crown
	15 Nov.	Yet another moment of discontent in Banér's army, on the verge of mutiny
	7 Dec.	Banér defeats Saxons at Goldberg
	17 Dec.	Torstensson defeats Saxons at Kyritz
1636	9 Jan.	Gustavsburg surrenders, Sweden loses Mainz

	11 Jan.	Knyphausen falls at Haselünne, in Emsland in the Lower Saxon Circle
	22 Jan.	The first of Banér's units cross the Elbe on their way into Saxony
	26 Jan.	Through the Advocatorial Edict, which orders all Imperial subjects to leave Swedish service or face an Imperial ban, George William of Brandenburg effectively declares war on Sweden
	1 Feb.	John George of Saxony issues an Imperial ban on all Germans in Swedish service, in the Emperor's name but probably on his own initiative; as a result, Banér devastates Saxony
	30 Mar.	Treaty of Wismar between France and Sweden; France agrees to play an active role in the war
	23 June	William of Hesse-Kassel and Swedes under Alexander Leslie relieve Hanau
	13 July	The Swedish garrison in Magdeburg surrenders to the Imperial Field Marshal Melchior von Hatzfeldt and the Saxon Lieutenant General Baudissin, then departs to join Banér
	14 July	Oxenstierna returns to Sweden
	13 Sept.	Banér gathers his forces at Parchim, Mecklenburg
	4 Oct.	Banér defeats a joint Imperial–Saxon army under Hatzfeldt and John George of Saxony at Wittstock; Brandenburg de facto withdraws from the war with Sweden
	10 Oct.	Field Marshal Herman Wrangel takes Gartz, on the Oder
1637	15 Jan.	Having moved into Saxony, Banér takes Torgau
	15 Feb.	As Imperial reinforcements approach, Banér abandons the siege of Leipzig, withdrawing to Torgau; *death of Ferdinand II; his son Ferdinand III succeeds as Holy Roman Emperor, appointing Gallas his overall military commander*
	29 June	Seriously outnumbered by Gallas's Imperial army, Banér's army retreats
	6 July	Banér reaches Landsberg, where he finds himself cut off from Pomerania by a second Imperial army
	9 July	Banér burns his supply train, sends the civilians eastwards to the border with the Polish-Lithuanian Commonwealth
	10 July	Banér orders his men on a forced march to the west; he orders the civilians to turn around
	14 July	Banér's army reaches Eberswalde, Brandenburg, where he joins forces with Herman Wrangel

	21 Sep.	*Death of William, Landgrave of Hesse-Kassel; he is succeeded, as regent, by his wife Amalie Elisabeth, Countess of Hanau-Münzenberg*
1638	12 Feb.	Jacob Ramsay's Swedish garrison in Hanau surrenders
	15 Mar.	Treaty of Hamburg between France and Sweden
	21 Mar.	Swedish garrison in Warnemünde surrenders
	2 Apr.	Sweden establishes Fort Christina, its first American colony (in modern-day Delaware)
	12 Apr.	Death of Sten Bielke, Governor-General of Pomerania; Banér nominated acting Governor-General of Pomerania in addition to his de facto role as commander-in-chief of Swedish military forces in Germany
	27 July	Banér takes Gartz, on the Oder
	24 Aug.	Field Marshal Alexander Leslie resigns from Swedish military service and returns to Scotland
	8 Dec.	Banér's appointment as Governor-General of Pomerania endorsed
1639	10 Jan.	Banér leads his army into the field
	1 Feb.	Banér crosses the Elbe at Lauenburg and moves south to relieve Erfurt
	2–20 Mar.	Banér lays siege to Freiberg, an important Saxon town which also contains the family tomb of John George of Saxony, but without success
	28 Mar.	Banér formally appointed Sweden's commander-in-chief in Germany
	14 Apr.	Banér defeats an Imperial–Saxon army under Rudolf von Morzin at Chemnitz
	26 Apr.	Banér reaches Pirna
	3 May	Banér takes Pirna; he then invades Bohemia
	19 May	*Field Marshal Leslie assumes command of the Army of the Covenant as Lord General; with the outbreak of the first Bishops' War between Scottish Covenanters and Royalists, many British veterans in Swedish service return home, where they eventually put their military experience of the Swedish model of war to good use in the English Civil Wars*
	29 May	Banér defeats and captures Imperial commanders Georg Lorenz von Hofkirchen and Raimondo Montecuccoli while crossing the Elbe at Brandeis, after which he takes Melnik
	30 May	Banér reaches Prague, but he lacks the manpower to lay siege to the city
	21 June	Hans Christoph von Königsmarck, recently appointed Swedish commander at the Weser, moves out of Minden for Erfurt, which he reaches in early August

	22 Aug.	*Amalie Elisabeth of Hesse enters into an agreement with France; henceforth, she becomes a major ally of France and Sweden*
	Nov.	Unable to find popular support in Bohemia, Banér orders its devastation so as to deny Bohemia's resources to the Empire
	5 Dec.	Ottavio Piccolomini brings Imperial reinforcements from the Spanish Netherlands to Prague
1640	14 Mar.	Banér leaves Leitmeritz, departing from Bohemia
	20 Apr.	An Imperial army under Major General Johann Rudolf von Bredau defeats the Swedish army under Major General Arvid Wittenberg at Plauen, Saxony
	29 Apr.	Banér arrives in Erfurt
	16 May	Banér joins forces with French, Hessian, and Lüneburgian allies in Erfurt
	17 May	The allied army moves to Saalfeld, where it establishes a fortified camp opposite Piccolomini's Imperial camp
	18 May	The artillery battle of Saalfeld commences, in which the artillery of the two camps exchange fire
	12 June	The allied army moves out in the direction of the Rhine
	17 June	Piccolomini joins the Bavarian army at Königshofen; henceforth, he devastates Hesse and later attempts to accomplish the same in Lüneburg
	11 Oct.	Piccolomini moves into Westphalia; the allied army splits up to go into winter quarters in the Weser region
	3 Dec.	Banér leaves his winter quarters on the Weser
	16 Dec.	Banér reaches Erfurt
1641	22 Jan.	Banér and the French commander Jean Baptiste Budes de Guébriant briefly attack Regensburg in an attempt to snatch the Emperor
	28 Jan.	Guébriant returns to the Rhineland
	20 Mar.	Piccolomini lays siege to Neunburg, reducing its walls and taking the town on the following day
	27 Mar.	Banér, alerted to the danger from Piccolomini, crosses the River Eger into Saxony
	29 Mar.	Guébriant rejoins Banér at Zwickau, Saxony
	20 May	Death of Banér; Swedish army mutinies
	29 Jun.	Carl Gustav Wrangel's Swedish army, Guébriant's French army, and contingents from Brunswick-Lüneburg and Hesse defeat an Imperial–Bavarian army under Archduke Leopold William and Piccolomini at Wolfenbüttel
	30 June	Treaty of Hamburg between France and Sweden, to last until peace is concluded, renews their alliance

	24 July	Sweden and Brandenburg sign the Peace of Stockholm, which formally ends Brandenburg's participation in the anti-Swedish coalition
	14 Oct.	Torstensson, promoted to Field Marshal and Governor-General of Pomerania, returns to Germany, landing in Stralsund
	25 Nov.	Despite his illness, Torstensson arrives in Saxony to take command of Swedish military forces in Germany
	2 Dec.	Guébriant's French army returns to the Rhineland
1642	13 Feb.	Torstensson carries out the execution of Colonel Joachim Ludwig von Seckendorf for treason, and as a means to reimpose discipline in the army
	24 Mar.	Horn released from captivity, exchanged for three Imperial generals: Johann von Werth, Georg Lorenz von Hofkirchen, and Hans Christoph von Puchhaim
	5 Apr.	Torstensson invades Saxony on the way to Silesia and Moravia
	4 May	Torstensson takes Glogau, Silesia
	31 May	Torstensson defeats a Saxon army under Francis Albert, Duke of Saxe-Lauenburg, at Schweidnitz, Silesia; Francis Albert falls in the battle
	14 June	Torstensson takes Olmütz, Moravia; soon after, his cavalry patrols, under Colonel Helmuth Wrangel, threaten Vienna
	5 Sep.	Torstensson receives reinforcements under Carl Gustav Wrangel
	14 Sep.	Torstensson initiates negotiations with Prince George Rákóczy of Transylvania through his emissaries, Colonels Derfflinger and Plettenberg
	28 Oct.	Torstensson arrives at Leipzig
	30 Oct.	Torstensson attempts to storm Leipzig but fails
	2 Nov.	Torstensson defeats Imperials under Archduke Leopold William and Piccolomini at Second Battle of Breitenfeld
	4 Dec.	*Richelieu dies; in the following year, Mazarin succeeds him as French chief minister*
	7 Dec.	Leipzig surrenders to Torstensson
	27 Dec.	Torstensson lays siege to Freiberg, Saxony, but without success
	29 Dec.	Wittenberg takes Chemnitz
1643	27 Feb.	Torstensson abandons siege of Freiberg
	22 May	Swedish regency government, under Oxenstierna and with Christina present, decides to invade Denmark
	26 Apr.	Sweden enters into an alliance with George Rákóczy of Transylvania

	19 May	*French victory over Spain at Rocroi (Louis, Duke d'Enghien, later Prince of Condé, defeats Francisco de Melo)*
	14 June	Oxenstierna dispatches a secret order to Torstensson to invade Denmark
	3 Oct.	Torstensson takes Eulenburg (near Olmütz); on the same day, he receives Oxenstierna's order to invade Denmark
	26 Oct.	Cautious preparations for the planned invasion of Danish Scania begins with a survey of available forces
	24 Nov.	*Bavarian general Franz von Mercy defeats a French army under Josias Rantzau at Tuttlingen; on the same day but in Rottweil, Guébriant dies from a previously sustained mortal wound; he is replaced by Henri de La Tour d'Auvergne, Viscount of Turenne*
	22 Dec.	Torstensson invades Holstein; Torstensson's dispatch about having received the order to go to war against Denmark reaches Stockholm only on 5 January 1644.
	28 Dec.	Torstensson storms Christianspreis outside Kiel
1644	14 Jan.	Torstensson leaves Kiel, moving into Jutland; Königsmarck initiates conquest of Bremen and Verden
	18 Jan.	Horn appointed commander of the planned campaign in Scania, with instructions to cross the border in February
	19 Jan.	Torstensson defeats a Danish cavalry corps near Kolding; Danish survivors retreat into the nearby camp at Snoghøj
	24 Jan.	Danish commander-in-chief Anders Bille evacuates those men he can to the island of Fyn; the rest of the Danish army at Snoghøj surrenders
	3 Feb.	Appointed day for the muster of Horn's Swedish army destined for the invasion of Scania; however, the muster cannot be carried out on time
	9 Feb.	Torstensson's attempt to cross the Little Belt fails
	18 Feb.	Two weeks behind schedule, Horn's army musters in Värnamo
	21 Feb.	Horn's army marches out from Markaryd in southern Sweden
	23 Feb.	*Transylvanian units move into Habsburg Hungary*
	24 Feb.	Horn's army crosses the border to Danish Scania
	27 Feb.	Horn takes Helsingborg
	10 Mar.	Horn takes Lund
	17 Mar.	Henrik Fleming leads a Swedish invasion force into the Norwegian province of Jämtland
	20 Mar.	Torstensson's final attempt to cross the Little Belt fails

22 Mar.	Henrik Fleming's Swedes defeats Jacob Ulfeldt's Norwegians at the battle of Brunflo, Jämtland
28 Mar.	Daniel Buscovius leads a Swedish invasion force into Norway from the province of Dalecarlia
11 and 12 Apr.	Norwegian units from Bohus Fortress cross the river near Gothenburg, but are repulsed
15 Apr.	Danish King Christian IV, personally commanding a fleet, arrives at Gothenburg which he attempts to blockade
17 Apr.	Horn takes Landskrona
21 Apr.	Norway's Governor Hannibal Sehested attempts an offensive into the Swedish province of Värmland from the north, from Vinger, but is stopped at the border
26 Apr.	Stenbock leads reinforcements into Gothenburg
10 May	Christian IV abandons the attempt to blockade Gothenburg
24 May	Horn takes Laholm
26 May	Christian IV defeats Louis De Geer's auxiliary fleet under Maerten Thijssen in the battle of Lister Dyb
27 May	Ulfeldt returns into Jämtland to recapture the province
4 June	Thijssen again confronts Christian IV; a storm interrupts the battle, after which Thijssen returns to the Dutch Republic
11 June	Swedish main fleet under Admiral Claes Fleming and inshore fleet under Major Henrik Hansson set out from Dalarö in the southern Stockholm archipelago
16 June	Swedish main fleet reaches the island of Bornholm
18 June	Swedish main fleet reaches Dornbusch, off Rügen
21 June	Swedish inshore fleet arrives at Kalmar
23 June	Having received current intelligence, picked up pilots, and loaded supplies, the Swedish main fleet sets out to locate the Danish fleet
25 June	Norwegian units again cross the river near Gothenburg; they are repulsed, but not before burning villages, manufacturing facilities, and river-locks
28 June	Horn lays siege to Malmö; Fleming's fleet enters the Bay of Kiel
29 June	Norwegian units from Uddevalla cross the border into the province of Dal to burn the town of Vänersborg
2 July	Horn reports to Stockholm that he cannot take Malmö unless a Swedish fleet blockades it from the sea; Christian IV's fleet returns to Copenhagen
9 July	Transported by Fleming's fleet, Torstensson lands on the island of Fehmarn, over which he on the following day gains full control; Christian IV leaves Copenhagen with his fleet

11 July	Inconclusive naval battle at Kolberger Heide; Christian IV wounded, losing an eye
13 July	Fleming's fleet enters Kiel; within days, the Danish fleet successfully blockades the port
29 July	Gallas crosses into Holstein, moves into Oldesloe
2 Aug.	Danes establish a fort with a gun battery within reach of the Swedish main fleet at Kiel; Gallas sends a raiding party into Kiel
5 Aug.	Admiral Claes Fleming falls by a stray cannonball; dying, he hands over command to Torstensson's chief of staff, Carl Gustav Wrangel
11 Aug.	Swedish fleet leaves Kiel
13 Aug.	Gallas takes Kiel
15 Aug.	Wrangel arrives at Dalarö
18 Aug.	Having returned, but this time to Gothenburg, Thijssen's auxiliary fleet again leaves port
19 Aug.	Thijssen's auxiliary fleet arrives at Landskrona, having passing through the narrow Straits without loss
20 Aug.	Last Swedish soldiers in Jämtland surrender to Ulfeldt
21 Aug.	Thijssen's auxiliary fleet arrives at Kalmar
25 Aug.	Hansson's inshore fleet leaves Ystad; en route to Kalmar (where he arrives around 2 September) the Danish fleet sinks seven and captures eight of his vessels
Sep.	Torstensson divides his forces: sending Helmuth Wrangel with a small army back to Jutland, Torstensson returns with the rest of the main army to Germany where he corners Gallas at Aschersleben
16 Sep.	Christian IV crosses the Straits to Malmö
20 Sep.	Thijssen, then in Stockholm, commissioned as a Swedish admiral and ennobled as Anckarhielm
27 Sep.	Anckarhielm back in Kalmar
7 Oct.	Under pressure from Christian IV's army, Horn breaks camp, gradually retreating towards the north
8 Oct.	Wrangel sails from Dalarö with main fleet, arriving in Kalmar on the following day
15 Oct.	Wrangel sails from Kalmar with both main and auxiliary fleet
19 Oct.	Wismar squadron joins Wrangel's fleet
23 Oct.	Swedish victory over Danes in the naval battle off Fehmarn (Wrangel and Anckarhielm defeat Pros Mund)
8 Nov.	Learning of the defeat off Fehmarn, Christian IV rapidly returns from Scania to Zealand
28 Nov.	Sehested breaks through the Swedish border defences and enters Värmland from the north
3 Dec.	Torstensson defeats a part of Gallas's army at Jüterbog

	18 Dec.	Coming of age at 18, Queen Christina assumes personal rule
	27 Dec.	Sehested takes Eda in Värmland
1645	1 Jan.	Sehested defeats Swedes at the battle on the ice of Lake Bysjön, Värmland
	2 Jan.	Königsmarck defeats Gallas and his survivors at Frohse near Magdeburg; Torstensson moves into Saxony to push John George out of the war by ravaging the area around Dresden
	19 Jan.	Torstensson's army leaves winter quarters, at first under Wittenberg in interim command
	12 Feb.	Having continued towards the south, Sehested attacks Vänersborg in the province of Dal, but is repulsed; he retreats into Norway
	15 Feb.	Horn receives his orders for the summer campaign
	25 Feb.	Königsmarck takes Stade
	28 Feb.	Königsmarck takes Buxtehude
	29 Feb.	Having made repeated attempts against Gothenburg without success, Sehested begins to pull out his men on the Gothenburg front, retreating into Norway
	6 Mar.	Torstensson defeats Imperials under Hatzfeldt at Jankow, Bohemia
	16 Mar.	Königsmarck takes Bremervörde, completing the conquest of Bremen and Verden
	25 Mar.	Torstensson reaches Krems on the Danube
	9 Apr.	Torstensson takes Wolfsschanze, the outermost bastion guarding Vienna; the fleeing Imperials burn the bridge across the Danube
	22 Apr.	*With the Treaty of Munkacz, George Rákóczy of Transylvania enters into an alliance with France in exchange for subsidies*
	5 May	Helmuth Wrangel defeats a Danish corps under Colonel Friedrich von Buchwald at Heide in Dithmarschen, capturing Buchwald; *Turenne's French army defeated at Herbsthausen near Mergentheim by an Imperial-Bavarian army under Franz von Mercy*
	3 May	Lacking the men to invest Vienna, Torstensson decides instead to lay siege to Brünn, Moravia
	25 May	Danish Admiral Ove Giedde leaves Copenhagen with a Danish fleet
	31 May	Admiral Erik Ryning, the new commander of the Swedish main fleet, receives his orders
	1 June	Ryning leaves Dalarö with the main fleet, but contrary winds push him back
	3 June	Gustav Otto Stenbock retakes Eda in Värmland

6 June	Danes attempts to move against Gothenburg, with Danes from Varberg and Norwegians under Sehested acting in co-operation with Giedde's fleet, but Anckarhielm blocks the maritime approach to Gothenburg
9 June	Imperial troops recover Wolfsschanze at Vienna
10 June	Wrangel's fleet leaves Wismar
19 June	Wrangel lands on the island of Bornholm
23 June	*Ottoman sultan goes to war with the Venetian Republic over Candia (modern-day Crete), abandoning his support for Transylvania's participation in the anti-Habsburg alliance*
27 June	Bornholm surrenders
30 June	Ryning, severely delayed by contrary winds, finally leaves the Stockholm archipelago
12 July	Ryning takes Visby on the island of Gotland
15 July	Ryning's main fleet and Wrangel's Wismar fleet join forces; Ryning assumes overall command
31 July	Sehested initiates a new offensive from Norway against Gothenburg
3 Aug	*The combined French-Hessian army under Enghien defeats Mercy's Bavarian army in the battle of Alerheim; Mercy falls in the battle*
15 Aug.	Torstensson attempts to storm Brünn; Swedish main fleet returns to Dalarö, outside Stockholm
16 Aug.	Transylvanian contingent abandons the joint campaign
23 Aug.	Torstensson abandons siege of Brünn, Moravia; siege of Bohus Fortress, north of Gothenburg (abandoned on the following day); Peace of Brömsebro ends the war between Denmark and Sweden
6 Sep.	Truce of Kötzschenbroda between Sweden and Saxony halts Saxony's participation in the anti-Swedish coalition
25 Sep.	Torstensson abandons the campaign in Bohemia and Moravia
2 Dec.	Königsmarck joins Torstensson at Landshut, then marches to Greifenberg, both in Bavaria
13 Dec.	Torstensson too ill to continue the campaign, leaves interim command to Wittenberg
14 Dec.	Königsmarck escorts Torstensson towards Leipzig, with 22 companies of horse
16 Dec.	*George Rákóczy concludes the Treaty of Vienna with Ferdinand III, abandoning the anti-Habsburg alliance*
22 Dec.	Torstensson and Königsmarck arrive in Eilenburg, north-east of Leipzig

	23 Dec.	Arriving from Holstein, Wrangel meets Torstensson in Eilenburg; Wrangel assumes command of the main army, while Torstensson maintains overall command over Swedish military forces in Germany from his present location
	25 Dec.	Wittenberg, in interim command, takes Leitmeritz, Bohemia
1646	23 Mar.	Wrangel confers with Torstensson in Leipzig
	31 Mar.	Peace of Eilenburg between Sweden and Saxony ends Saxony's participation in the war
	16 Apr.	Königsmarck retakes Bremervörde
	18 Apr.	Wrangel leads out the army towards Höxter, north of Kassel
	1 May	Siege of Höxter begins
	5 May	Wrangel takes Höxter
	8 May	Wrangel promoted to field marshal and formally appointed overall commander of Swedish military forces in Germany (the warrant only reaches Wrangel in late July or early August)
	15 May	Wrangel takes Paderborn
	23 May	Königsmarck takes Vechta
	25 May	Wrangel takes Stadtberge (Marsberg), where he stays until 31 May
	1 June	Königsmarck takes Lemgo
	15 June	Königsmarck joins Wrangel at Wetzlar
	22 June	Wrangel leaves Wetzlar; Mazarin finally authorises Turenne to join forces with Wrangel
	23 June	Wrangel reaches Amöneburg, near Marburg in Hesse
	26 June	Wrangel takes Amöneburg
	4 July	Archduke Leopold William advances to Amöneburg with an Imperial–Bavarian army, where he remains until 16 July
	17 July	First French units join Wrangel
	19–20 July	Turenne's main army crosses the Rhine
	10 Aug,	Turenne joins Wrangel (between Wetzlar and Giessen)
	16 Sep.	Königsmarck defeats Bavarians at Pfaffenhofen, south of Ingolstadt
	21 Sep.	Wrangel and Turenne take Rain-am-Lech
	28 Sep.	Wrangel and Turenne lay siege to Augsburg
	1 Oct.	Wittenberg defeats an Imperial army under Major General August von Hanau at Horschitz, Silesia
	11–12 Oct.	Wrangel and Turenne attempt to storm Augsburg

	13 Oct.	Wrangel and Turenne abandon the siege of Augsburg; soon after, Paris recalls Turenne's army
	4 Nov.	Wrangel takes Landsberg-am-Lech
1647	4 Jan.	Wrangel takes Bregenz
	13 Feb.	Wrangel takes the island of Mainau
	8 Mar.	Wrangel abandons the siege of Lindau
	11 Mar.	Königsmarck, with a joint Swedish-Hessian army, takes Kirchhain (east of Marburg), which hitherto had constituted a major threat to neighbouring Hesse
	14 Mar.	Maximilian of Bavaria, together with his brother Ferdinand, the Elector of Cologne, signs the Truce of Ulm with Sweden, France, and Hesse-Kassel
	25 Mar.	Banér and Turenne suspend operations in Bavaria
	25 Apr.	Wrangel takes Schweinfurt
	26 May	Königsmarck takes Vechta
	10 June	Königsmarck takes Fürstenau
	14 June	Wrangel's army leaves Bamberg
	24 June	*Bernardine army in Strasbourg mutinies against Turenne, sets off to join the Swedes; eventually, Wrangel enlists the remnants*
	15 July	Königsmarck takes Wiedenbrück
	27 July	Wrangel takes Eger, western Bohemia
	30 July	Major General Helmuth Wrangel raids Ferdinand III's camp
	12 Aug.	Wrangel moves out of Eger
	13 Aug.	Wrangel establishes a fortified camp in Plan, in front of Triebel Castle
	15 Aug.	Ferdinand, the Elector of Cologne, withdraws from the Truce of Ulm
	19 Aug.	Holzapfel storms Triebel Castle
	22 Aug.	During a failed assault on the Swedish camp, Imperial troops defeat a cavalry force under Helmuth Wrangel, who falls in the battle
	7 Sep.	Ferdinand III signs a treaty with Maximilian of Bavaria in Pilsen, which confirms Bavaria's resumption of the war as part of the Imperial alliance
	14 Sep.	Maximilian of Bavaria withdraws from the Truce of Ulm and resumes the war against Sweden, hoping that France will stay out of the conflict (Holzapfel is made commander-in-chief of both the Imperial and Bavarian armies); learning of the renewed threat from Bavaria, Wrangel's army returns north, abandoning Bohemia
	20 Nov.	Wrangel's army arrives in Oldenburg, Hesse
	23 Nov.	Bavarians take Memmingen, held by Swedish troops

	27 Nov.	Turenne resumes operations against the Bavarian army; he sends a trumpeter to Munich to announce France's withdrawal from the Truce of Ulm
	7 Dec.	Imperials take the Bohemian town of Iglau, held by Swedish troops
1648	*30 Jan.*	*Peace of Münster between the Dutch Republic (the United Provinces) and Spain concludes the Eighty Years' War*
	23 Mar.	Wrangel and Turenne again join forces
	20 Apr.	Wrangel and Turenne take Göppingen, south-east of Stuttgart
	21 Apr.	Wrangel and Turenne take Dinkelsbühl
	17 May	Joint Swedish–French army under Wrangel and Turenne defeat joint Imperial–Bavarian army under Holzapfel and Bronckhorst-Gronsfeld at Zusmarshausen, near Augsburg; Holzapfel falls mortally wounded in the battle
	22 May	Wrangel dispatches Königsmarck to raid Bohemia; he also orders Wittenberg to invade Bohemia from Silesia
	29 May	Wrangel's and Turenne's Swedish–French army successfully crosses the River Lech at Rain, after which it ravages Bavaria
	2 June	Christina appoints her cousin Charles Gustavus commander-in-chief of Swedish military forces in Germany; Wrangel is instructed to remain in Germany to assist Charles Gustavus
	16 June	Charles Gustavus receives his instructions
	1 July	Königsmarck takes Falkenau
	16 July	Charles Gustavus sails from Dalarö in the southern Stockholm archipelago, together with Swedish reinforcements
	26 July	Swedish fleet arrives in Germany, Charles Gustavus lands at Wolgast; Königsmarck takes Prague Castle, gaining the richest booty ever taken by a Swedish army, and then lays siege to the city of Prague
	30 July	Wittenberg joins Königsmarck at Prague
	11 Aug.	Wittenberg continues south towards Tabor
	20 Aug.	*A French army under the Prince of Condé defeats the Spanish Army of Flanders under Archduke Leopold William at Lens, Flanders*
	23 Aug.	Wittenberg storms Tabor
	19 Sep.	Wittenberg again sets out towards the south, making the Imperial commanders fear that he will advance to Linz, the location of the Imperial court
	23 Sep.	Wittenberg defeats and captures Imperial Field Marshal Hans Christopher von Buchheim

4 Oct.	Charles Gustavus brings reinforcements to Königsmarck's army at Prague, assumes command of the siege
5 Oct.	Wrangel and Turenne surprised by Imperials under Piccolomini while on a hunting party at Dachau, near Munich; Wrangel saves himself but Imperials take 94 prisoners
10 Oct.	Wrangel and Turenne return across the Lech at Landsberg-am-Lech
13 Oct.	Swedish army attempts to storm Prague, but without success
16 Oct.	Wrangel and Turenne cross the Danube at Donauwörth, abandoning the devastated Bavaria
24 Oct.	Peace of Westphalia; formal end of the Thirty Years' War
25 Oct.	Swedish army makes another attempt to storm Prague, but again without success
2 Nov.	Rumours of the expected signing of the peace agreement reach Prague, an armistice is agreed
4 Nov.	Charles Gustavus receives a letter from the Swedish negotiators in Westphalia stating that a peace agreement is imminent
6 Nov.	News of the peace agreement reaches Prague
9 Nov.	Confirmation of the peace agreement reaches Wrangel and Turenne; confirmation of the agreement also reaches Prague, hostilities between Sweden and the Empire cease

Introduction

After the death of Sweden's King Gustavus Adolphus in 1632, his Lord High Chancellor, Axel Oxenstierna, assumed overall political and military command of the Swedish and Protestant alliance in Germany. Although the Swedish army had been successful, neither side could yet be said to have gained any decisive advantage. The prolonged military operations devastated further many of those territories that already had seen considerable destruction. As Oxenstierna struggled to retain control over the Protestant alliance, the depredations of its soldiers soon gave his name an ominous meaning in the Catholic regions. This is revealed in a children's rhyme from one of the regions of operations, here presented in English translation:

> *Pray, child, pray!*
> *Tomorrow comes the Swede,*
> *Tomorrow comes the Oxenstierna,*
> *He will soon teach you to pray.*
> *Pray, child, pray!*[1]

This book describes and analyses the early modern Swedish army during the Thirty Years' War after 1632. In this period, Swedish military operations were led by field marshals under the overall command of Chancellor Oxenstierna. The book aims to expand our understanding of the Swedish army and navy during the Thirty Years' War by also focusing on the later operations, including those against Denmark, and not only on the better-known operations in Germany against the Catholic League and the Holy Roman Empire. It describes the 1643–1645 Swedish invasion of Denmark, the operations on the border with Norway, and the battles and sieges, including those of Vienna and Prague, which led up to the Peace of Westphalia, which concluded the Thirty Years' War. Finally, the book covers the military aspects of the establishment of Sweden's first colonies in North America and West Africa.

Oxenstierna could not have brought Sweden to a successful peace without able field marshals. In the first years after the King's death, Oxenstierna was nominally in personal command of the army and refrained, for political reasons, from making formal appointments as overall military commander.

---

1   Author's translation. For the German original, see Appendix 2.

However, it was obvious to him and others that he could not lead the army at the same time that he simultaneously managed all political affairs, in Germany and Sweden. Oxenstierna therefore always chose a purely military officer as overall commander of the Swedish military forces in Germany. In the early years, these appointments were implicit only, which sometimes caused all manners of confusion in the alliance's chain of command. Later, the appointments were mostly official, which reduced the capacity for misunderstandings. Either way, there was always a senior Swedish general in overall command of military operations in Germany. These generals were, in chronological order, Gustav Horn, Johan Banér, Lennart Torstensson, Carl Gustav Wrangel, and Charles Gustavus. The first three were all exceptional commanders who had served Gustavus Adolphus since his early campaigns in the Polish-Lithuanian Commonwealth, or in the case of Horn, already during the 1612 campaign in Muscovy.

Horn was the most experienced of the generals, but he was not a lucky commander. Several times he had to face insurmountable natural obstacles or, possibly worse, superior enemy numbers under talented generals, as a result of which he was captured and had to spend many years as a prisoner of war. Contemporaries emphasised his self-control, decorum, and modesty as much as his wisdom, courage in battle, and presence of command.[2] Following the period of captivity, Horn again made a name for himself in the war against Denmark.

Banér was a soldier's general, a bold, imaginative fighter who liked women, food, and drink in excessive quantities, and had a laissez-faire attitude to discipline. Despite usually being outnumbered, he restored the fighting reputation of the Swedish army following the death of Gustavus Adolphus and the subsequent disaster at Nördlingen, in which Horn fell into captivity.

Torstensson, almost fully incapacitated by what may have been rheumatoid arthritis, was trained in the sciences and viewed his soldiers similarly to his beloved artillery: as clockwork components to be deployed in the manner best suited to achieve the desired outcome. This made him the most cold-blooded of the three, a harsh disciplinarian but an imaginative tactician who despite his incapacitating illness carried out a series of fast, powerful campaigns which because of their capacity to unbalance the enemy through continuously changing fronts perhaps can be best described as an early form of *Blitzkrieg*. This would not be an anachronism, since already his contemporaries awarded Torstensson the nickname 'The Lightning Bolt' (Swedish: *Blixten*; German: *Der Blitz*) due to the speed with which his army marched.

Wrangel, who earned his spurs during the war in Germany but after the death of the King, belonged to a younger generation. Torstensson rated him highly, and Wrangel was a skillful and aggressive commander. However, those who knew him also described Wrangel as polite and generous. In

---

2   Robert Monro, *Monro, His Expedition with the Worthy Scots Regiment (Called Mac-Keyes Regiment)*, Vol. 2 (London: William Jones, 1637), p.143.

addition, Wrangel was interested in French fashion, literature, and art, much of which he brought home to decorate his newly built palaces.[3]

In the last year of the war, when Queen Christina had come of age and assumed royal power in Sweden, she appointed her cousin and one-time sweetheart Charles Gustavus overall commander in Germany. A bold, experienced, and capable commander in his own right, Charles Gustavus would later succeed Christina as King of Sweden.

Each will be described in turn, in their respective period of overall command. Yet, there were other influential field commanders as well, including men such as the Scotsman Field Marshal Alexander Leslie, and Field Marshal (so promoted after the war) Hans Christoph von Königsmarck, a Brandenburger. Each played an important role in the Swedish war effort, and their contributions will be described, too.

Meanwhile, Oxenstierna continued his administrative reforms, which enabled Sweden consistently to raise troops, despite the small population of Sweden and its territories, and enabled an intelligence and logistics system which could supply the armies, despite the vast geographical depth of operations. While the Swedish army of Gustavus Adolphus positioned Sweden as an emerging great power, it was the subsequent developments of the army under Oxenstierna that enabled the Swedish rise to regional great power status.

The focus of the present volume is the Swedish Army and, in extension, the Swedish military state during the final phases of the Thirty Years' War. It is not intended as a comprehensive history of the war, which beyond and above the religious divide between Catholics and Protestants brought together several different conflicts (to be precise, the Habsburg attempt to assert authority in the Holy Roman Empire and on the southern Baltic coastlands, an ongoing war between Spain and the Dutch Republic, a struggle between Spain and France which in 1635 escalated into open war, rivalry over the Baltic Sea between Denmark and Sweden, and within Sweden and the Polish-Lithuanian Commonwealth, a dynastic conflict between different lines of the Swedish Vasa family). Such an endeavour would demand considerably more space than the present format allows. Nor does this volume aim to provide a comprehensive military history of Sweden, with full details on all battles and campaigns, even though several lesser-known engagements will be described in some detail to illustrate how the Swedish army functioned in battle. It will also not describe the opposing forces of the Commonwealth, the Catholic League, and the Holy Roman Empire, since they are covered in other books of the series. What this volume hopes to achieve is to describe all aspects of the Swedish army during the war – recruitment, organisation, weapons, equipment, training, and tactics – that are relevant for an understanding of how the Swedish army emerged and built a foundation for Sweden as a great power. For the Swedish army in the earlier phases of the war, see the already

---

3   When the personal traits of the four men are summarised, they display an uncanny but unintended resemblance to Athos, Porthos, Aramis, and D'Artagnan as described by Alexandre Dumas.

published first volume, *The Lion from the North: The Swedish Army during the Thirty Years' War, 1618–1632*, vol. 1 (Helion, 2020).

After the death of Gustavus Adolphus, a major change took place with regard to tactical doctrine. He had advocated the primacy of the infantry. However, after his death his general, Duke Bernard of Saxe-Weimar, instead advocated the primacy of the cavalry. Bernard retained many aspects of the Swedish model but ordered the cavalry to charge at the gallop, independent of infantry support. Cavalry and dragoons also grew increasingly important, and numerous, because of their mobility, a necessary factor in the foraging for supplies. This change in thinking is also reflected in this volume, and henceforth cavalry units will be listed before infantry units. We will see that this change was also reflected in the Instrument of Government adopted by the Swedish Crown in 1634 (more on which below).

At the time of the war, some of the belligerent powers followed different calendars. The Gregorian calendar, named after the sixteenth-century Pope Gregory XIII who introduced it, had been developed as a correction to an observed error in the old Julian calendar. The visible result of the correction was that the date was advanced 10 days, that is, 4 October 1582 was followed by 15 October 1582. France and the Holy Roman Empire changed calendar on this date, as did most Catholic nations. However, many Protestant countries including Sweden, initially objected to adopting a Catholic innovation. They retained the Julian calendar, which for this reason differed from the one used in Catholic nations and at present. Old Style (O.S.) and New Style (N.S.) are terms commonly used with dates to indicate that the calendar convention used at the time described is different from that in use at present. Unless noted otherwise, the dates given here will be N.S., since the events described primarily took place in Catholic nations. However, Swedish archival documents relating to the war commonly use the O.S. calendar, and most Swedish-language works describing the war still follow this style. This frequently leads to confusion among historians. I have yet to see a work on the Thirty Years' War without the occasional wrongly calculated date, and no doubt there will be mistakes in the present volume, too. The different calendars caused confusion already at the time; the Swedish chancellery in Germany received letters and dispatches without knowing if the date was O.S. or N.S., so Oxenstierna's working documents might refer to either calendar style.[4]

---

4   See, for example, Oxenstierna to the Council of the Realm, 3 January 1633 (O.S.), *Rikskansleren Axel Oxenstiernas skrifter och brefvexling* (henceforth cited as *AOSB*) 1:8, pp.1–10, on p.8.

Prologue: Axel Oxenstierna, Lord High Chancellor of Sweden

Axel Oxenstierna (1583–1654), Lord High Chancellor of Sweden, descended from one of Sweden's most powerful noble families. Following a conventional education, which naturally included Latin and major modern languages such as German and French, in 1599–1602 he studied at the universities in Rostock, Wittenberg, and Jena. Following his return, he went into the service of Gustavus Adolphus's father, the unpredictable and frequently brutal King Charles IX.

The 20-year-old Oxenstierna was talented and rose rapidly in rank and position. He had already joined the Swedish Council of the Realm (Swedish: *Riksrådet*) in 1609, and in January 1612, at age 28, became Lord High Chancellor. This was in the middle of the Kalmar War, days after Gustavus Adolphus had to assume sole military command after the death of his father Charles IX.

Oxenstierna was only 11 years older than the young king, and the two rapidly developed a mutual respect. Although they did not always agree, the two young men complemented each other. Moreover, Gustavus Adolphus trusted Oxenstierna. The King allowed the Chancellor to develop the state machinery as needed, without fear that Oxenstierna one day might conspire against him. Indeed, Sweden at the time of Gustavus Adolphus's ascension to the throne can be said not yet to have had a machinery of state, and without Oxenstierna, it is unlikely that the country would have left the Thirty Years' War a victorious great power, or even a functioning state.

The historian often attempts to understand a significant historical person through his or her writings, such as letters, treatises, and above all memoirs. Oxenstierna did not write memoirs, nor did he explain his actions to posterity. But he was a prodigious writer. During his long life of state service, he drafted innumerable reports, memorandums, letters, and orders. He also maintained a substantial correspondence with friends and relatives. In 1888, the Royal Swedish Academy of Letters, History and Antiquities began to publish Oxenstierna's copious correspondence. The project only came to a conclusion of sorts in 2018, and resulted in multiple volumes and a database, maintained by the Swedish National Archives (*Riksarkivet*). If there is any key to Oxenstierna's character to be found in these thousands of documents, it is his devotion to affairs of state. His personal character remains in the shadow of the statesman and, to some extent, in the shadow of the King (and, later, Queen) whom he served. He worked throughout the day, either in the Chancellery in Stockholm or during his long periods abroad. He knew all important statesmen of his time, and such was his family background, power, and influence that he could speak freely to kings and first ministers everywhere. In his time, Oxenstierna was one of three European statesmen who literally changed the world in which they lived. In Spain, Gaspar de Guzmán y Pimentel, Count-Duke of Olivares (1587–1645), took care of policy in the same manner as Oxenstierna did in Sweden. In France, it was Cardinal Armand Jean du Plessis, Duke of Richelieu (1585–1642). All three relied on their closeness to their king, capacity for work, personal intelligence, and ability. These were the men who shaped seventeenth-century Europe. Sweden was smaller, and had fewer resources, than Spain and France, but in power and ability, Oxenstierna was not their inferior. Indeed, Cardinal Jules Mazarin (1602–1661), Richelieu's successor, famously said that if all of Europe's ministers were on the same ship, the helm should be handed to the Swedish Chancellor. Oxenstierna was also the oldest of the three, and he stayed in power the longest.

Like his French and Spanish counterparts, Oxenstierna was a political creature. Although known for bluntness when addressing minor allies who failed to live up to expectations, Oxenstierna worked behind the scenes as much as in the open. He had to; where the late Gustavus Adolphus simply could have ordered, Oxenstierna had to persuade, convince, and, when needed, manipulate. He did not hesitate to sacrifice those whom he considered pawns in the game for what really mattered, that is, safeguarding the interests of Sweden and the Swedish Crown. For instance, in 1634 he de facto dismissed Field Marshal Dodo von Innhausen und zu Knyphausen, who had known Gustavus Adolphus when the latter was a mere boy of 13, had been instrumental in saving the King's army at the battle of Lützen, and was one of the most experienced officers in the Swedish army. Knyphausen was unfortunate in that Oxenstierna previously had appointed him to keep an eye on George, Duke of Brunswick-Lüneburg, who only stayed loyal to the Swedish Crown as long as he found it beneficial. However, now Oxenstierna needed the support of the dukes of Brunswick in an upcoming political meeting and it was well known that Duke George resented Knyphausen. As a result, Oxenstierna, in his own words, 'let him [Knyphausen] fall'.[1] It is, perhaps, telling that one of the individuals who fanned the Duke's dislike for Knyphausen was Erik Andersson Trana who had been ennobled in 1626 for his years of valuable service to Oxenstierna on the Muscovite frontier as an intelligence officer. Although there is no conclusive evidence of a conspiracy to blacken Knyphausen's reputation, Oxenstierna certainly did not hesitate to make full use of the opportunity when it arose.

Chancellor Oxenstierna did not personally command major armies, nor did he play a battlefield role. However, before his death Gustavus Adolphus

---

1   Lars Tingsten, *Huvuddragen av Sveriges politik och krigföring i Tyskland efter Gustav II Adolfs död till och med sommaren 1635* (Stockholm: Militärlitteraturföreningens förlag 157, 1930), p.171.

had made Oxenstierna his sole authorised representative, with full political and military control over Swedish affairs in Germany. Besides, it was due to Oxenstierna's success in maintaining Sweden's course in foreign policy that the Thirty Years' War could be fought to, for Sweden, a successful conclusion. So, although Oxenstierna was in no way a field commander, he certainly led the Swedish armies in the ongoing wars.

In 1608 Oxenstierna wed Anna Åkesdotter Bååt (1579–1649). By all accounts, the couple were happily married for 41 years; they had 12 children (although only three survived their parents), but Anna only seldom had the opportunity to spend extended periods with her husband. Affairs of state always took precedence, and Oxenstierna spent many years abroad. Instead Anna managed, on her own and with considerable skill, the numerous manor houses and palaces that the couple acquired over the years, throughout the Swedish realm. Her husband had little or no time for such minor matters, since his task was the maintenance of the machinery of state.

1

The Wars of Axel Oxenstierna

Oxenstierna Takes Command

After the death of King Gustavus Adolphus at the battle of Lützen, Oxenstierna was the only Swedish military or civilian officer who simultaneously had the authority, ability, and resolve to take full political and military command in the late King's stead. The King's heir, Princess Christina, was six years old. While the King was alive, Gustavus Adolphus and Oxenstierna had effectively shared the burden of command. The King had led the field army and handled military affairs, while Oxenstierna had taken care of political relations, with the Council of the Realm in Stockholm, foreign rulers, and not least in importance, the numerous German princes who for understandable reasons all wanted to have a say in what went on in their respective domains now when the Swedish army was operating there. Henceforth, Oxenstierna would have to take responsibility for both political and military affairs. This meant that his already heavy workload doubled overnight.

Axel Oxenstierna, late 1640s. (David Beck)

Oxenstierna was a servant of the Crown, a deputy; he would not claim the Crown itself. Nor could he, since there was an heir to the throne. Oxenstierna had met Gustavus Adolphus for the last time on 3 November 1632, less than a fortnight before the King's death. Gustavus Adolphus had then explained his views on the strategic goals of the campaign and given Oxenstierna two instructions. The first directive was military. As the King's authorised representative, Oxenstierna should assume political and military control of the Franconian, Swabian, Upper Rhenish, and Electoral Rhenish Circles.[1] Gustavus Adolphus wanted Oxenstierna to establish four new armies,

---

1   For military and taxation purposes, the Empire was divided into regional groupings of states known as Imperial Circles. When discussing military strategy and operations within the Empire,

in addition to the main field army under the King. Each new army should consist of 15 regiments of foot and 50 companies of horse. Except for the already existing garrison units, Gustavus Adolphus wanted his military disposition in Germany to be as in Table 1.

Table 1. Disposition of the Swedish armies in Germany, as envisaged by Gustavus Adolphus in his last instruction. (Source: Tingsten, *Huvuddragen*, p.7)

- The main field army under Gustavus Adolphus
- An army of the Rhine under Christian, Count Palatine of Birkenfeld-Bischweiler, or in his absence, Otto Louis, Wild- and Rhinegrave of Salm-Kyrburg-Mörchingen (who presently was in Gustav Horn's army)
- An army in Alsace (technically in the Upper Rhenish and southern Burgundian Circles) under Field Marshal Gustav Horn
- An army in the Swabian and Bavarian Circles under General Johan Banér
- An army in the Franconian Circle temporarily under Count Kraft von Hohenlohe or Major General Balthasar Jacob von Schlammersdorff, until an army commander could be appointed

The second directive was political. Oxenstierna should promote and establish an alliance of the Protestant powers at the upcoming meeting with the German Protestant princes in Ulm, for which the King had already issued the necessary authorisation.[2]

The two directives were the last of a long series of instructions from Gustavus Adolphus to his Chancellor. They were never intended as the King's political or military last will. Yet, it will be shown that Oxenstierna, loyal to his late friend and ruler, set out to follow the King's instructions as if they had carried this weight. Oxenstierna received the news about the King's death on 22 November, while at Hanau, that is, less than a week after the event.[3] At the time, the Swedish field armies in Germany only in part conformed to the late King's intentions (Table 2).

Table 2. Disposition of the Swedish armies in Germany immediately following the King's death. (Source: Tingsten, *Huvuddragen*, pp.8–9)

- The main field army, formerly under Gustavus Adolphus but presently under Lieutenant General Bernard, Duke of Saxe-Weimar, combined with an army under George, Duke of Brunswick-Lüneburg, in the Upper Saxon Circle
- An army presently on the Rhine under Lieutenant General Wolf Heinrich von Baudissin
- An army in Alsace under Field Marshal Gustav Horn
- An army in the Swabian Circle, in the absence of General Johan Banér (who was recuperating from his wounds) under Christian, Count Palatine of Birkenfeld-Bischweiler
- An expeditionary corps in Silesia under Colonel Jacob Duwall (subordinated the Saxon army)

In addition, there were allied armies, notably the Saxon army, under John George (1585–1656), the Elector of Saxony, and his general Hans Georg von

---

it for practical and geographical reasons remained common to regard them as separate theatres of operations.

2 Tingsten, *Huvuddragen*, p.7.
3 *Ibid.*, p.8.

Arnim (1583–1641), which operated in Silesia, and the Hessian army, under William (1602–1637), Landgrave of Hesse-Kassel. There was also the Brandenburgian army, under George William (1595–1640), the Elector of Brandenburg, which, however, like the Swedish contingent in Silesia operated under Saxon command.

With the exception of the allies, all armies were in Swedish service, and their commanders, even when German princes, were serving Swedish army officers, having sworn an oath to the Swedish Crown. Yet here was a problem, now the King was dead. The German princes had not considered subordinate status to the King of Sweden as a problem. However, they did not willingly accept a subordinate status merely because a Swedish officer held higher military rank or was senior in service. Oxenstierna had the rank and reputation of a man who spoke to kings on an equal basis, so they accepted, willingly or not, to follow his instructions. Yet, the princes were not willing to take orders from a mere field marshal. Oxenstierna had to take these facts of political life into account when he made his dispositions.

Besides, among the Swedish generals, it was only Gustav Horn (1592–1657) who was currently available and sufficiently experienced to command an army. Johan Banér (1596–1641) was still recuperating from his wounds. The hard-fighting Åke Tott (1598–1640) had been relieved of his command and, besides, had not quite made it as an army commander. Lennart Torstensson (1603–1651) was a prisoner of war in Ingolstadt.

As a result, military command of Swedish forces in Germany fell to Field Marshal Gustav Horn. He came from a distinguished noble family and had a long and notable military career. Horn had served since 1612, first under his brother, Field Marshal Evert Horn, who had fallen while Gustavus Adolphus laid siege to Pskov in 1615, then in Dutch service, and then again in Swedish service in all the King's campaigns. At the battle of Breitenfeld in 1631, Horn at one crucial moment was instrumental in saving the army, and thus winning the battle. So, while the German princes were too proud to serve under a Swedish general, regardless of his titles, experience, and achievements, Horn, likewise, refused to serve under any of the German princes, and since Oxenstierna was his father-in-law, he told him so.[4]

Horn was popular with those who served under him. The Scottish officer Robert Monro described Horn as a beloved commander who in a time dominated by unruly princes exercised unusual self-control and willingness to follow the King's orders:

John George, Elector of Saxony.

Hans Georg von Arnim. He was occasionally called Johann Georg von Arnim.

William, Landgrave of Hesse-Kassel.

---

4   *Ibid.*, p.120.

Gustav Horn, 1640.
(Jacob Heinrich Elbfas)

Dodo von Innhausen und zu
Knyphausen.
(Matthäus Merian)

Gustavus Horne, being a valiant cavalier, without either gall or bitternesse (as they say) but on the contrary he was wise, valiant, sober, modest, vigilant, and diligent, striving in all his actions to please God, and his Master the King of *Sweden* … *Gustavus Horne* was remisse in advising, but very resolute and couragious in the execution; partes most worthy praise in a Commander, being Subalterne to anothers command, as he was unto His Majesty of *Sweden*, who could never enterprize of himselfe, more then was allowed unto him by his instructions had in writing, so as he attempted nothing rashly, he feared no danger, once being entred, and he was so meeke in his command, that with love he obliged the Cavaliers that followed him, to obedience, more then another could doe by austerity: being the best meanes to conquer with, and the safest way to maintaine reputation and credit; Thus beloved of all men, he was very wise, and silent, keeping a *Decorum* in his actions and gestures, being to my judgment powerful to command himselfe, as he did command others.[5]

For sure, Oxenstierna had experienced German and Scottish generals as well. Major General Dodo von Innhausen und zu Knyphausen (1583–1636) was a skilled soldier who had fought in a variety of armies. These included Dutch service from 1602, then under Ernst von Mansfeld (*c.* 1580–1629), a prominent commander who despite being a Catholic served on the side of the Bohemian Revolt in the early stages of the Thirty Years' War, and finally English service during which time Knyphausen raised troops for the 1628 attempt to raise the siege of La Rochelle. Then, in 1629, Knyphausen had again gone into Swedish service. Knyphausen, who first met Gustavus Adolphus when the latter was a mere boy of 13, was one of the most experienced officers in the Swedish army.

Then there was Major General Alexander Leslie (1582–1661), a Scotsman who may have fought in Dutch service against Spain in 1605, certainly went into Swedish service in 1608 or 1609, and in 1609–1610 participated in the campaign in Muscovy under Jacob De la Gardie (1583–1652).[6] Following the relief of Stralsund in 1628, he had been in charge of the town's defences. Later, he had served as major general under Åke Tott.

---

5   Monro, *His Expedition*, p.143.
6   On Leslie, see Steve Murdoch and Alexia Grosjean, *Alexander Leslie and the Scottish Generals of the Thirty Years' War, 1618–1648* (Abingdon: Routledge, 2016).

Lieutenant General Wolf Heinrich von Baudissin (also known as Bauditz; 1579–1646) was a Silesian who was regarded as the army's best cavalry commander. Baudissin had entered Imperial service already while young, and in 1613 he had gone into the service of Venice. In 1620, he had taken part, as a cavalry captain, in the battle of White Mountain outside Prague on the side of the Bohemian Revolt. Baudissin went into Danish service in 1625 and in the following year fought under Ernst von Mansfeld. Entering into Swedish service in 1628, he had in 1632 replaced Åke Tott as the Swedish commander in the Lower Saxon Circle.

An up-and-coming officer in this group was Otto Louis (1597–1634), Wild- and Rhinegrave of Salm-Kyrburg-Mörchingen. Not yet a general, he had fought in Danish service during Danish King Christian IV's failed intervention in Germany in 1626. However, in 1628, Christian IV's morganatic wife fell in love with the dashing Otto Louis. Predictably, the King did not take this well. As a result, Otto Louis chose to go into Swedish service during the war in Pomerania, in which he participated as a colonel of a cavalry regiment. Gustavus Adolphus disliked the poor discipline maintained by Otto Louis, but since the latter fought bravely, he never took action against him. At the time of the King's death, Otto Louis served in Horn's army, but as noted, Gustavus Adolphus had considered promoting him to commander of an army.

These men were both talented and experienced. However, the German princes were no more willing to take orders from them than from a Swedish general. In fact, they would have been more likely to accept a Swedish noble of high rank such as Horn, if Oxenstierna had enjoyed the luxury of pressuring them.

The German princes were a talented but mixed lot. Besides, they had private responsibilities, family ties, and lands in Germany which they had to take into account when deciding upon a course of action. For these reasons, Oxenstierna could never take their loyalty to the Swedish Crown for granted, even when they fought under Swedish banners.

George (1582–1641), Duke of Brunswick-Lüneburg, was an experienced soldier. King Christian III of Denmark was his maternal grandfather, and following studies at the university of Jena, he had in 1612 gone into Danish service, fighting for Denmark in the Kalmar War against Sweden. Following Danish King Christian IV's failed intervention in Germany in 1626, George went into Imperial service. In 1631, he transferred to Swedish service because it was advantageous for him. Although Oxenstierna knew that George would only stay loyal to the Swedish Crown as long as he found it beneficial, George knew how to lead an army and he had sworn loyalty to the Crown. George was politically well-connected; after the death of Gustavus Adolphus, he was according to the old Imperial system elected Commander of the Lower Saxon Circle.

Alexander Leslie.

Wolf Heinrich von Baudissin, 1633.

Otto Louis, Wild- and Rhinegrave of Salm-Kyrburg-Mörchingen. (Cornelis Danckaerts)

George, Duke of Brunswick-Lüneburg.
(Residenzmuseum, Celle)

Christian, Count Palatine of Birkenfeld-
Bischweiler. (Matthäus Merian)

Christian (1598–1654), Count Palatine of Birkenfeld-Bischweiler, had gone into Swedish service in 1630 when Gustavus Adolphus landed in Germany. In Swedish service, he was appointed general of cavalry. Although an able commander, Christian was less experienced in warfare than his peers.

Finally, there was Bernard, Duke of Saxe-Weimar (1604–1639), possibly the best commander of the German princes in the Swedish army. The talented Bernard was born as a younger son of a duke, so he went into military service early. When Bernard in 1631 went into Swedish service, he had already fought in several armies, including under Ernst von Mansfeld in 1622, Christian IV of Denmark in 1625, and from 1627 in Dutch service. He was made colonel after having shown his skills at Werben in 1631, and in 1632, Gustavus Adolphus appointed him general. Meanwhile, Gustavus Adolphus had made Bernard's elder brother, Duke William of Saxe-Weimar, lieutenant general and Gustavus Adolphus's deputy commander of the main field army. However, William had grown ill, so he had bestowed the title and position of lieutenant general to his younger brother Bernard. Whether because of lack of time or alternatives, Oxenstierna now accepted William's transfer of his position to his brother. At Lützen, Bernard *had*, after all, assumed command of the Swedish field army after the death of Gustavus Adolphus, and his personal military ability was a major factor in saving the army and holding the battlefield after the King's death.

Yet, this did not make Bernard the overall commander of the Swedish military forces in Germany. As noted, it was Oxenstierna himself who according to the late King's wishes should assume political and military control in Germany.[7] And with the list of available candidates for the position of overall military commander being what it was, Oxenstierna had no choice but to retain the role of military commander-in-chief for himself.

Yet, Oxenstierna lacked the time to take personal command of a field army, as Gustavus Adolphus had done, and simultaneously continue his political duties. Besides, he was not a soldier and had no particular military skills beyond the general knowledge of military affairs expected of any senior noble. Furthermore, Oxenstierna rightly deemed it more important to manage the royal succession at home and the establishment of the planned Protestant alliance in Germany so that both could be achieved without problems. What Oxenstierna *could* do was to assume overall, not field, military and political command. In doing so, Oxenstierna also tried to reconcile the military situation with the late King's wishes. Of course, reorganising the senior levels

---

7   Or, to be precise, in the four named Imperial Circles; however, there is no reason to believe that Gustavus Adolphus had wanted anybody else to assume overall responsibility on his death.

of command and the entire setup of Sweden's military forces in Germany under conditions of ongoing warfare posed its own set of problems.

The Swedish Field Armies and the German Princes

The first internal problem of Swedish military setup, it was soon revealed, was that the still recuperating Johan Banér was dissatisfied with how Christian, Count Palatine of Birkenfeld-Bischweiler, handled the army in the Swabian Circle. Johan Banér (1596–1641) had seen his first action at the siege of Pskov in 1615. He had also distinguished himself at the siege of Riga 1621, for which he was promoted to colonel. Since then he had followed Gustavus Adolphus as a trusted commander. Banér had commanded the right wing at the battle of Breitenfeld in 1631. In the following year, he had taken a bad wound in his right arm from a musket shot at Alte Feste, a

Bernard, Duke of Saxe-Weimar. (Photo: Medströms)

wound that never fully healed. Banér's experience and ability as a soldier was not in doubt, even though Oxenstierna at times complained of his 'insolent, presumptuous, and ambitious head'.[8] Oxenstierna accordingly agreed with Banér, suggesting that if Banér had recovered sufficiently to return to duty, Oxenstierna would send the Count Palatine to take command of an army of the Rhine, as the late King had directed. Banér replied that although he had not yet fully recovered, he would return to resume command.[9] In December 1632, Banér returned to the army in the Swabian Circle (which, he then reported, had a strength of 1,500 to 2,000 horse and 3,000 foot), relieving Christian. Soon after, in January 1633, Horn brought reinforcements and also assumed command of the army in the Swabian Circle, which then had a strength of 3,100 horse and 3,700 foot.[10] Henceforth, this became Horn's field army. Otto Louis, Wild- and Rhinegrave of Salm-Kyrburg-Mörchingen, was given command of the army in Alsace. Soon after, Banér left the army. His wound was not yet healed, and he may have resented that he no longer had an independent command. Banér had no need to worry; from February 1634 he was given independent command of and orders to reconstitute the Swedish field army in the north-east, in the Upper Saxon Circle, which remained a theatre of key importance to Sweden but where Swedish military forces were comparatively weak.

8   Oxenstierna to Gabriel Gustafsson Oxenstierna, 29 March 1636, *AOSB* 1:15, pp.326–36, on p.329.
9   Tingsten, *Huvuddragen*, p.11–12.
10 *Ibid.*, p.34.

The next step was to sort out the late King's field army. In January 1633, Oxenstierna reported to the regency government that the main field army formerly under Gustavus Adolphus would be divided into two armies. One army, under George, Duke of Brunswick-Lüneburg, assisted by the reliable Knyphausen, would move to the River Weser with orders to defeat the Catholic League army in the Westphalian Circle under Jost Maximilian von Bronckhorst-Gronsfeld (1598–1662), the successor of Gottfried Heinrich zu Pappenheim whose army previously had operated in the region with great success. Bronckhorst-Gronsfeld was already engaged by Baudissin along the Rhine, so his strongholds in the Westphalian Circle were poorly manned. Besides, William of Hesse-Kassel would lead the allied Hessian army, too, into Westphalia from the south.[11] A week later, Oxenstierna promoted Knyphausen to the rank of field marshal.[12] This was, no doubt, a means to give the experienced Knyphausen additional status vis-à-vis George, and also to safeguard Swedish interests in case George chose to focus on his personal goals at the detriment to the Swedish cause.

The other army, under Bernard of Saxe-Weimar, would move to Franconia, with the task of defending the Franconian Circle. Bernard would be assisted by Major General Wilhelm von Calcum, better known as Lohausen (1584–1640).[13] Lohausen was another of those experienced officers who for years had fought in a variety of armies. Having lost his right leg in an early battle, he employed a wooden one. He was an educated man who knew several languages, and while in Imperial captivity after the 1626 battle of Lutter-am-Barenberge, he had translated several classics from Latin and Italian into German.

Then the turn came to the expeditionary corps in Silesia, which hitherto had been under the command of Colonel Jacob Duwall (c. 1589–1634), an experienced Scotsman who had been in Swedish service since 1607. In reality, the Swedish expeditionary corps had been lent to the allied Saxon army under John George of Saxony, who like William of Hesse-Kassel was an ally, not a subordinate. In February, Oxenstierna appointed Count Heinrich Matthias von Thurn commander of the Swedish troops in Silesia, which until then had been subordinated Jacob Duwall.[14] Thurn was the one who in 1618 had led the Bohemian Revolt, which caused the outbreak of the Thirty Years' War. He had subsequently gone into Swedish service, but lately as ambassador to Brandenburg. As for the Swedish troops in Silesia, they remained under Saxon command. Duwall stayed with the corps to assist Thurn.

Although apparently nowhere stated in writing, a pattern is visible in these appointments. This would seem to be Oxenstierna's design, and no mere coincidence. George, Duke of Brunswick-Lüneburg, the newly appointed commander of the important Weser army, received Field Marshal

11 Oxenstierna to the Council of the Realm, 3 January 1633 (O.S.), *AOSB* 1:8, pp.1–10, on p.7.
12 Oxenstierna to Knyphausen, 10 January 1633 (O.S.), *AOSB* 1:8, pp.57–9.
13 *Ibid.*, 59 n.3; Tingsten, *Huvuddragen*, pp.14–15.
14 Oxenstierna to George William of Brandenburg and John George of Saxony, 9 February 1633 (O.S.), *AOSB* 1:8, pp.189–91; Tingsten, *Huvuddragen*, pp.18, 38.

Knyphausen as his deputy. Likewise, Bernard, Duke of Saxe-Weimar, received Major General Lohausen as his deputy. In the same manner, the Bohemian noble Heinrich Matthias von Thurn was told to retain Colonel Duwall as his deputy. Clearly, Oxenstierna put these armies under the command of German princes, but in each case with an experienced soldier as second in command who already had proven himself and, perhaps more importantly, had proven his loyalty in Swedish service. It is notable that both Horn and Banér remained in full command of their respective armies, without the need for such a deputy.

Following these appointments, Oxenstierna only needed to make sure that the new army of the Rhine was properly taken care of, too. Because one German prince remained eligible for army command: Christian, Count Palatine of Birkenfeld-Bischweiler.

The last directive of Gustavus Adolphus had been to give Christian command of an army of the Rhine. Hence, Oxenstierna had given Christian the appropriate orders when he by the end of 1632 was relieved by Banér.

In late March, Christian assumed command of what now became the army of the Rhine, replacing Lieutenant General Wolf Heinrich von Baudissin. Christian had orders to take command of all units on the Rhine, except those in Frankfurt-am-Main and Mainz, which remained under the direct authority of Oxenstierna and, for a few years, functioned as Sweden's second capital.[15] We can presume that Oxenstierna intended Baudissin to remain in the Rhine army as Christian's deputy, in a similar arrangement to what Oxenstierna had established elsewhere. However, Baudissin was dissatisfied with the new arrangement. He accordingly left Swedish service, thus inadvertently spoiling what seems to have been Oxenstierna's cunning scheme.

In spring 1633, there were accordingly five Swedish field armies and one large expeditionary corps in Germany, with a total strength of some 72,000 to 76,000 men (Table 3). In addition, there were some 37,000 men in garrisons throughout the theatres of operations.[16] Furthermore, there were three allied field armies: the Saxon army under John George of Saxony and his general Hans Georg von Arnim; the Hessian army under William of Hesse-Kassel; and the Brandenburgian army, which, as noted, like the Swedish contingent in Silesia operated under Saxon command. The allied armies had a total strength of some 30,000. Besides, the allies had garrison troops, too. The grand total of the loose Protestant alliance was accordingly close to 150,000 soldiers, and so far, they were loyal to the Swedish cause.

15 Tingsten, *Huvuddragen*, p.50. Although Christian assumed command of the army of the Rhine on 13 March 1633, Oxenstierna had planned this appointment together with the others already in January, if not before. Oxenstierna to Ambassador Jacob Steinberg in Brunswick, 9 January 1633 (O.S.), *AOSB* 1:8, pp.43–53, on pp.47–8.
16 Tingsten, *Huvuddragen*, p.115.

Table 3. Disposition of the Swedish armies in Germany, spring 1633, with estimated number of men. (Source: Mankell, *Uppgifter* 2, pp.169–71; Tingsten, *Huvuddragen*, p.39)

- The Swabia army under Gustav Horn, in the Swabian Circle, with 14,000 men
- The Alsace army under Otto Louis, Wild- and Rhinegrave of Salm-Kyrburg-Mörchingen, in Alsace, with 9,000 to 10,000 men
- The Franconia army under Bernard of Saxe-Weimar and Major General Lohausen, in the Franconian Circle, with 13,500 men
- The army of the Rhine under Christian, Count Palatine of Birkenfeld-Bischweiler, in the Electoral and Upper Rhenish Circles, with 10,800 men
- The Weser or Lower Saxon army under George, Duke of Brunswick-Lüneburg, and Field Marshal Knyphausen, in the Lower Saxon and Westphalian Circles, with 15,000 to 18,000 men
- The Silesia corps under Count Heinrich Matthias von Thurn and Colonel Duwall, in Silesia, with 10,000 men (subordinated to the Saxon army)

Oxenstierna wanted Sweden to lead a coalition of German Protestant powers, and he wanted the war in Germany primarily to be fought with German soldiers. Oxenstierna had accordingly devised a policy to include the German princes in the Swedish army, reward them with high rank, and give them important commands. Johan Banér was against this policy. He argued that Oxenstierna committed a strategic error in insisting on realising the late King's plans for five separate Swedish field armies in Germany instead of concentrating his forces for a decisive strike against the heart of the Empire. Banér instead suggested the formation of two strong, wholly Swedish field armies, respectively commanded by Horn and himself. These two armies would then go on the offensive against the Habsburg heartland, until the Emperor agreed to peace.[17] While political realities certainly influenced Oxenstierna's choice of army commanders, Banér's criticism fails to take into account three problems. First, the need not to leave the Swedish core territories undefended against potential attacks from Denmark or the Polish-Lithuanian Commonwealth. Second, the importance to provide a measure of security to those Protestant territories which were at risk of enemy reconquest. Third, the logistical constraints. In fact, the King's intention, which was realised by Oxenstierna, to divide his military forces into several, separate armies may have been the necessary outcome of logistical limits. With many parts of Germany already ravaged by war, there were increasing difficulties in finding supplies. It was simply impossible to supply as large forces as in the early years of the war. Even in the early years, it should be remembered, armies were frequently split up for logistical reasons and only rejoined for battle.[18]

Johan Banér.
(Photo: Medströms)

17 Banér to Oxenstierna, 20 November 1632 (O.S.), *AOSB* 2:6, pp.81–3.
18 Oxenstierna explained the disposition as in accordance with the wishes of the late King. Oxenstierna to the Council of the Realm, 4 February 1633 (O.S.), *AOSB* 1:8, pp.159–66, on p.163.

The Heilbronn League

In mid March 1633, Oxenstierna opened the planned-for meeting to unite the Protestant party in Germany. Originally intended to take place at Ulm already in December, the King's death delayed the proceedings and the meeting had to be moved to Heilbronn, which in addition was a less exposed location. Arguments about rank were invariably a key obstacle in diplomatic negotiations, but Oxenstierna evaded the issue by dispensing with chairs and arranging for the participants to stand throughout the discussions. After a month of negotiations under these conditions, the Heilbronn League was formed on 23 April out of the Protestant parties of the Electoral Rhenish, Franconian, Swabian, and Upper Rhenish Circles, with Axel Oxenstierna as Director-General. Brandenburg refused to commit to the League, and Saxony did not wish to participate. Hence, neither of the two Saxon Circles joined the League.

By then, Oxenstierna had also renewed the Franco-Swedish treaty. As before, France would pay 400,000 Reichsthalers annually to subsidise Sweden's war effort. In return, Sweden promised to maintain 6,000 horse and 30,000 foot in Germany. The subsidy was important but not critical to Sweden's finances. In 1633, for instance, the Dutch Republic paid the very same amount (600,000 Gulden, corresponding to 400,000 Reichsthalers[19]) for the use of only 1,600 national Swedish and Finnish cavalry under Colonel Torsten Stålhandske (1593–1642), to operate together with Hessian cavalry against the Spanish Netherlands.[20] Incidentally, the mission against the Spanish Netherlands was a success, and Stålhandske, already a well-known Finnish cavalry commander, was promoted to Major General after the campaign. Stålhandske had grown up with his step-father, the Scottish Major Robert Guthrie, and in his youth once followed Patrick Ruthven to Scotland on an enlistment drive. He then fought under Gustavus Adolphus, first in Prussia and then at both Breitenfeld and Lützen.

Torsten Stålhandske.
(Photo: Medströms)

19 Exchange rate as specified in the Heilbronn League agreements. Haupt- und Nebenrezesszu Heilbronn, 1633 IV 15, Reichsarchiv, Vol. 5 (1713), PSpec I–1, pp.290–297, on p.294 (Dokumentenarchiv der Universitätsbibliothek Augsburg).
20 Detlev Pleiss, "Der Zug der finnischen Reiter in die Niederlande via Wesel 1633", Jutta Prieur (ed.), *Stadt und Festung Wesel: Beiträgezur Stadtgeschichte der frühen Neuzeit* 1 (Wesel: Stadtarchiv Wesel, Studien und Quellenzur Geschichte von Wesel XX, 1998), pp.1–48.

The Heilbronn League agreed to maintain an army of what most understood to be 16,000 horse and 40,000 foot.[21] The French and Dutch subsidies would go into the League treasury. In addition, the League agreed to pay the arrears of the units already in service. This was necessary, since within days of the formation of the League, parts of Horn's and Bernard's armies, then at Donauwörth on the Danube, mutinied, refusing to carry out any duties until their arrears had been paid. It was not so much a popular rising as one engineered by the colonels hired on the Continent, who depended on payments for both their personal needs and to maintain discipline among their enlisted troops. Many colonels formed an association to secure their interests. The impact of the mutiny was considerable, since a majority of the army consisted of Continental enlisted units. It took some time before Sweden and the League had gathered sufficient money to pay the troops, and the disturbances continued for several weeks.[22] Finally, a significant payment, some in the form of cash but most in German lands, was handed over. This fulfilled the demand at least in part, and the most turbulent officers were pacified with gifts of estates in Germany. Chief among the beneficiaries was Bernard, who indeed may have helped to set the mutiny on foot.

Many colonels quickly sold their new estates, since their cash needs were immediate and ownership in any case might change due to the fortunes of war. Others took recourse to seeking contributions, followed by looting. To give but one minor example: when Horn and Bernard in the summer of 1634 led the main Swedish field army and its Heilbronn League allies deep into Bavaria, they in July stormed and took Landshut. 'We stayed eight days and plundered the town', noted Peter Hagendorf, a former Imperial soldier who then served in the Swedish army, in his field diary.[23] This kind of behaviour was hardly conducive to long-term economic development. As a result, the League found it increasingly difficult to finance its commitments, and all arrears could not be paid. In fact, the League never succeeded in raising more than a minor share of the funding that had been agreed upon.

Successes in the West, Defeats in the East

The key importance of the army of the Rhine was that it blocked the important Habsburg route to the Spanish Netherlands, known as the Spanish Road (el Camino Español). In the past, Spain had repeatedly used this route to bring reinforcements for its war against the Dutch Republic. The route had also been used in reverse, to bring troops from the Spanish Netherlands in support of the Imperial army in Germany. For Sweden and the Protestant

---

21 *The Swedish Intelligencer* (London: Nathaniel Butter and Nicolas Bourne,1632–1633), Vol. 3, 225. The calculation of the numbers of men committed to and the corresponding pay to which the League agreed was complex and, no doubt, to some extent open to interpretation.

22 Horn to Oxenstierna, 4 May 1633 (O.S.), *AOSB* 2:8, pp.124–5; Horn to Oxenstierna, 21 May 1633 (O.S.), *AOSB* 2:8, pp.125–7.

23 Peter Hagendorf, *Sedan stack vi staden i brand: En legoknekts dagbok från trettioåriga kriget* (Stockholm: Ordfront & Armémuseum, 2006), p.50.

Germany.

alliance, it was vital to block such troop movements. France shared this interest, because of its ongoing rivalry with both Spain and the Empire. On the Rhine, the centre of opposition to the Protestant cause was the town of Cologne. But there were also complications with Charles, Duke of Lorraine, who attempted to navigate his own foreign policy, between the stronger powers of France and the Empire.

In early June 1633, Christian of Birkenfeld-Bischweiler and the Swedish army of the Rhine took Heidelberg, hitherto held by Imperial troops. The defenders then moved to Hagenau, located directly on the Spanish supply line. As Christian laid siege to Hagenau, the Duke of Lorraine first took some of the Imperial troops into his own service, and then attacked the besieging Swedish army. Lorraine alone was no match for the Swedish army of the Rhine, and in August, Christian of Birkenfeld-Bischweiler's Swedish army defeated Charles of Lorraine at Pfaffenhofen, south of Ingolstadt. Richelieu had no intention to permit either Lorraine or the Empire again to secure the Rhine route for the Habsburg cause. In the following year, Richelieu summarily deposed Charles of Lorraine and subjected his duchy to French administration.[24]

Despite the importance of the Rhine route, it was the Weser army which was the strongest of the Swedish armies. This may well have been because of what Oxenstierna knew of Gustavus Adolphus's plans for the near future just before his death. Gustavus Adolphus had first planned to deal with the Imperial commander-in-chief, Albrecht von Wallenstein (1583–1634), in the Upper Saxon Circle. After this had been accomplished, the King had intended to sort out the situation in the Lower Saxon Circle, that is, around the Weser. This was the region where Pappenheim so efficiently had harassed Tott's Swedish army earlier in 1632. However, after the fall of Pappenheim at Lützen, and the retreat of his surviving men towards Bohemia, the situation around the Weser was no longer as critical as it had been. The current Catholic League commander there, Jost Maximilian von Bronckhorst-Gronsfeld, at the time had only 4,000 men at his disposal (most of it horse). The late King's concerns for the Weser region were accordingly no longer urgent. Nonetheless, Oxenstierna reinforced the Weser army, possibly out of respect for the judgement of his late friend and ruler.[25] The fact that it was commanded by the influential George, Duke of Brunswick-Lüneburg, no doubt played a role, too (from January 1634, George simultaneously held the position of Swedish general and the old Imperial position of Commander of the Lower Saxon Circle, which constituted the theatre of operations of his army). While Bronckhorst-Gronsfeld was an able soldier, he was not as aggressive as his predecessor Pappenheim. In fact, he was an educated man who published comments about the history of the war and also, most likely, invented the Gronsfeld cypher, a variant of the well-known Vigenère cypher

---

24 Tingsten, *Huvuddragen*, pp.52–3, pp.106–9.
25 *Ibid.*, 39. As noted, Oxenstierna explained the disposition as in accordance with the wishes of the late King. Oxenstierna to the Council of the Realm, 4 February 1633 (O.S.), *AOSB* 1:8, pp.159–66, on p.163.

which became widely used in Europe among those who needed to send encrypted messages.

The Swedish Weser army operated in close cooperation with the allied Hessian army. In March 1633, a joint Hessian–Swedish army laid siege to Hameln, a key town on the Weser. The joint force was led by the Hessian Lieutenant General Peter Melander von Holzapfel (1589–1648) and the Swedish Colonel Lars Kagg (1595–1661). Holzapfel was another of those officers who had fought for many countries, including in Dutch, Venetian, and Swiss service. In 1633, Landgrave William of Hesse-Kassel appointed Holzapfel his lieutenant general, which put him immediately under the Landgrave in military rank. As for Kagg, his first wars had been the Kalmar War against Denmark in 1611 and the campaign against Pskov in Muscovy in 1615;he had also trained in the Life Guard of Maurice of Nassau for three years, and then gone into

Peter Melander von Holzapfel.

the service of Frederick V of Bohemia. In 1621, Kagg was back in Swedish service, fighting at Riga, and he also took part in the battles of Dirschau and Stralsund. In 1631, he had been beaten by Pappenheim in the same region where he now was fighting.

Soon, an Imperial army under General Jean de Merode (c.1589–1633; also known as Johann von Merode) joined forces with Bronckhorst-Gronsfeld's League units. In July, they moved against Hameln. Merode was a skilled soldier, but his name was, apparently already in or close to his life-time, in folk etymology most associated with the concept of marauding. For instance, in the contemporary novel *Simplicius Simplicissimus* by the German writer Grimmelshausen, who participated in the Thirty Years' War, marauders were called Merode Brothers.[26]

In response, a joint Swedish–Hessian army under Knyphausen, Holzapfel, and Kaggin July offered battle at Oldendorf (modern-day Hessisch-Oldendorf). The Imperial and League commanders had deployed on two hills, one of which they regarded as unassailable. However, Knyphausen's men found a small path which admitted a column of cavalry, one horseman at a time. Bronckhorst-Gronsfeld believed that he could defeat Knyphausen's cavalry on the hill itself, so he allowed them to approach. However, Knyphausen's men not only repulsed Bronckhorst-Gronsfeld's charge, but then successfully counter-attacked. In effect, both wings of the Swedish–Hessian army successfully enveloped the Imperial army. The efficient Swedish artillery fire played a major role, too. As a result, the Imperials panicked and fled. It was a conclusive Swedish victory, which left almost

---

26 Hans Jakob Cristoph von Grimmelshausen, *Der abenteuerliche Simplicissimus Teutsch* 4:13 (1669); Universal-Bibliothek edn published by Philipp Reclam, Stuttgart (1990), pp.417–18. In reality, the term *marauder* is believed to derive from Old French.

4,000 Imperial and League soldiers dead and some 3,000 captured. Merode fell in the battle, and Bronckhorst-Gronsfeld barely escaped, losing his horse. In comparison, Swedish and Hessian losses were small.[27] A few days later, Hameln surrendered to the joint Swedish–Hessian army.

Then there were the armies in the Swabian and Franconian Circles. In March 1633, Horn and Bernard of Saxe-Weimar joined forces at Oberndorf in the Black Forest. Their intention was to march into Bavaria. However, at the end of April, as noted, parts of their army mutinied at Donauwörth, refusing to carry out any duties until their arrears had been paid. Horn went there in an attempt to sort out the problem. However, since it took time before Sweden and its Heilbronn allies had gathered sufficient money to pay at least some of the troops, the disturbances continued for several weeks.

Then, as the mutinous officers slowly were falling in line, a new problem arose. During the summer, the Spanish Governor of Milan, Gómez Suárez de Figueroa y Córdoba (1587–1634), Duke of Feria, had raised a substantial Spanish army in Italy. He had, at first, intended to lead it to the Spanish Netherlands by way of Tyrol, but then he changed plans, instead deciding to recover the parts of Alsace that were needed to restore access to the old Spanish route along the Rhine. And Feria was not alone. In late September, Feria joined forces with the Catholic League Field Marshal Johann von Aldringen (1588–1634) at Lake Constance (German: *Bodensee*). For the Swedes, this was bad news. Both Feria and Aldringen were experienced soldiers with distinguished records. Aldringen was known to the Swedes; in the previous year, Gustavus Adolphus had defeated the Catholic League's commander-in-chief, Johann t'Serclaes von Tilly, at the battle of Rain-am-Lech, and Aldringen had succeeded Tilly in this position after Tilly's death in the aftermath of the battle.

Johann von Aldringen.
(*Theatrum Europaeum*)

Now the problem for the Swedes was that they did not know where to expect the Habsburg army. Horn and Bernard decided once again to lead their armies on separate ways. Horn moved south, intending to prevent the Habsburg army from reaching the Rhine and crossing into Alsace. Bernard moved east, so as to apply pressure on the enemy closer to his home.

By October, it was obvious that Feria's and Aldringen's combined army was on its way to Alsace. Feria took Bregenz, Konstanz, Rheinfelden, and Breisach. However, Horn's army blocked any further movement. As for Bernard, he laid siege to Ratisbon (Regensburg), which he took in November. Regensburg was an important Protestant town in the predominantly Catholic Bavaria, so it had a political value beyond that of its strategic location.[28] The siege lasted less than two weeks, since the besiegers had some 12,000

---

27 Bertil C:son Barkman, Sven Lundkvist, and Lars Tersmeden, *Kungl. Svea Livgardes Historia* 3:2: *1632 (1611)–1660* (Stockholm: Stiftelsen för Svea Livgardes Historia, 1966), pp.24–31.

28 Regensburg was, together with Vienna, Worms, and Speyer, one of Germany's key political centres.

men, while the defenders were no more than 2,000. The fall of Regensburg had ramifications far beyond its immediate surroundings. Wallenstein, the Imperial commander-in-chief, had to abandon his, until then, successful campaign against Saxony, Brandenburg, and Pomerania.[29] For Feria and Aldringen, the implications were far worse. Since Horn blocked them in the west, where their army was harassed by Horn's men, and Bernard now blocked them along the Danube, their only available recourse was to retreat into Bavaria. There their men went into winter quarters. Soon after, Feria died from typhoid.

Kagg was nominated Swedish commandant in Regensburg, not because he wanted that, but due to his medical condition. Kagg had suffered several wounds in previous battles, including at Oldendorf, which prevented him from horse riding. Most of all, Kagg wanted to retire and return to Sweden. However, Oxenstierna needed a reliable commandant for the important town, so Kagg had to stay.

By the end of 1633, Oxenstierna had reasons to be satisfied with his achievements. He had faced a series of challenges after the death of Gustavus Adolphus. Politically, Oxenstierna had brought about the royal succession in Sweden according to the late King's intentions and introduced a regency government for the heir, young Princess Christina. In Germany, the newly established Heilbronn League seemed to fulfil its purpose of placing the burden of the costs for the war on the shoulders of Sweden's allies. Militarily, the Swedish armies in the Swabian, Franconian, Rhenish, Lower Saxon, and Westphalian Circles were victorious. Alsace, too, did fine, which meant that the entire western half of the Empire as well as the Baltic shore were controlled by Swedish or allied armies. Despite the fall of Gustavus Adolphus, Oxenstierna had succeeded in maintaining the momentum of the Protestant alliance.

In the east, the military situation was not so good. The Imperial commander-in-chief Wallenstein, the Empire's most capable surviving general, remained undefeated. In late summer 1633, Wallenstein had moved out of Prague, He sent General Rudolf von Morzin (c. 1585–1646) into Silesia. Morzin was a Bohemian who previously had been in Commonwealth and Muscovite service, before he became an Imperial officer. He had fought both at Breitenfeld and Lützen. In October, Morzin rapidly defeated the Swedes under Heinrich Matthias von Thurn and Jacob Duwall at Steinau-an-der-Oder in Silesia. Thurn's Swedish cavalry managed to extricate itself, but the enlisted infantry (5,000 men) was captured and immediately enlisted into Wallenstein's army. Thurn was taken prisoner, too, but he was turned loose by Wallenstein without ransom. Then Thurn and Duwall signed orders to surrender addressed to the commandants of several fortified towns in the vicinity, many of whom were Bohemians like Thurn and Wallenstein. Those in Liegnitz and Glogau followed the order; several others, under

---

29 Tingsten, *Huvuddragen*, pp.61–2. On the siege of Regensburg, see Barkman, Lundkvist, and Tersmeden, *Kungl. Svea Livgardes Historia* 3:2, pp.45–9. On Feria's army, see also Pierre Picouet, *The Armies of Philip IV of Spain, 1621-1665: The Fight for European Supremacy* (Warwick: Helion, 2019), pp.45–8.

Rudolf von Morzin.

Saxon officers, refused. As a result, the combined Saxon-Brandenburgian army had to save itself by retreating across the Elbe. Wallenstein followed them into Saxony and Brandenburg, where he among other locations occupied Berlin. Frankfurt-an-der-Oder fell, too, when attacked by Johann von Götz (1599–1645), another of Wallenstein's commanders. Some Imperial raiding parties reached as far as Pomerania. For Sweden, the campaign was a failure. Moreover, it was a shameful failure. Thurn was dismissed from Swedish service. Duwall died in Breslau in the following year.[30]

Oxenstierna's Strategy and Chain of Command

The regency government had already on 21 January 1633 officially appointed Oxenstierna the senior representative of the Swedish Crown in Germany and commander-in-chief of the Swedish armies there.[31] He suddenly had more formal powers than any other subject of the Swedish Crown, then or later.

This was a formality, not a promotion, since the late King's instruction already had made Oxenstierna his representative. Besides, as chancellor he was still responsible for other aspects of Swedish policy. In the winter of 1632/1633, Oxenstierna submitted and then discussed with the regency government in Stockholm an extensive memorandum on domestic and foreign policy after the death of the King. Out of 36 clauses, only six dealt with Germany.[32] Oxenstierna explained that he was creating a double-security arrangement that consisted of, first, a permanent Swedish presence in Pomerania and Prussia, in order to secure the Baltic Sea against both the Empire and the Polish-Lithuanian Commonwealth, with which there was a dynastic conflict, and, second, the formation of a confederation of allied Protestant princes in central Germany to serve as a buffer against further Imperial aggression. Most of the Swedish national units would be withdrawn to garrisons on the Baltic shore (where, in fact, most Swedish units in Germany already were deployed). The main field army would then

---

30 Tingsten, *Huvuddragen*, pp.77–9.

31 *Svenska riksrådets protokoll* 3 (Stockholm: RA, 1885), 12 (11 January 1633 O.S.); Council of the Realm, 12 January 1633 (O.S.), *Handlingar rörande Skandinaviens historia* 24 (Stockholm: Hörberg, 1840), pp.310–12. The appointment was made on 11 January while the warrant was dated 12 January 1633 (O.S.).

32 The memorandum resulted in an ongoing discussion, by letter, between Oxenstierna and the Council. Oxenstierna to the Council of the Realm through Secretary Lars Grubbe, 5 December 1632 (O.S.), *AOSB* 1:7, pp.699–717; Council of the Realm to Oxenstierna, 14 January 1633 (O.S.), *Handlingar rörande Skandinaviens historia* 24 (Stockholm: Hörberg, 1840), pp.315–37; Oxenstierna to the Council of the Realm through Secretary Lars Grubbe, 13 February 1633 (O.S.), *AOSB* 1:8, pp.226–33. See also Council of the Realm to Oxenstierna, 7 January 1633 (O.S.), *Handlingar* 24, pp.291–310. Oxenstierna's initial memorandum of 5 December 1632 (O.S.) can also be found in *Handlingar* 24, pp.249–74.

The fortified camp of Gustavsburg, 1633.

be dissolved. However, Sweden would retain a few outposts further south, including Mainz, where a vast fortified camp, known as Gustavsburg and with capacity to host 17,000 men, was constructed at the junction of the Rivers Main and Rhine as a centre for Swedish power and to ensure that nobody else gained control of this important region. For a few years, Mainz functioned as Oxenstierna's residence and a second Swedish capital.

Following the strategy outlined in the memorandum, Oxenstierna continued the policy of retaining most Swedish troops in garrisons in northern Germany.[33] So was, for instance, the Swedish Brigade, the core of which was the Östergötland Regiment (sometimes called the New Blue Regiment) dissolved, and the survivors of its national components sent to Pomerania.[34] Since the Scottish units, too, were regarded as particularly loyal, many of them were also moved into the northern garrisons.[35] Henceforth, almost all soldiers in the field army were enlisted on the Continent.

However, unsure of Denmark's and the Polish-Lithuanian Commonwealth's intentions, Oxenstierna made sure that an increasing number of new conscripts were retained in Sweden and Finland as well, so as to defend against any external threats. Oxenstierna had never forgotten that Denmark remained a latent threat and that Sweden still technically was at war with the Commonwealth. Oxenstierna had never been as enthusiastic about the war in Germany as Gustavus Adolphus. As late as 1634, Oxenstierna wrote to Banér that 'The Polish war is our war; win or lose, it is our gain or loss. This German war, I do not know what it is, only that we pour out blood here for the sake of reputation, and have naught but ingratitude to expect.'[36]

In Oxenstierna's opinion, the formation of the Heilbronn League was a step in the right direction. Before the League had been put together, he had written to the Swedish regency government that henceforth, the war should, if at all possible, be waged by proxy. Sweden would lend her name to the war, but Germans would have to fight it, as allies or in Swedish service. Sweden would, as a secret policy, not invest either men or funding in the war, except where so was necessary to maintain the north German garrisons.[37] The withdrawal of most national units to the Baltic shore formed part of this secret policy, and secrecy seems to have been maintained. The removal of national units did not seem to upset Sweden's allies, who may not have noticed the gradual redeployment.

One outstanding question was who would become operational commander of Swedish military forces in Germany. We have seen that for political reasons, Oxenstierna had to take the position of overall commander upon himself. Yet, Germany was not Oxenstierna's first war, and he was, no doubt, aware of the difficulties inherent in the management of army operations from afar and the frequently negative results of a failure to maintain unity of

33 Oxenstierna to the Council of the Realm, 3 January 1633 (O.S.), *AOSB* 1:8, 1–10, on p.7.
34 Gustaf Petri, *Kungl. Första livgrenadjärregementets historia 2: Östgöta regemente till fot 1619–1679* (Stockholm: P. A. Norstedt & Söner, 1928), p.188.
35 On the loyalty of the Scots, see, for example, Oxenstierna to Queen Christina, 28 September 1635 (O.S.), *AOSB* 1:14, 71–77, on p.73.
36 Oxenstierna to Banér, 28 October 1634 (O.S.), *AOSB* 1:12, pp.629–34, on pp.632–3.
37 Oxenstierna to the Council of the Realm, 4 February 1633 (O.S.), *AOSB*1:8, pp.159–66, on p.162.

command. Now he faced a situation of operations continuing simultaneously in different theatres of war. It became impossible for Oxenstierna personally to direct operations. He received reports by letter, and sent out orders, but by the time his letters arrived, the operational situation had already changed. Oxenstierna realised this, and in his orders, he generally told his senior commander to act as they saw fit within the given parameters.[38]

Due to the aforementioned need to retain the cooperation of the German princes, Oxenstierna did not at this time formally appoint anybody else as overall operational military commander in Germany. Yet, there are reasons to believe that in Oxenstierna's eyes, Field Marshal Gustav Horn played this role. The rank of field marshal was the highest in the Swedish army, and it was reserved for those who might execute independent command in a theatre of operations. Even though Horn was not formally appointed overall operational commander, Oxenstierna still trusted him more than other generals and de facto paid more attention to his suggestions than those of other senior commanders when strategy was being formulated. First, Horn was the most experienced and trusted Swedish commander. Second, he held the senior military rank among those commanders who were available. Third, Horn was Oxenstierna's son-in-law. Fourth, Horn on occasion appears to have had veto rights over suggestions by other generals in Swedish service. This particularly affected the decisions and wishes of Bernard of Saxe-Weimar. Not only because Horn and Bernard at times combined their armies, but also because Bernard generally seems to have been the most ambitious for personal advancement of the generals in Swedish service. Bernard wanted an independent command and regarded himself, a German prince, as of higher worth than any Swedish nobleman. In fact, within months of the battle of Lützen he demanded the title of *Generalissimus* and independent command of both Swedish and Heilbronn League forces. Unsurprisingly, Oxenstierna did not agree.[39] Neither did Horn, who in late May 1633 advised Oxenstierna to offer Bernard a rank no higher than that of lieutenant general, if even that, and only as long as Oxenstierna saw fit to do so;[40] soon after, Horn informed Oxenstierna that he would not serve under Bernard.[41] When Bernard demanded the title of *Generalissimus*, the League directors instead had discussed giving the title to Horn. Although this, no doubt, would have corresponded with Oxenstierna's personal wishes, presumably for political reasons he did not push the issue.[42]

The choice between Horn and Bernard went beyond personal ambitions. Horn, like Oxenstierna, was cautious when it came to strategy, since he saw his key duty as defending Sweden's interests in Germany and the Protestant areas already liberated from Imperial rule. Bernard, on the other hand, may have regarded the overthrow of the Catholic powers, the Emperor and the

---

38 Oxenstierna to George of Brunswick-Lüneburg, 9 March 1633 (O.S.), *AOSB* 1:8, pp.324–6; Oxenstierna to Knyphausen, 22 March 1633 (O.S.), *AOSB* 1:8, pp.356–8.
39 Tingsten, *Huvuddragen*, p.143.
40 Horn to Oxenstierna, 21 May 1633 (O.S.), *AOSB* 2:8, pp.126–7.
41 Horn to Oxenstierna, June 1633 (O.S.), *AOSB* 2:8, pp.129–32, on 130 (no exact date given).
42 Tingsten, *Huvuddragen*, p.144 n.1.

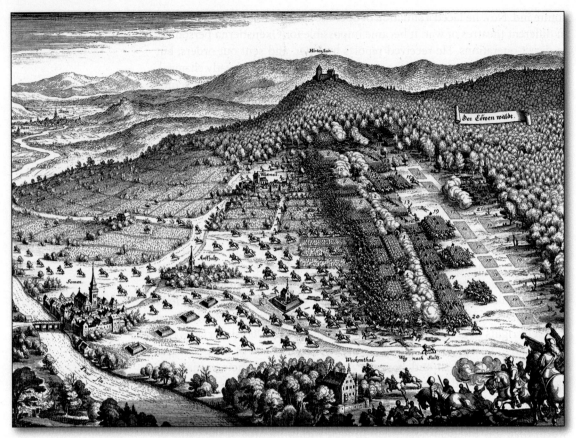

Important victories took place also in the peripheral theatres of war. In 1634, Otto Louis, Wild- and Rhinegrave of Salm-Kyrburg-Mörchingen, took several towns in and around Alsace, including Sulz, Gebweiler, Thann, Belfort, Altkirch, Neuburg, and Freiburg. In this print, he drives Imperial troops and their allies from Lorraine.

Elector of Bavaria, as the more important objective and was willing to gamble to achieve this goal.

The Battle of Nördlingen

George William of Brandenburg had insisted on a resolution to the issue of who should control Pomerania before committing to the Heilbronn League. Nonetheless, Johan Banér and Alexander Leslie prepared to operate in conjunction with Arnim's Saxon army with Swedish troops from Pomerania (previously under Leslie) and some Brandenburgian units. In May 1634, Banér mustered 14,000 men (6,000 horse and 8,000 foot) in Müncheberg, north-west of Frankfurt-an-der-Oder. To this had been added 3,600 Brandenburgers.[43] Banér's army henceforth became a new Swedish field army, that of Silesia. During the summer, the allies moved into first Silesia, and then Bohemia. Although Arnim's Saxon army operated in the same area, cooperation was less than perfect, not least because Saxon and Imperial

---

43   Julius Mankell, *Uppgifter rörande svenska krigsmagtens styrka, sammansättning och fördelning sedan slutet af femtonhundratalet, jemte öfversigt af svenska krigshistoriens vigtigaste händelser under samma tid*, Vol.2 (Stockholm: C.M. Thimgren, 1865), pp.196–7; Tingsten, *Huvuddragen*, p.163.

representatives were engaged in peace negotiations at the same time as the Swedish and Saxon armies moved further into Bohemia.[44] In late July, they reached as far as Prague, the capital of Bohemia and as the Empire's second most important city the long-time residence of the Emperor.

Meanwhile, Horn and Bernard led the main Swedish field army and its Heilbronn League allies deep into Bavaria, where they stormed and took Landshut, an action that resulted in the death of Johann von Aldringen, the senior commander of the Catholic League army.

However, the Imperial cause had successes, too. Following the assassination of Wallenstein in February 1634, the Emperor's son, Archduke Ferdinand (then better known as the King of Hungary, subsequently Emperor under the name Ferdinand III; 1608–1657) had been appointed commander-in-chief of the Imperial army. In this role, the young Archduke was assisted by two Italians: Matthias Gallas (Matteo Gallasso; 1588–1647), who had enjoyed a long, successful military career (which is often forgotten by historians in light of his later, less fortunate endeavours), and Ottavio Piccolomini (1599–1656), who had fought with distinction throughout the war including at the battle of Lützen. In July, the Archduke's Imperial field army recaptured Regensburg. Out of gunpowder, the Swedish commandant, Lars Kagg, had no choice but to surrender.[45] This Imperial success was in August followed by the conquest of Donauwörth.

Two days later, Archduke Ferdinand laid siege to Nördlingen.[46] Following the death of Aldringen,

Matthias Gallas.

Ottavio Piccolomini.

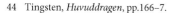

44 Tingsten, *Huvuddragen*, pp.166–7.
45 Barkman, Lundkvist, and Tersmeden, *Kungl. Svea Livgardes Historia* 3:2, pp.57–74.
46 The literature on the siege and battle of Nördlingen is vast. The best account of the mutually conflicting sources is Göran Rystad, "Vem vållade Nördlingen katastrofen" 1634? En studie i propaganda", Göran Rystad (ed.), *Historia kring Trettioåriga kriget* (Stockholm: Wahlström & Widstrand, 1963), pp.81–114 (first published 1959). Recent Swedish works include Lars Ericson, "Nördlingen 1634", Lars Ericson et al., *Svenska slagfält* (np: Wahlström & Widstrand, 2003), pp.139–46; Lars Ericson Wolke, Göran Larsson; and Nils Erik Villstrand, *Trettioåriga kriget: Europa i brand 1618–1648* (Lund: Historiska Media, 2006), pp.226–39. See also Peter Engerisser and Pavel Hrnčiřík, *Nördlingen 1634: Die Schlacht bei Nördlingen – Wendepunkt des Dreißigjährigen Krieges* (Weißenstadt: Verlag Heinz Späthling, 2009); Lothar Höbelt, *Von Nördlingen bis Jankau: Kaiserliche*

Ferdinand also controlled important contingents of the chiefly Bavarian Catholic League army. Besides, he knew that reinforcements were on the way under his cousin, the Cardinal-Infante Ferdinand (1609/1610–1641), who was the younger brother of King Philip IV of Spain. The new Spanish strategy of direct intervention against the Swedes in Germany was the creation of the Count-Duke of Olivares who regarded this as crucial for Spain's ability to project power in the Netherlands. After all, Spain relied on the supply line along the Rhine to maintain communications with the Spanish Netherlands, which Gustavus Adolphus had cut and the Duke of Feria had failed to reopen. The Cardinal-Infante brought an experienced Spanish army of 15,000 men from Italy, which greatly bolstered the Imperial cause.

The Cardinal-Infante arrived in early September. The two cousins Ferdinand, young men of the same age, immediately became good friends. They prepared a fortified camp in the hills south of Nördlingen, and there awaited the Swedish main field army under Horn and Bernard. They were confident and, no doubt, eager for military glory. The united Habsburg army consisted of at least some 36,500 to 39,000 men.[47]

In comparison, Horn's and Bernard's total strength was 23,000 to 25,000 men (probably 9,000 horse, 16,000 foot, and some 70 cannons).[48] Nördlingen had no real military significance, and relieving the town was primarily a political objective. However, Horn and Bernard were determined to save Nördlingen because of its symbolic value. Besides, early intelligence reports suggested that the opposing forces were much weaker in numbers than they actually were. When last-minute intelligence reports reassessed the enemy strength, the Swedish commanders did not heed the new information. Perhaps Horn and Bernard thought it was too late to disengage. As we have seen, Horn was the overall commander of the Swedish army, the senior field marshal, and accordingly, at least in his and Oxenstierna's eyes, Bernard's superior. However, Bernard was a German prince who although technically in Swedish service also, as will be shown, was an autonomous ruler in free alliance with Sweden. Horn and Bernard were used to commanding their own, separate armies. Now they would have to fight together, with Horn in charge of what effectively constituted the senior, right wing of the army, while Bernard commanded the left wing.

The Habsburg army had settled down in a camp on the hill named Schönfeld, south of Nördlingen, and in addition deployed units on a series of other hills that extended in a westerly direction from Schönfeld: Albuch, Heselberg, Lachberg, Ländle, and Himmelreich. The hills were smooth and rounded, but between them were narrow valleys of dense forest. Besides, while the slopes were not steep, they were extensive and took time to climb. To assault any of the fortified positions entailed first marching down into the

---

Strategie und Kriegführung 1634–1645 (Vienna: Heeresgeschichtliches Museum, 2016); Picouet, *Armies of Philip IV*, pp.47–8, pp.231–44.

47 Engerisser and Hrnčiřík, "Nördlingen 1634", p.289; Höbelt, *Von Nördlingen bis Jankau*, p.21; Picouet, *Armies of Philip IV*, p.237.

48 Jonas Hedberg (ed.), *Kungl. Artilleriet: Yngre vasatiden* (Stockholm: Militärhistoriska Förlaget, 1985), p.254; Ericson, "Nördlingen 1634", p.139; Ericson Wolke, Larsson; and Villstrand, *Trettioåriga kriget*, p.227.

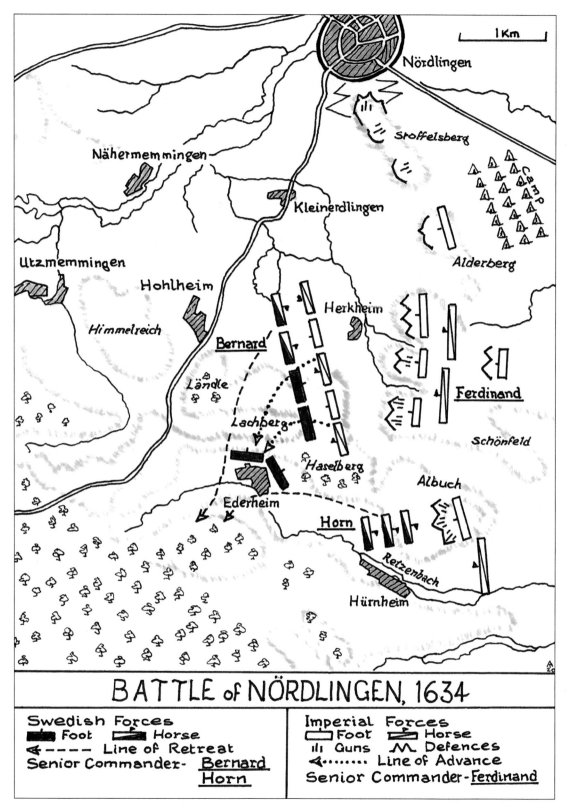

1 Km

Nördlingen

Stoffelsberg

CAMP

Nähermemmingen

Kleinerdlingen

Alderberg

Utzmemmingen

Hohlheim

Herkheim

Himmelreich

Bernard

Ferdinand

Ländle

Lachberg

Schönfeld

Haselberg

Albuch

Ederheim

Horn

Retzenbach

Hürnheim

BATTLE of NÖRDLINGEN, 1634

Swedish Forces
- ◼ Foot ⬜→ Horse
- ◀----- Line of Retreat
- Senior Commander- <u>Bernard</u>
  <u>Horn</u>

Imperial Forces
- ⬜ Foot ⬜→ Horse
- ⅲ Guns ᴍ Defences
- ◀········ Line of Advance
- Senior Commander- <u>Ferdinand</u>

Nördlingen.

Battle of Nördlingen, 1634, as seen from the Imperial side. Horn's men attempt to take the Albuch, on the left and easily recognisable by its three bastions behind of which a huge explosion is taking place. Horn's cavalry, on the extreme left, attempt to bypass the bastions, while his infantry, in the brigade formation of Gustavus Adolphus, attempt to storm them. The Rezenbach valley is visible behind Horn's units, and here the drawing illustrates a later phase of the battle, as Bernard's cavalry flees down into the valley,

valley below. This exposed the troops to fire from the Habsburg outposts, before they even could attempt to climb and storm their objective. The forested valleys were too narrow to allow the units to move in proper order. It was also hard to get an overview of the area, since the hills and forested valleys prevented easy observation. As it turned out, when the ensuing battle got underway, Horn and Bernard failed to see each other's movements, while the two Ferdinands found a hill that gave them an overview of the entire area.

Upon approaching Nördlingen, Horn and Bernard first took up positions at the little town of Bopfingen, to the west of the Habsburg lines. On 5 September, the Swedish army moved out. Because of the hilly terrain, neither the Swedish nor the Imperial–League–Spanish army deployed with any real centre. Bernard, commanding the vanguard, assaulted and rapidly gained

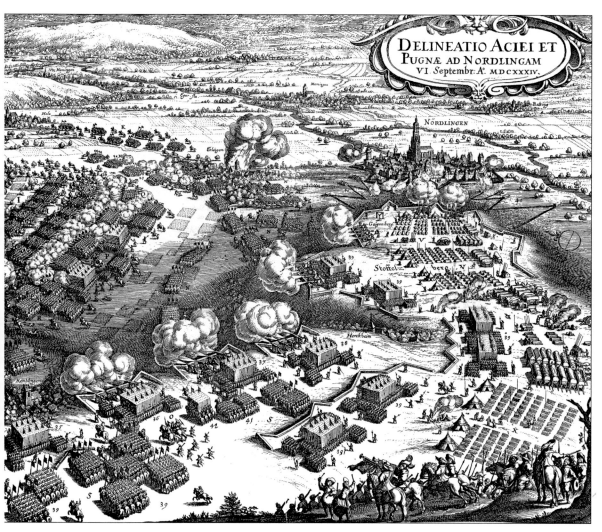

disrupting Horn's units. However, there are numerous inaccuracies in the print. Most obvious, the obsolete form of the Imperial tercio formation was no longer used. Even some events of the battle illustrated in the print can be disputed, as they were based on propagandistic pamphlets produced after the battle. (Matthäus Merian, *Theatrum Europaeum*)

control over Himmelreich, Ländle, Lachberg, and Heselberg, which were defended by only small forces of infantry. The next target would be Albuch, which was fortified and strongly defended by three redoubts. And behind Albuch stood the Imperial main force, on the hill Schönfeld. If the Swedes could gain Albuch, they might be able to push the Habsburg troops down onto the plains around Nördlingen, which probably would result in an untenable position, since the garrison of Nördlingen then could sally out against the enemy (which they indeed appear to have done during the ensuing battle[49]).

---

49 Sydnam Poyntz, *A True Relation of These German Warres* (Camden Society, 1908), p.111.

Battle of Nördlingen, 1634. The last of three paintings by the Cardinal-Infante's court painter Peeter Snayers. Left: The two Ferdinands in the final charge, with the Swedish army fleeing. Upper left: Albuch. Upper centre: Heselberg. The painting is more reliable in its details than the Merian print.

Horn ordered his men to move into position at night, and then at dawn, on 6 September, storm Albuch. Thus began the battle of Nördlingen 1634.

The battle essentially consisted of a Swedish assault on a series of fortified hills. It was a risky plan. If they failed, their only line of retreat went through the Rezenbach valley, south of the hills. If the Imperials managed to gain control of this valley, Horn's men would be surrounded.

Unfortunately for Horn and his men, the night march had resulted in difficulties, with cannons and wagons overturning in muddy lanes which, moreover, caused noise that alerted the enemy. The assault on the hill failed, too, with the cavalry and infantry failing to coordinate their attacks. There were instances of friendly fire, and when one of the three redoubts finally had been taken, a store of abandoned gunpowder apparently exploded, causing yet more casualties and confusion. Besides, the Habsburg forces were no easy opponents. In particular the Spanish infantry was highly trained and disciplined. When Horn's men seemed to have gained the hill, Spanish infantry moved in to support the failing defenders. Horn's infantry could not withstand the Spanish counter-attack, and soon they again lost control of the hill, having to begin all over again. During the day, Horn's men made 14, or according to the Spanish accounts, 15 attempts to storm the redoubts above them on Albuch. However, in the end they could not break through the Habsburg defences. Horn accordingly halted the attack and began to withdraw his men through the Rezenbach valley, under cover of musketeers. In addition, Horn ordered Bernard to cover the retreat. The retreat took place in good order, Horn later explained, but this may be too charitable a description of what due to the terrain likely was a disordered withdrawal. Besides, suddenly Bernard's cavalry fled down into the Rezenbach valley, followed by his infantry, all of them pursued by Habsburg troops. Bernard had engaged the Habsburg troops on the plain at the village of Herkheim, just south of Nördlingen itself. This had not gone well. The two retreating Swedish forces collided around the village of Ederheim in the Rezenbach

THE WARS OF AXEL OXENSTIERNA

valley. Bernard's fleeing men disrupted the already disordered retreat, which turned into a chaotic, wholesale flight. An English officer who commanded a Habsburg company of dragoons in the battle, Sydnam Poyntz, claimed to have heard Bernard "swearing intolerably" in an attempt to restore order.[50] He also noted that "the bottome wherein they fought was but small and had more horse and men then they could well order there already being betwixt two great Hills."[51] In other words, the terrain caused as many problems as the disengagement and withdrawal.

As a result, the entire operation ended in disaster. The Swedish army lost some 8,000 dead or wounded and some 3,000 to 4,000 captured. Most were infantry. Naturally, many captives went into Imperial service. Horn was captured, too, being the most senior Swedish officer to fall into captivity during the entire war. The Swedish army also lost all of its artillery and the supply train. Imperial losses were much lower, an estimated 1,600 dead and wounded.[52] While we should not disregard Gallas's and Piccolomini's input, the two Ferdinands were, rightly, triumphant.

Archduke Ferdinand and the Cardinal-Infante Ferdinand, the victors at Nördlingen. (Cornelis Schut)

They had won a great victory and distinguished themselves as generals, maintaining command and control where Horn and Bernard failed to do so. Their exposed observation post, described as "always amidst the Musquet-shot", had not been without risk.[53] However, remaining in position, they simultaneously managed to control the battle and provide an example to their men, who praised the pair after the battle.

Soon afterwards, Nördlingen fell, too. The Swedish survivors, under Bernard, took refuge with the approaching Swedish Alsace army under Rhinegrave Otto Louis, which until then had been busy attempting to recover Rheinfelden and Breisach. These reinforcements had not reached the battle in time, but they could at least serve as a refuge for the survivors. Bernard then retreated into Alsace with his men. Most Swedish garrisons south of the River Main were withdrawn to the north.

Horn remained in captivity for eight years. From his jail, he blamed Bernard for the disaster. Bernard, in turn, held Horn responsible. The

---

50 *Ibid.*, p.111. Poyntz had served in the Swedish army in 1631, and it remains possible that he then had encountered Bernard and now recognised him.
51 *Ibid.*, p.112.
52 Engerisser and Hrnčiřík, "Nördlingen 1634", pp.144–5; Picouet, *Armies of Philip IV*, p.243.
53 Galliazo Gualdo Priorato, *An History of the Late Warres and Other State Affaires of the Best Part of Christendom* (London: John Hardesty, Thomas Huntington, and Thomas Jackson, 1648), p.267.

Johann von Werth.
(Pieter de Jode)

Habsburg generals offered yet other explanations for their great victory, with Imperial, Spanish, and Bavarian commanders arguing over who had the best right to take credit for the victory. For this reason, it was for a long time difficult to disentangle the facts of the battle. Yet, it seems fairly certain that Horn failed to disengage his exhausted men in good order. Pursued by Imperial and Spanish troops, they collided with Bernard's men who were also in retreat, pursued by the Bavarian cavalry under the able Johann von Werth (1591–1652), another of those senior officers who had risen from the ranks during the war, in his case in Spanish service. Both the Swedish commanders failed to reach their objectives. Besides, both Horn and Bernard disregarded the risks inherent in an attack on superior numbers of enemy forces in prepared positions in difficult terrain.

The Peace of Prague and the Truce of Altmark

Politically, the disaster at Nördlingen signified the end of the Heilbronn League. In November, its German members asked France to intervene in the war. In December, Oxenstierna withdrew himself from the League. By then, John George of Saxony had already entered into peace negotiations with the Emperor, which resulted in an agreement eventually signed in Prague in late May 1635. Soon Maximilian of Bavaria (1573–1651) agreed to same terms as Saxony, dissolved the Catholic League, and placed his Bavarian army under Imperial command. For a considerable time, the Bavarian army had constituted the bulk of the Catholic League's army, so this changed little in practical terms. With the Peace of Prague, both the Saxon and Bavarian armies were subordinated the Imperial army. Henceforth, the religious aspects of the struggle played a lesser role. No longer were Catholics ranged against Protestants. Nor was the Imperial cause any longer as firmly wedded to the Catholic cause as in the past.

The Peace of Prague had other implications as well. Based on the articles of the peace agreement, the Emperor ordered all Germans in Swedish service to change sides. Those who did not were threatened, as Imperial subjects, with an Imperial ban (*Reichsacht*), which in effect meant that Germans no longer were allowed to serve the Swedish Crown. In August 1635, George, Duke of Brunswick-Lüneburg, formally withdrew from his position as a Swedish general and agreed to the terms of the Peace of Prague. Christian, Count Palatine of Birkenfeld-Bischweiler, relinquished his rank and position too, seeking reconciliation with the Emperor. It was only Landgrave William of Hesse-Kassel who remained loyal to the Protestant and Swedish cause, but he, too, formally withdrew from his service as a Swedish general. William could not withstand Imperial pressure, was driven out of his territory, and died, destitute, in exile.[54]

Without an effective chain of command, the Swedish army of the Rhine effectively disintegrated. After the resignation of Christian of Birkenfeld-Bischweiler, the Swedish camp outside Mainz, the Gustavsburg, came under siege. In January 1636 its garrison marched out with military honours, abandoning the area. In the Rhineland only Hanau held out, and this stronghold, too, fell in early 1638. However, in Alsace the Swedish garrison of Benfeld, south of Strasbourg, held out throughout the war and departed only in 1650.

In September 1635, Sweden and the Polish-Lithuanian Commonwealth renewed, at Stuhmsdorf, the Truce of Altmark for a further 26 years, but this time under, for Sweden, less favourable terms. Yet, Oxenstierna needed a renewed truce, since the King of Poland, Ladislaus IV Vasa (Polish: Władysław; 1595–1648; r. 1632–1648) still claimed the Swedish Crown. and the Commonwealth by then was finally free to go to war against Sweden again, if it so wished. The Smolensk War with Muscovy had ended in the previous year, and so had the Commonwealth's war with the Ottoman Empire. Fortunately for Oxenstierna, the Polish magnates were unwilling to be led into a new war, and the Commonwealth agreed to a renewed truce.

The Rise of Bernard of Saxe-Weimar

Meanwhile, the able Bernard of Saxe-Weimar was growing into a liability for Oxenstierna. In the summer of 1633, Bernard had demanded the duchy of Franconia for himself, and Oxenstierna drew him a patent, in June creating him Duke of Franconia under the Swedish Crown.[55] Bernard was allocated the bishoprics of Würzburg and Bamberg to pay for his troops, whose pay was in arrears. Although still technically in Swedish service, a few days later he entered into an alliance with Sweden.[56] Bernard henceforth simultaneously had the same status of a free alliance with Sweden as Landgrave William of Hesse-Kassel, with whom the previous alliance had recently been renewed.[57]

France had already in April 1633 attempted to negotiate a deal to attract Bernard to French service.[58] Now both Saxony and the Empire made him similar offers. Neither Oxenstierna nor Richelieu wanted Bernard to desert the alliance; they had lost Horn already and could not afford to lose Bernard as well. As a result, in March 1635, Bernard was appointed commander-in-

54 Lars Tingsten, *Fältmarskalkarna Johan Banér och Lennart Torstensson såsom härförare* (Stockholm: Militärlitteraturföreningens förlag 164, 1932), p.23.

55 Patent, 10 June 1633 (O.S.), Carl Hallendorff (ed.), *Sverges Traktater med främmande magter jemte andra hit hörande handlingar* 5:2 (1632–1645) (Stockholm: P. A. Norstedt & Söner, 1909), pp.92–100.

56 On 14 June 1633 (O.S.), Sweden entered into an alliance with Bernard as a sovereign ruler. Hallendorff, *Sverges Traktater*, pp.105–9.

57 The alliance with William is reprinted in Hallendorff, *Sverges Traktater*, pp.71–4.

58 Cicely Veronica Wedgwood, *The Thirty Years War* (New York: Book-of-the-Month Club, 1995), p.367.

chief in Germany on behalf of both the increasingly irrelevant Heilbronn League, in which Sweden formally remained a member, and the King of France.[59] Since he had lost his duchy of Franconia after the battle of Nördlingen, he instead wanted the landgravate of Alsace. By June 1635, Richelieu accordingly promised him Alsace, under the assumption that Bernard should first conquer the territory for France and then hold it under French rule. Bernard would also receive the county of Hagenau.[60] On 27 October 1635, France signed a formal agreement with him, hiring him and what Richelieu expected to be an army of 18,000 men for 1.6 million Reichsthalers a year (about four times the French subsidy to Sweden).[61]

Bernard's existing army followed its commander into French service, yet, both he and his army continued to operate essentially like an independent Protestant power. Henceforth, the Bernardine army (frequently and somewhat confusingly usually known as the Weimar army, after Bernard's duchy in Saxony) primarily operated out of Alsace, Bernard's new domain. When in 1639 he died following a sudden illness, on his deathbed he appointed four directors of the Bernardine army. They were tasked to keep the army together, and keep it independent, following Bernard's own example.

It has frequently been argued that formally, Bernard remained in Swedish service.[62] He had, after all, gone into Swedish service already under Gustavus Adolphus, received Swedish military rank and position, and enlisted troops under the authority of Swedish patents. Bernard was appointed commander-in-chief of the Heilbronn League before the Peace of Prague, at the time when Sweden formally remained a member, which meant that although he and his army were seconded to the League, they remained in Swedish service. He also never formally relinquished his Swedish rank and position. Moreover, Bernard's army included famous Swedish enlisted regiments such as the Yellow Regiment, which still formally was the late King's Household Regiment and, in later centuries, constituted an important part of the heritage of the Swedish Life Guard. Bernard's army also included the Green Regiment, in which served German and Scottish soldiers who for years had distinguished themselves in Swedish service. Since years later, after Bernard's death, some of his men returned into that service, it would perhaps seem appropriate to count them as Swedish soldiers for the duration of their service under Bernard. Yet, this would be an incorrect description of the relationship. After Bernard in October 1635 went into French service, and brought his army with him, he no longer formed part of the Swedish command structure and neither requested nor received orders from either Oxenstierna or the Swedish regency government, or any Swedish officer. He remained an important ally, but henceforth neither he nor his men were Swedish soldiers.

Richelieu regarded Bernard as his overall commander in Germany, due to his experience and because he already had an army at his disposal. However,

---

59 Bernard wrote his commission himself. Bernard's commission, 2 March 1635 (O.S.) *AOSB*: 1:13, pp.162–7.

60 Wedgwood, *Thirty Years War*, pp.402–4.

61 Parker, *Thirty Years' War*, p.148.

62 See, for example, Tingsten, *Fältmarskalkarna*, p.23; followed by later Swedish military historians.

he did not trust Bernard with French troops. The French units in Lorraine and Germany accordingly had their own field marshal, Louis de Nogaret d'Épernon (1593–1639), known as Cardinal de La Valette. France had not yet declared war against the Empire (war broke out only in 1636). In 1635, the non-Bernardine French troops in Germany accordingly fought under the nominal authority of Sweden,[63] yet, like the situation with Bernard, it was an authority in name only.

Banér Takes Command

In spring 1635, only one Swedish army in Germany remained intact: that in Thuringia commanded by Johan Banér. He had been promoted to field marshal and de facto operational commander of Swedish military forces in Germany after the loss of Horn. Learning of the defeat at Nördlingen, Banér had in September marched from Leitmeritz (modern-day Litoměřice) in Bohemia over Pirna into Thuringia, where he in October reached Weimar. The Brandenburgian regiments had abandoned him, instead joining the Saxon army. Banér then went into winter quarters at Erfurt.[64]

The situation was now quite different from before. After the King's death, Sweden had controlled five field armies and an army-sized corps distributed throughout Germany. Operations took place in every theatre of war simultaneously, and there was the problem of maintaining a unified command. No longer. The Swedes had pulled out of southern Germany and much of the Rhineland. Following the Peace of Prague between John George of Saxony and the Emperor in late May 1635 and, in early September, the shift of George William of Brandenburg to the Imperial cause, the Swedes pulled out of Saxony as well. On the Weser, George of Brunswick-Lüneburg formally left Swedish service in August 1635 and switched his loyalty to the Imperial cause for a while (sadly for the Duke, the Swedish garrisons of some of his towns refused to surrender; George only returned to the side of Sweden and France when conditions changed in 1639–1640). Major General Nicolaus Dietrich Sperreuter briefly assumed control of the Swedish Weser army, bringing together eight regiments and four companies, which he sent to Banér.[65] Then Sperreuter, too, resigned from the Swedish army (in the following year, he went into Imperial service). The loyal Knyphausen, who previously had been dismissed by Oxenstierna but in November 1635 was appointed commander in the Westphalian Circle, persuaded four of Sperreuter's regiments to remain in Swedish service, and some of them stayed with him until in January 1636 he fell in the battle of Haselünne, in Emsland in the Lower Saxon Circle.[66]

---

63 Parker, *Thirty Years' War*, p.147.
64 Tingsten, *Huvuddragen*, pp.167–8.
65 *Ibid.*, p.204. On Sperreuter, see Christian Kodritzki, "Sperreuth, Claus Dietrich von", Markus Meumann (ed.), *Lexikon der Heerführer und hohen Offiziere des Dreißigjährigen Krieges* (2017; https://thirty-years-war-online.net/prosopographie/heerfuehrer-und-offiziere/sperreuth-claus-dietrich-von/).
66 Tingsten, *Fältmarskalkarna*, pp.88–9.

Dodo von Innhausen und zu Knyphausen on horseback. He carries a Swedish-style rapier, typical of his time, and wears a gorget for protection.

As a result, there was now only one important theatre of operations for the Swedes and only one Swedish field army, under Banér. Its existence depended on his ability to maintain lines of communication to the Baltic Sea and, beyond, to Sweden itself. The Swedish commanders accordingly did what they could to gather the Swedish units on other fronts, bringing them over to Banér.

Meanwhile, John George of Saxony made repeated attempts to subvert the Germans of the Swedish army. Based on the articles of the Peace of Prague, he ordered all Germans, as Imperial subjects, in Swedish service to change sides. Those who did not were threatened with an Imperial ban; in effect, he threatened to make all Germans in Swedish service outlaws. The Saxons, or possibly somebody else, even planned to have Banér assassinated. The conspiracy was revealed to him by a Colonel Erasmus Platow and there were, apparently, different versions of the plan. Either Banér would be shot by a sniper, or a group of conspirators would destroy the gate of his residence with a petard, and then have a company or two of cavalry ride in to catch him, his aides, and field chancellery. However, the conspiracy was thwarted.[67]

Banér was not in an enviable position. Ahead of him was the hostile Saxony. In his rear was Brandenburg, which although not yet openly hostile, certainly had abandoned its former position of cautious support.

In early August 1635, Banér mustered his army between Stassfurt and Kalbe, south of Magdeburg. It consisted of 12,000 horse and 14,000 foot, in total 26,000 men. His regiments were undermanned. He had 24 regiments of horse, which means that the average strength was 500 men. His 18 regiments of foot had an average strength of less than 800.[68] The vast majority of his men were German nationals. Not all had signed up for mercenary motives. Many had fought for the Protestant cause and remained loyal to their German identity. Some owned lands and had family obligations. Many were Saxons. Besides, as Imperial subjects they were susceptible to an Imperial ban. Of the 26,000 men in the army, only 2,000 to 3,000 were national Swedish troops. This was a serious problem, since in conjunction with the muster, Banér's army mutinied, refusing to carry out any duties until their arrears had been paid. The situation was the same as at the time of the colonels' mutiny in late April 1633, except that now it was worse, since the mutiny was instigated by letters from Saxony. Three days after mustering the army, Oxenstierna met a group of major generals, colonels, and lieutenant colonels in Magdeburg to discuss the matter. It turned out that John George of Saxony had sent proposals to several of these officers, asking them to abandon the Swedes and, if they so wished, join his army instead – or face an Imperial ban. At first the discussions were friendly; however, soon the situation grew more ominous.[69]

---

67 Birger Steckzén, *Johan Banér* (Stockholm: Hugo Geber, 1939), pp.185–6. Although the best biography of Banér, it is a popular history without notes.

68 Tingsten, *Huvuddragen*, p.205; Tingsten, *Fältmarskalkarna*, p.24.

69 Tingsten, *Huvuddragen*, pp.205–7.

On 28 September, Oxenstierna learnt that a delegation of three senior officers, including Major General Lohausen, had departed to the headquarters of John George. Although no violence had yet taken place, a mutiny had de facto occurred. Oxenstierna had in all but name become a hostage. During the night of 29 September Banér sent a group of trusted officers with a unit of Livonians to escort Oxenstierna out of the town to Wismar, where he arrived four days later.

With Oxenstierna safely out of the way, Banér had no reason to remain idle. The army would have to march out. As second in command, Banér chose the experienced Lieutenant General Patrick Ruthven (c. 1572–1651), who had been in Swedish service since 1509. As for Lohausen, he could not reconcile being in Swedish service with the new conditions after the Peace of Prague, so he resigned, in the following year instead going into the service of Duke Adolph Frederick of Mecklenburg. The army left camp in early October.

Patrick Ruthven, 1623.
(Skokloster Castle)

On 16 October, John George declared war on Sweden. However, he was too intransigent to offer the mutineers better terms than Banér, thus wasting his best chance to dismember the Swedish army. As a result, as Banér's army marched north, outspoken opposition in the army to its Swedish commanders gradually vanished and then was heard no more. However, not all regiments followed orders, and while Banér's army was impressive on paper, in reality he could only count on parts of it. Banér's concerns, which he expressed in letters to Stockholm, were well-founded.

Possibly the best cavalry commander in the Swedish army under Gustavus Adolphus had been Wolf Heinrich von Baudissin. However, we have seen how Baudissin by 1633 was dissatisfied with his situation. He accordingly left Swedish service and in 1635 joined the Saxon army instead, in which John George of Saxony appointed him lieutenant general in replacement of Arnim, who had resigned following the Peace of Prague.[70] Baudissin knew many Swedish officers and had contacted them. Although not the only cause for the mutiny, Baudissin's letters had played a role. When John George in mid October declared war on Sweden, he ordered Baudissin to clear Saxony of any remaining Swedes. Saxon troops attacked the Swedes as they were retreating. Banér and his commanders fought several, mostly successful, engagements against the Saxons. Colonel Erik Slang and his cavalry regiment played a key role in these engagements, since he was good at the small war and, moreover, his regiment was one of few cavalry units which obeyed orders.

Baudissin moved north through Brandenburg and into Mecklenburg, where he laid siege to Dömitz, a fortified town on the Elbe. However, Banér sent Patrick Ruthven to relieve Dömitz. Ruthven brought 4,000 to

---

70 Baudissin's infant son, named Gustav Adolph after the Swedish King whom Baudissin had admired, in time became a noted cavalry general, too, eventually went into Danish service, and later fought Sweden with some success in the Scanian War.

5,000 horse and 1,000 musketeers, while Baudissin had only infantry at his disposal, although the numbers were higher, some 6,000 to 7,000 men. On 1 November 1635, Ruthven managed to attack the Saxon infantry from behind, at the same time as the Dömitz garrison made a sortie. Baudissin lost most of his army (reportedly 6,000 of his 7,000 men, including 2,500 men who were captured and went into Swedish service) and had to abandon the siege. He reportedly only saved himself by swimming across the Elbe.[71]

So far, the short war against the Swedes had not gone well for John George of Saxony. By the end of 1635, his remaining units accordingly joined forces with an Imperial army under Rudolf von Morzin. However, Banér had received reinforcements, too. The Swedes had retained substantial forces in Prussia under the Grand Marshal of the Realm, Jacob De la Gardie, in preparation for a renewed outbreak of war with the Polish-Lithuanian Commonwealth. Among his officers were General of Artillery Lennart Torstensson, Major General Lars Kagg, Major General of Cavalry Henrik Fleming (1584–1650), and Major General of Infantry Alexander von Essen (1594–1664).[72] Fleming had fought in the Kalmar War and the war in Muscovy, while Essen from 1615 had been in Dutch and then Venetian, Spanish, and (against the Ottoman Empire) Commonwealth service before he joined Gustavus Adolphus for the wars in Livonia and Prussia. These men knew each other well. Alexander von Essen, for instance, had served in the Life Guard of Maurice of Nassau from 1615 to 1616, where in the latter year, Lars Kagg had joined him. Following the Truce of Stuhmsdorf, concluded in September 1635, the army in Prussia could be redirected to join Banér's army. The army in Prussia consisted of some 18,600 men. Of these, Oxenstierna wanted 7,700 (1,500 horse and 6,200 foot) to return to Sweden. However, to support Banér, he ordered Torstensson and Kagg to bring to Pomerania the enlisted units – some 9,700 men – and the Östergötland Regiment – almost 1,200 men under the one-legged Colonel Axel Lillie (1603–1662).[73] Travelling by road, Torstensson and Kagg brought a first batch consisting of 2,500 horse and 4,500 foot (including the Östergötland Regiment and Lillie, who despite his wooden leg was promoted to Major General of Cavalry[74]). They had already arrived in Wollin in October. The rest, all infantry, had to follow later in February 1636, under Field Marshal Herman Wrangel (1585–1643), since the Commonwealth had not allowed the use of the road for more men.[75]

Lennart Torstensson, who commanded the army from Prussia, had fought under Gustavus Adolphus since the siege of Riga in 1621. The King had then sent young Torstensson, at the time a barely 18-year-old dispatch rider, with

71   Tingsten, *Fältmarskalkarna*, p.45; Ericson Wolke, Larsson; and Villstrand, *Trettioåriga kriget*, p.144.

72   Mankell, *Uppgifter* 2, pp.213–14.

73   Petri, *Kungl. Första livgrenadjärregementets historia* 2, pp.202–3; Tingsten, *Huvuddragen*, p.211. The Östergötland Regiment consisted of 144 officers and 939 common soldiers, that is, 1,083 men, to which was added 89 men to ill to serve who joined later, which produces a total of 1,172 men or two battalions. Petri, *Kungl. Första livgrenadjärregementets historia* 2, pp.202–3.

74   *Ibid.*, p.203.

75   Tingsten, *Fältmarskalkarna*, p.46.

an order to one of the colonels. However, while riding to his destination, Torstensson noticed that the circumstances that warranted the King's order had changed. He accordingly, on his own initiative, changed the order to fit the evolving situation better. Returning to the King, the young man reported what he had done. Amazed, Gustavus Adolphus agreed that Torstensson had done the right thing. It was accordingly unsurprising that Gustavus Adolphus soon gave Torstensson increased responsibilities. He had since then worked to develop the Swedish artillery, a task in which Gustavus Adolphus had taken a keen interest. In 1633, Torstensson was one of the officers who accompanied the King's corpse back to Sweden, and during the 1634 state funeral, he carried the national banner (*riksbanér*). In 1634, he was also appointed national chief of artillery (*rikstygmästare*) and head of all Swedish artillery. However, Torstensson suffered from bad health. In 1632, he had been captured at Alte Feste,

Lennart Torstensson, c. 1647–1651. (David Beck)

after which he was imprisoned in a damp jail in Ingolstadt. Henceforth, Torstensson was increasingly crippled by gout (as it was then diagnosed, a more likely diagnosis is perhaps rheumatoid arthritis).[76]

Lillie and most of the Östergötland Regiment deployed in garrisons primarily on the islands of Wollin and Usedom, while Torstensson, most enlisted units, and 300 Östergötland foot joined Banér. This temporarily increased Banér's army to some 20,000 men by the end of the year.[77] The presence of the Östergötland Regiment may have brought back memories to Banér, who in the 1620s had been its colonel.

Banér's army desperately needed reinforcements, since it had rapidly been shrinking in size. When the unreliable units had been discarded, its strength had been reduced to about 18,000 men.[78] By November 1635, Banér had some 15,000 men.[79] Despite the reinforcements, the army shrank further. By February 1636, only some 12,000 men remained.[80]

76 Modern-day physicians do not agree about how to diagnose Torstensson's illness, which possibly began even before his imprisonment. Ido Leden, "En kortfattad berättelse om fältmarskalk Lennart Torstenssons liv och sjukhistoria", *Reuma Bulletinen* 94 (2013), pp.31–5.

77 Petri, *Kungl. Första livgrenadjärregementets historia* 2, p.204.

78 Mankell, *Uppgifter* 1, p.152; Petri, *Kungl. Första livgrenadjärregementets historia* 2, p.202.

79 Tingsten, *Fältmarskalkarna*, p.48.

80 *Ibid.*, p.53.

Besides, Banér was well aware that mutinous sentiments were not completely gone. In mid November, another moment of discontent took place in the army. However, as negotiations got underway, Oxenstierna promised the men pay and new clothes. Moreover, he promised the men that he would not distinguish between the men in Banér's army, who were mostly Germans, and those who came with Torstensson from Prussia, many of whom were Swedes. This was a message well received in Banér's army.[81]

Banér's Choice

In January 1636, Brandenburg, too, effectively declared war on Sweden through the Advocatorial Edict, which ordered all Imperial subjects to leave Swedish service or face the effects of an Imperial ban. At around the same time, Oxenstierna made a campaign plan for the year. He wanted to focus on defending what Sweden already held. Oxenstierna wanted Banér to base the main field army (12,000 men) on Magdeburg, where it would hold parts of northern Saxony so as to protect the Swedish maritime base areas of Pomerania and Mecklenburg. In addition to the main field army, Oxenstierna wanted a small army (6,000 men) under Leslie, who had replaced the unfortunate Knyphausen and himself now was promoted to field marshal, to grab hold of the Weser and, based on Nienburg, Osnabrück, and Stade, protect the right flank of the main army. Likewise, another small army (6,000 men) under Field Marshal Herman Wrangel would grab hold of the Oder and, based on Stettin, protect the left flank of the main army.[82] Henceforth, this became the standard disposition of the Swedish military forces in Germany: a major field army for deployment wherever needed and two smaller field armies for flank protection in the Weser and Oder regions, respectively.

The setup decided by Oxenstierna was not without its problems. Technically, Herman Wrangel was senior in service to Banér, and he was not content with being subordinated the 11 years younger Banér who had only been a field marshal for a short time. Yet, Oxenstierna nominated Banér commander of the main field army in Germany and, like Horn before him, in overall operational command under Oxenstierna's personal authority. As a result of this decision, relations between Banér and Wrangel were not without difficulties.

However, the situation was grim, in particular following Brandenburg's de facto declaration of war. Besides, soon after Brandenburg, John George of Saxony, too, issued the Imperial ban, which he for so long had threatened to do, in the Emperor's name but probably on his own initiative. Banér reacted quickly. Before Brandenburg had time to mobilise, Banér chose to move against not Brandenburg, but Sweden's key Protestant enemy, Saxony. Banér accordingly, together with his principal lieutenants Torstensson and Ruthven, prepared for an offensive down the Rivers Elbe and Saale to Naumburg (in

---

81 *Ibid.*, pp.46–7.
82 *Ibid.*, pp.53–4.

the end, old Ruthven did not join the offensive, since in spring he was sent instead to Scotland to enlist more men; having returned home, he in mid 1637 resigned his post in the Swedish army). In late January 1636, the first of Banér's units crossed the Elbe into Saxony, and soon these were followed by the entire army. In February, Banér devastated Saxony. This was a deliberate decision, not the effect of poor discipline. Banér needed to overwhelm the Saxons, showing them that it did not pay to join the anti-Swedish coalition. He also needed to reduce Saxony quickly. Henceforth, Banér ordered the devastation of enemy territories, not as a means to find supplies but to reduce the enemy's territory to prevent him from feeding his own forces. It was a strategy of what can only be called total war, in which enemy-held resources and non-combatants were targeted just as much, or more, than enemy combatants. The key objective was now to prevent the enemy from waging war against the Swedes. That the strategy of devastation was no joke is obvious since at times the devastation grew too vicious even for the hard-edged Banér, who had to step in to prevent the worst excesses.

In March, Imperial troops under Field Marshal Melchior von Hatzfeldt (1593–1658) were sent to Brandenburg in an attempt to move against Banér's army from the rear. Banér did not wish to be caught between two fires, so he retreated to the north. Hatzfeldt then joined the Saxons, under Lieutenant General Baudissin. The joint Imperial–Saxon army of 23,000 men laid siege to Magdeburg, which had a Swedish garrison.

Banér now had to choose: to follow Oxenstierna's orders to defend the Baltic shore, which was vital for safeguarding the Swedish sea lines of communication, or to go on the offensive, ignoring Oxenstierna's orders. Banér chose the offensive.

Melchior von Hatzfeldt.

Although the Swedish army by then had acquired an increasing focus on the offensive, Banér's choice was not merely a matter of habit or doctrine. First, he knew that Pomerania was too poor to supply the Swedish army. A retreat into defensive positions there would ultimately and irrevocably result in the destruction of his army, even if the enemy did nothing. Second, there were reports that Imperial reinforcements were on their way. Finally, there was always the risk that Denmark might join the Imperial coalition to strike against the Swedish heartland. Banér accordingly drew the conclusion that it was better to confront and defeat the enemy here and now, outside Swedish-held territory. However, he needed significantly more men to confront Hatzfeldt's army. Banér began to gather reinforcements to the field army from those garrisons which could spare them. Banér also restored order in the army, in which discipline had deteriorated further through the total war strategy implemented in Saxony. When in May, some officers again made demands, Banér immediately stopped the attempt, warning them that if they tried this again, they would be executed. No more general mutinies were attempted in his army as long as Banér was alive.

In July 1636, Hatzfeldt and John George finally took Magdeburg, to which they had laid siege for some time. By coincidence, this was at the same time that Oxenstierna finally returned to Sweden, leaving affairs in Germany to be handled by Banér. The conquest of Magdeburg was a success for the Imperial cause, but it was not decisive. The Swedish Magdeburg garrison departed, later joining Banér's army. Moreover, Baudissin was badly wounded during the siege, so he was replaced by Francis Albert, Duke of Saxe-Lauenburg (1598–1642), who had been close to Gustavus Adolphus in his last moments at Lützen but later gone into Saxon service.

In the western theatre of operations, Alexander Leslie had joined his units (2,500 horse and 1,500 foot[83]) to the Hessian army. In June, they relieved Hanau, the ancestral home of Landgravine Amalie Elisabeth and still held by Swedish troops under another Scotsman, Jacob Ramsay (1589–1639). Hanau had been under siege for nine months. Leslie then took Lüneburg, which together with Dömitz would secure his communication line to Hamburg, which in its role as Germany's banking centre was a major source of funding and supplies of all kinds, ranging from war materials to foodstuffs.[84] Leslie and his men then joined Banér.

Banér also received reinforcements from Pomerania, dispatched by Herman Wrangel. First, Major General Stålhandske with one squadron each of Nyland and Småland cavalry, in total 600 men. Then, Lieutenant General Johann Vitzthum von Eckstädt with 1,300 horse and 700 foot.[85]

In mid September, Banér prepared a fortified camp at Parchim, Mecklenburg. With the reinforcements, the last of which were those brought by Vitzthum von Eckstädt who arrived by the end of the month, Banér's army consisted of some 16,000 to 17,000 men.[86]

Banér then led his men against the joint Imperial–Saxon army, at the time based between Werben and Perleberg in Brandenburg, to which he offered battle. Although Banér had received reports that the enemy had the advantage of numbers, he had received all reinforcements that he might expect, and the army was under control again. Besides, as one of his Scottish officers noted: "As soon as these [reinforcements] were arrived we tooke a firme resolution to provoke the Enemy to battaile: Whereunto indeed our Necessitys constreyned us, for want of meanes to support our army and though they were farre stronger, then we."[87] However, Hatzfeldt left Perleberg and retreated, despite his superior numbers, preferring to await the expected Imperial reinforcements. Banér followed Hatzfeldt's army in forced marches.

83 *Ibid.*, p.60.
84 The key financial centres in Germany were Hamburg, Bremen, Magdeburg, Leipzig, Frankfurt-am-Main, and Nuremberg.
85 *Ibid.*, p.63.
86 *Ibid.*, p.64.
87 Lieutenant General James King's report, reprinted in Steven Murdoch, Kathrin Zickermann, and Adam Marks, "The Battle of Wittstock 1636: Conflicting Reports on a Swedish Victory in Germany", *Journal of the Scottish Society for Northern Studies* 43 (2012), pp.71–109, on p.93.

Saxon supply train. Detail from a print depicting the Saxon victory at Liegnitz, 1634. The beer barrels constitute an important part of the supplies.

He finally managed to intercept the enemy army at Wittstock on the Dosse, a tributary of the River Havel, where the Imperials and Saxons had begun to prepare fortified positions, setting up batteries and forming their supply train into a stockade.

The Battle of Wittstock

Banér attacked on 4 October 1636, in the engagement that would become known as the battle of Wittstock.[88] Banér had never before been in sole command in a set battle, and ever since the disastrous defeat at Nördlingen, he had felt the pressure on the Swedes rise. Yet, he was sufficiently experienced to know that at some point he would have to risk battle to turn the tide of the war. Besides, Banér had rebuilt the Swedish field army and restored order in it. Even so, it must have been disconcerting to learn that his army was somewhat inferior in numbers, which was the intelligence that he and his officers had received.[89] Still, Hatzfeldt had attempted to avoid battle, which perhaps gave some encouragement.

Neither contemporary sources nor modern historians agree on the number of men in the opposing armies. Banér probably had some 16,000

---

88 For a detailed description of the battle of Wittstock, see Tingsten, *Fältmarskalkarna*, pp.63–72. Recent works of the battle of Wittstock include Lars Ericson, "Wittstock 1636", Lars Ericson et al., *Svenska slagfält* (np: Wahlström &Widstrand, 2003), pp.147–54; Murdoch, Zickermann, and Marks, "Battle of Wittstock", pp.71–109; Sebastian Jägerhorn, *Hårdast bland de hårda: En kavalleriofficer i fält* (Stockholm: Medströms, 2018), pp.136–43. Of the modern works, each emphasises the contribution to the victory of a specific national group: Swedes, Scots, and Finns, respectively. The pre-Second World War Swedish General Staff project resulted in additional materials on Wittstock, currently deposited in the Swedish Military Archives but unpublished.

89 Lieutenant General James King's report, reprinted in Murdoch, Zickermann, and Marks, "Battle of Wittstock", p.93.

men (9,000 horse and 7,000 foot; Table 4). About a third of them were national troops, with the rest mostly being of British and German origin. The Imperial–Saxon army under Hatzfeldt, Morzin, and John George consisted of some 18,000 to 20,000.[90]

Hatzfeldt and John George of Saxony had deployed their army on a ridge, in prepared positions of their own choosing, in the hope that Banér would order a frontal assault. Hatzfeldt commanded the right wing, which consisted of the Imperial cavalry. John George and Morzin commanded the centre. The Saxon cavalry, again under John George and Morzin, constituted the left wing.

Banér had no intention to oblige the enemy, especially since his army was inferior in numbers. Instead, he aimed to carry out a double envelopment of the Imperial–Saxon army. First, out of sight, Banér sent his left wing, under Lieutenant General James King (and with Major General Torsten Stålhandske in vanguard) on a flank march, around Hatzfeldt's right wing. Then, he ordered the rest of the army simply to march around the enemy's prepared positions in a flanking manoeuvre so as to envelop them. When Hatzfeldt noticed this move, he found himself forced to abandon his positions and move the entire line so as to meet the expected Swedish attack.

Banér and Torstensson led the Swedish right wing, consisting of roughly half the cavalry, about 500 commanded musketeers under Colonel William Gunn, and some artillery, with Torstensson in the vanguard. The Swedish artillery opened fire to cover the movement. As soon as they were in position, they attacked the Saxon left wing and centre.

Meanwhile, the Swedish centre, commanded by Field Marshal Alexander Leslie with the support of Major General Thomas Kerr, had orders to await the flank attack before taking action. The same, for obvious reasons, held for Lieutenant General Johann Vitzthum von Eckstädt who commanded the reserve, with the support of Major General John Ruthven (a nephew of Patrick Ruthven and son-in-law of Alexander Leslie).

Even though the Imperial–Saxon army had managed to redeploy, Hatzfeldt feared that the Saxons might lose heart by the Swedish attack. He accordingly sent the cavalry from his right wing in support of the Saxons. Indeed; the Saxon units were already shaken. Yet, inferior in numbers, the Swedish attack on the Saxons went nowhere. Hatzfeldt's reinforcements arrived gradually, until the Swedish cavalry squadrons were greatly outnumbered.

In response, Banér ordered Leslie to bring the centre into action, and then the reserves as well. Leslie's infantry charged the Imperial–Saxon lines. Outnumbered, the Swedish infantry suffered significant losses. The 'Swedish Brigade' (with one battalion each from the Kronoberg and Jönköping Regiments and some units from Finland) was reduced from 892 to 308 men, while the 'Scottish Brigade' was reduced from 800 to 450. Banér's life regiment, the Old Blue, also suffered significant losses.[91] Banér later wrote that this fight was so hard fought that he had "not in his entire life witnessed

---

90   Mankell, *Uppgifter* 2, p.238; Tingsten, *Fältmarskalkarna*, pp.65–6; Ericson, "Wittstock 1636," p.147, pp.149–50; Jägerhorn, *Hårdast bland de hårda*, p.136.
91   Ericson, "Wittstock 1636", p.153.

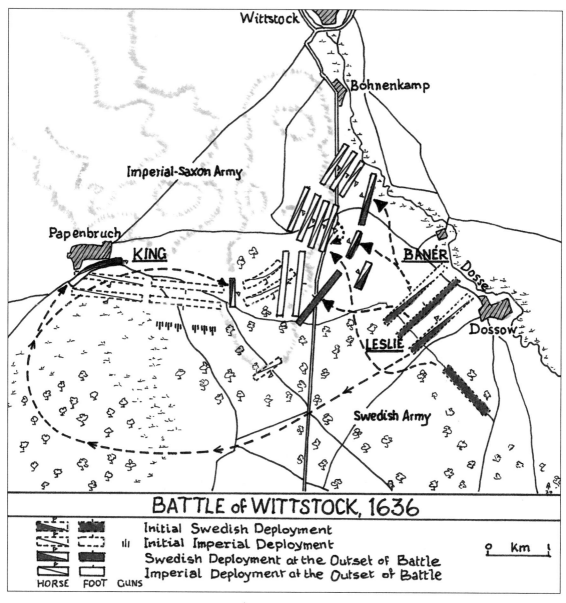

Wittstock.

the like".[92] The older and yet more experienced Leslie, too, noted that the enemy attacked with such fury that he had 'almost never' seen the like.[93] But where were the reserves? They had been ordered into action, but none had shown up.

92 Banér's report to the Queen on the battle of Wittstock, 24 September 1636 (O.S.), *AOSB* 2:6, pp.856–66, on p.859.
93 Leslie's report to Oxenstierna on the battle of Wittstock, 27 September 1636 (O.S.), *AOSB* 2:9, pp.465–8, on p.467.

Nonetheless, Banér, Leslie, and their men fought on. A retreat at this point would have ended in disaster, and there was still the chance that King's flank march would appear.

And finally, by the end of the day, King and Stålhandske appeared in the Imperial rear. They had found the terrain impassable, so had taken a long detour. They also had marched on parallel roads, until they finally united in time to attack. Stålhandske attacked first, with two cavalry regiments (the combined Nyland Cavalry and Småland Cavalry Regiment and Johann Arend von Goldstein's Cavalry Regiment). They rapidly dispersed three Imperial regiments. This was too much for the Imperials, especially since the Swedish reserves were pouring in as well. Hatzfeldt's centre now suddenly faced a fresh opponent, while he had already brought units from his right wing to the centre, thus weakening the right wing which now was under attack in the flank and rear by King. It is a testament to Hatzfeldt's skill that the Imperial–Saxon army did not disintegrate but managed to retreat under reasonably controlled conditions.

King's force then slowed down, since night was falling. The last Swedish reserves of the centre finally attacked, too. There were reports that Vitzthum von Eckstädt had feared that the hard-fought battle would turn into another Nördlingen, for which reason he intentionally had refused to engage. In the end, it was likely Ruthven and the colonels who took the initiative to attack

Contemporary depiction of the battle of Wittstock, 1636. The Swedish units (below) push back the Saxon and Imperial troops (above), who have begun to flee from the field. Part of a series of battle paintings completed in the 1670s by Johan Hammer, who in turn based them on drawings by Conrad Mardefelt published in *Theatrum Europaeum*. Mardefelt (born as Maesberg; 1610–1688) joined the Swedish army in 1628 and fought in the battle of Wittstock. (Photo: Medströms)

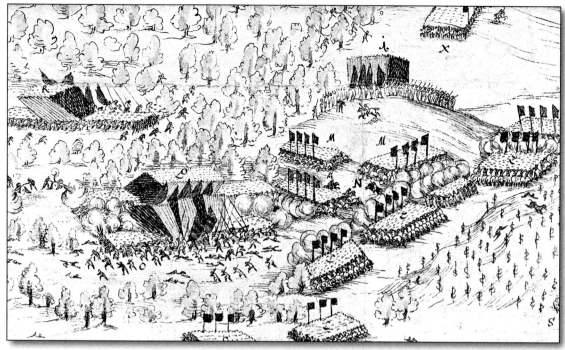

Detail from a depiction of the battle of Wittstock, 1636, believed to have accompanied Johan Banér's report to the regency government, Stockholm, in early 1637. Lower right side: Swedish units, marked by blue standards. Upper left side: Imperial and Saxon units, marked by red flags. Centre left: A Swedish infantry brigade is sorely pressed by an Imperial unit. Centre right: Banér (marked N) leads cavalry and musketeers to the rescue.

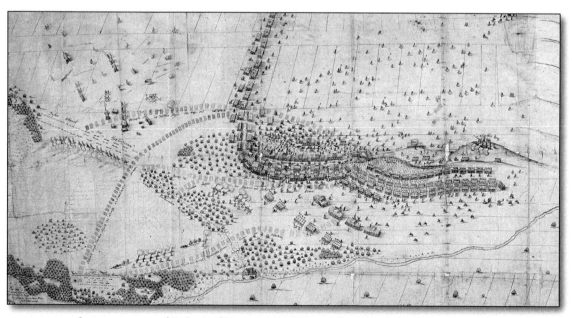

Contemporary map of the battle of Wittstock, 1636. (Military Archives, Stockholm; Photo: Medströms)

(Vitzthum von Eckstädt was subsequently accused of treason because of his lack of initiative; he absconded and joined the Imperial army).

The Swedes camped on the field of battle, while Banér gave King orders to attack again at dawn. However, John George and the Saxons retreated under the cover of darkness towards the safety of the River Elbe. Realising that the battle was lost, Hatzfeldt abandoned the field too.

At dawn, King set off after the retreating enemy. He carried out this task with admirable efficiency. First, he captured John George's supply train. Then, he continued, reaching the retreating infantry, many of whom were cut down. The pursuit ended only when King reached the River Elbe, which Hatzfeldt's survivors crossed opposite the town of Werben.

Swedish losses were 3,369 dead and wounded, or more than a fifth of the total army, which gives testimony to how hard-fought the battle was. The Imperial–Saxon army lost between 4,000 and 5,000 men and on the following day, the Swedes captured some 2,000 stragglers. The Swedes also seized 151 standards, 33 cannons, and the supply train including the Elector's field chancellery and field treasury.[94]

The two key features of the battle were Banér's march around Hatzfeldt's fortified position, which forced the Imperial commander to abandon it for a less advantageous one, and King's flank march, which although delayed, arrived just in time to break the enemy's will to fight. Raimondo Montecuccoli (1609–1680), who fought in the battle on the Imperial side, explained the Swedish victory at Wittstock with the laconic observation that "we strongly reinforced our front against one side, but the enemy came from the other." He also observed that one had to form up the troops with sufficient reserves so that they could fight several times. "He who in the end has more men will win." In Montecuccoli's view, Banér won the battle because King's fresh squadrons arrived at sunset when the Imperials were already exhausted.[95]

Yet, the battle of Wittstock only eliminated parts of the Imperial army. Hatzfeldt managed to disengage many units. Even so, the battle was decisive to the extent that it shattered the Imperial momentum gained with the victory at Nördlingen. The Swedish army regained its reputation for efficiency, and it no longer seemed preordained that the Emperor would win the contest, despite the greater resources of the Habsburgs.

Moreover, the battle of Wittstock effectively eliminated Brandenburg from the contest. Although without direct participation by Brandenburgian forces, the battle had taken place in the Brandenburg heartland. Henceforth, George William of Brandenburg preferred to sit out the war from the safe distance of Königsberg in East Prussia until he died in December 1640 (his son, Frederick William, then assumed power and proposed a separate peace

---

94 Banér's report to the Queen on the battle of Wittstock, 24 September 1636 (O.S.), *AOSB* 2:6, pp.856–66, on pp.861–2, 865–6. See also Tingsten, *Fältmarskalkarna*, pp.70–1; Ericson, "Wittstock 1636", pp.147, 154; Ericson Wolke, Larsson; and Villrand, *Trettioåriga kriget*, p.151.

95 Raimondo Montecuccoli, *Ausgewählte Schriften* 2 (Vienna: Kriegs-Archiv/W. Braumüller, 1899), pp.580–1.

with Sweden, the Peace of Stockholm between Sweden and Brandenburg, which was signed on 24 July 1641).

For Banér, his choice to go on the offensive had paid off spectacularly. Henceforth, he would consistently go on the offensive. And not only Banér. It can be argued that the offensive henceforth became the standard Swedish operating procedure. Banér had chosen the offensive over the defence of his supply lines. By releasing his field army from the communication lines with the north, he was able to gain mobility, while supplies could be gathered in the area of operations, deep in enemy territory. Although Banér probably found inspiration in the strategy and operations of the late Gustavus Adolphus, Banér's strategy henceforth was bolder than that of his predecessor. However, he was no fool, and we will see that Banér also knew how to follow a defensive strategy, when this was more advantageous.

Table 4. Swedish order of battle at Wittstock, 4 October 1636 (sources: Banér's report to the Queen on the battle of Wittstock, 24 September 1636 (O.S.), AOSB 2:6, pp.856 66, on pp.864–5; drawing by Conrad Mardefelt, who participated in the battle; Mankell, *Uppgifter* 2, p.238)

Commanding officer/Regiment	Strength
Commander-in-Chief: Field Marshal Johan Banér	
Right Wing	
Commanders: Field Marshal Johan Banér and General of Artillery Lennart Torstensson	
Gadow's Cavalry	200 (Uppland Cavalry Regiment)
Klingspor's Cavalry	200 (Östgöta Cavalry Regiment)
Ture Bielke's Cavalry	500 (Åbo Cavalry Regiment)
Johan Wittenberg's Cavalry	500 (Åbo Cavalry Regiment)
Hans Wachtmeister's Cavalry	600 (Livonians)
Gustav Gustavson's Cavalry	450 (Livonians)
Billinghausen's Cavalry	300 (Courlanders)
Krockow's Cavalry	400
Duke Francis Henry of Saxe-Lauenburg's Cavalry	350
William Gunn's Regiment Jeschwitzki's Regiment Wrangel's Regiment	738 (musketeers detached in support of right wing; some may instead have been deployed in the reserve)
Centre	
Commanders: Field Marshal Alexander Leslie and Major General Thomas Kerr	
First Line	
Hans Drake's Regiment Caspar Ermes's Regiment Salomon Adam's Regiment	892 (in 'Swedish Brigade', consisting of the former Magdeburg garrison including units from Kronoberg and Jönköping Regiments and Ermes's Savolax Regiment)

Commanding officer/Regiment	Strength
Thomas Kerr's Regiment Lindsay's Regiment Cunningham's Regiment	} 800 (in Kerr's 'Scottish Brigade')
Abel Moda's Regiment Banér's Life Regiment of Foot ('Old Blue')	} 856 (in 1 brigade)
Goltz's Regiment Zabeltitz's Regiment	} 896 (in 1 brigade)
Leslie's Regiment	900 (in 1 brigade)
Second Line	
Banér's Life Regiment of Horse	600
Torstensson's Life Regiment of Horse	300

Reserve

Commanders: Lieutenant General Johann Vitzthum von Eckstädt and Major General John Ruthven

Thomas Thomson	438 (Värmland Regiment, in 1 brigade)
Peter Linde's Regiment Herberstein's Regiment Kriegbaum's Regiment John Forbes's Regiment Bauer's Regiment Strahlendorf's Regiment	} 1,012 (in 1 brigade)
Berghofer's Cavalry Regiment	150
Pfuel's Cavalry Regiment	400
Duwall's Cavalry Regiment	300
Douglas's Cavalry Regiment	200
Claes Wopersnaw's Cavalry Regiment	300
Stewart's Cavalry Regiment	200
Würzburg's Cavalry Regiment	300

Left Wing

Commanders: Lieutenant General James King and Major General Torsten Stålhandske

King's Cavalry	250
Hoditz's Cavalry	250
Beckerman's Cavalry	150
Glaubitz's Cavalry	250
Boy's Cavalry	200
Birkenfeld's Cavalry	150
Dewitz's Cavalry	250
Jens von Habersleben's Cavalry	350
Goldstein's Cavalry	500
Stålhandske's Cavalry	550 (Nyland Cavalry and Småland Cavalry Regiments)
Magnus Hansson's Regiment Ruthven's Regiment Claes Bengtsson's Regiment	} 698 (musketeers detached in support of left wing; some may instead have been deployed in the reserve)
Total cavalry	9,150

Commanding officer/Regiment	Strength
Total infantry	7,230
Grand Total	16,380

Banér on the Defensive

After Wittstock, Banér's aims were to deny enemy armies access to Sweden's Baltic Sea possessions, support (if needed) Sweden's sole remaining ally, Landgrave William of Hesse-Kassel, and continue to intimidate Saxony. Meanwhile, Herman Wrangel maintained the defensive line in Pomerania.

Immediately following the battle of Wittstock, Banér accordingly again moved south into Saxony. In December, he pushed through an agreement with the town of Erfurt, which henceforth would support the Swedes, in the same way that Magdeburg had done until retaken by Hatzfeldt.

In January 1637, Banér first took Torgau on the Elbe, and then laid siege to Leipzig. Supply conditions were difficult in the devastated Saxon territories, to a great extent because of his own depredations in the previous year. Moreover, in February Banér learnt that an Imperial–Bavarian–Saxon army under Hatzfeldt and Johann von Götz, who now commanded the Bavarian army, was on its way. Banér abandoned the siege. He hoped to entice the Imperials into battle, but as additional Imperial reinforcements arrived, Banér, realising that he was seriously outnumbered, withdrew to Torgau.

Gallas, recently appointed overall Imperial military commander, brought more men. Banér's army had to withdraw further. In late June, Banér retreated east of the Oder. Pursued by one Imperial army, Banér found another waiting for him in early July when he reached Landsberg. The combined Imperial armies had amassed at least 45,000, probably some 50,000 men against Banér's 14,000.[96] Banér was cut off from Pomerania. It was, of course, possible to move further east, into the Polish-Lithuanian Commonwealth, but moving a Swedish army into the Commonwealth could easily result in renewed war, for which Sweden was unprepared.

The Imperials thought that Banér was trapped. However, he had no intention to surrender. First, he burned his supply train. All civilians within the army were sent eastwards, against the Commonwealth. The order encompassed the officers' wives, including Elisabeth Juliana of Erbach, Banér's wife. This was a diversion in the hope that Imperial scouts might believe that the entire army was moving east. Instead Banér ordered his men on a forced march in the opposite direction. Then, he ordered the civilians to turn around. Before the Imperial commanders realised what was happening, Banér's entire army had crossed the Oder, after which the retreat turned to the north. In mid July, Banér's army reached Eberswalde, Brandenburg, where he could join forces with Herman Wrangel. Banér had outmanoeuvred

---

96 Tingsten, *Fältmarskalkarna*, p.84; Ericson Wolke, Larsson; and Villstrand, *Trettioåriga kriget*, p.152.

his enemies. His skillful retreat attracted much praise, and a satisfied Banér commented on the operation with the words: 'They had me in the sack but forgot to tie it up.'

However, the supply situation in Pomerania was no better in 1637 than before, or indeed later. Short of funds and supplies, Banér's army would remain confined in Pomerania for over a year, unable to break out. Instead, the Swedes concentrated their defences on Stralsund, Greifswald, and Anklam. As long as the sea lines of communication remained under the control of the Swedish navy, supplies could be brought in – although this was contrary to how Oxenstierna had envisaged financing the war.

By July 1637, Pomerania was defended by Banér with a field army of 10,000 men and Wrangel with close to 5,000. In addition, reinforcements were sent from the Swedish heartland, primarily to the Swedish garrisons which consisted of possibly some 9,000 men in Pomerania and 1,200 in adjacent Mecklenburg.[97] By the end of 1637, the garrisons in Pomerania had increased to around 15,000 men. In addition, Sweden still controlled Wismar and Warnemünde in Mecklenburg; Minden, Nienburg, Osnabrück, and Vechta in the Weser region and Westphalia; Hanau on the Lower Main; Erfurt in Thuringia; and Benfeld in Alsace. The total garrisons in these locations consisted of some 8,000 men.[98]

During the autumn, Gallas made several attempts to go on the offensive into Pomerania. He took many Swedish fortresses, including those at Demmin and Wolgast. However, he failed to dislodge the Swedish presence at the coast. Besides, now it was Gallas's Imperial army which suffered from the lack of supplies in northern Germany. He eventually had to move out of the region to find winter quarters.

The Battle of Chemnitz

Following increasing difficulties in cooperation between Banér and Herman Wrangel, the latter was in April 1638 recalled to Sweden. At around the same time, Sten Bielke, Governor General of Pomerania, died of natural causes. Although Bielke had held a civilian post, his death and Wrangel's departure significantly consolidated Banér's position of overall command. Banér became acting governor general. At least the chain of command was no longer ambiguous, and Banér was henceforth in sole charge of all military and many political activities (Banér's appointment as Governor General of Pomerania was formally endorsed in early December, and in late March 1639, his de facto appointment as Sweden's commander-in-chief in Germany was also formalised.[99])

Even so, the Swedish situation in Pomerania remained weak. Moreover, in spring Gallas returned to Pomerania. Meanwhile, both the Swedish and the Imperial army suffered from lack of supplies, and possibly yet worse, an

---

97 Mankell, *Uppgifter* 2, pp.235–6; Tingsten, *Fältmarskalkarna*, p.97.
98 Mankell, *Uppgifter* 2, p.241; Tingsten, *Fältmarskalkarna*, p.101.
99 Tingsten, *Fältmarskalkarna*, p.96.

outbreak of plague in late spring 1638 which ravaged garrisons and army camps alike. Repeating the defensive strategy of the previous year, which then was forced upon him but now was voluntary, Banér waited as Gallas's Imperial army gradually shrank in size due to the lack of supplies.

Even so, reinforcements were sorely needed. Oxenstierna had to reverse his policy on avoiding the use of national Swedish troops in Germany. In June, Oxenstierna sent 14,000 men (9,000 men from Sweden and 5,000 from Finland) to Pomerania to reinforce Banér's army. Previously, reinforcements had been fewer in numbers and mostly intended for garrison duty. Besides, following the March 1638 Treaty of Hamburg with France, which ratified the two-year-old Treaty of Wismar, French funding again became available. Both the men and the funding were welcome additions to Banér's army. By late July, Banér's field army consisted of 21,000 men (11,000 horse and 10,000 foot).[100]

In September 1638, after some cavalry skirmishes in which Torstensson, Stålhandske, and Slang had harassed the enemy, Banér finally went on the offensive. Gallas, concluding that his remaining forces were too weak to fight, retreated south. Later in the year, Banér also defeated a corps of Saxon reinforcements under Morzin, who just before (in October) had gone into Saxon service with the rank of Field Marshal.

In early January 1639, Banér again led his army into the field. A month later, he crossed the Elbe at Lauenburg and moved south to relieve Erfurt, where there still was a Swedish garrison under siege. Having relieved Erfurt, Banér laid siege to Freiberg, an important Saxon town which also contained the family tomb of John George of Saxony. Soon he found two enemy armies approaching, an Imperial one under Hatzfeldt and a joint Imperial–Saxon one under Morzin.

Banér temporarily abandoned the siege, which so far had not gone well, and then turned first against Morzin's army, attempting to attack it before the Imperial armies could unite. However, Morzin retreated. Even so, following the example of his operations before the battle of Wittstock two years previously, Banér managed, through forced marches, to intercept Morzin at Chemnitz. The battle of Chemnitz was fought on 14 April 1639. Banér used his cavalry to defeat first the left, and then the right wing of Morzin's army. The enemy cavalry fled, and the Swedish army was then free to move against the infantry, which had no way to escape. The Swedes lost 250 men, while Morzin's army was essentially "destroyed", as Banér, probably correctly, put it. It was a decisive victory. The Swedes took 1,500 prisoners, including 300 officers, 63 standards, the supply train, chancellery, artillery, and ammunition. Morzin, wounded in the battle, managed to escape to Prague, but only to be imprisoned and prosecuted as responsible for the defeat.[101]

Chemnitz was taken under Swedish control, and a contingent of the Västgöta Cavalry Regiment was moved into the town as its garrison. The Västgöta contingent had come to Germany in 1638 under its larger-than-life colonel Harald Stake, who once had saved the life of Gustavus Adolphus. Now

---

100 *Ibid.*, p.103.
101 *Ibid.*, pp.110–11.

Stake had returned home, handing over command to Lieutenant Colonel Johan Printz (1592–1663), another extraordinary character who accordingly assumed command of the garrison. Printz, at least in his later life an unusually big and heavy man, had when young studied theology at various universities in Germany, until he was forcibly enlisted, he said, into an Imperial regiment. He later also served in Venetian and Danish regiments. After the defeat of the Danish army, he in 1625 returned home, where he joined the Swedish army to fight in Prussia. By 1630, he had become captain in the Åbo Cavalry Regiment, learnt Finnish, and been appointed quartermaster. In 1636, Printz fought at Wittstock. He was once captured by Imperial troops, purchased his release, and in 1638, transferred to the Västgöta Cavalry Regiment.

Banér's Invasion of Bohemia

After the battle of Chemnitz, Banér continued towards Bohemia. In late April he reached Pirna, which he took a week later. In May, Stålhandske pushed on with nine cavalry regiments and 500 musketeers to Leitmeritz in Bohemia, which he took.[102] To protect Bohemia, the Imperial commander Georg Lorenz von Hofkirchen (d. 1657) attempted to defend the Elbe line, assisted by the aforementioned Raimondo Montecuccoli (1609–1680), who in time would become far better known and had fought the Swedes repeatedly, in the battles of Breitenfeld, Nördlingen, Wittstock, and Chemnitz. Hofkirchen, who previously had been in both Saxon and Swedish service (after Baudissin's resignation, he had commanded the latter's cavalry regiment), prepared positions at Altbunzlau, where there was a pontoon bridge across to Brandeis. However, Banér crossed the river further downstream, near Melnik. Employing similar tactics as Gustavus Adolphus when crossing the Lech back in 1632, Banér only sent some artillery and foot to Brandeis, in order to create a diversion through artillery fire. The Swedish infantry was shipped across the river on some 30 boats and barges on the evening of 28 May. In addition, Banér had a redoubt built to protect his artillery while it gave fire upon the opposite shore. The artillery fire pushed back Montecuccoli's men who contested the crossing. Meanwhile, the Swedish cavalry forded the river in another location, not far away. On 29 May 1639, Hofkirchen led 10 cavalry regiments against the crossing point, but they were defeated and pursued, losing a thousand dead, in Banér's assessment, and several hundred who were captured, including both Hofkirchen and Montecuccoli.[103]

Montecuccoli had to spend the years from May 1639 to May 1642 (when he was exchanged for Slang) in captivity in Stettin, which gave him the opportunity to put his conclusions on the art of war into writing. His book, when published, became highly influential as a source of military theory.

Meanwhile, Banér continued to Prague, which he reached on 30 May. Learning of the fate of Morzin's army at Chemnitz, Hatzfeldt hastened to Prague, where the Imperial commander Gallas had already prepared a

---

102 *Ibid.*, p.127.
103 *Ibid.*, pp.127–8.

fortified camp at White Mountain outside Prague. Now safe in Prague, Gallas and Hatzfeldt refused battle. Banér considered his forces insufficient to storm the city. Besides, it had been impossible to bring siege artillery on his many forced marches.

In October 1639, Archduke Leopold William (1614–1662) assumed overall command of the Imperial army. Since the Archduke was Emperor Ferdinand III's younger brother, he had sufficient authority to put an end to the personal rivalry between Gallas and Hatzfeldt, which had hampered their co-operation. As a result, Hatzfeldt was ordered to leave Prague and return to the west in forced marches. Banér followed for a while, but then reversed course back to Prague. Gallas was less fortunate, he was dismissed and returned to Vienna.

So far, Banér had issued stern orders not to pillage Bohemia. He claimed to have come to liberate the oppressed Bohemians, and possibly he believed that the Protestant spirit of the Bohemian Revolt still lingered there. However, in the 1620s, Emperor Ferdinand II had

Raimondo Montecuccoli.

carried out a harsh campaign of recatholicisation in Bohemia, which formed a major part of his ancestral lands. Two decades later, a majority of Bohemians were Catholics. It was impossible to raise popular support for the Swedish army. When Banér realised this, he also realised that since he could not gain control of Bohemia, he would have to deny its abundant resources to the enemy, just as he had done in Saxony. In early November 1639, Banér issued orders to devastate Bohemia, and also those parts of Silesia and Moravia that were within his reach. The Swedes in Bohemia began primarily to engage in small war: raids and foraging. So did Hatzfeldt, who responded in kind.

Archduke Leopold William of Austria. (Pieter Thijs)

Just as in Saxony, Banér devastated Bohemia as a deliberate policy, so as to prevent the Imperial army from using the territory for its own purposes, but also to apply pressure on the Emperor, since Bohemia formed an important part of his ancestral lands and core territories. Prague, the capital and administrative centre of Bohemia, was as important as Vienna, the Empire's political centre.

In early December, Archduke Leopold William received reinforcements in the form of Ottavio Piccolomini with 6,000 horse and 124 companies of foot, mostly Walloons, recently enlisted in the Spanish Netherlands. The combined Imperial army in Bohemia then counted 8,350 horse and 13,500 foot, in addition to the Croats who, according to reports available to Banér,

were uncountable. In comparison, Banér had some 16,000 men in the field army and an additional 4,000 at the Elbe.[104]

In March 1640, Banér moved out of Leitmeritz, departing from Bohemia, where he had stayed for more than nine months. He marched through Saxony, arriving in Erfurt in late April. Banér left Stålhandske in charge of the field army on the Oder, which he henceforth used to apply pressure on Silesia and eastern Saxony.[105]

Swedes and French Join Forces

In May, Banér's army at Erfurt (which then consisted of 15,000 to 16,000 men[106]) joined forces with the French army under the Henri d'Orléans, Duke de Longueville (1595–1663), assisted by Jean Baptiste Budes de Guébriant (1602–1643), and the armies of two German allies: those of the late William of Hesse-Kassel's widow, Amalie Elisabeth (1602–1651), Countess of Hanau-Münzenberg, and George, Duke of Brunswick-Lüneburg. Both German rulers had suffered reverses in the past. William and Amalie Elisabeth of Hesse-Kassel had lost access to Hesse in 1637 and had to retreat into Frisia where William died in the same year. Amalie Elisabeth had entered into an agreement with France in August 1639, according to which she again allied with France and Sweden. Under the guidance of Amalie Elisabeth, the Hessian army from 1640 onwards became one of the most active participants in the war. George of Brunswick-Lüneburg had agreed to the terms of the Peace of Prague in August 1635. Now, however, he, too, returned to the war, on the side of Sweden and France. The combined allied army then constituted some 36,000 men.[107]

Amalie Elisabeth of Hesse-Kassel, as a young woman. Most surviving portraits depict Amalie Elisabeth in the last few years of her life, when illness had taken its toll. However, those portraits are not representative of her appearance until at the very end of the war.

The allied army immediately moved to Saalfeld, where it established a fortified camp opposite Piccolomini's Imperial camp. The two camps soon exchanged artillery fire in what became known as the artillery battle of Saalfeld. Colonel Slang was hit in the right arm, which had to be amputated. However, since the Imperial army was smaller in numbers, Piccolomini refused to march out for battle. Instead, he hoped for the arrival of a Bavarian relief army. Nor did the allied army find conditions suitable to storm the camp. As a result, a number of skirmishes took place, but no decisive action.

In June, the allied army moved out, instead turning west towards the Rhine. This plan suited the French, and Banér, who may have been the originator of the plan, supported it, too. There were still Swedish forces in the west. Previously, they had been commanded by James King. When King in

---

104 *Ibid.*, p.133.
105 Petri, *Kungl. Första livgrenadjärregementets historia 2*, p.229.
106 Tingsten, *Fältmarskalkarna*, p.138.
107 Ericson Wolke, Larsson; and Villstrand, *Trettioåriga kriget*, p.159.

the summer of 1639 left his command at the Weser and Westphalia and went to Sweden, Banér had appointed Hans Christoph von Königsmarck (1605–1663) commander of the remaining Swedish forces at the Weser.[108] Königsmarck was a Brandenburger who served as ensign in Wallenstein's army when Gustavus Adolphus landed in Germany in 1630. He went into Swedish service in 1631 as a captain of an enlisted company within Baudissin's Dragoons. Königsmarck fought at Oldersdorf in 1633 and according to some reports at Nördlingen in 1634. He was a good cavalry officer and, in the Weser army, rose in rank to colonel, in which position he (around 1638) succeeded Sperreuter. Königsmarck was promoted to major general in 1640. Due to his personality and unwillingness to take orders, Königsmarck primarily distinguished himself in small war or with independent commands.[109]

Hans Christoph von Königsmarck, 1651. (Matthäus Merian the Younger, Skokloster Castle)

The Bavarian army now joined Piccolomini at Königshofen. He then took Neustadt, where his position was even stronger than at Saalfeld. The rest of the summer was spent in attempts at outmanoeuvring the other, but neither side gained an advantage. A further problem for the allies was that Piccolomini in August moved into Amalie Elisabeth's Hesse, which he devastated. Frequent skirmishing took place as the Imperials ravaged Hesse. The allies needed supplies, too, which they brought in food convoys from Lüneburg so as not to devastate Amalie Elisabeth's territory further. Meanwhile, both sides attempted to prevent the other from gaining supplies. Both sides also had to disperse their forces for reasons of sustaining themselves. Too big armies simply could not find the supplies they needed.

Meanwhile, things were not going so well for the Swedes in the east. An Imperial army under a Portuguese noble, Eduardo de Braganza (Duarte de Bragança; 1605–1649), in early May 1640 turned up to lay siege to Chemnitz. Eventually the town's commandant, Printz, had to surrender under humiliating conditions. Printz was the aforementioned lieutenant colonel of the Västgöta Cavalry Regiment which was garrisoned in the town. The Swedish cavalrymen, deprived of horses, weapons, and standards, had to march north, where they ultimately were shipped to Kalmar. Upon his return to Sweden Printz was arrested, court-martialled, and dismissed from military service. This would normally have been a footnote in history, but nonetheless, we will see that he later made a spectacular comeback (but not so his adversary Eduardo de Braganza, whose brother later in the year

---

108 Tingsten, *Fältmarskalkarna*, pp.95–6, pp.128–9.

109 Königsmarck remained in Swedish service after the Thirty Years' War and eventually reached the rank of field marshal. His son, Otto Wilhelm von Königsmarck (1639–1688), was a distinguished Swedish Field Marshal during the Scanian War.

rebelled against Spanish rule as King John IV of Portugal, for which Eduardo was imprisoned in Milan until the end of his life).

Soon things were not going well in the western theatre of operations, either. The allies fundamentally disagreed about strategy, not least because of the inability of Stockholm and Paris to agree on what the anti-Habsburg alliance should aim to achieve. The French wanted to fight the Emperor but they did not wish to fight the Bavarians, with whom they had an understanding. Since the Bavarian army was a major component of the enemy forces, Banér never really trusted the French. There was strife among the Hessians, too. The Hessian military commander, Peter Melander von Holzapfel, could not agree on policy with Amalie Elisabeth, who accordingly took effective command into her own hands. Rumour said that at the time she even slapped his face. Be that as it may, Holzapfel left Hessian service (and, after a while, joined the Imperial army). Meanwhile, all armies suffered serious losses to attrition from famine and disease.

In early September, Longueville, worn down by fever, returned to Paris. He left the French troops in the hands of Guébriant. By then, Piccolomini attempted to move the war into Brunswick-Lüneburg. However, the allies managed to prevent his crossing the Weser.

In October, Piccolomini accordingly moved into Westphalia, where, the allies assumed, he would go into winter quarters. The allies moved into winter quarters, too. Banér's second in command, Torstensson, was so ill that he had to take his leave and return first to Stralsund, and then to Sweden. The entire campaign season had produced no decisive results for either side. However, since the allies were the stronger party, and in fact fielded the strongest anti-Habsburg army since Gustavus Adolphus's 1632 assault on the Alte Feste outside Nuremberg, the campaign can only be described as a failure for their cause. For the first time, Swedes and French had joined forces and both fielded significant numbers of experienced men. Yet, they had achieved nothing. The winner was undoubtedly Piccolomini, who despite his smaller force remained undefeated and had retained the initiative throughout the campaign.

Banér did not stay long in his winter quarters on the Weser. Departing already in early December, he led the army back to Erfurt. There news arrived from Regensburg, where the Emperor Ferdinand III had called an Imperial Diet (*Reichstag*). In fact, this was the only occasion when this institution convened during the Thirty Years' War. Learning of the meeting, Banér devised an audacious plan to capture the Emperor, thus in one stroke ending the war. Banér called out his troops and, taking advantage of the frozen rivers, marched rapidly against Regensburg, intending to surprise the participants of the meeting. The plan might have worked. However, a sudden thaw reduced the bearing capacity of the ice, which delayed the raid. Although both Banér and Guébriant, who rejoined Banér for the operation, reached and briefly attacked Regensburg in January 1641, Banér did not achieve his goal. Swedish cavalry did capture several Imperial courtiers out for a hunt, but the Emperor had been delayed and was not among them. The Swedes only captured his cart.

Banér then moved east to the border of Bohemia, where he again went into winter quarters, at Schwandorf near Cham in Bavaria. In March, an Imperial army under Piccolomini attempted to catch him there. However, first the Imperials aimed to subdue Neunburg, north-west of Cham, where the one-armed Erik Slang was in command. Piccolomini laid siege to Neunburg in March. Although stubbornly defended by Slang, the garrison was greatly outnumbered, short of ammunition, and the town walls were obsolete and rapidly collapsed when under the onslaught of the Imperial siege artillery. Slang had to surrender on the following day, and his situation was so desperate that Piccolomini did not allow him to withdraw with military honours. Slang and his men had to go into captivity.

However, the siege of Neunburg had alerted Banér to the danger. He broke camp and left for Saxony. In late March, Banér crossed the River Eger into Saxony on a pontoon bridge. In early April, the Swedish field army camped down in the Leipzig area.

As a tactician and strategist, Banér was innovative. He appreciated fighting skills, but he had less patience for other virtues, in particular civilian ones. In a letter to Oxenstierna in spring 1641, a customarily grumpy Banér assessed his senior officers. He found Torstensson acceptable, but as for the rest, Banér was not very pleased:

> [Torsten] Stålhandske is too slow, and [Adam von] Pfuel – although useful – spends too much time thinking about his new wedded life. [Hans Christoph von] Königsmarck is a good soldier, but he lacks knowledge of military affairs. [Carl Gustav] Wrangel is useless. After his time in France, he is a fop with the habit of sleeping late. If he is ordered to rise before dawn, he shows up no earlier than eight o'clock.[110]

The war had made Banér a harsh man. He also regularly engaged in heavy drinking, which gradually destroyed his health and made him yet more short-tempered. Thus, the only person who could manage Banér was his wife since 1636, Elisabeth, who followed him on his campaigns. Gentle but determined, Elisabeth was the one influence that could rein in her husband. Both soldiers and burghers often asked her to intervene when Banér's callousness and exactions grew too strong. When Elisabeth died in June 1640, Banér was deeply affected. Although he remarried in a scandalously short time, with Johanna Margareta of Baden-Hochberg, the young daughter of the Margrave of Baden, whom he had met at his wife's funeral, the loss of Elisabeth made him increasingly reckless. His health deteriorated, too. In May 1641, Banér died of a sudden illness.

Banér was popular with his men because he was a successful general, but even more so because he generally overlooked their customary depredations, looting, and general lack of discipline. Admittedly, he had few means at his disposal to do otherwise. Besides, devastating the enemy's territory by then had become an established strategy.

---

110 Rosander, *Sveriges fältmarskalkar*, p.108.

Torstensson Takes Command

Without Banér, his army again grew close to mutiny. Again, it was the colonels who put forth demands. Before his death, Banér had recommended Torstensson as his successor, indeed we have seen it argued that Torstensson was the only one of his senior officers who would do, but Torstensson was still convalescing in Sweden. The three major generals Carl Gustav Wrangel (1613–1676; a son of Field Marshal Herman Wrangel), Arvid Wittenberg von Debern (1606–1657), and Adam von Pfuel (1604–1659;) accordingly assumed temporary command of the main army. Major General Stålhandske remained in command of the units in Silesia, while Major General Königsmarck commanded the units in the west.

The oldest of the three major generals with the main army was Pfuel, a Brandenburger, who had gone into Swedish service with an enlisted regiment in 1634. He was also the brother-in-law of Banér. Next in age and with considerably more experience came Wittenberg von Debern, or only

Arvid Wittenberg, 1649.
(Matthäus Merian)

Wittenberg as he was commonly called. Wittenberg was born in Sweden. He had begun his military career in 1622 and had fought in Prussia, at Oldendorf, Nördlingen (where he was captured), Wittstock, and Chemnitz.

Wrangel was the youngest. Even so, he had been promoted to major general of cavalry already in 1638 and accordingly was the senior in service. Wrangel was the son of Field Marshal Herman Wrangel. As a 13-year-old, young Wrangel had joined his father who was then fighting in Prussia. Four years later, in 1630, the young man had joined Gustavus Adolphus's field army. Despite Banér's cranky complaint that Wrangel was a fop with French manners, there is no doubt that the young general had fighting experience. There is a tradition that he took part in the battle of Lützen in 1632 as a dispatch rider. In 1635, Wrangel as a lieutenant colonel certainly participated in battles in the River Elbe region. There he was shot twice, once through his hat and then at his shot-proof breastplate, but he escaped wounds. Wrangel was promoted to colonel in 1636. In 1639, he fought at Chemnitz. While young Wrangel's promotion to major general may have been prompted by Oxenstierna's need to appease old Herman Wrangel after his recall from Germany, it was only Banér who found faults in the young man's military skills. It may have been the bad feelings between Banér and old Herman Wrangel which made Banér grumble also over the younger Wrangel. Or perhaps it was the French manners, after all. Young Wrangel was "in dress and manners like a born Frenchman", the exasperated Banér once complained.[111] Perhaps it also mattered that Wrangel was 17 years younger. Nonetheless, the ill and cantankerous Banér did not prevent

---

111 *Ibid.*, p.117.

young Wrangel from marrying Anna Margareta von Haugwitz, a German orphan girl who due to chance and the misfortunes of war had become his and his wife's ward. Young Wrangel's marriage with Anna Margareta was a love match opposed by his father, since the girl had neither high rank nor inheritance.

There were only 500 national troops in the field army. Of the army's 30 colonels, 23 united in a mutinous association similar to the one at Donauwörth in 1633, with a Dutch colonel, Caspar Cornelius de Mortaigne (d. 1647), as one of their most outspoken leaders. Another was an Austrian, Georg Derfflinger (1606–1695), who after the Thirty Years' War was ennobled as Georg von Derfflinger, became a field marshal and in many ways was the professional founder of the Brandenburg-Prussian army. In effect, this was yet another labour strike, in which the colonels refused to have their men fight before the arrears had been settled and their monetary demands fulfilled. Ultimately, as we will see, both Mortaigne and Derfflinger continued to serve in the Swedish army, and both acquired high rank. At this point, however, they were unhappy – and presumably not a little worried about what would happen after the death of Banér.

Carl Gustav Wrangel, 1646 or 1647. The 33-year-old new commander of Swedish military forces in Germany, Wrangel enjoyed Torstensson's confidence but had not yet made a name for himself among the more experienced senior officers. (*Theatrum Europaeum*)

But there was still fighting to be done. Wrangel, together with Guébriant's French army and contingents from Brunswick-Lüneburg and Hesse, in late June 1641 beat off an Imperial–Bavarian army under Archduke Leopold William and Piccolomini at Wolfenbüttel in the Lower Saxon Circle. The two armies were fairly evenly matched, although the Imperial side seems to have been somewhat superior in numbers. For Wrangel, the battle was a clear victory, but because of difficulties in cooperation between the Swedish, French, and Lüneburgian contingents, not a decisive one.[112]

Carl Gustav Wrangel, 1647. His moustache is barely discernable, which makes him look younger than he was. (Medal self-commissioned by Wrangel in Nuremberg)

However, young Wrangel had not yet developed the authority to restore order in the army. This had to wait until the arrival from Sweden of Banér's replacement, for which Oxenstierna had selected the experienced but seriously ill Torstensson, who also had been Banér's choice for a successor.

It took Oxenstierna some persuasion to get Torstensson, crippled by rheumatoid arthritis, to assume command. However, eventually he agreed. Torstensson was accordingly promoted to Field Marshal and Governor-General of Pomerania, that is, the same position that Banér had held before him. Torstensson then sailed for Germany. The sea voyage severely taxed his health, which meant that immediately upon arriving he was laid up in bed in Stralsund. When Torstensson joined the army in Saxony in late November 1641, he brought with him replacements (3,000 horse, although mostly without horses, and 5,000 foot) and all the funding that Oxenstierna

---

112 Tingsten, *Fältmarskalkarna*, pp.187–9.

had managed to raise to pay the troops.[113] He also met Guébriant, who, however, in December returned to the Rhineland. This was bad news for Torstensson, who had brought Swedish cavalrymen but few horses. Now he was too weak in cavalry to operate efficiently.[114]

The illness had made Torstensson ruthless. The greater part of time he was confined to a cumbrous horse-litter, since he could not ride a horse or even sit upright in a wagon. Torstensson immediately set out to restore harsh discipline. Gone was the laissez-faire attitude of Banér. Torstensson handled the mutinous attitude among the German colonels quickly and ruthlessly by arresting one of the ringleaders, Colonel Joachim Ludwig von Seckendorf (1591–1642), who was court-martialled for having engaged in conspirative negotiations with senior Imperial commanders, sentenced to death, and executed in front of the entire army. When Seckendorf, on the execution ground, asked for mercy for the welfare of his wife and children, Torstensson promised to provide for them out of his personal funds (a promise which he kept), and then proceeded with the execution. Torstensson acted harshly, but he did not take chances. For instance, he did not unite the reinforcements whom he had brought from Sweden with the army in Germany before discipline was fully restored. He also did not act against Mortaigne and Derfflinger, whom he regarded as good officers. Instead he promoted them, within a couple of months making Mortaigne a major general. Both officers henceforth served loyally. Had Torstensson not been such a capable commander, he would soon, no doubt, have faced a full-blown mutiny. He offered his men victories and the accompanying loot. In return, he rode them hard, through hangings, shootings, and floggings. Torstensson never tried to court favour with his men, yet, because of his combination of harsh discipline and success, nobody would rise against him.

Torstensson's bad health had one direct effect on the war. Unlike his predecessor Banér, Torstensson generally avoided campaigning in winter, since he then suffered from illness far more than in warmer seasons. Banér had often left winter quarters already in January, or dispensed with winter quarters altogether. Not so Torstensson. But when he left camp, he generally moved rapidly. In early April 1642, Torstensson crossed the Elbe to invade Saxony. The Swedish army (5,000 horse, 3,000 unmounted cavalrymen, and 7,000 foot[115]) crossed the river at Werben, and then moved south. Since Imperial units in Silesia might threaten his flank, he then moved into Silesia, where he, having joined with Stålhandske, in early May took Glogau. His total strength was then 7,000 horse, 3,000 unmounted cavalrymen, and 10,000 foot.[116] In late May, Torstensson defeated a Saxon army under Francis Albert of Saxe-Lauenburg at Schweidnitz in Silesia. Francis Albert died in the battle, and Schweidnitz surrendered after the defeat. Torstensson then moved into Moravia, where in June, he took Moravia's capital Olmütz (modern-day Olomouc). The booty from Olmütz was huge, and besides money, food

---

113 *Ibid.*, p.185.
114 *Ibid.*, pp.200–201.
115 *Ibid.*, p.206.
116 *Ibid.*, p.207.

supplies, weapons, and ammunition, the Swedish army collected (and sent to Sweden) almost 10,000 books and old manuscripts. Torstensson was now in a position to threaten the Habsburg heartland. Soon his cavalry patrols, under Colonel Helmuth Wrangel (1600–1647; the elder half-brother of Carl Gustav Wrangel), were within a day's ride of Vienna. Because of his daring exploits, then and later, Helmuth Wrangel became known, in German, as 'the Mad Wrangel' (*der Tolle Wrangel*).

Torstensson, it will be remembered, had served under Banér, and it appears that it was Banér's initiative in taking the war to the Imperial hereditary lands that inspired Torstensson to do likewise. However, Torstensson had also learnt caution from Gustavus Adolphus. Instead of marching on Vienna, which the Emperor could easily abandon, he returned through Silesia across the Elbe at Torgau into Saxony to vanquish John George, the Elector of Saxony, once and for all.

Helmuth Wrangel. (Joachim von Sandrart; Skokloster Castle)

Having in early September received reinforcements of 300 horse and 4,000 foot under Carl Gustav Wrangel, Torstensson's army consisted of some 16,000 men as compared to Piccolomini who reportedly had 25,000. Soon, Major General Axel Lillie arrived with another 1,750 horse.[117] Torstensson first marched to Glogau, which was under siege by the Imperials. When Piccolomini avoided battle, Torstensson moved to Leipzig, where he arrived in late October. The plan was to secure the abundant supplies expected to be found in Leipzig. These would be sorely needed during the coming winter. Torstensson and his commanders also expected that a siege of Leipzig would force the Imperial army to offer battle, or else see the important town fall. At Leipzig, Torstensson received additional reinforcements under Königsmarck.

In late October, Torstensson attempted to storm Leipzig, but failed. Torstensson was laying siege to Leipzig when the Imperial army under Archduke Leopold William and Piccolomini finally advanced against him. When the Imperial army approached Leipzig, Torstensson abandoned the siege and withdrew, deliberately giving Piccolomini the impression that he tried to avoid battle with the superior numbers brought by the Imperial general. He also took measures to give the impression to Imperial scouts that the Swedish army was retreating in disorder. Piccolomini pursued, only to find, on the morning of 2 November, that the Swedish army was deployed for battle just ahead of him. Torstensson had decided to meet the Imperials at Breitenfeld.

---

117 Mankell, *Uppgifter* 1, p.179; Petri, *Kungl. Första livgrenadjärregementets historia* 2, pp.236–7.

Siege of Pleissenburg Castle in Leipzig, 1642. Two batteries of cannons (marked G, D) and a battery of mortars (E) are firing against a bastion (B). Meanwhile, Swedish snipers in a trench (P) and in a row of houses keep the defenders away from the walls. An assault party is advancing against the bastion in a trench (F). The besiegers have hung sheets of cloth (M) to prevent the defenders from observing their activities.

The Second Battle of Breitenfeld

The battle would be fought on the same terrain (but not the identical spot) where Gustavus Adolphus 11 years before had won his great victory over Tilly. However, at this time the Saxons of John George were on the side of the Emperor. As for Torstensson, he surely remembered how in 1631 he had commanded the artillery, positioned in the centre, ahead of the Swedish infantry. This time, he commanded the entire Swedish army.[118]

Torstensson had his army deploy for battle in the evening and stay overnight in this position, with the town of Breitenfeld at their back. To hide his intention he allowed very few fires, so as give any observers the impression that his was only a temporary camp for a part of the retreating Swedish army. Piccolomini had received faulty intelligence that Guébriant's French army was only three days' march away (in reality, he was far to the north-west, near Hanover), and believing that Torstensson moved to join forces with the French, Piccolomini hoped to defeat the Swedes first. On 2 November 1642, the two armies met at Breitenfeld, in what would become known as the Second Battle of Breitenfeld.

---

118 Recent works of the second battle of Breitenfeld include Lars Ericson, "*Leipzig 1642*", Lars Ericson et al., *Svenska slagfält* (np: Wahlström &Widstrand, 2003), pp.155–61. See also Tingsten, *Fältmarskalkarna*, pp.213–20.

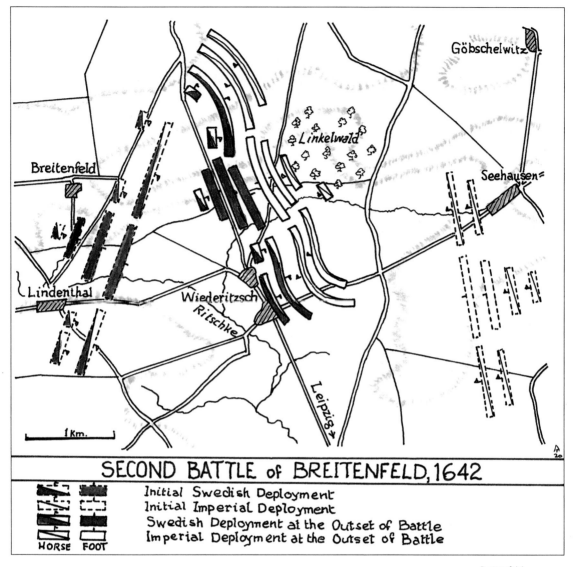

Göbschelwitz

Linkelwald

Breitenfeld

Seehausen

Lindenthal

Wiederitzsch

Ritschke

Leipzig →

1 Km.

A 20

SECOND BATTLE of BREITENFELD, 1642

		Initial Swedish Deployment
		Initial Imperial Deployment
		Swedish Deployment at the Outset of Battle
		Imperial Deployment at the Outset of Battle
HORSE	FOOT	

Breitenfeld.

There is some uncertainty about the number of men on both sides. Due to the attrition among the new reinforcements from Sweden, the traditional Swedish interpretation is that no more than some 15,000 (9,000 horse and 6,000 foot) Swedes stood against 18,000 to 19,000 (12,000 to 13,000 horse and 6,000 foot) Imperials.[119] Based on somewhat later, but still not recent, research, the Swedish army consisted of some 20,000 men (10,000 horse and 10,000 foot, and 70 cannons), while the Imperial army consisted of some

119 Mankell, *Uppgifter* 1, p.180; Mankell, *Uppgifter* 2, pp.208–9; Ericson, *"Leipzig 1642"*, p.155; Ericson Wolke, Larsson; and Villstrand, *Trettioåriga kriget*, p.164.Ultimately, this calculation derives from the nineteenth-century Swedish military historian Mankell, who noted that the 'numbers seem not quite reliable'.

Lennart Torstensson on horseback. Although often incapacitated by illness, there were days when Torstensson was less ill than usual.

26,000 men (16,000 horse and 10,000 foot, and 46 cannons).[120] Later historians have attempted to reconcile the figures by suggesting that an estimated 18,000 Swedes stood against 25,000 Imperials (Table 5).[121]

Torstensson was less ill than usual, spending the day on horseback. On most days, he could barely manage an hour, and then had to have an attendant lead the horse, since his decrepit hands were unable to grasp the reins. As during the battle in 1631, Torstensson had deployed his artillery well forward of his lines, and it immediately opened fire. Torstensson had adopted a traditional deployment. The Swedish right wing was led by Arvid Wittenberg in charge of the first line, and Torsten Stålhandske of the second line. The centre was commanded by Caspar Cornelius de Mortaigne on the right and Carl Gustav Wrangel on the left. The left wing was commanded by the one-armed Erik Slang in the first line and Hans Christoph von Königsmarck in the second. General of Artillery Johan Lilliehöök led the artillery (and possibly also the entire centre), while Axel Lillie commanded the reserve behind the centre. Torstensson deployed detached musketeer units between the cavalry squadrons.

Although not noted at the time, within the Swedish units were several men who later would become famous generals. These included Simon Grundel (1617–1677), who at Jankow in 1645 would fight as a major, in 1646 become quartermaster-general under Wrangel, from 1649 serve as head of all artillery, and from 1676 be the commander-in-chief of the Swedish army. Another was Rutger von Ascheberg (1621–1693), a Courlander who served as a common cavalryman. At Jankow in 1645, he would lead, as an ensign, a squadron from the Landgrave Frederick of Hesse's Cavalry Regiment, and in 1673 become military mentor to Swedish King Charles XI. During the Scanian War, Ascheberg and Grundel would reintroduce the aggressive tactics of the Thirty Years' War into the Swedish army, which had forgotten about them, and this played an important role in winning the war.[122] In the present battle, Ascheberg was wounded and captured. Fortunately for him

120 Tingsten, *Fältmarskalkarna*, pp.215–16. Tingsten refers to later research, although still from the nineteenth century and, since he considered his book a popular history, he added only few references.

121 For example, Tom Gullberg, *Krigen kring Östersjön 3: Lejonet vaknar 1611–1660* (Helsingfors: Schildts, 2008), p.141.

122 For further details on these men, see Michael Fredholm von Essen, *Charles XI's War: The Scanian War between Sweden and Denmark, 1675–1679* (Warwick: Helion, 2019).

(and Sweden), he was saved by Hans Walter, a cavalry captain from Schleswig who served under Stålhandske. In 1677, the two men would meet again but on opposing sides, at the battle of Landskrona, in which Walter fell.

The two armies were not properly lined up against each other, so the Swedish infantry advanced under cover of the artillery fire. The Imperial army advanced to meet them. The cavalry on the wings moved into contact earlier than the infantry and the cavalry battle was more fluid. The Swedish right wing under Wittenberg and Stålhandske rapidly defeated their opponents, despite the Archduke galloping there in person in a vain attempt to rally the fleeing cavalry. However, the Swedish left wing did not fare so well. Slang fell in the battle, hit by a gunshot. Königsmarck managed, barely, to maintain order, with the help of Derfflinger, by bringing in the reserves. In this recovery also participated the young Charles Gustavus (1622–1660), who recently had joined Torstensson's army and in due time would become King of Sweden.

In the centre, the fight was hard, too, not least because the Imperial artillery used chain shot, a type of cannon projectile formed of two sub-calibre balls chained together. When used against line infantry, chain shot caused terrible slaughter. However, eventually the Swedish infantry pushed back the Imperials.

Seeing the danger that his left wing was in, Torstensson personally took charge of some of the cavalry squadrons from Wittenberg's and Stålhandske's wing, which then was engaged in the pursuit of the fleeing Imperial cavalry. Torstensson then ordered these squadrons around the lines and into the rear of the Imperial army, where he charged the remaining Imperial cavalry, trapping them between his own squadrons and those of Wrangel. However, with Torstensson's customary coolness, he left some squadrons east of the Imperial lines, too. As the Imperial infantry collapsed, and men began fleeing eastwards, they were shocked to find Swedish cavalry waiting for them there, blocking their flight. Many of the panicking Imperial soldiers were cut down. This completed the battle, which had lasted for four hours.

The Imperial army lost at least 4,000 dead and wounded and a further 5,000 as prisoners (most of whom went into Swedish service), the Archduke's field treasury, field chancery, and open coach, and the supply train, including 46 cannons, 69 standards, 116 colours, and 50 ammunition wagons. Archduke Leopold William survived the battle through pure luck; on one occasion, he found himself face to face with a Swedish cavalryman who pointed his pistol straight at him. However, the pistol misfired, and Leopold William managed to escape.

The Swedish army lost 2,000 dead, including Johan Lilliehöök and Erik Slang, and about 2,000 wounded.[123] Torstensson, too, only survived by pure chance. A piece of Imperial chainshot hit Torstensson's command group, killing his horse and slashing through his coat. The same chainshot cut Colonel Lars Grubbe, the former resident in Hamburg, in half, killing him

---

123 On casualties for both sides, see Ericson, *"Leipzig 1642"*, pp.155, 161. Ericson at least in part bases the figures on Mankell, *Uppgifter* 1, p.180, who estimates the Imperial casualties as "5,000 lost, almost as many captured".

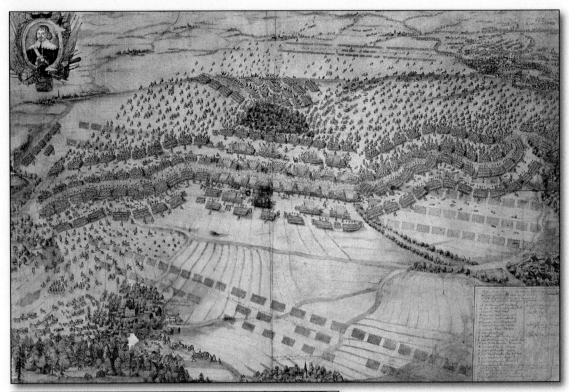

Contemporary depiction of the second battle of Breitenfeld, 1642. The Swedish army (below) is pushing the Imperial army (above) backwards, and some Imperial troops have begun to flee. In the upper centre, the wood of Linkelwald causes problems for the Imperial cavalry. Original deployment indicated by shadowed squares marking the individual units. (Military Archives, Stockholm; Photo: Medströms)

Detail of the second battle of Breitenfeld, 1642, showing the attack of the Swedish right wing, with the Imperial units and supply train in the foreground. Some Imperials are already withdrawing in face of the Swedish attack. In the upper right corner, Swedish cavalry units attack the Imperial foot.

Torstensson's open coach, used by him while on campaign and possibly the one taken from Archduke Leopold William at the second battle of Breitenfeld, 1642. The coach is painted red while the undercarriage displays traces of pink colour. (Royal Armoury, Stockholm)

instantly, smashed into Grubbe's secretary, Martin Qvast, who also died at once, and, in addition, slaughtered the horses of both Charles Gustavus and a cavalry captain named Rabenau, both of whom, like Torstensson, survived splattered with blood but without physical wounds. It is a testament to Torstensson's coolness that after this event he was still able not only to take control of the pursuing Swedish cavalry to lead them against the Imperial rear, but also remembered to deploy some units so as to prevent the enemy's flight.

Table 5. Swedish order of battle at Breitenfeld, 2 November 1642. (Source: Mankell, *Uppgifter* 2, pp.268–9)

Squadrons	Brigades	Commanding Officer or Unit
Overall Commander: Lennart Torstensson		
Right Wing		
First Line		
Commander: Arvid Wittenberg		
3	–	Torstensson's Life Regiment
3	–	Landgrave of Hesse
3	–	Duwall
3	–	Höking
2	–	Kinsky
Second Line		
Commander: Torsten Stålhandske		
3	–	Derfflinger

Squadrons	Brigades	Commanding Officer or Unit
2	–	Wittkopff
3	–	Helmuth Wrangel
2	–	Polish cavalry

In total: 24 squadrons

Centre

Commander: Johan Lilliehöök

First Line

Commanders: Caspar Cornelius de Mortaigne (right) and Carl Gustav Wrangel (left)

Squadrons	Brigades	Commanding Officer or Unit
–	1	Carl Gustav Wrangel (incl. Dalecarlia Regiment)
–	1	Mortaigne
–	1	Lilliehöök
–	1	Banér

Second Line

Commander: Axel Lillie

Squadrons	Brigades	Commanding Officer or Unit
–	1	Axel Lillie
–	1	Schlieben
–	1	Pfuel
–	1	Jeschwitski

Third Line

Squadrons	Brigades	Commanding Officer or Unit
–	1	William Maul
–	1	Plettenberg
–	1	'Old Blue'

In total: 11 brigades

Squadrons	Brigades	Commanding Officer or Unit
3	–	Detached squadrons

Left Wing

First Line

Commander: Erik Slang

Squadrons	Brigades	Commanding Officer or Unit
3	–	Stålhandske
2	–	Wittenberg
2	–	Cratzenstein
2	–	Robert Douglas
2	–	Billinghusen
2	–	Schulman
2	–	Pfuel
2	–	Seckendorf
2	–	Mitzlaff

Second Line

Commander: Hans Christoph von Königsmarck

Squadrons	Brigades	Commanding Officer or Unit
3	–	Tideman
2	–	Lilliehöök

In total: 24 squadrons

In total, 51 squadrons and 11 brigades

A month later, Leipzig fell, too. The town had to pay an indemnity of 150,000 Reichsthalers. However, Torstensson made sure not to loot the town, or tax it too hard, since he found the long-term control of the town more valuable than what could be acquired immediately.

Torstensson then laid siege to Freiberg, but like Banér's attempt before him, the effort failed and after two months he abandoned the endeavour.

Again, Torstensson's illness prevented any major winter campaign. In March 1643 Torstensson, with some 18,000 men, led his army into Bohemia and Moravia.[124] By then, Archduke Leopold William had left for his bishopric of Passau, while Piccolomini, with the Emperor's permission, had gone into Spanish service. As a result, the Emperor reappointed Gallas as his supreme commander. Gallas now commanded a newly raised Imperial army in Moravia. However, he attempted to avoid battle. First, the Emperor had forbidden him to offer battle; second, his army primarily consisted of newly enlisted men. As a result, the Swedish army ravaged Bohemia and Moravia. Cavalry detachments including units from the Östgöta Cavalry Regiment under Wittenberg and Wrangel, respectively, raided as far south as in the vicinity of Vienna. In early October, Torstensson took Eulenburg (near Olmütz). To outsiders, he seemed poised to invade the Habsburg heartlands in Bohemia and Austria (yet, he was not; no more than 800 men in reinforcements had reached him from the north during the entire campaign[125]). Then, reportedly on the same day Torstensson took Eulenburg, a courier from Stockholm arrived with an urgent dispatch from Stockholm. It was an order from Oxenstierna, and it had been encyphered.

Torstensson's War against Denmark

In previous decades, Denmark had been a persistent threat to Sweden, and since the war in Germany began, King Christian IV of Denmark had done nothing to change this impression. To the contrary, he had, among other recent actions, in 1641 signed a commercial treaty with Habsburg Spain, married his son to a daughter of John George of Saxony, and in the spring of 1643 blockaded Hamburg, which in its role as Germany's banking centre was an important source of supplies and funding for the Swedish army. There was also information that Christian IV was mobilising his fleet and army. Danish emissaries were agitating among Swedish peasants in the border region, attempting to arouse them against Oxenstierna, the regency government, and the Swedish nobility. Danish propaganda pamphlets were smuggled into the country. There were even reports that Christian IV was secretly negotiating an alliance with the Empire – and was angling for an anti-Swedish coalition with the Commonwealth and Muscovy. Then there were the Sound tolls. Goods on Swedish ships were supposed to be exempted. However, Christian IV interpreted this as meaning that only goods on its way to or from Sweden or Finland would be exempted – not goods to or from Estonia, Livonia, or the Swedish territories in northern Germany. Yet more annoyingly, he interpreted the Swedish exports of war materials, in particular cannons, as subject to the Sound tolls, despite being carried on Swedish ships from

---

124 Petri, *Kungl. Första livgrenadjärregementets historia* 2, p.244; based on Mankell, *Uppgifter* 1, p.182.
125 Tingsten, *Fältmarskalkarna*, p.231.

Scandinavia

Sweden. This hit the Swedish exports of cannons to the Dutch Republic particularly hard. It also made Christian IV, who received the proceeds from the tolls as a personal income, very rich.[126]

By May 1643, Oxenstierna had had enough. He decided to initiate a pre-emptive war against Denmark so as to neutralise this clear and present threat to Sweden's security.[127] Oxenstierna based the campaign plan on one that Gustavus Adolphus had outlined in Stettin in 1630.[128] The key role in this war would be played by the efficient Torstensson and his experienced army in Germany.[129]

The Swedish regency government devised an elaborate strategy that was well ahead of its time. Torstensson would attack Denmark from the south, through Germany. He would conquer Jutland and then ship his army to Danish islands of Fyn, Lolland, and Zealand so that he could attack Copenhagen. Simultaneously, a smaller corps from Pomerania (200 cavalrymen on foot and 2,000 infantry under Colonel Erik Hansson Ulfsparre[130]) would invade southern Zealand. At the same time Field Marshal Gustav Horn, who after eight years of captivity had finally been able to resume command after his exchange in 1642 for three Imperial generals including Johann von Werth

Christian IV of Denmark. (Karel van Mander)

---

126 In 1618, Christian IV received an annual income of some 200,000 Reichsthalers from the Sound tolls. In 1636, this income had grown to 226,000 Reichsthalers, which in 1637 increased to 229,000. In 1638 the revenue rose to a staggering 482,000 Reichsthalers, which in 1639 grew into 616,000 or even 618,000 Reichsthalers. The increase in revenue took place even as the volume of shipping diminished. Försvarsstabens krigshistoriska avdelning, *Slaget vid Femern 1644 13/10 1944: Minnesskrift* (Gothenburg: Sjöhistoriska samfundet, 1944), p.33; Tom Gullberg, *Krigen kring Östersjön 3: Lejonet vaknar 1611–1660* (Helsingfors: Schildts, 2008), p.146.

127 Modern historians tend to be critical of Oxenstierna's decision to invade Denmark at this point, before first ending the devastating war in Germany. Instead, they argue, Oxenstierna should have devoted all efforts to invade the Habsburg core territories in order to push the Emperor into accepting a peace agreement. In effect, they echo, knowingly or unknowingly, Banér's proposal from late 1632. See, for example, the arguably best general history of the war in the Swedish language, Dick Harrison, *Ett stort lidande har kommit över oss: Historien om trettioåriga kriget* (Stockholm: Ordfront, 2014), p.472. However, such criticism disregards the frequently divergent war aims of Sweden and France. It is unlikely that Sweden could have ended the war by itself, even if Oxenstierna had devoted all of Sweden's resources to the task. Second, Denmark remained a serious latent threat to Sweden and might have taken advantage of a too single-minded Swedish focus on the Habsburg hereditary lands. Besides, from the Swedish perspective, the time Oxenstierna chose was as good as any to deal with the Danish menace.

128 Petri, *Kungl. Första livgrenadjärregementets historia* 2, p.249.

129 In traditional Danish historiography, the wars between Denmark and Sweden were commonly named after the leading commander. The Swedish invasion of Denmark from the south accordingly became known as Torstensson's War, while the war in Scania was called Horn's War, after the Swedish commander Gustav Horn. Likewise, the Norwegian incursions into Sweden during the conflict became known as Sehested's War, after the Danish governor of Norway, Hannibal Sehested.

130 *Slaget vid Femern*, p.61.

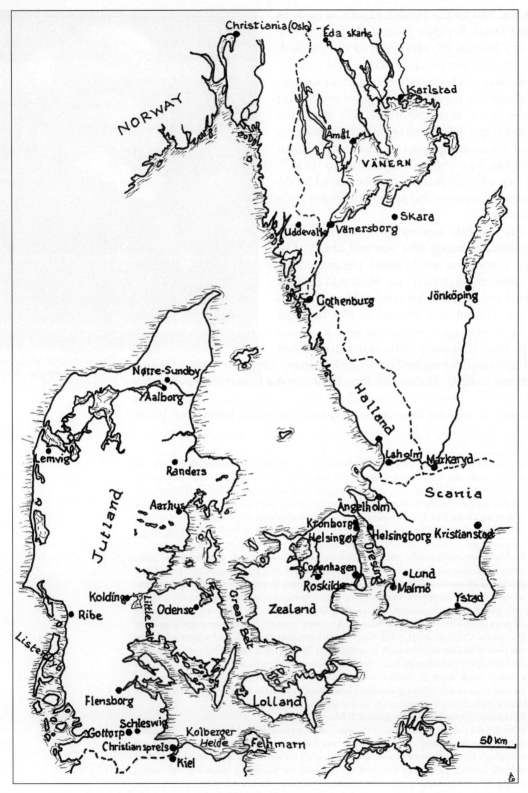

Denmark and Southern Sweden.

who had been held captive in Paris, would attack Scania and the other Danish provinces in modern-day southern Sweden. Horn, too, would then ship his army across the sea to Copenhagen, where he and Torstensson would join forces. By then, Danish King Christian IV would have no choice but to surrender, or so the regency government argued.

Simultaneously, the regency government ordered an invasion of Jämtland, a province of Norway which protruded into Sweden. There was also talk of a diversion from Livonia against the nearby island of Ösel (modern-day Saaremaa), which belonged to Denmark.

The plan was intended as a surprise attack. No war preparations would be undertaken that could be observed by the Danes. It was a true Blitzkrieg plan, and in its outline, the plan was brilliant. However, it was also too far ahead of its time, since the slow communication lines simply did not allow such exact coordination over such large distances. Torstensson received Oxenstierna's order to attack Denmark only in early October 1643. The dispatch also explained why he would receive no reinforcements for the task; Oxenstierna found it necessary to retain the newly raised men at home, so as to counter the Danish threat. Torstensson did not waste time; he rapidly prepared his defences on the borders of Bohemia and Moravia, and then marched his army to the north-west without informing his officers of the ultimate destination. The army then consisted of the reliable core of Torstensson's men, many of whom were national troops, which meant 12,000 men; with officers and under-officers added, the total has been estimated as some 16,000 men which corresponds to the army before the march.[131] To move yet faster, and to facilitate the provision of supplies, Torstensson divided his army in three columns, which marched along parallel roads. This was not yet common practice in Europe, but the method was already in use in Sweden, for instance when regiments marched to Stockholm for a general muster, or to ports to be shipped overseas.[132] Although details are unknown, we can probably assume that some of Banér's forced marches, too, were carried out along parallel roads. Torstensson brought three major generals: Wrangel, Wittenberg, and Mortaigne. Wrangel essentially functioned as Torstensson's chief of staff, so we can assume that the columns were commanded by Torstensson, Wittenberg, and Mortaigne.

The Danish King was also the suzerain of Schleswig-Holstein, which extended south of Jutland to the River Elbe in the vicinity of Hamburg and accordingly constituted the Danish territory closest to Germany. Torstensson invaded Holstein in late December. In January 1644, he stormed the well-defended but small Danish fortress of Christianspreis (modern-day Friedrichsort) outside Kiel. Torstensson took no prisoners, since the Danes had refused to surrender. Torstensson's reputation, the speed with which he advanced, and the deliberate ruthlessness which he displayed at

---

131 Tingsten, *Fältmarskalkarna*, p.241; the estimate of 4,000 officers and under-officers: *Slaget vid Femern*, p.72.

132 In Sweden, the practice of marching along parallel roads was well-established no later than 1630. John Rumenius, *Wästgöta Ryttare i 30:åriga kriget: 1000 frivilliga bönder drar ut i kriget 1630* (Stockholm: Nyblom, 1987), p.110.

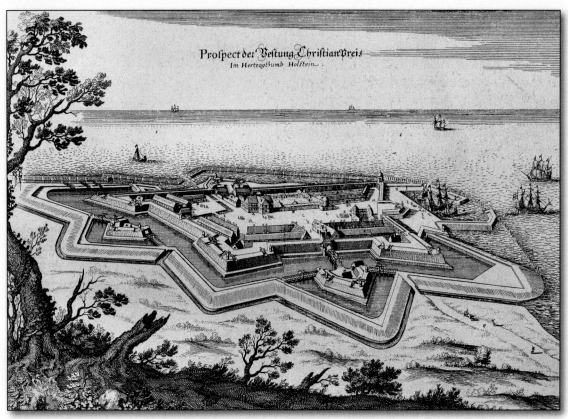

Christianspreis, 1653.
(Matthäus Merian,
*Topographia Saxoniae
Inferioris*)

Christianspreis terrified the Danes. When the news of the storm reached the other fortresses, most surrendered. Only Glückstadt and Krempe in southern Holstein refused, thus remaining in Danish hands. Henceforth the garrisons there, together with nearby peasants, continuously sent out small raiding parties to harass the Swedes.

Torstensson's original intention seems to have been to collect ships in Kiel, with which he would land on the Danish island of Fyn. However, with the approaching cold, he abandoned this plan. He accordingly continued by land, into Jutland.

There, near Kolding, Torstensson also encountered, and defeated, the first Danish corps that attempted to meet him. This was an all-cavalry force of some 1,400 men under the experienced soldier Friedrich von Buchwald (1605–1676).[133] The Danes were scattered by Swedish cavalry under Colonel Robert Douglas. Although some Danes escaped into the nearby bastion at Snoghøj, Buchwald was captured. Torstensson first took Kolding itself, and then quickly moved against Snoghøj. The Danish commander-in-chief Anders Bille (1600–1657), realising that resistance was futile since he was greatly outnumbered, evacuated those he could to the island of Fyn. The rest of the Danish Jutland army surrendered. By late January 1644, Torstensson had taken most of Holstein and all Jutland. Some peasants gathered to

---

133 *Slaget vid Femern*, p.73.

Propaganda print from 1644, illustrating the Danish–Swedish rivalry over the Straits. Christian IV and Lennart Torstensson play a game over victory in the war 1643–1645. To the right is Kronborg, to the left Helsingborg. The Straits are full of ships, and its owners pay the Sound toll into the chests behind Christian. Torstensson (to the left) wagers weapons of war, while Christian (to the right) wagers goods, pigs, and cattle.

resist the Swedes, but they were soon dispersed or slaughtered. Meanwhile, Torstensson sent Hans Christoph von Königsmarck into Verden and Bremen, which Sweden had restored to Danish control after Nördlingen, to occupy these territories as well.

At this point, communications interfered with the Swedish war plans. Torstensson had moved so rapidly that when he marched into Holstein, his dispatch to Stockholm with confirmation of the plan to attack Denmark had not yet reached the regency government. In Stockholm, the regency government despaired over why Torstensson had not yet confirmed receipt of his orders. Oxenstierna's order to Torstensson should have reached him in, at most, four to six weeks, but because of difficulties in Silesia and Moravia, the courier's travels had taken almost four months. Stockholm had no way of knowing this, or for that matter, where Torstensson was. It was common for letters to arrive late, but without news, the regency government could not know that Torstensson had commenced the war and already stood in Holstein. Stockholm only found out in early January that the invasion of Holstein had been initiated, exactly as Oxenstierna had planned. This upset the entire war schedule. So as to avoid giving warning to the Danes, the regency government had not yet given Horn his marching orders for the invasion of Scania. So, while Torstensson despite the delayed order carried out his part of the plan on time, Horn was unable to cross the border into Scania before February 1644. In addition, the planned maritime invasion of Zealand from Pomerania could no longer be carried out, since the Danish navy now was alerted and surely would act to prevent such an attempt.

Horn's War in Scania

Preparations for Horn's Scanian campaign had begun in late October 1643, although with due caution so as not to alert the Danes. Major General Lars Kagg was put in charge of preparations. Kagg had the border defences reinforced and mobilised men, with plans to muster them in Värnamo in early February 1644. In mid January, the Crown formally appointed Horn commander of the planned campaign in Scania and instructed him to cross the border in February. He would bring an army of 3,100 horse and 7,700 foot. As for cavalry, he would use the Västgöta and Småland Cavalry Regiments and two cavalry squadrons from Uppland and Östergötland, respectively. The instructions to Horn also specified under which conditions sieges were permissible. He should, if possible, take the coastal towns but the inland ones should be bypassed. The ultimate target was the Danish islands, and before crossing the Straits, Horn was instructed not to waste time on unnecessary sieges.[134]

However, the muster could only be held in mid February, two weeks behind schedule. Horn's army then consisted of 2,900 horse, 7,700 foot, and artillery in the form of six 12-pounders, 22 3-pounders, and two small mortars.[135] These were fresh troops, in most cases recently conscripted and untried in war. More siege artillery was on its way, but it had not yet arrived.

Horn's army constituted a major share of the total number of soldiers available in Sweden. The military forces then in Sweden and Finland consisted of 7,229 horse and 16,980 foot, that is, a total of 24,209 men. Not all men were available for campaigns, since the borders had to be defended and garrisons had to be maintained as well. Garrisons consisting of national troops were expected to account for 1,126 men in Sweden and Finland and 5,775 men in Estonia, Livonia, and Ingria. This would leave only some 17,300 men available for campaigns against Denmark and Norway, of which Horn's army received 10,600. In comparison, there were at the same time almost as many national troops in Germany: 22,040 men (2,387 horse and 19,653 foot).[136] The military establishment in Germany included 12,900 national troops in garrisons in the northern German territories of Pomerania and Mecklenburg.[137] Most of the rest were in Torstensson's army.

Despite the Swedish delays, the Danes had neglected their defences. In late February, Horn's army moved out from Markaryd in Sweden, crossing the border in forced marches. There was virtually no resistance. Six days later, he reached the fortified Danish port of Helsingborg, which he immediately took. It is likely that Horn had hoped to find ships in sufficient quantity to

134 Barkman, Lundkvist, and Tersmeden, *Kungl. Svea Livgardes Historia* 3:2, pp.106–7.
135 *Slaget vid Femern*, p.78; Barkman, Lundkvist, and Tersmeden, *Kungl. Svea Livgardes Historia* 3:2, p.109.
136 Mankell, *Uppgifter* 1, p.181; Mankell, *Uppgifter2*, pp.273–4; citing data from 16 October 1643 (O.S.) when preparations for the campaign began. Note that either Mankell or the original document miscalculated the total. In the present calculation, unlike the one provided by Mankell, the total number of available men in Sweden and Finland is assumed also to include the garrisons in Estonia, Livonia, and Ingria, since these garrisons were manned by men from Sweden and in particular Finland.
137 Mankell, *Uppgifter* 1, p.181; Mankell, *Uppgifter* 2, pp.274–5; citing data from 1643.

cross the Straits there. However, the Danish navy was prepared, so if this was the plan, it was a futile hope. Horn soon also took the unfortified Lund. However, to take the much larger, and better defended, Malmö (Denmark's second largest town, after Copenhagen), Horn needed siege artillery, which did not arrive before early April. With the siege artillery, Horn first moved against the other of the two remaining Danish strongpoints in Scania: the well-fortified port of Landskrona, which fell within days.

Another problem was that the emergence of pro-Danish guerrillas. The Swedish authorities referred to the guerrillas as *snapphanar* (singular *snapphane*), a pejorative term of unclear origin that most likely was an old expression for brigand or robber. However, the *snapphanar* came in two main varieties: genuine *snapphanar*, who were outlaws in the true sense of the word, who made a living from crime, and 'freeshooters' (in Danish German: *Freyschützen*), paramilitary soldiers who were recruited for Danish military service and regarded themselves as soldiers. The first such unit had been recruited already in 1559 and the use of such men grew common in the Nordic Seven Years' War (1563–1570), when Danish irregulars repeatedly fought the Swedes.

The Danish Crown had attempted to replace the old levy system of local defence in Scania with a more up-to-date military organisation, consisting of men who had received some military training. The Danish noble Ebbe Ulfeldt (1616–1682) accordingly organised units of voluntary freeshooters, recruited from the locals, who would operate as guerrillas against the Swedish communication lines, including in operations that reached into Swedish territory.[138] Ulfeldt, a Scanian noble in Imperial and Spanish service during the Thirty Years' War, had returned to Denmark in 1641, married a daughter of King Christian IV, and become county governor in the Scanian town of Kristianstad.

By the time of Horn's invasion of Scania, Torstensson had run into problems. He had probably hoped to march across the ice of the Little Belt, the waterway between Jutland and the island of Fyn. However, the winter was mild, the ice did not bear weight, and insufficient shipping was available. An attempt in February to cross to Fyn with 70 to 80 boats failed. The plan was to cross under the cover of darkness. However, the Danes, alerted, opposed the crossing with artillery and musket fire. Having lost several boats, the Swedes attempted to abort the operation. However, then several Danish warships which had been patrolling nearby moved in to attack. They destroyed several more boats, and dispersed the rest. The failed crossing resulted in the loss of about 1,000 Swedes, most of them dead, many from exposure to the ice-cold water when their boats were destroyed. Although a second attempt at crossing was made later, this, too, failed. Christian IV had taken personal command of the Danish troops on Fyn, and Danish warships continued to prevent any crossing. The Danish warships from to time also opened fire with their shipboard artillery on any Swedes who appeared on the shore, at one time almost hitting Torstensson himself and his staff.

---

138 Bo Knarrström and Stefan Larsson, *Hans Majestäts friskyttar av Danmark* (Stockholm: Riksantikvarieämbetet, 2008), pp.70–74.

Meanwhile, pro-Danish guerrillas appeared on Jutland, too. The first may have been freeshooters recruited by one Jesper von Buchwald in Dithmarschen, a district in Holstein. Although they occasionally harassed the Swedish supply lines, Torstensson ordered his men to deal with any armed peasants in the same way that they would have done in Germany, that is, ruthlessly and without mercy. All peasants caught armed were summarily killed. Soon, the Swedish army in Scania adopted the same measures to fight the pro-Danish guerrillas there, who in any case was a more serious problem than those on Jutland.

In April it was clear to the Swedish regency government that it was unlikely that Torstensson and Horn would be able to unite their forces on the Danish islands. The government accordingly instructed Horn instead to take control of Scania, with Malmö the key objective. In late June, Horn moved against Malmö. However, in early July he had to report to Stockholm that there was no way to take the town unless a Swedish fleet blockaded it from the sea. Horn was an able commander; he could handle the Danes, but without a fleet, he lacked the means to take command of the sea.

In western Sweden there were problems, too. Gothenburg, located on a narrow strip of land that separated the Danish and Norwegian territories and the only Swedish port facing the North Sea, was exposed to attacks from the neighbouring provinces in both Denmark and Norway. In April 1644 Danish King Christian IV personally led around 10 warships in an attempt to blockade Gothenburg. He also ordered Danish troops from Scania under Ebbe Ulfeldt and units from the Norwegian province of Bohuslän under Norway's governor, Hannibal Sehested (1609–1666), to move against Gothenburg, to invest the town from the land as well. However, this attempt was thwarted by Horn, who led his army north in pursuit of the Danes and, by taking the town of Laholm in late May after a short siege, prevented the Danish troops from the south to join up with the Norwegians from Bohuslän. In May, Christian IV abandoned the operation against Gothenburg. Being hemmed in, Ulfeldt in June evacuated his men to Zealand.

Hannibal Sehested, c. 1650. (Karel van Mander)

In June and July Sehested continued to send units across the river in the direction of Gothenburg. Norwegian raids also took place in the neighbouring Swedish province of Dal. By August, however, sufficient Swedish reinforcements had arrived to repulse the Norwegians.

By July Horn controlled almost the entire provinces of Scania, Blekinge, and Halland. However, he did not yet control Malmö.

Torstensson Devastates Saxony

In early 1644, the Emperor sent Gallas with an Imperial army to support the Danes against Torstensson. The plan was to attack Torstensson in the rear. In hindsight, the plan was not very realistic, since Gallas had only some 12,000 men, which surely was not enough to deal decisively with

Torstensson.[139] We have seen that before Torstensson set out, he had some 16,000 men;[140] by some accounts, and despite the losses and attrition of the campaign, he now had 18,000.[141] Moreover, Transylvanian forces had invaded Habsburg Hungary. This was no coincidence. In April 1643 Sweden had, through Torstensson, concluded an alliance with George Rákóczy (1593–1648; Rákóczi György), successor to Gabriel Bethlen (Bethlen Gábor) as ruler of Transylvania. To further encourage Rákóczy, France promised subsidies for his participation in the war. Moreover, Rákóczy had secured the approval of the Ottoman sultan, on whom he depended. As a result, the Emperor recalled Gallas's army. By then it was too late: Gallas was already on his way to Denmark.

In late July, Gallas reached Danish Holstein. His army moved into Oldesloe between Hamburg and Lübeck. There Danish reinforcements, some 3,500 enlisted men from Glückstadt and 1,000 national troops, joined him. This increased the strength of Gallas's field army to approximately 15,000 to 16,000 men (some 8,000 cavalry, perhaps 400 dragoons, 600 Croats, and some 6,000 foot).[142]

In early August some of the Imperial units pushed on to Kiel, where the Swedish main fleet was locked in (see below). They raided the town, killing some of the wounded Swedish sailors in the process. Torstensson now had to defend the fleet in addition to safeguarding his own position in Jutland and Holstein. The fleet which was supposed to support him now needed his protection. And for sure, within days, Gallas arrived with the main army, which took Kiel – but not before the Swedish fleet left port.

Torstensson withdrew his forces from Jutland in order to confront Gallas. However, Gallas did not accept battle, preferring a campaign of manoeuvre. For the time being, he remained in his camp at Oldesloe. Unfortunately for Gallas, Torstensson did not intend to allow his adversary to set the pace of the campaign. In September, Torstensson first sent Colonel Helmuth Wrangel, now promoted to major general, with 5,600 men (4,000 cavalry, 400 dragoons, and 1,200 foot[143]), back to Jutland. Torstensson himself then returned to Germany with the main army, bypassing the Imperial defences.

Gallas followed him, but Torstensson first cornered his army at Aschersleben, and then, in early December, destroyed a part of it, under Albert Gaston Spinola de Bruay (1601–1645), at Jüterbog, near Magdeburg. Torstensson moved towards his enemy during the night and attacked at dawn. The Imperials fled. The battle began at Niemegk, but the pursuit continued until Jüterbog, where the Imperials suffered most losses. The Imperial losses remain unclear but were significant. Torstensson captured 1,500 men and 3,500 horses.[144] The remnants of the Imperial army, including Gallas, took refuge in Magdeburg. Torstensson left Königsmarck with a small

139 Hedberg, *Kungl. Artilleriet*, p.271.
140 Tingsten, *Fältmarskalkarna*, p.241; *Slaget vid Femern*, p.72.
141 *Slaget vid Femern*, p.76.
142 Tingsten, *Fältmarskalkarna*, p.251; *Slaget vid Femern*, p.75.
143 Mankell, *Uppgifter*, p.191; *Slaget vid Femern*, p.77.
144 Tingsten, *Fältmarskalkarna*, p.253.

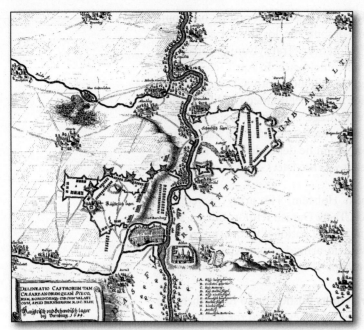

Swedish and Imperial camps facing each other at Bernburg (Saale), Saxony, 1644. The Swedish camp is located on the right side of the river, while the Imperial camp is on the left, next to the town of Bernburg itself. (*Theatrum Europaeum*)

force at Magdeburg. When the Imperials under Gallas attempted to break out in early January 1645, Königsmarck defeated them, killing or capturing more than half. Gallas himself escaped with between 1,000 and 2,500 men, and he and the survivors returned along the Elbe to Bohemia. Gallas then resigned his command and retired. The disastrous retreat gave him the nickname *Heerverderber* ('army wrecker').

Gallas had brought some Saxon cavalry units. With Saxony still an enemy, Torstensson's communication lines through Pomerania to Sweden could not be safe. Torstensson accordingly moved his army into Saxony. He let John George of Saxony know that he would tolerate no more hostilities, and if the Elector persisted Torstensson would turn the area around Dresden into a desert.[145] To prove his point, he destroyed several towns and castles in the region. In an age and region already hardened to destruction, Torstensson showed that he was serious. John George had to accept negotiations for peace.

The Norwegian Frontier

The war between Denmark and Sweden was not limited to Jutland and Scania: King Christian IV of Denmark was also King of Norway. In spring 1643 the Swedish regency government had discussed an invasion of Norway. However, the idea was rejected with one exception, since Norway was too mountainous and poor to allow for efficient offensive operations. Besides, it was argued, correctly, that even if Christian IV lost Norway it was unlikely that he would accept defeat, so long as he retained his Danish territories.

However, in any war with Denmark, Norway was a threat. The Norwegian army was small but could easily go on the offensive independently of the Danes. The long border was impossible to close, or even defend, with the means available – which mainly consisted of levied peasants. As in the past, Sweden depended on levies for its border defences. In times of war, the Crown still had the right to levy troops among the peasants. This was done through a quota that the peasants had to fill. Levied troops would not be trained, and they would have to pay for their own weapons and supplies. On the other hand, they were only required to serve at home. Levied troops were

---

145 Dresden was the capital of Saxony and, in similarity to Prague, Kassel, and Berlin, a key administrative centre.

usually used to man defensive bastions along the external borders, in effect operating as a border guard. The levied peasants would serve for a time, then be replaced by other levies from the same area. The Crown directed that former soldiers should be selected as leaders of the levies.

In times of need, the Crown also had the right to raise a general levy. A general levy consisted of all men able to bear arms and usually was called out to defend an external border. The levied troops would have to arm and supply themselves. Their use was accordingly restricted, for practical reasons, to certain geographical areas and short durations of time. Levies could also be called out in the form of burgher militias, which would have to take some responsibility for defending their towns when under siege.

The lack of regular soldiers was not the only problem. The border was fragmented and sometimes poorly defined. Conditions were not conducive to large-scale operations. The borderlands were forested and often mountainous, and neither side had the agricultural capacity to sustain major armies. In the same way that several modern-day southern Swedish provinces by this time belonged to Denmark, two modern-day northern Swedish provinces (Jämtland and Härjedalen) belonged to Norway. The northern provinces were marginal to Danish and Swedish economic activities, but the long common border between the two countries meant that in case of war, hostilities would break out there as well. Hence the exception alluded to when the regency government ruled against a full-scale invasion of Norway. The province of Jämtland had to be occupied so as to secure the border.

The regency government accordingly did not allocate regular troops to the Norwegian border, except for the border with Jämtland and Härjedalen. If possible, these two provinces would be conquered, preferably by persuading the few inhabitants to accept Swedish rule. As a result, the first Swedish incursions into Norwegian territory took place in March 1644.

Warfare on the northern frontier was not like warfare on the Continent. Terrain, climate, and number and characteristics of troops were all different. It accordingly makes sense to describe some of the operations in more detail.

In early March some 100 dragoons and 1,400 foot (in companies each consisting of 100 men) from the Västerbotten Regiment and Hälsinge Regiment were mobilised on the border with the Norwegian province of Jämtland. The Hälsinge troops gathered in the Swedish province of Medelpad, while the Västerbotten men, under Colonel Hans Strijk, came from the province of Ångermanland further to the north.[146] The invasion force also included 100 artillerymen with four heavy and four light cannons.[147] At the time, there were 1,270 Norwegian regulars in Jämtland, commanded by Lieutenant Colonel Jacob Ulfeldt.[148] Under Henrik Fleming, the Swedes crossed the border in mid March. In the battle of Brunflo in Jämtland, the invaders defeated the few Norwegians defenders. It was more a skirmish

146 The most thorough description of the operations in Jämtland is Birger Steckzén, "Striden om Jämtland 1644–1645", Gustaf Näsström (ed.), *Jämtländska studier: Festskrift till Eric Festin XII.X.MCMXXVIII* (Östersund: Heimbygda, 1928), pp.263–93.

147 Hedberg, *Kungl. Artilleriet*, pp.155, 279.

148 Steckzén, "Striden om Jämtland", pp.265, 269.

than a battle. According to the Swedish report, six Swedes died in the fight, as compared to some 70 Norwegians. The reported casualty figures seem reasonable for the circumstances. As the Norwegian commandant, Ulfeldt, retreated into Norway, the inhabitants of Jämtland swore fealty to the Swedish Crown. In April, the regency government appointed Strijk commandant in Jämtland. The Swedes built redoubts in strategic locations and provided small garrisons for them. In reality, these were no more than outposts. Then the regular infantry left the province, since they were needed for the war in the south.

Meanwhile, the regency government had ordered the governor of Falun in the Swedish province of Dalecarlia, Peter Kruse, to conquer the Norwegian settlements of Särna, Idre, and Hede (in Härjedalen), which happened to be located on the eastern side of the border mountains. He knew the region, since he employed two agents who frequently travelled there to report on local conditions. Kruse mobilised levies from the neighbouring Dalecarlian community of Älvdalen, in total 112 men who in exchange for a year's tax exemption agreed to participate in some border warfare. The levies were armed with bows and arrows, spears, hunting guns, and improvised weapons. They brought their own skis for easier transportation. Kruse appointed the local chaplain, Daniel Buscovius (1599–1677), commander of the detachment, commissioning him as major. An ex-soldier with a musket, and a parish clerk, were added as his staff unit. Some locals made a cloth standard for the unit. In late March 1644, Buscovius and his men put on their skis and moved north, and four days later, they reached Särna. Buscovius called the inhabitants of the settlements together, offered that they become Swedes, and warned that if they did not accept, he would burn their settlements. For the inhabitants of Särna, Idre, and Hede the choice was easy – and it was sweetened by the fact that Buscovius was a chaplain. The Norwegian Crown had neglected to provide a priest to the community, and Buscovius immediately applied soft power: he delivered a Sunday sermon, carried out

Daniel Buscovius.

several baptisms and weddings, and attended to the long-neglected spiritual needs of the locals. He then returned home with his men, accompanied by representatives of the three most recent additions to the Swedish realm, who in front of governor Kruse swore fealty to the Swedish Crown. Kruse later calculated that the entire campaign of conquest had cost the Crown no more than 94 Dalers of silver, a minuscule amount compared to expenses elsewhere. In return, he had added these vast although sparsely populated territories to the province of Dalecarlia.

The new Dalecarlian possessions easily reconciled to Swedish rule. Not so the occupied province of Jämtland. Although the Norwegian reaction was delayed (it will be shown that the Danish governor in Norway, Sehested, first focused on the Swedish province of Värmland), already in late May 1644 a Norwegian force of 1,100 to 1,200 men, under the aforementioned Jacob Ulfeldt, moved into Jämtland. Only some 450 Swedish soldiers remained in the province, and they were dispersed in small outposts. Most were surprised and massacred. Sweden had no resources available to counter the Norwegian offensive. Levies were raised, but the Dalecarlians refused further service, and they also did not want to cross into another province (which, to be fair, was technically not required of levies). Another force of mostly levies did move into Jämtland, but it soon turned back. The last Swedish regulars, under Strijk in the redoubt on Frösö island, surrendered in August 1644. The few survivors were escorted back to the border with the Swedish province of Medelpad, where they were released.

As noted, the able Danish governor in Norway, Hannibal Sehested, had no intention of sitting idle during the war. In April 1644, roughly at the same time that Christian IV attempted to blockade Gothenburg, Sehested also attempted an offensive into the neighbouring Swedish province of Värmland from Vinger (modern-day Kongsvinger) in the north.

However, the Värmland levies under the governor Colonel Olof Stake (1593–1664; the elder brother of Harald Stake who had distinguished himself in the war in Germany), stopped the Norwegians at Magnor, a border settlement. Then, almost immediately, Sehested was recalled. He was needed elsewhere, further to the south on the Gothenburg front. With the recall of Sehested, the Norwegian offensive never acquired momentum. Both sides dug down, and during the summer of 1644, they built redoubts facing each other. Meanwhile, skirmishing continued, until after several months Sehested, back from the Gothenburg front, resumed the offensive into Värmland. In late November, Sehested and his Norwegian army (some 1,200 horse, 2,800 foot, and 18 cannons) broke through the Swedish defences and, a month later, took Eda. Stake was considerably inferior in numbers, so he led a fighting withdrawal deeper into Sweden.

Well-to-do Swedish peasant, seventeenth century. Dressed for winter conditions, he wears a fur hat, jacket with undergarment, baggy breeches, and mittens. Swedish peasants still generally wore full beards.

Near-contemporary watercolour painting of a peasant from Österbotten in Finland, dated to the late seventeenth century. He wears essentially the same clothes (jacket, baggy breeches, stockings, and a woollen cap) as found on the Swedish warship *Vasa*, lost in 1628. The faded red jacket has greenish cloth inserted in the seams, cuffs, and shoulder wings, while the cap is lined in blue. Swedish peasants still generally wore full beards.

The Battle of Kolberger Heide

In mid 1644, Christian IV was isolated on the Danish islands. On the other hand, the Danish fleet was undefeated and prevented the Swedish armies from reaching Copenhagen and ending the war.

Horn commenced the siege of Malmö in June 1644. It was an important port which was easily supplied by sea across the Straits from Copenhagen, and he needed warships to cut the Danish sea lines of communication, at least at this spot.

Claes Fleming.

Stockholm was well aware of this. The able Admiral Claes Fleming (1592–1644) had prepared to move the Swedish main fleet towards Danish waters. Logistics presented many problems for the Swedish navy. Stockholm, the key naval base, was closed by ice for much of the year, and certainly for a longer period than Copenhagen and the Danish ports. The Swedish navy also found it difficult to find experienced crews, not least because the icy winter conditions made the usual sailing season quite short. Although Swedish warships already had experience in sailing throughout the year – and had done so during the war against the Commonwealth in the 1620s – in winter there were no ice-free friendly ports to enter for supplies or repairs. This produced excessive wear and tear on the ships, and serious loss of life to disease and famine among the crews. However, if the warships did return to port in autumn, the crews had to await until spring before they could leave port again.

Because of these problems, the regency government had sent the Swedish–Dutch industrialist Louis De Geer (1587–1652) to hire ships and men in Amsterdam to form an auxiliary fleet. This was something that De Geer did very willingly, because it was his cannons exported to the Dutch Republic that Christian IV had made subject to the Sound toll. Since Louis De Geer had relocated to Sweden in 1627, he had developed the Swedish armaments industry until it could simultaneously satisfy the needs of the Swedish army and sustain a healthy export business. This trade had made him very wealthy. In the Swedish mercantile world, Louis De Geer held a

Louis De Geer, c. 1650. (David Beck)

stature comparable to that of Oxenstierna in the political realm. Through his actions, the Danish King had unwisely managed to annoy the two individuals in Sweden who had the influence to cause most damage to Danish interests.

Louis De Geer accordingly went to the Dutch Republic to hire himself a war fleet, and after some initial difficulties he managed to hire 22 armed merchantmen and 10 transports.[149] Commanded by the experienced Dutch Admiral Maerten Thijssen (d. 1657), this essentially private fleet henceforth operated on behalf of the Swedish navy. Thijssen left port in April, sailing north along the coast of Jutland. In late May, the auxiliary fleet encountered the

---

149   *Slaget vid Femern*, pp.88–9.

Danish main fleet, nine warships under the personal command of Christian IV.[150] The two fleets met in a battle at Lister Dyb, near the village List on the island of Sylton the coast of western Jutland, where Thijssen was supposed to embark Torstensson's troops for transportation to Zealand. The Danish warships were fewer but significantly larger than the armed merchantmen of Thijssen's auxiliary fleet. The outcome was a Danish victory, and after a second battle some days later, Thijssen had to return to the Dutch Republic to reorganise his damaged fleet, enlist more men, and carry out necessary repairs.

Meanwhile the Swedish main fleet, commanded by Fleming, embarked soldiers at Dalarö, and then gathered at Älvsnabben, a natural harbour in the southern Stockholm archipelago which functioned as the summer naval base for the Swedish navy. The fleet consisted of 33 warships, eight fireships, one pinnace, and one galiot.[151] The fleet left port in mid June.

At the same time, the inshore fleet left port too. Commanded by Major Henrik Hansson, it consisted of around six vessels of the *struts* type and some 60 rowing vessels of the *lodja* type (on these types, see chapter 7).[152] The inshore fleet could not accompany the main fleet at sea, so followed the shore to Kalmar, where those soldiers embarked who were intended for the invasion of Zealand. They were eventually landed at Ystad in Scania, since the Danish fleet prevented the inshore fleet from crossing the Straits. The inshore fleet was then ordered to support Horn's siege of Malmö by blockading the town from the sea; however, being too small to threaten the Danish warships, the inshore vessels proved unable to maintain the blockade (this was proven beyond doubt when Hansson in late August left Ystad, with orders to return the inshore fleet to Kalmar. En route, the Danish fleet sank seven vessels of the *lodja* type and captured two of the *struts* and six of the *lodja* type.)[153]

After a week at sea Fleming's fleet arrived at the island of Rügen, where it received current intelligence, picked up pilots, and loaded supplies. The fleet then set out to locate the Danish fleet. The two fleets encountered each other on 11 July 1644 at Kolberger Heide, the waters between Kiel and the island of Fehmarn, which the Swedes had occupied a few days previously. Both Fleming and Christian IV sought battle. Fleming's fleet consisted of the aforementioned 43 ships (except for three smaller ships detached for duty elsewhere). Christian IV's fleet was equal in size, numbering some 40 ships.[154]

This was the first full-scale naval battle between Swedes and Danes since 1566. However, the outcome of the battle was inconclusive and both sides claimed victory. There were few losses on either side (39 dead and 69 wounded Swedes, 37 dead and 170 wounded Danes, including the 67-year-old Christian IV, who lost an eye but shrugged off the injury, and his

150 *Ibid.*, pp.92–2.
151 *Slaget vid Femern*, p.97.
152 S. Artur Svensson (ed.), *Svenska flottans historia* 1(Malmö: Allhem, 1942), p.430.
153 *Ibid.*, p.436.
154 *Slaget vid Femern*, pp.97–8; Martin Peterson (ed.), *Stormaktstidens soldater i krig: Från nordiska sjuårskriget till trettioåriga kriget* (np: SMB, 2015), pp.164–5, which lists the Swedish and Danish ships.

Admiral-General, Jørgen Vind, who fell in the battle[155]). Neither Christian IV nor Fleming was satisfied with the conduct of their captains. The Danes withdrew for repairs, while the Swedes stayed at the location of the battle. Possibly this could qualify as a tactical victory for the Swedes. However, then the Swedish fleet sailed into the Kieler Förde, the inlet to the port of Kiel, for repairs. Having learned of this, the Danish fleet positioned itself at the exit of the inlet, so as to blockade Fleming's fleet. Stuck in Kiel, Fleming thus found himself unable to support Horn's siege of Malmö. The blockade was unmistakably a strategic victory for Christian IV, albeit one that had little to do with the outcome of the recent battle.

Besides, the Swedish fleet suffered its most significant loss after the battle, while in the Kieler Förde. By then, both Gallas's Imperial army and units from the Danish army had reached the vicinity of the port, but on opposite sides of the Kieler Förde. In early August, the Danes established a fort with a gun battery within reach of the Swedish fleet. Three days later, Admiral Fleming was killed on his flagship, the *Scepter*, by a stray cannonball from the Danish fort, as he was doing his morning ablutions in his cabin. Dying, Fleming handed over command of the fleet to Torstensson's chief of staff Carl Gustav Wrangel, who had just arrived for a meeting on behalf of the Field Marshal. Torstensson calmly accepted Wrangel's unexpected secondment to the navy. Due to fortunate winds, Wrangel a few days later managed to bring the fleet out of the Kieler Förde. By then, the Danish fort had been taken by Torstensson's army. Still, it was at the last moment, because on the following day Gallas's army marched into Kiel. Christian IV had replaced his fallen Admiral-General, Jørgen Vind, with Peder Galt, who during the 1620s had served as Danish agent in Stockholm.[156] Galt, who had the disadvantage of the winds, could do nothing to stop the Swedish fleet, for which Christian IV had him executed.

For Major General Carl Gustav Wrangel, this was his first truly independent command. Now he was given command of the entire Swedish main fleet, despite having spent his entire military career in the army. This was surprising, but perhaps Fleming knew what he was doing. Already when young, Wrangel had shown an interest in naval affairs and studied them abroad. Wrangel would later play a very prominent part in Sweden's wars and, in time, attain the rank of Field Marshal, Grand Admiral of the Realm, and Grand Marshal of the Realm.

Wrangel returned the fleet to Dalarö, in the southern Stockholm archipelago, which it reached in August. The Danes thought that the Swedish fleet would not return until next year, so they felt safe. In early September the Danish commander-in-chief, Anders Bille, soon followed by Christian IV, led an army of 4,000 horse and 10,000 foot across the Straits to Malmö.[157] The Danes then attacked Horn's camp. Horn defended his position for several

---

155 Hedberg, *Kungl. Artilleriet*, p.271. The Swedish casualty report also included the men lost during the capture of the island of Fehmarn.

156 Michael Fredholm von Essen, *The Lion from the North: The Swedish Army during the Thirty Years' War, 1618–1632*, vol. 1 (Warwick: Helion, 2020).

157 *Slaget vid Femern*, p.82.

weeks, but broke camp in early October, and then gradually had to withdraw further north, until by the end of the month he had almost returned to the Danish–Swedish border.

Horn's army then consisted of some 10,200 men (3,955 horse and 6,229 foot). A preserved year-end summary of the state of Horn's army, including the cause of losses since the beginning of the campaign, gives insights into the conditions of warfare at the time (Table 6). The campaign in Scania had been one of manoeuvres and sieges, not set battles. As usual, the main source of deaths was disease, not combat. Two conclusions are obvious. First, losses to disease were significantly higher in the infantry than the cavalry, including among officers. This was the result of the cavalry's higher mobility, which also meant that they tended to receive better, or at least less disease-ridden, lodgings than the infantry. Officers were not exempted. It is notable that many infantry officers succumbed to the same diseases which ravaged the rank and file of the crowded army camps. By adding the total number of officers (available and lost) and comparing this figure to the casualty rate due to disease, we find a death rate of less than one percent for the cavalry officers and almost six percent for their infantry counterparts. For the common soldiers, death rates were far higher, in this campaign nine percent within the cavalry and 32 percent within the infantry.

Table 6. Horn's army in Scania, 30 December 1644. (Source: Barkman, Lundkvist, and Tersmeden, *Kungl. Svea Livgardes Historia* 3:2, p.124; citing an extract dated 20 December 1644 (O.S.), currently in the RA)

	Officers	Common Soldiers
Cavalry		
In units (field or garrison)	771	3,184
of whom fit	755	2,335
of whom ill	16	849
Prisoners of war or missing	3	74
Dead from disease	8	349
Killed in action	7	185
Sent home	22	31
Deserters	–	21
Stragglers or deserters	–	3
Infantry		
In units (field or garrison)	759	5,470
of whom fit	720	3,877
of whom ill	39	1,593
Prisoners of war or missing	1	7
Dead from disease	53	2,738
Killed in action	15	125
Sent home	87	34
Deserters	–	231
Stragglers or deserters	–	43

Second, the rate of desertion was much lower in the cavalry than in the infantry. This can be explained by the fact that most cavalrymen were peasants who each provided a horse and equipment and then served themselves, in exchange for tax exemption, according to the institution referred to as a cavalryman's holding (*rusthåll*), which consisted of one or more farms which individually or collectively contracted to support a cavalryman.[158] As a result, they had incentive to remain with their units, unlike much of the national infantry, which was conscripted.

Third, the figures also show that the ratio of officers to men was significantly higher in the cavalry than in the infantry. In the cavalry the ratio approached 1:5, while in the infantry it was close to 1:10. This can in part be explained by the smaller units within the cavalry. However, the ratios also probably reflect the generally better conditions within the cavalry.

The Battle off Fehmarn

In August, Thijssen's auxiliary fleet returned from the Dutch Republic. After a brief stopover in Gothenburg to drive off several Danish ships there, the auxiliary fleet passed through the Straits without loss. Thijssen even captured several Danish ships en route, thus gaining additional strength. With characteristic boldness, he fired a Swedish salute (two cannon shots in rapid succession) from each ship as the auxiliary fleet passed the Danish castle Kronborg at Helsingør (immortalised by Shakespeare as Elsinore).[159] Thijssen's fleet continued into the Baltic Sea, where it went into the Swedish port of Kalmar. With the prizes taken en route, Thijssen had increased the strength of the auxiliary fleet to 22 armed merchantmen, three transports, and three fireships.[160] For this feat Thijssen was commissioned as a Swedish admiral and ennobled. Receiving the Swedish name Mårten Anckarhielm, Thijssen became the founder of a family which would provide a couple of other noted Swedish naval officers.

As noted, the Swedish main fleet had in August 1644 returned to Dalarö, in the southern Stockholm archipelago. However, since Sweden controlled the Baltic Sea ports in Germany, Sweden retained naval forces there as well. There was already a naval squadron in Wismar. Besides, in Stockholm the Admiralty equipped a new fleet already in the autumn. Carl Gustav Wrangel was appointed overall commander of both main and auxiliary fleet as well as the Wismar squadron, with instructions to report to Torstensson in his capacity of overall commander of Swedish military forces in Germany. In early October, 16 selected ships of the Stockholm fleet (12 warships, two galiots, and two fireships[161]) left Dalarö. Under the command of Wrangel, it joined up with Anckarhielm's auxiliary fleet in Kalmar. Soon after, Wrangel

---

158 For further details, see Fredholm von Essen, *Lion from the North* 1.
159 A Danish salute consisted of three cannon shots in rapid succession, which was the same as the Imperial salute.
160 *Slaget vid Femern*, p.119.
161 *Ibid.*, p.108.

also incorporated the Wismar squadron (three warships and a fireship[162]) into his fleet.

Since Christian IV had thought that the Swedish fleet would remain in port until spring, he had demobilised most of the Danish warships for the winter. The Danish fleet then consisted of only 17 ships (15 warships and two smaller ships).[163] The fleet was commanded by a Norwegian, the able Admiral-General Pros Mund (c. 1589–1644). The fleet also lacked soldiers. Mund possibly had some 730 soldiers onboard, although a Swedish source claims that there were none. In any case, the Danish ships did not carry as many soldiers as would have been considered normal in Scandinavia.[164]

Within a few days of bringing in the Wismar squadron, Wrangel's combined fleet located the Danish fleet off the island of Fehmarn, in a location not far from the previous engagement at Kolberger Heide.[165]

Wrangel's fleet consisted of two dissimilar components, the Swedish navy fleet and the Dutch auxiliary fleet. The Swedish contingent consisted of 15 warships, two galiots, and three fireships, while the auxiliary fleet was composed of 19 armed merchantmen, one pinnace, and one galiot.[166] Wrangel also had some 1,500 soldiers, distributed among all ships in his combined fleet.[167]

The combined Swedish and auxiliary fleet was clearly stronger than the Danish one. However, all Danish ships were warships, and thus larger and more strongly built than the Dutch ships. They also carried heavier cannons. Still, there is no doubt that the Danes were at a disadvantage. Wrangel's fleet was superior in numbers, combined tonnage, cannons, and men. Besides, the Swedish tactics again focused on boarding the enemy vessels, not engaging in artillery duels with them.

We do not know why Mund accepted battle, despite the Swedish superiority in numbers. It is possible that he saw an engagement as the only way to prevent the expected Swedish invasion of the Danish islands. However, it is also possible that in light of Galt's execution he realised that he had little choice. Fight or not, either way he would suffer the blame – unless he won, of course. Mund may have counted on the generally superior quality of the Danish crews, as compared to their Swedish counterparts. However, since the Swedes began operations in support of the campaign in Prussia in the 1620s, they had, in fact, acquired plenty of experience in naval operations.

The battle began around 10:00 a.m. on 23 October 1644 and continued until 6:00 p.m. Mund immediately advanced against Wrangel's fleet. He probably hoped to penetrate Wrangel's formation, separating the Swedish from the Dutch ships. However, the wind changed in the favour of the

---

162 *Ibid.*, p.126.

163 *Ibid.*, p.128.

164 *Ibid.*, p.143.

165 The essential work on the battle off Fehmarn is *Slaget vid Femern*. Recent works include Ingvar Sjöblom, "Femern 1644", Lars Ericson et al., *Svenska slagfält* (np: Wahlström & Widstrand, 2003), pp.162–72; Ericson Wolke, Larsson; and Villstrand, *Trettioåriga kriget*, pp.250–7; Lars Ericson Wolke and Martin Hårdstedt, *Svenska sjöslag* (np: Medströms, 2009), pp.82–7.

166 *Slaget vid Femern*, pp.130–1, which lists the vessels.

167 *Ibid.*, p.142.

Swedes. Eventually, the Danish formation was disordered, and the three largest Danish warships, the flagship *Patientia*, *Lindormen*, and *Oldenburg*, were isolated from the others. The *Lindormen* was set on fire by the fireship *Meerman*, exploded, and sank. The survivors, including Admiral Joachim Grabow, were saved by the Swedes and surrendered. The other two large ships were captured. Although Wrangel attempted to board the *Patientia* with his own flagship, *Smålands Lejon*, the attempt failed. His flagship was badly damaged from cannon fire and had to withdraw from the battle. However, two other Swedish warships, *Regina* and *Göteborg*, eventually managed to close with and board the *Patientia*. The battle on the *Patientia* lasted for an hour, and at the end Admiral Pros Mund defended himself, ultimately quite alone, with his admiral's command sword. This was a broad longsword that had no point or only a blunt one, of a type that was given to admirals in a sixteenth-century custom that survived throughout the seventeenth century. When Mund resolutely refused to surrender, two Swedish sailors shot him dead. The loss of the three largest Danish warships decided the battle. In total, the Danes lost 15 out of 17 ships (although one which went aground could be saved later, raising the number of surviving ships to three). Of those lost, 10 were taken as prizes. The Swedish fleet lost only one ship, *Swarte Arent*, from the auxiliary fleet, but its crew could be saved. *Swarte Arent* was destroyed by the fourth and last Danish flagship, the *Tre Løver* under Vice Admiral Corfitz Ulfeldt. However, *Tre Løver* was boarded, too, and surrendered. Ulfeldt fell severely wounded, having lost a leg. He died from his wound a few days later.

After the battle, Wrangel wrote an extensive report, in which he described the fate of all individual officers, on both sides, as well as the crews. About 100 Danes died in the battle, half of them on the *Lindormen*. At least 1,000 Danes were captured. The Swedes lost 59 dead.[168]

The Swedish victory at sea was decisive. Denmark had lost a third of its war fleet. Learning of the defeat, Christian IV in early November rapidly crossed to Zealand in a fishing vessel, after which he withdrew most of his men from Scania, since he feared an imminent Swedish landing near his capital. This enabled Horn to return south, where he went into winter quarters near the town of Ystad. Under the threat of a Swedish invasion of the Danish islands, peace talks began in November. Meanwhile, Wrangel's fleet spent the winter in Wismar.

Battle off Fehmarn, 1644. Left: The burning *Lindormen*. Right: The Danish flagship *Patientia* fighting for her life with the Swedish warships *Regina* on the left and *Göteborg* on the right. (Willem van de Velde the Elder; Photo: Medströms)

168 *Ibid.*, p.145. Wrangel's report to Queen Christina is reprinted in Svensson, *Svenska flottans historia* 1, pp.520–21.

Danish fleet escapes after the battle off Fehmarn, 1644. (Skokloster Castle; Photo: Medströms)

Detail depicting the Danish flagship *Patientia* fighting for her life with the Swedish warships *Regina* on the left and *Göteborg* on the right, battle off Fehmarn, 1644. (Willem van de Velde the Elder)

Could the victory off Fehmarn have been utilised to land an army on the Danish islands of the kind envisaged in the original war plan? This seems unlikely, since Torstensson's army by then was elsewhere and Horn at the time lacked sufficient forces. Besides, disease began to spread in Wrangel's fleet soon after the victory, which resulted in a severe shortage of sailors.

The Conclusion of the War against Denmark

When the year 1645 began, Sehested continued his ongoing offensive into northern Värmland. On 1 January he defeated the Swedes at the battle on the ice of Lake Bysjön. Although a minor engagement, the battle had serious consequences, since even a small army could make an impact in the borderlands. Sehested led from the front; he took two bullets in his hat during the engagement but suffered no wounds. In Stockholm, the Norwegian invasion of Värmland was assessed as a serious threat, since it was a strike into the Swedish heartland. In late December the Crown (Queen Christina had come of age, so had assumed direct rule) instructed Colonel Gabriel Gabrielsson Oxenstierna (1619–1673), a distant relative of Chancellor Oxenstierna, to lead four companies of horse and four companies of foot to Värmland to confront Sehested.[169] In January 1645 Oxenstierna's corps, reinforced with levies from Bergslagen, a large mining district in the northwestern parts of the Swedish heartland, and six cannons, reached the area around Karlstad. Other troops were sent from Gothenburg through Dal so as to intercept the Norwegian force from the south.

Queen Christina of Sweden. Christina was well-trained and notably skilled in shooting, fencing, and horseback riding (she was also known for favouring practical shoes and a skirt instead of high-heeled shoes and full dress and many noted that her face was suntanned and generally without makeup). Like her father, Christina was highly educated, speaking Swedish, German, Danish, Dutch, French, Italian, Spanish, Latin, and Greek, in addition to some Finnish and Hebrew. (National Museum, Stockholm; photo: author)

However, Sehested had already moved straight south into Dal. Fearing that his small army might be cut off if he moved too deep into Sweden, Sehested had avoided the road to Karlstad, Värmland's chief town, and the Swedish heartland. Instead, moving south, he took Åmål. Sehested then continued south, in February attempting an attack on Vänersborg, but he was repulsed. His ultimate destination was the Gothenburg front, although he now had to retreat into Norway to get there. Still, some Norwegian troops remained in Värmland: Colonel Gunde Lange and six companies. Henceforth, the operations in Värmland were unconnected to Sehested's operations further to the south.

By then, Major General Gustav Otto Stenbock (1614–1685) had been put in command of the Swedish operations in Värmland and Dal.[170] Stenbock had fought in Germany from 1632, including at Nördlingen, Wittstock, Chemnitz, and in the second battle of Breitenfeld. In March and April, he and Colonel Oxenstierna pushed the remaining Norwegians in Värmland back to Eda. In May, Stenbock

---

169 Hedberg, *Kungl. Artilleriet*, p.282.
170 Stenbock's military career continued after the Thirty Years' War. He was later promoted to Field Marshal and, eventually, Grand Admiral of the Realm.

Plate 1

The Swedish army at Wittstock, 1636
1.1: Resting pikeman after the battle
1.2: Resting musketeer after the battle
(Illustrations by Sergey Shamenkov, © Helion & Company 2020)
See Colour Plate Commentaries for further information

Plate 2

The Swedish army at Breitenfeld, 1642
2.1: Well-to-do dragoon
2.2: Swedish musketeer
(Illustrations by Sergey Shamenkov, © Helion & Company 2020)
See Colour Plate Commentaries for further information

Plate 3

The Swedish army of Jankow, 1645
3.1: Cavalry officer
3.2: Infantry officer
(Illustrations by Sergey Shamenkov, © Helion & Company 2020)
See Colour Plate Commentaries for further information

Plate 4

The Swedish army at the siege of Prague, 1648
4.1: Infantry Officer
4.2: Musketeer
(Illustrations by Sergey Shamenkov, © Helion & Company 2020)
See Colour Plate Commentaries for further information

Plate 5

The Swedish artillery at the siege of Prague, 1648
5.1: Artilleryman
5.2: Artillery under-officer
(Illustrations by Sergey Shamenkov, © Helion & Company 2020)
See Colour Plate Commentaries for further information

Plate 6

Swedish levies on the Norwegian border, 1644
6.1: Levied irregular in winter clothes
6.2: Levied irregular in summer clothes
(Illustrations by Sergey Shamenkov, © Helion & Company 2020)
See Colour Plate Commentaries for further information

Plate 7

The Swedish army in New Sweden
7.1: Musketeer, New Sweden
7.2: Navy Sailor
(Illustrations by Sergey Shamenkov, © Helion & Company 2020)
See Colour Plate Commentaries for further information

Plate 8

The Swedish army on the Gold Coast
8.3: Navy under-officer
8.4: African officer, Swedish Gold Coast
(Illustrations by Sergey Shamenkov, © Helion & Company 2020)
See Colour Plate Commentaries for further information

Plate 9

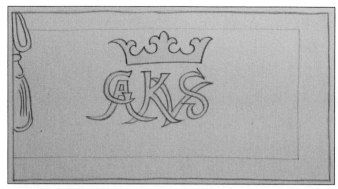

General Johan Banér's Life Regiment of Horse
(Riksarkivet, Stockholm. Author's photos)
See Colour Plate Commentaries for further information

Plate 10

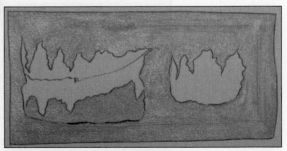

Duke Bernard of Saxe-Weimar's Life Regiment of Horse
(Riksarkivet, Stockholm. Author's photos)
See Colour Plate Commentaries for further information

Plate 11

Major General Patrick Ruthven's Cavalry Regiment
(Riksarkivet, Stockholm. Author's photos)
See Colour Plate Commentaries for further information

Plate 12

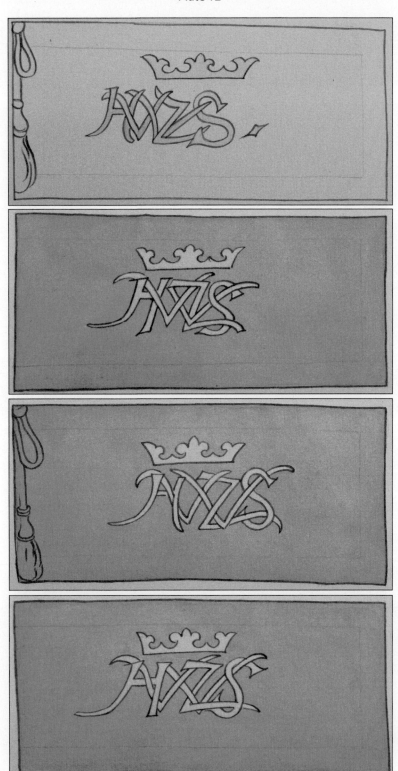

Duke William of Saxe-Weimar's Life Regiment of Horse
(Riksarkivet, Stockholm. Author's photos)
See Colour Plate Commentaries for further information

Plate 13

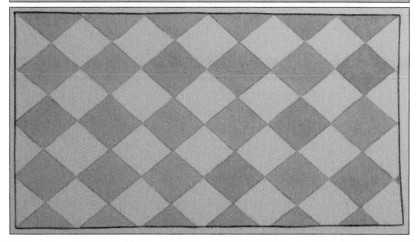

Duke Hans Ernst of Saxe-Weimar's Life Regiment of Horse (13.1);
Captain Gottfried Holtzmüller's Dragoon Company (13.2);
Colonel Wolf Ebert Horneck's Regiment of Foot (13.3)
(Riksarkivet, Stockholm. Author's photos)
See Colour Plate Commentaries for further information

Plate 14

Colonel Nicolaus Dietrich Sperreuter's Cavalry Regiment
(Riksarkivet, Stockholm. Author's photos)
See Colour Plate Commentaries for further information

Plate 15

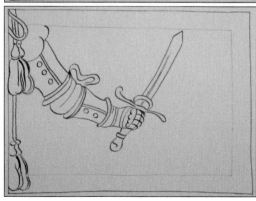

Colonel Robert Munro of Foulis's Cavalry Regiment
(Riksarkivet, Stockholm. Author's photos)
See Colour Plate Commentaries for further information

Plate 16

Colonel Robert Munro of Foulis's Cavalry Regiment (continued)
(Riksarkivet, Stockholm. Author's photos)
See Colour Plate Commentaries for further information

Plate 17

Colonel Jürgen Ernst von Wedel's Cavalry Regiment
(Riksarkivet, Stockholm. Author's photos)
See Colour Plate Commentaries for further information

Plate 18

Colonel Jürgen Ernst von Wedel's Cavalry Regiment
(Riksarkivet, Stockholm. Author's photos)
See Colour Plate Commentaries for further information

Plate 19

Johann Bernhard von Öhm's Cavalry Regiment
(Riksarkivet, Stockholm. Author's photos)
See Colour Plate Commentaries for further information

Plate 20

Colonel Georg aus dem Winckel's Old Blue Regiment of Foot, *c.* 1633–1635 (20.1);
Colonel Georg aus dem Winckel's Dragoon Company, 1635 (20.2)
(Riksarkivet, Stockholm. Author's photos)
See Colour Plate Commentaries for further information

Plate 21

Colonel Thomas Sigmund von Schlammersdorff's 'New' Regiment of Foot
(Riksarkivet, Stockholm. Author's photos)
See Colour Plate Commentaries for further information

Plate 22

Colonel Thomas Sigmund von Schlammersdorff's 'New'
Regiment of Foot (continued)
(Riksarkivet, Stockholm. Author's photos)
See Colour Plate Commentaries for further information

Plate 23

Colonel John Forbes's Regiment of Foot
(Riksarkivet, Stockholm. Author's photos)
See Colour Plate Commentaries for further information

Plate 24

Colonel John Forbes's Regiment of Foot (continued)
(Riksarkivet, Stockholm. Author's photos)
See Colour Plate Commentaries for further information

Plate 25

Colonel Johann Michael Rau's Regiment of Foot
(Riksarkivet, Stockholm. Author's photos)
See Colour Plate Commentaries for further information

Plate 26

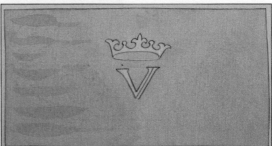

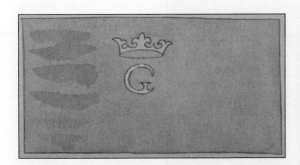

Colonel Johann Schneidewind's Regiment of Foot
(Riksarkivet, Stockholm. Author's photos)
See Colour Plate Commentaries for further information

Plate 27

Colonel Johann Schneidewind's Regiment of Foot (continued)
(Riksarkivet, Stockholm. Author's photos)
See Colour Plate Commentaries for further information

Plate 28

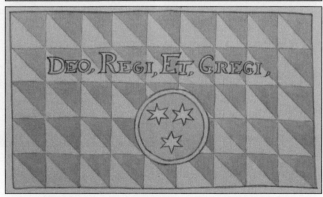

Colonel Philipp von Liebenstein's Regiment of Foot
(Riksarkivet, Stockholm. Author's photos)
See Colour Plate Commentaries for further information

Plate 29

Colonel Philipp von Liebenstein's Regiment of Foot (continued)
(Riksarkivet, Stockholm. Author's photos)
See Colour Plate Commentaries for further information

Plate 30

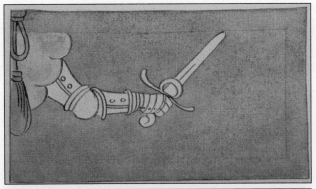

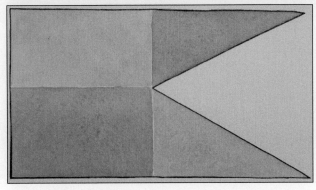

Formerly Catholic cavalry and dragoon units
(Riksarkivet, Stockholm. Author's photos)
See Colour Plate Commentaries for further information

Plate 31

Formerly Catholic infantry units
(Riksarkivet, Stockholm. Author's photos)
See Colour Plate Commentaries for further information

Plate 32

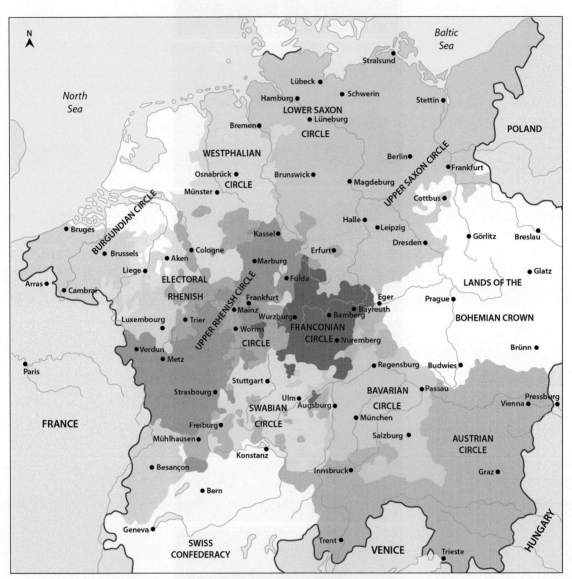

The Imperial Circles
(Illustration by George Anderson, © Helion & Company 2020)
See Colour Plate Commentaries for further information

received reinforcements, reaching a total of some 2,000 men, in addition to approximately 600 levies. He thought that the redoubt at Eda was manned by 400 Norwegians, but they were only 268. When Stenbock attacked in early June, the Norwegians surrendered. Stenbock immediately continued across the border, where the Norwegian border defences surrendered, too, on the same day. Having taken control of the border defences, the Swedes then returned to the Swedish side.[171] Stenbock had orders not to move into Norway, instead to hold and defend the border crossings. In June, he and most of his men moved into the province of Västergötland, where it was feared the Norwegians would go on the offensive.

As for Sehested, he and his Norwegians in February made repeated attempts to push against Gothenburg. However, by the end of the month, Sehested began to pull out his men. The Norwegians retreated into Norway.

Meanwhile, on the Scanian front, Horn had received his orders for the summer campaign in mid February. His main task was to take Malmö. Scania and the surrounding Danish provinces should be taken under control if possible and certainly be used as sources of supplies. No real fighting took place in the south during the winter, since most Danes had withdrawn across the Straits after the battle off Fehmarn. In May, Horn moved against the province of Blekinge to gain supplies. He also looked for ports which were easier to access for the expected Swedish fleet than Ystad, which was uncomfortably close to the Danish islands.[172]

Horn's army again prepared to attack Malmö in June. However, his expected reinforcements did not arrive since Stockholm, as noted, was concerned about an expected Norwegian attack on Västergötland and accordingly reinforced defences there instead of sending reinforcements to Horn.

These concerns were well founded. In early June, a Danish fleet under Admiral Ove Giedde (1594–1660), in cooperation with Sehested and his Norwegians, indeed made another attempt to advance against Gothenburg. However, Denmark no longer controlled the seas. Giedde could not overcome Anckarhielm, who successfully blocked maritime access to Gothenburg, thus preventing the Danish offensive.

In late May, the Swedish main fleet at Stockholm, 23 warships, three fireships, and a couple of small vessels under Admiral Erik Ryning, again went to sea. Although he was ordered to confront the Danish fleet, if it left port, the Danes were actually expected to concentrate on maintaining communications with Malmö. Ryning was accordingly ordered to focus on blocking all Danish communications across and through the Straits. Finally, he should support Horn's attack on Malmö. If Ryning gained supremacy at sea, he should also carry out an attack on Zealand. However, winds were unusually adversarial, even for Stockholm, so Ryning was six times driven back into port before he managed to move south. On the way south, he took the town of Visby on the island of Gotland, a conquest long desired by Oxenstierna. Meanwhile, Wrangel's fleet from Wismar had in June landed at

---

171 Barkman, Lundkvist, and Tersmeden, *Kungl. Svea Livgardes Historia* 3:2, pp.125–32.
172 *Ibid.*, pp.137–40.

and occupied the Danish island of Bornholm, with troops he requested and received from Horn's army. Wrangel took Hammershus Castle later in the month, after which the population on Bornholm surrendered.

In mid July, the Wismar fleet under Wrangel and the Stockholm main fleet joined forces at Bornholm. Ryning assumed overall command.

In late July, Horn reported that he was poised to attack Malmö. The necessary reinforcements had finally arrived, from Stockholm and from the overseas territories. Among them was also the newly re-established Life Guard regiment, under its equally new colonel, the young Magnus Gabriel De la Gardie (1622–1686), the son of Jacob De la Gardie who had led campaigns in Muscovy and Livonia when Gustavus Adolphus was young. Horn had some 9,600 men at his disposal (2,841 horse and 6,772 foot, including officers). He requested naval support to cut off Malmö from the sea. However, Ryning's fleet was not yet ready to provide the requested ships.[173] Still, yet more reinforcements arrived to Horn's army, and in early August, he had 20,855 men (7,417 horse and 13,438 foot) at his disposal, although many, no doubt, were in garrisons. Horn sent a force of 8,258 men (3,141 horse and 5,117 foot) against Malmö.[174] If he could get naval support, this should be sufficient to take the town.

Meanwhile, Sehested and his Norwegians had not given up the struggle. In early August, they made another determined attempt to go on the offensive against Gothenburg. After serious fighting, Colonel Harald Stake and Lieutenant General Kagg pushed them back. Moreover, at this time the Dutch Republic finally abandoned its role as mediator and joined the Swedish side against Denmark. A Dutch fleet of 49 warships and 400 merchant ships passed through the Straits in a show of force that the Danes could do nothing to prevent. Not wishing to give the Swedes the opportunity to land troops on Zealand, Christian IV had no choice but to agree to negotiations for peace. Horn was ordered to hold the siege of Malmö while peace negotiations went on.

The war between Sweden and Denmark ended with the Treaty of Brömsebro in August 1645. Denmark surrendered the province of Halland for 30 years, which gave Sweden a significantly more secure access to the North Sea (previously, Sweden had to rely on the narrow strip of land around Elfsborg and subsequently Gothenburg). Sweden also gained the provinces of Jämtland and Härjedalen from Norway and received the Baltic islands of Gotland and Ösel from Denmark. Unofficially, Sweden also retained control over Idre and Särna, the northern settlements that Governor Kruse had occupied and incorporated in the province of Dalecarlia, since the Danish side did not remember these two remote territories when the Treaty was concluded. Finally, Denmark agreed to extend Sweden's exemption from the Danish Sound tolls.

---

173 *Ibid.*, p.141.
174 *Ibid.*, p.143; citing a document dated 30 July 1645 (O.S.).

The Battle of Jankow

By early 1645, Gallas had been discharged and replaced by Melchior von Hatzfeldt as Imperial commander. The latter gathered his troops at Prague. Hatzfeldt had orders to engage in battle, by some accounts because the Emperor said that the Virgin Mary had promised him victory in a dream.

Torstensson, too, was inclined to go on the offensive, at least into Bohemia and Moravia but, if possible, into Austria as well. In January 1645, as soon as the cold enabled easier road travel, Torstensson led his army of some 15,500 men into Bohemia.[175] The immediate plan was to attack and defeat Hatzfeldt's Imperial army and Johann von Werth's Bavarian corps before they could join forces. Torstensson's broader strategy was to carry out the offensive in conjunction with the Transylvanians and at the same time when the French army of the Rhine, under Henri de La Tour d'Auvergne, Viscount of Turenne, would invade Bavaria. In the end, the French failed to defeat the Bavarians under Franz von Mercy (1597–1645) and retreated with great losses.[176]

Henri de La Tour d'Auvergne, Viscount of Turenne.

Nonetheless, by the end of February, Torstensson was deep within Bohemia. The campaign in Bohemia became one of manoeuvre. Torstensson was unable to prevent the rendezvous of the enemy contingents. On the other hand, Hatzfeldt was unable to prevent Torstensson from moving forward. On 5 March, Swedish and Imperial cavalry units encountered each other. Some skirmishing followed, but the main outcome was that Torstensson learnt the position of Hatzfeldt's army near the village of Jankow. The terrain around Jankow consisted of forested hills and was very uneven, but it was dry, so even the artillery was easy to move. We do not know if the ground was covered with snow, but if so, the snow cover was not deep.

On 6 March 1645, the two armies confronted each other in what became known as the battle of Jankow.[177] Torstensson had some 15,500 men (8,800

---

175 Försvarsstabens krigshistoriska avdelning, *Slaget vid Jankow 1645 24/2 1945: Minnesskrift* (Stockholm: Försvarsstabens krigshistoriska avdelning, 1945), pp.42–4, 65–8. See also Mankell, *Uppgifter* 1, p.200; Mankell, *Uppgifter* 2, pp.278–82. Again, Mankell's reprinted documents seem to include some printing errors, and in addition, the number of officers has to be estimated. On Torstensson's artillery, see Hedberg, *Kungl. Artilleriet*, p.257.

176 Mercy had early on fought for the Empire against the Ottoman Empire. Later, he was in the service of the Duke of Lorraine, after which he returned to Imperial service in time to participate in the battle of Breitenfeld 1631. Since 1638, he had been the most able Imperial–Bavarian commander on the Rhine. Unusually among generals, he did not enrich himself from his campaigns. When Mercy eventually fell in battle, Maximilian of Bavaria had to step in to support Mercy's family.

177 The best discussion of the battle is *Slaget vid Jankow*, pp.58–124. Previously, the best description of the battle of Jankow was Tingsten, *Fältmarskalkarna*, pp.267–79, now superseded. For more recent works, see Hedberg, *Kungl. Artilleriet*, pp.257–9; Lars Ericson, "Jankow 1645", Lars Ericson et al., *Svenska slagfält* (np: Wahlström &Widstrand, 2003), pp.173–80.

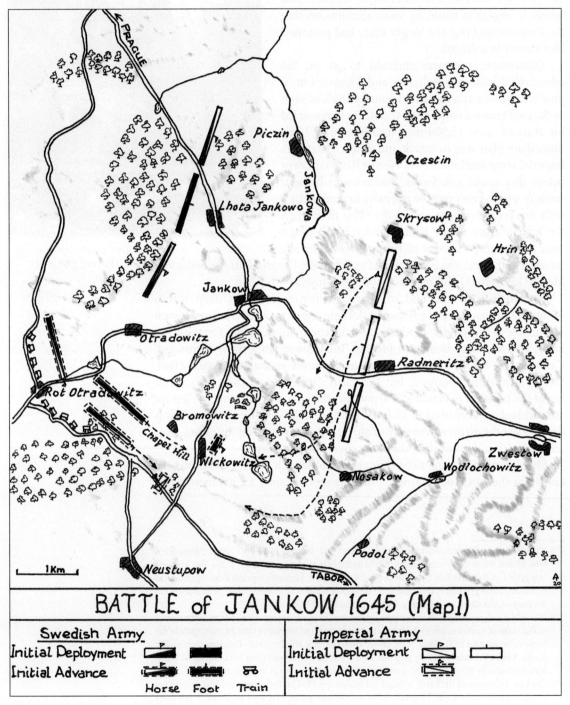

Jankow Phase 1.

First phase of the battle of Jankow, 1645, with the initial deployment of the two armies. Left: Swedish army. Right: Imperial army. (Based on drawings by Conrad Mardefelt published in *Theatrum Europaeum*)

horse, 6,700 foot, and 60 cannons; see Table 7).[178] Hatzfeldt's army was of comparable size, consisting of some 15,000 to 16,000 Imperial, Bavarian, and Saxon troops (10,000 to 11,000 horse, some 5,000 foot, and 26 cannons). It was a coalition, including about 9,000 Imperials, 5,000 Bavarians, and 1,400 Saxons,[179] and accordingly Hatzfeldt was stronger in cavalry but weaker in infantry and artillery. The terrain did not favour the cavalry, in which Hatzfeldt was the stronger.

The two armies had formed up already on the previous day. Torstensson had deployed the Swedish right wing under Arvid Wittenberg and Johann Arend von Goldstein, the centre under Caspar Cornelius de Mortaigne, and the left wing under Robert Douglas. Torstensson deployed his cavalry squadrons interspersed with 40-man-strong musketeer infantry platoons to provide direct fire support to those cavalry units to which they were attached. His heavy artillery deployed before the front.

Hatzfeldt had deployed on a number of hills, with his right wing under the Bavarian cavalry commander Johann von Werth, the centre under Ernst Roland de Suys, and the left wing under Johann von Götz.

---

178 *Slaget vid Jankow*, pp.65–8.
179 *Ibid.*, p.74.

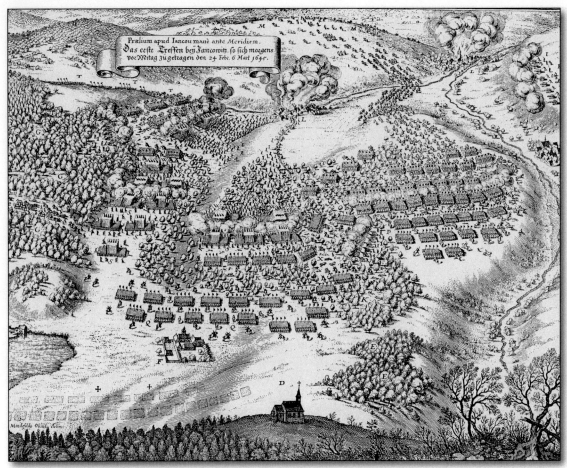

Second phase of the battle of Jankow, 1645, with Chapel Hill in the foreground. Following the fall of Johann von Götz, yet more Imperial troops advance against the Swedes; however, they are pushed back. (Based on drawings by Conrad Mardefelt published in *Theatrum Europaeum*)

Johann von Götz.

Torstensson, for once comparably free from his debilitating illness, ordered his army to carry out a flank march, led by the right wing so as to envelop the Imperial left flank. The army set out already at dawn, and by 8:00 a.m., it had reached its first destination, a small hill henceforth known as Chapel Hill. Although the hill was held by Imperial dragoons, they failed to warn Götz about the Swedish advance in time. Having gained control of the hill, the Swedish army opened fire with both infantry and artillery against the Imperial left wing which was caught in a narrow valley. Götz lost four horses killed under him and then fell himself, having mounted his fifth horse.

Meanwhile, Hatzfeldt redeployed his centre and right wing so as to face the Swedes. In time, more and more units became engaged in the battle, which was complicated because of the difficult terrain. Just before noon, the fighting gradually died down. Hatzfeldt's men withdraw some distance, and then formed up again in a valley out of

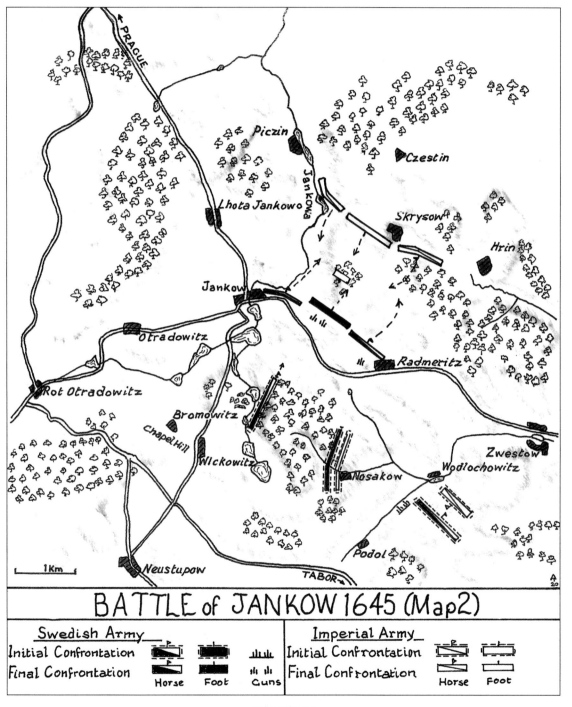

Jankow Phase 2.

sight of the Swedish army. His plan was to await nightfall, at which point he expected to withdraw. The Swedish army, likewise, formed up again. Having captured most of the Imperial artillery, and knowing that Götz and several other Imperial officers were dead or captured, the Swedish commanders, too, thought that the battle was mostly over.

However, when Torstensson noticed that a small Imperial musketeer unit had occupied a minor hill in front of his battle line, he ordered his detached infantry and 10 regimental cannons to take it. It was then around 1:00 p.m. This was accomplished, but as a result some Imperial units which had then re-formed attacked again. Having lost control of some of his men, Hatzfeldt did the best of the situation by ordering his other units to charge, too.

For a moment, the result looked spectacular. The Bavarian and Imperial cavalry under Johann von Werth broke through the Swedish lines and even gained control of the Swedish supply train, including the wives of the senior Swedish officers, among whom was Beata De la Gardie, Torstensson's wife. However, the looting of the supply train released the pressure on the Swedes and gave them time to recover, and soon Swedish cavalry rushed in to liberate the ladies. The Bavarian and Imperial cavalry was disrupted and pushed back. Again, the fighting was very hard. Johann von Werth was captured twice, but was rescued by his own men both times. Hatzfeldt was captured, too. The Imperial infantry, surrounded, was essentially destroyed. The battle was over around 4:00 p.m.

Third and final phase of the battle of Jankow, 1645. Following another bout of fighting, the Imperials abandon the battle. (Based on drawings by Conrad Mardefelt published in *Theatrum Europaeum*)

Battle of Jankow, 1645. Part of a series of battle paintings completed in the 1670s by Johan Hammer, who in turn based them on drawings by Conrad Mardefelt published in *Theatrum Europaeum*. Colonel Mardefelt joined the Swedish army in 1628 and fought in the battles of Wittstock and Jankow. In 1646, Mardefelt was appointed inspector general of the Swedish fortifications in northern Germany. In March 1647, he received a new assistant, the young Erik Jönsson (1625–1703, later ennobled and better known as Dahlbergh), a civilian who in 1638 had been sent to Germany as a boy for training and work and soon became involved in the war effort. Henceforth, Mardefelt trained the young man to become a military engineer and fortification officer. Both Mardefelt and Dahlbergh became key actors in Sweden's subsequent wars. (Photo: Medströms)

The Swedish artillery played a major, perhaps a decisive, role in the victory. Certainly, the Swedish artillery employed tactics at Jankow that were not yet in common use anywhere else, and would not become commonplace in other armies for many years to come. During the battle, the Swedish artillery was constantly in use, in different ways and deployed in various locations. Even the 24-pounders seem to have changed firing position more than once during the battle; perhaps a first in history.[180]

The Imperials lost all their artillery, more than half the army (8,500 men, including at least 4,000 dead and 4,400–4,500 captured), the field chancery, and their leading commanders. Götz was dead, as were several colonels and other officers. Hatzfeldt and five other senior commanders were captured: Field Marshal Lieutenant Albert Gaston Spinola de Bruay, who later died of his wounds, Field Marshal Lieutenant Heinrich von Mercy, Major General Don Felix de Zúñiga y Guzmán, Major General Georg Adam von Trauditsch, and Major General Václav Zahrádecký. The Swedes lost 3,000 to 4,000 men dead and wounded. In the Old Blue Regiment, all officers were dead or wounded, and among Charles Gustavus's Courlanders, Charles

Charles Gustavus, 1645. By this time, hat fashion had changed into a flat crown and small brim. The painting is believed to depict Charles Gustavus at the time of the battle of Jankow.

---

180 *Ibid.*, p.118.

Gustavus himself was the only officer who was neither killed nor wounded. The two colonels Seestedt and Reuschel were dead.[181] As usual, many of the captives immediately went into Swedish service.

Although Charles Gustavus survived the battle unharmed, he counted one hole each in his hat, shirt, and coat, all caused by enemy fire, and had even lost a lock of hair, which likewise had been cut off by enemy fire.[182]

When the Imperial regiments a week after the battle were gathered at Prague, they counted only 2,697 men, and the survivors derived from 36 different regiments. The average regimental strength had been reduced to 75 men.[183] The battle broke the back of the Imperial army, at least for now. In addition, it shattered the Bavarian cavalry.

Table 7. Swedish order of battle at Jankow, 6 March 1645. Figures specify the number of squadrons (in the wings) and brigades (in the centre). Note that most brigades consisted of units from more than one regiment. (Source: *Slaget vid Jankow*, pp.65–71)

Squadrons	Brigades	Strength	Commanding Officer or Unit
Commander-in-Chief: Field Marshal Lennart Torstensson			
Quartermaster: Colonel Conrad Maesberg (Mardefelt)			
Heavy artillery: Lieutenant Colonel Andreas Sommerfeldt			
(18 cannons; the 42 regimental cannons were distributed among the infantry units)			
Right Wing			
Commander: Major General			
Arvid Wittenberg			
First Line			
2		600	Torstensson's Life Regiment of Horse
2		400	Major General Arvid Wittenberg
2		300	Colonel Reinhold Jordan (Livonians)
2		300	Count Palatine Charles Gustavus (Courlanders)
2		300	Margrave Frederick of Baden-Durlach's Regiment
1		200	Lieutenant Colonel Raabe
2		350	Colonel G. M. von Witzleben
Second Line			
Commander: Major General Johann Arend von Goldstein			
2		330	Colonel Georg Derfflinger
2		300	Major General Johann Arend von Goldstein
2		300	Colonel Christofer von Galbrecht
1		220	Major General Axel Lillie
2		350	Colonel M. A. (Moritz August?) von Rochow
2		300	Colonel Johan von Wittkopff
In total: 24 squadrons			

181 *Ibid.*, pp.105–6.
182 *Ibid.*, p.102.
183 *Ibid.*, p.107.

Squadrons	Brigades	Strength	Commanding Officer or Unit
Centre			
Commander: Major General Caspar Cornelius de Mortaigne			
First Line			
	1		Major Per Christofersson Ribbing (one company each from the Skaraborg Regiment and Elfsborg Regiment)
		500	Colonel Axel Axelsson Stålarm (Björneborg Regiment)
	1	776	Torstensson's Life Regiment of Foot ('Old Blue' Regiment)
	1	383	Major General Carl Gustav Wrangel
		427	Colonel Lorenz von der Linde
	1	670	Major General Caspar Cornelius de Mortaigne
	1	342	Colonel Jürgen Paikull
		613	Colonel Paul Seestedt
	1	676	Colonel Daniel von Wolckmar
Second Line			
	1	434	Major General Axel Lillie
		329	Colonel Johan von Koppy
	1	323	Colonel Gustav Adolph Lewenhaupt
		662	Colonel Michael(?) Jordan
In total: 8 brigades			
Left Wing			
Commander: Major General Robert Douglas			
First Line			
2		360	Colonel Joachim Tideman
1		250	Colonel Charles de Bretagne-Dubois d'Avaugour
2		300	Major General Robert Douglas
1		150	Colonel Gustav Evertsson Horn af Marienborg
2		300	Colonel Johann Christofer von Hammerstein
1		150	Colonel Gustav Evertsson Horn af Marienborg
3		500	Landgrave John of Hesse-Darmstadt
Second Line			
2		350	Colonel Carl Abraham von Reichart
1		270	Colonel Otto von Dannenberg
2		200	Colonel Sigmund von Riesengrün
1		150	Colonel Fritz Buttler
2		250	Colonel Jacob Reuschel
1		250	Colonel Kuno Ulrich von Pentz
2		400	Colonel Burchard Müller von der Lühnen
In total: 23 squadrons			

Detached units of 40 musketeers, taken from the numbers above, were deployed between each of the squadrons of the first line in both wings; in addition, there were 400 dragoons in an unknown location (including a company of 60 dragoons raised by Major General Johann Arend von Goldstein)

Two days after the battle, Emperor Ferdinand III, who was in Prague, learnt of the Swedish victory. With a few picked servants, he immediately fled to Regensburg, thence down the Danube to Linz, where he joined his wife. The flight continued to Vienna, where Ferdinand III remained, but he sent his children onwards to Graz. He also evacuated his treasury to Graz.

On the same day the Emperor received the news, Torstensson led his remaining men, who cannot have been more than 16,000 in number even with the enlisted prisoners, into the Habsburg heartland. By way of Znaim, in late March 1645 he reached Krems on the Danube. The town soon fell, but Torstensson was unable to cross the Danube into Lower Austria. The water level of the Danube was at a high level, and Lower Austria was well defended by fortified strongpoints. Still, Vienna was within easy reach; indeed, Torstensson in early April took the outermost bastion (Wolfsschanze, at Jedlersdorf) which guarded one of Vienna's main bridges across the Danube, the Wolfsbrücke, near the modern-day Floridsdorf Bridge. The fleeing Imperials burned the bridge as they evacuated. However, Torstensson knew that a successful operation against Vienna depended on whether he would receive Transylvanian support. He did not have enough men to invest Vienna on both sides of the river. Torstensson had no intention of putting his entire field army at risk without a reasonable hope of success. This would have jeopardised the strong position which Sweden had already gained, and on which Sweden depended in the already ongoing peace negotiations in Westphalia.

However, the Emperor initiated negotiations with George Rákóczy, offering him concessions. Rákóczy now negotiated with both sides, and also with the French, who offered subsidies if he would join Torstensson, to which Rákóczy agreed. In late April or early May, some 1,100 of Rákóczy's men under Gabriel Bakos (Bakos Gábor) joined the Swedish army outside Vienna. However,

Jean-Louis Raduit de Souches.

they mutinied almost at once, demanding additional pay. Without real reinforcements, Torstensson had too few men to lay siege to Vienna. Instead, in June he moved on and laid siege to Moravia's capital Brünn (modern-day Brno). Brünn had only a small garrison, but the town carried out a spirited defence, based on its burgher militia, students from the Jesuit seminary, and many other townsmen, led by Jean-Louis Raduit de Souches (1608–1682). He was a French Huguenot who had formerly been in Swedish service. Since he had deserted, reportedly after having challenged his superior officer, the late Torsten Stålhandske, to a duel (an act forbidden in the Swedish army and subject to capital punishment), Souches was highly motivated to fight on.

Another Transylvanian contingent, under Sigismund (1622–1652; Rákóczi Zsigmond), George Rákóczy's son, joined Torstensson at Brünn. This increased the number of the Transylvanian contingent

Contemporary painting of the siege of Brünn, 1645. Swedish and Transylvanian officers discuss the ongoing operations.

to some 7,000 men.[184] By all accounts, Sigismund Rákóczy fought bravely, but the same could not be said of all of his units. Most Transylvanians were irregular light cavalry or light infantry, and some served only for plunder, not pay.[185] They were of little use in siege warfare. Then, in June 1645, the Ottoman sultan went to war with the Venetian Republic over Candia (modern-day Crete). This ended the Ottoman support for George Rákóczy, who backed down and in December 1645 concluded the Treaty of Vienna with Emperor Ferdinand III, defecting from the anti-Habsburg alliance.

Regardless, Brünn fought on, and in August 1645, with the plague rampant in the Swedish camp, Torstensson abandoned the siege. Although the original plan to take Brünn so as to take control of Silesia and the communication lines to the north had been sound, the siege had taken far too long. If ever there had been a chance to move against Vienna with hope of success, which is doubtful, it is certain that this no longer was possible, even had the Transylvanians provided more reliable support than they ultimately

---

184 Based on Torstensson's reports; cited in Försvarsstabens krigshistoriska avdelning, *Från Femern och Jankow till Westfaliska freden: Minnesskrift* (Stockholm: Generalstabens Litografiska Anstalt, 1948), p.99 n.6.

185 Zsolt Schäfer (ed.), *Soldiers from the Age of Gábor Bethlen* (np: Bethlen Gábor Hagyományőrség Egyesület, 2017; available online).

did. It has been noted, wryly but with some truth, that the chief contribution of the Transylvanian contingent to the Swedish army was the plague.

Torstensson again marched to the vicinity of Vienna in early September. However, the Imperial forces remained south of the Danube, unwilling to confront the Swedes north of the river. In late September, Torstensson returned towards northern Bohemia. By then, his army consisted of 8,000 horse and 2,500 foot.[186]

We have seen that France attempted to enlist the support of the Transylvanians through the offer of subsidies, but where was the allied French army at the time of Torstensson's operations against the Imperial heartland? Would not a Swedish–French–Transylvanian coalition have been able to invest Vienna and force the Emperor to concede defeat? The answer is that the French army by then was in no shape to provide support to Torstensson. After several defeats (primarily at Herbsthausen near Mergentheim on 5 May 1645), the French army needed more support than Torstensson. Indeed, Swedish reinforcements, under Königsmarck, had to reinforce Turenne's army after the battle. Then Louis, Duke d'Enghien (1621–1686; later Prince of Condé) assumed command of the French army. He also brought further reinforcements. Expecting the French henceforth to be able to carry their own weight, Torstensson ordered Königsmarck into Saxony, with some 5,500 men, to apply pressure on John George of Saxony.[187] It turned out that Torstensson's assessment was correct. At the battle of Alerheim (near Nördlingen; the battle is sometimes referred to as the second battle of Nördlingen) on 3 August, the combined French–Hessian army under Enghien defeated Mercy's Bavarian–Imperial army. Mercy fell in the battle.

After Jankow and Alerheim, it was clear to all that the Emperor no longer had any field army that was able to stand up to the Swedes and their allies. On 6 September, John George of Saxony felt compelled to sign the Truce of Kötzschenbroda with Sweden. This ended Saxony's participation in the war. Emperor Ferdinand III drew the same conclusion, instructing his chief negotiator, Count Maximilian von und zu Trauttmannsdorff (1584–1650), to agree to significant concessions in the ongoing peace negotiations in Westphalia.

Wrangel Takes Command

By late 1645, Torstensson had to spend weeks at a time in bed. He could barely speak and, because of his failing hands, not even sign an order. Torstensson accordingly handed over interim command to Major General Arvid Wittenberg, awaiting the arrival of Carl Gustav Wrangel, whom Torstensson had recommended as his successor.

Wrangel was then in Holstein. He met Torstensson in late December 1645 in Eilenburg, north-east of Leipzig, which also was the location of the Swedish–Saxon peace negotiations. Oxenstierna still wanted Torstensson to

---

186 Mankell, *Uppgifter* 1, p.202; *Från Femern och Jankow*, p.101.
187 *Från Femern och Jankow*, p.101.

be in overall command of military operations. Wrangel accordingly received command of the main field army only, while Torstensson retained overall command over Swedish military forces in Germany. Although Wrangel received operational responsibility for the main field army, it was decided that Torstensson would assist him with advice and retain overall command. In short, it was obvious that Oxenstierna hoped that Torstensson would be able to resume command after a period of rest.[188] Wrangel, still only a major general, for the time being had neither formal nor real authority to plan the ongoing campaign on his own. As a result, some of Wrangel's subordinates, in particular Lieutenant General Königsmarck who both was older and of higher rank, did not always follow his instructions to the letter.[189]

The main field army in early 1646 consisted of 23,500 men (14,000 cavalry, 1,500 dragoons, and 8,000 foot, and 70 cannons).[190] Torstensson instructed Wrangel eventually to continue operations in the Habsburg hereditary lands. However, he should not aim for a decisive battle, unless he had to. The reason was obvious to the two generals: peace negotiations went on in Westphalia, and while it was sound policy to apply pressure on the Emperor, there was much at risk, and little to be gained, by a major battle. If the Swedish army lost the engagement, this would jeopardise the Swedish position in the negotiations. For the immediate future, Torstensson accordingly advised Wrangel to remain in northern Bohemia, near Saxony, since a Swedish military presence there would serve to apply the required pressure on John George of Saxony to conclude the peace negotiations.

On 31 March, the Peace of Eilenburg between Sweden and Saxony ended Saxony's participation in the war. Wrangel again conferred with Torstensson in Eilenburg. Henceforth, Torstensson and Wrangel agreed, the best course of action would be to join forces with Turenne's French army on the Rhine. Both Torstensson and Wrangel regarded cooperation between French and Swedish military forces as the real key to victory over the Empire. But first, they wanted to focus on Bavaria, not Austria, in order to force Bavaria out of the war in the same way that they had dealt with Saxony.

Since Turenne had sent messages that his army could not join the Swedes before the end of May, Wrangel's army would first provide necessary support to Sweden's most dependable ally, Hesse-Kassel. Wrangel and Königsmarck would join forces with Amalie Elisabeth of Hesse-Kassel to lay siege to those fortresses that remained in enemy hands around her lands, primarily Höxter to the north of Kassel.

Yet, the Swedes would not neglect the Habsburg hereditary lands. Wittenberg would lead 4,900 men (3,000 cavalry, 900 dragoons, and 1,000

---

188 Lars Tingsten, *De tre sista åren av det trettioåriga kriget jämte den västfaliska freden* (Stockholm: Militärlitteraturföreningens förlag 171, 1934), p.5.

189 Later historians have sometimes, incorrectly, explained Wrangel's lack of authority by blaming his personal characteristics and alleged lack of experience. See, for example, Peter Englund, *Ofredsår* (Stockholm: Atlantis, 1993), pp.421–2. At the time, Wrangel still had only limited formal authority, and Königsmarck was not subordinated to him.

190 Tingsten, *De tre sista åren*, p.6.

foot) into Silesia, where he would maintain a presence and, if possible, also move the war into Moravia and Austria.[191]

Königsmarck was ordered to Bremen to enlist more men and to support Amalie Elisabeth. Königsmarck, who was not keen to follow young Wrangel's instructions and in any case always was most efficient when acting independently, retook Bremervörde in mid April, then in turn successfully laid siege to several other fortresses, including Vechta in May and Lemgo in June, before he somewhat reluctantly joined Wrangel at Wetzlar in mid June. On the way, Königsmarck also gathered the Hessian army, which meant that upon arrival his total forces consisted of 7,700 men (3,500 cavalry, 1,200 dragoons, 3,000 infantry).[192]

Meanwhile, Wrangel led the main army towards Höxter in mid April, taking the fortress in early May. Wrangel then turned towards Paderborn, which he took in mid May. Amalie Elisabeth asked Wrangel also to take Stadtberge (Marsberg), which he did 10 days later. In late June, Wrangel and Königsmarck took Amöneburg, near Marburg in Hesse.

However, where was Turenne? The French army was supposed to meet the Swedes in Hesse-Kassel. Delayed, Turenne was not ready to march before the end of May. He also did not move very fast, and at the appointed meeting time, Wrangel received intelligence that an Imperial–Bavarian army was on its way. In reality what had happened was that France's Cardinal Mazarin had ordered Turenne not to join the Swedes, since this might endanger his ongoing negotiations with Maximilian of Bavaria over a separate peace between France and Bavaria. In addition, to show his good faith, Mazarin had secretly handed over the joint Swedish–French campaign plan to the Bavarians.[193]

Maximilian was no fool. He continued negotiating with Mazarin. Meanwhile, with the benefit of full knowledge of the Swedish–French campaign plan, he made sure that a strong Imperial–Bavarian army under Archduke Leopold William advanced towards Hesse-Kassel.[194] Wrangel, outnumbered, dug in at Amöneburg. The two hostile camps faced each other for a while. However, Wrangel could easily receive supplies from his Hessian allies, while Leopold William faced considerable supply problems.

Turenne only received his marching orders after Mazarin's plan to conclude a separate peace with Bavaria had failed. When Turenne finally arrived, in early August, two and a half months late according to the common campaign plan, the Imperials withdrew.

Archduke Leopold William's Imperial–Bavarian army had consisted of 31,400 men (18,100 horse and 13,300 foot). Wrangel had 20,000 men (11,000 horse and 9,000 foot). Turenne's army and the Hessian army together

191 Mankell, *Uppgifter* 1, p.204; Tingsten, *De tre sista åren*, p.9.
192 *Från Femern och Jankow*, p.171. An earlier interpretation was 7,800 men (3,500 cavalry, 800 dragoons, 3,500 infantry). Mankell, *Uppgifter* 1, p.204; Tingsten, *De tre sista åren*, p.10.
193 Englund, *Ofärdsår*, p.421.
194 Mankell, *Uppgifter* 1, p.205; Tingsten, *De tre sista åren*, p.12.

consisted of 13,800 men (8,000 horse and 5,800 foot). In total, the coalition had 33,800 men versus the Emperor's 31,400.[195]

In late July or early August, letters arrived from Stockholm with the Queen's promotion of Wrangel to the rank of field marshal and overall commander of Swedish military forces in Germany. Wrangel finally had undisputed authority to function as the Swedish overall commander in Germany as Torstensson's replacement. At the same time, Torstensson was at last allowed to return home (but not into retirement: in Stockholm the Queen, Oxenstierna, and other senior leaders regularly consulted him on German affairs).[196] The other senior Swedish generals were promoted, too, Wittenberg to chief of artillery (*generalfälttygmästare*), Königsmarck to general of cavalry, and Mortaigne to general of infantry.

There was also a letter from Torstensson. He instructed Wrangel to move into and ravage first Bavaria, preferably together with Turenne, and then the Habsburg ancestral lands, so that the enemy would lose his ability to supply further operations. Sieges should be avoided, since they were too time-consuming and also produced difficulties in supplying one's own forces. Königsmarck and the Hessians should remain in Franconia to protect the rear of the advancing armies, while Wittenberg should continue into the Habsburg lands from Silesia.[197]

Wrangel and Turenne Invade Bavaria

Unable to initiate a battle with any hope of success, the Imperial army was forced back to Bohemia. The joint French–Swedish army then moved into Bavaria, which Wrangel had orders to ravage thoroughly, so that it would cease hostilities.

Swedish–French cooperation was not without its difficulties. Eventually, Wrangel and Turenne had to agree that they, in turn, would command the united army on alternate weeks.

Wrangel and Turenne took Rain-am-Lech in early October. Wrangel hoped that Augsburg would surrender, as the town years ago had surrendered to Gustavus Adolphus. However, Augsburg had no intention of surrendering either to Wrangel or Turenne, who both, separately, approached the town. They had to lay siege to Augsburg. However, news of approaching Imperial reinforcements under Archduke Leopold William reached Turenne and Wrangel. Having failed to storm the town in mid October, they abandoned the siege.

Unfortunately for Wrangel, news then arrived that France had concluded a truce with the enemy. Turenne was no longer permitted to move further into Bavaria. Preferring to avoid fighting with Bavaria, Paris worried that the joint operation might make Sweden too powerful. Not for the first time, Paris concluded that the Swedish military presence in southwestern Germany,

195 Tingsten, *De tre sista åren*, p.13.
196 *Från Femern och Jankow*, p.177.
197 *Ibid.*, p.178.

on the French border, seemed to grow too strong. Wrangel continued the campaign in Bavaria alone. The results, of the joint Swedish–French invasion of Bavaria as well as Wrangel's continued operations alone, were momentous. Fearing a peasants' revolt more than the Swedes, Maximilian of Bavaria refused to arm his subjects. Instead he ordered a scorched earth policy, including the destruction of mills and storehouses so as to starve the invaders and, coincidentally, his own subjects.

By the end of the year, Wrangel reached the region around Lake Constance on the Swiss border. In early January 1647, he took Bregenz. This produced a rich booty, since nobles and bishops from throughout upper Swabia had sought refuge there with their valuables. Wrangel then claimed the title Admiral of Lake Constance. Perhaps this was in mock retaliation for the 1628 Imperial appointment of Wallenstein as General of the Oceanic and Baltic Seas, which similarly had encroached on Swedish dignity. But there was substance to the title, since he captured 13 vessels in Bregenz, which he rearmed for operations on Lake Constance. In early January 1647, Wrangel wrote to a Swedish naval base in Pomerania, requesting a ship's master, two boatswains, and several naval specialists to his new fleet. These specialists, together with 200 soldiers, reportedly Finns, provided the core of the Lake Constance fleet. With the help of the fleet, in February 1647 Wrangel took the island of Mainau. He also attempted, but failed, to take Lindau. Imperial vessels, too, operated on the large lake, and hostilities between the Swedish and Imperial fleets continued throughout 1647. The Swedish Lake Constance fleet remained in operation until the end of the year.[198]

In spring 1647 Maximilian of Bavaria asked for a truce, and in March he signed, together with the Elector of Cologne, the Truce of Ulm with Sweden, France, and Hesse-Kassel. Wrangel and Turenne then suspended operations in Bavaria.

Meanwhile, Oxenstierna had issued an instruction for Field Marshal Wrangel. The instruction emphasised two conclusions. First, Sweden's real enemies in the war were the Emperor and the Elector of Bavaria. For this reason, the war should, if possible, be waged in their ancestral lands, not elsewhere in Germany. Second, Sweden's key interest was the Baltic shore in Pomerania and the Lower Saxon Circle. For this reason, when conducting operations in Bohemia and beyond, it was important always to maintain the ability to send a *corps volant* ("flying body", a mobile corps intended for rapid movements) to intervene against any enemy army that tried to take advantage of the main field army's remote location by moving against the Baltic shore. This could be Wittenberg's army in Silesia or Königsmarck's army in Westphalia.[199]

In late May, Wrangel received a message from Turenne. The latter had received orders from Paris to move the French army to Flanders. There could accordingly be no joint Swedish–French operations for the rest of 1647. Turenne's departure for Flanders with the French army, with the order to gather all French units there, was not to the liking of the remaining,

---

198 *Ibid.*, pp.190–3. Wrangel requested naval personnel from Usedom on 28 December 1646 (O.S.).
199 Tingsten, *De tre sista åren*, p.31; citing an instruction issued by the Swedish government dated 7 April 1647 (O.S.).

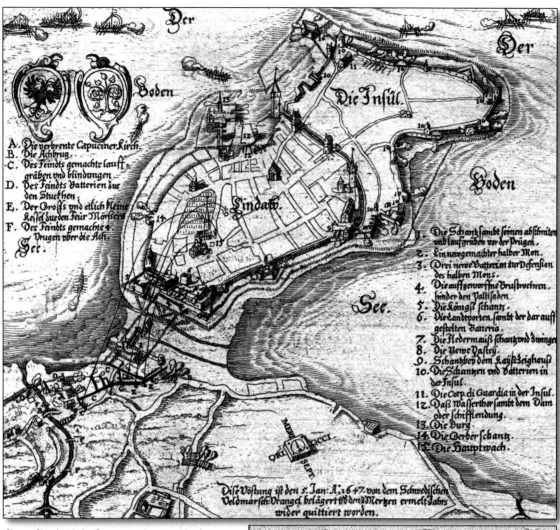

Siege of Lindau, Lake Constance, January–March 1647. Around the island, several cannon-armed sailing vessels from Wrangel's fleet give fire. (Photo: Medströms)

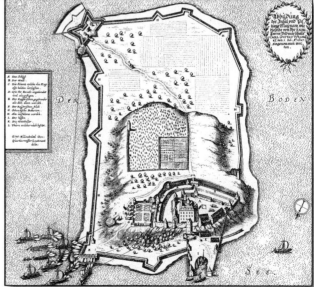

Wrangel takes the fortified island of Mainau, 13 February 1647. (*Theatrum Europaeum*, after a drawing by Swedish quartermaster-lieutenant general Georg Wilhelm Keinstretl)

139

4,000-strong Bernardine army on the Rhine (eight cavalry regiments sometimes known as the 'German Brigade'[200]). The Bernardines promptly mutinied, since they did not wish to be amalgamated into the French army or sent outside Germany. Most set off to join the Swedes, where eventually Wrangel enlisted them since the Bernardines threatened to join the enemy unless the Swedes took them in.[201] Turenne only managed to regain control of three weak regiments, which he then dissolved, dispersing the men among the French regiments. The remaining 1,660 Bernardines joined the army of Königsmarck, who reorganised them into four regiments.[202]

Meanwhile, Wrangel was going on the offensive into Bohemia, as per the instructions issued by Oxenstierna. In early June, he gathered his forces at Bamberg. He then controlled some 17,000 men (12,000 horse, 5,000 foot, and 22 cannons).[203] In late June, Wrangel reached Eger (modern-day Cheb) in western Bohemia, to which he laid siege. Eger soon surrendered. Three hours later, some 24,000 Imperial reinforcements under Peter Melander von Holzapfel and, unusually, Emperor Ferdinand III arrived in the area.[204] This was the same Holzapfel who in 1633 fought on the side of the Swedes in the siege of Hameln and the battle of Oldendorf and until 1640 had been in Hessian service. Imperial Field Marshal since 1642, Holzapfel had, following the death in spring 1647 of Gallas, succeeded him as the commander-in-chief of the Imperial army (Gallas had in late 1646 replaced Archduke Leopold William). The Swedish and Imperial armies faced off, but Wrangel did not wish to engage the superior numbers of the enemy.

Holzapfel had not yet fully fortified the Imperial camp, no doubt because the Swedish camp was on the other side of the River Eger. When the Swedes learnt this, Wrangel attempted to do what Banér had attempted at Regensburg, to strike at the very head of the enemy. Early in the morning, Major General Helmuth Wrangel forded the River Eger with 10 cavalry squadrons, including those from Witzleben's and Douglas's regiments, and carried out a surprise raid on the Imperial camp. The result was spectacular; in the panic that followed, three Swedish cavalrymen reached the Emperor's lodgings, where Ferdinand III slept. They rapidly killed the guards, then entered. However, a vigilant guard fought them off, killing one intruder, until more Imperial soldiers had time to intervene. At this point, the Imperial troops began to form up, too. The Swedes disengaged, and then recrossed the river. Ferdinand III returned the Swedish prisoners taken during the raid without ransom, as a gallant sign of appreciation of their bravery. Then, wisely, he left the army, leaving active command to Holzapfel.

Since the opportunity to retake Eger seemed small, the Imperial army soon left the area. Wrangel, too, moved out. He established a fortified camp

200 Tingsten, *De tre sista åren*, p.33.
201 Wrangel to Oxenstierna, 22 February 1648 (O.S.), *AOSB*2:8, pp.735–7, on pp.736–7. See also *Från Femern och Jankow*, p.223.
202 Mankell, *Uppgifter* 1, p.212; Tingsten, *De tre sista åren*, p.33.
203 Tingsten, *De tre sista åren*, p.32. Mankell suggests 30 regiments of horse, 11 regiments of foot, and 52 cannons. Mankell, *Uppgifter* 1, p.211.
204 *Från Femern och Jankow*, p.232. Mankell suggests some 25,000 men. Mankell, *Uppgifter* 1, p.212; Tingsten, *De tre sista åren*, p.34.

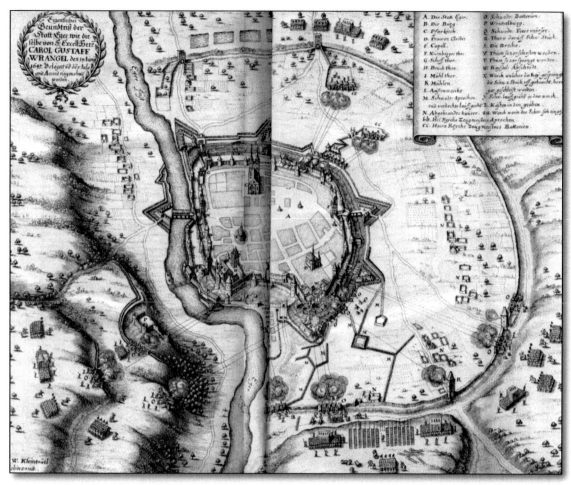

Siege of Eger, June–July 1647. Swedish engineers have established artillery batteries surrounding the town, while Swedish infantry dig trenches and other fieldwork as a means to prepare for storming the town. (*Theatrum Europaeum*)

in Plan, in front of the old castle of Triebel. However, soon after, Holzapfel stormed Triebel. The Imperial army built a fortified camp near the Swedish one. Several skirmishes occurred, and in late August, a larger engagement took place as Imperial troops attempted a surprise attack on the Swedish camp. The assault failed, but in the ensuing cavalry battle the Imperial cavalry under Johann von Werth, who had abandoned Bavaria after the peace agreement, managed to envelop Helmuth Wrangel and squadrons from 10 Swedish cavalry regiments. The Imperials were superior in numbers and artillery, so the Swedes lost more than 1,000 men, including Helmuth Wrangel who fell in the engagement. The rest of the Swedish army then moved out to offer battle, but Holzapfel had suffered numerous losses, too, including Werth who was wounded, and chose to return into camp.[205]

In September Holzapfel moved out from Triebel. On the following day Wrangel moved out, too. For a while the two armies attempted to outmanoeuvre each other. Yet more skirmishes followed. The Swedish

---

205 *Från Femern och Jankow*, p.234; Tingsten, *De tre sista åren*, p.35.

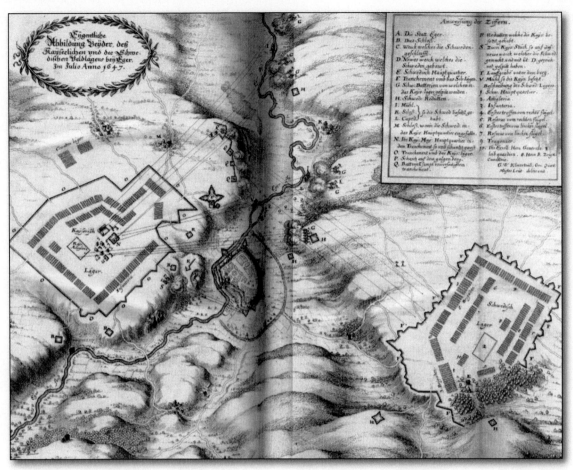

Swedish and Imperial camps facing each other on opposite sides of the River Eger and the town of Eger, early August 1647. Left: The Imperial camp, now properly fortified. Right: The Swedish camp. (*Theatrum Europaeum*)

army by then consisted of some 14,100 men (6,600 horse, 3,000 unmounted cavalrymen, and 4,500 foot). The Imperial army consisted of 19,000 men.[206]

Then, in late September, Wrangel received bad news. Maximilian of Bavaria had changed his mind about the Truce of Ulm. On 14 September 1647, he resumed the war against Sweden. Maximilian gambled that his peace with France would remain in force. He informed Mazarin that he was ready to uphold the Truce of Ulm with France, as long as the French did not join forces with the Swedes. The Bavarian army, under Bronckhorst-Gronsfeld, moved into Bohemia; Maximilian's change of heart put the Swedish army at risk of losing its lines of communication with the north. Wrangel had to gather the men from the various garrisons and head north again. Holzapfel did not pursue; instead he in November moved into Hesse, which he thoroughly devastated, possibly in part because of his aversion towards Landgravine Amalie Elisabeth. Wrangel, too, moved into Hesse, to Oldendorf, where he went into winter quarters. Suddenly the main theatre of operations had switched from Bohemia to Hesse. The Bavarian army moved into winter quarters in the bishoprics of Würzburg and Kulmbach in the

---

206 Mankell, *Uppgifter* 1, p.214; Tingsten, *De tre sista åren*, p.36.

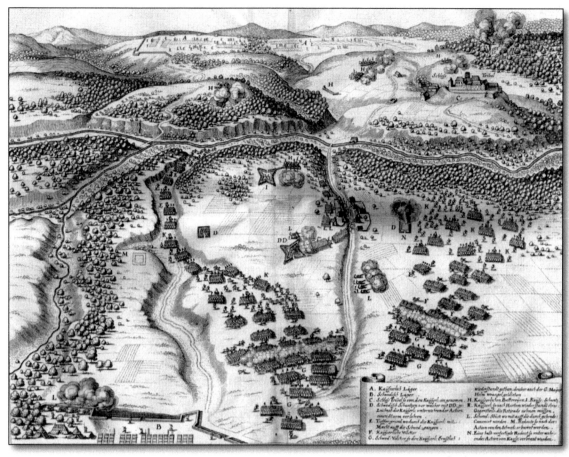

Combat operations around Triebel, Bohemia, 22 August 1647. Top: The Imperial camp. Centre: The Swedish camp. Right: The battle in which Helmuth Wrangel fell. (*Theatrum Europaeum*)

Franconian Circle. Some of the Imperial units went into winter quarters in Thuringia, while others, under Holzapfel, laid siege to Marburg in Hesse.

In France, Mazarin had not expected Bavaria to rejoin the war. He had hoped that with the withdrawal of both France and Bavaria, the Swedish and Imperial armies roughly would balance each other, so that France need not concentrate on events east of the Rhine. But, with Wrangel faced by both the Bavarian and Imperial armies, the Swedes were again outnumbered. Then Hesse again became the main theatre of operations. For Mazarin, this was far too close to French interests. As a result, France withdrew from the truce with Bavaria. Paris ordered Turenne back to the Rhine, where he could reunite with Wrangel.

The Battle of Zusmarshausen

In January 1648 Wrangel gathered his men at Oldendorf. His total strength was then 17,000 to 18,000 men. Most, some 10,000 to 11,000 were horse, while the rest was infantry.[207] Soon after, Turenne crossed the Rhine at Mainz

---

207 *Från Femern och Jankow*, p.255; Mankell, *Uppgifter* 1, p.218. Mankell concludes that different sources offer conflicting figures: either 11,000 horse and 6,000 foot or 10,000 horse and 8,000 foot.

with 8,200 men (3,800 horse and 4,400 foot).[208] Having operated near each other for a while, Wrangel and Turenne joined forces in late March.[209]

Despite being stronger, the Imperial and Bavarian armies retreated to first Nuremberg, then Ingolstadt, where Holzapfel planned a defensive line along the Danube.

Meanwhile, Wrangel and Turenne had difficulties agreeing on strategy. Wrangel wanted to move into Bohemia, as he was instructed, while Turenne, knowing the intentions in Paris, wanted to stay in Swabia, within reach of the Rhine. As a result, the two armies did not always act quite as decisively as they could have. Sweden and France still had different strategic goals.

Even so, the situation was worse between the Imperial and Bavarian commanders. In 1645, Bronckhorst-Gronsfeld had been appointed commander-in-chief of the Bavarian army. This was the same Bronckhorst-Gronsfeld whom Holzapfel had fought at Hameln and Oldendorf while he was in Hessian service. Moreover, Bronckhorst-Gronsfeld enjoyed the strong support of Maximilian of Bavaria, who took an active role in strategic decisions. He also commanded more men. In comparison, Holzapfel's support from the Emperor was less perceptible. As a result, issues of precedence and personality seriously hampered co-operation within the joint command.

On 17 May 1648, such issues enabled the joint Swedish–French armies under Wrangel and Turenne to surprise Holzapfel's Imperial–Bavarian army at the village of Zusmarshausen, to the west of Augsburg.[210]

At the time, the Imperial–Bavarian army is estimated to have consisted of some 24,000 to 25,000 men, divided into an estimated 10,000 Imperials and 14,000 Bavarians.[211] By then, Wrangel and Turenne were technically outnumbered. Wrangel's army consisted of 15,000 men (10,500 horse and 4,500 foot), while Turenne had 7,000. In total, this made 22,000 men.[212]

However, at the time of the engagement at Zusmarshausen, the Swedish–French force was stronger in numbers, since Bronckhorst-Gronsfeld and the Bavarian units were marching along a different route, further to the south, so were mostly unavailable. Moreover, the Imperial–Bavarian army was impeded by camp followers, at the rate of four to one by some accounts. Wrangel, Turenne, and Königsmarck led nine cavalry squadrons (from six Swedish and three French regiments) on a forced march to take the enemy by surprise. In the following morning, they attacked the Imperial–Bavarian army soon after it had broken camp and marched out. It was a strategic rather than tactical surprise. Holzapfel received words about the enemy approach before the attack, but he did not realise the strength of the attackers. As a result, he ordered the experienced Raimondo Montecuccoli to cover the retreat with 3,300 men (2,500 horse and 800 musketeers) and four

208 *Från Femern och Jankow*, p.258.
209 *Ibid.*, p.264.
210 *Ibid.*, p.274; Tingsten, *De tre sista åren*, pp.48–52. A more thorough description is Birger Steckzén, "Arriärgardesstriden vid Zusmarshausen 7 maj 1648", *Historisk Tidskrift* 41 (1921), pp.135–48, on which Tingsten based his work.
211 Steckzén, "Arriärgardesstriden", p.136; Tingsten, *De tre sista åren*, p.48.
212 Mankell, *Uppgifter* 1, p.219; Tingsten, *De tre sista åren*, p.47.

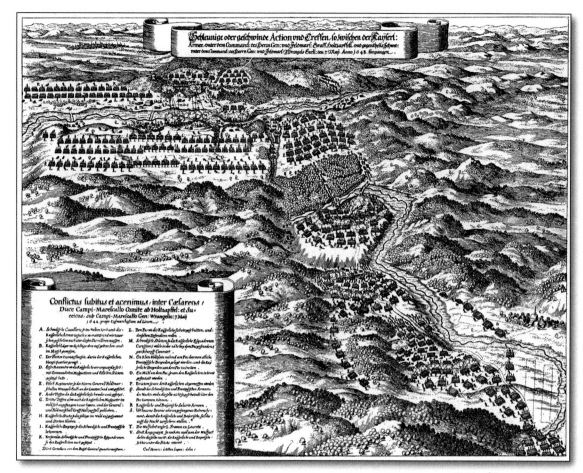

Battle of Zusmarshausen, 17 May 1648. (*Theatrum Europaeum*, after a drawing by Swedish quartermaster-general Cornelius von dem Busch)

cannons.[213] Montecuccoli began the action with a defiant Imperial salute (three cannon shots in rapid succession), then commenced what turned into a successful delaying action which lasted for four hours. Meanwhile, further up the road, Holzapfel had abatis prepared to provide a secure position from which his men could support Montecuccoli's retreat. He manned it with 400 horse, 500 musketeers, and two cannons, with himself in command.[214] In the ensuing attack Holzapfel was wounded, and when his men carried him off the field he was hit again, mortally this time. Montecuccoli then retreated to Landsberg-am-Lech, saving his men but abandoning the artillery and baggage. The Imperials and Bavarians lost some 1,900 to 2,200 dead, wounded, and prisoners. Bronckhorst-Gronsfeld, with the rest of the army, retreated to Augsburg, thus saving the army. He also, temporarily, assumed command of the combined Imperial and Bavarian army.[215]

213 *Från Femern och Jankow*, p.274; Tingsten, *De tre sista åren*, p.49. The General Staff work presumably copied Tingsten. In contrast, Steckzén, "Arriärgardesstriden", p.141, notes 1,500 horse, 800 musketeers, and four cannons. It would seem likely that either Steckzén or Tingsten made a typing error.

214 Steckzén, "Arriärgardesstriden", p.143; Tingsten, *De tre sista åren*, p.51.

215 *Från Femern och Jankow*, p.274; Steckzén, "Arriärgardesstriden", p.144.

After the battle, Bronckhorst-Gronsfeld attempted to defend the River Lech for several days. However, in late May the Swedish–French army successfully crossed the river, building a bridge at Rain, on the same spot where Gustavus Adolphus had crossed 16 years earlier. Bronckhorst-Gronsfeld retreated.[216]

This time Bavaria could not be saved. While Wrangel and Turenne overran Bavaria, devastating the territory, the Elector Maximilian fled with his court, ultimately all the way to Salzburg. Furthermore, Maximilian had Bronckhorst-Gronsfeld arrested for treason, since he had abandoned the defensive line along the Lech. However, Maximilian freed him in 1649, after which the general moved to Vienna to embark upon a diplomatic career.

The Emperor sent Piccolomini back from Spanish service and now the Duke of Amalfi, to assume command after the late Holzapfel. Piccolomini reorganised and reinforced the Imperial–Bavarian army in an attempt to rescue Bavaria. However, Bavaria was ravaged and out of supplies, while Wrangel and Turenne evaded open battle. Both sides awaited reinforcements. Besides, Piccolomini had orders not to move too far away from Austria, since the news from Bohemia were very bad (as will be shown, a Swedish army under Königsmarck occupied part of Prague in late July while Wittenberg took Tabor in August and threatened Linz, with the Imperial court, in September). In early October, Wrangel and Turenne left the devastated Bavaria. They returned across the Lech, then continued to Donauwörth, where they crossed the Danube. In early November, they received news about the peace agreement recently concluded in Westphalia. The Swedish army moved into the Franconian Circle, with headquarters in Schweinfurt. The French army returned to the Swabian Circle, with headquarters in Tübingen. Piccolomini, who received news about the peace at roughly the same time, returned to Austria.

Charles Gustavus Takes Command

Meanwhile, the Swedish armies in Germany had received a new commander-in-chief. In early June 1648, Christina appointed her 25-year-old cousin, Charles Gustavus (1622–1660), the Queen's Lieutenant General and commander-in-chief (*Generalissimus*) of the Swedish forces in Germany. Christina had planned this for several months, as a means to avoid marriage with him. Charles Gustavus received his instructions in mid June. He was ordered to cooperate with Field Marshal Wrangel and the newly appointed General Magnus Gabriel De la Gardie, who simultaneously was head of the Life Guard. Charles Gustavus should conserve his forces, yet "frighten" the enemy by moving as deep as possible into the Emperor's hereditary lands, Bohemia and Moravia. In addition, the war in Bavaria should be continued and Westphalia be kept safe. He should avoid uniting his forces with the French.[217] The instructions were guidelines, not direct orders, since Charles

---

216 *Från Femern och Jankow*, pp.299–300.
217 *Ibid.*, pp.287–90.

Gustavus was free to operate as the situation demanded, as long as he took counsel with Wrangel and the other generals. Wrangel was informed that the appointment was made "for higher reasons", with no blame on his conduct, and he was instructed to remain in Germany to assist Charles Gustavus.[218] In the end, there were no hard feelings. Charles Gustavus regarded Wrangel, nine years older, as his military mentor, and the two became close friends.

It was obvious that Christina wanted the army to act in support of the ongoing peace negotiations, by maintaining a strong presence and by acting as a deterrent on the Emperor by showing him what could be done, if he did not accept Sweden's demands. Christina had already made her position clear; she wanted peace and was in favour of the peace negotiations. However, her orders to Charles Gustavus show that she had no intention to appease the enemy. It would have to be a peace on Swedish terms.

Charles Gustavus, 1652 or 1653. (Sébastien Bourdon)

Charles Gustavus sailed from Dalarö in the southern Stockholm archipelago in mid July, together with the last national reinforcements sent to Germany during the war. These included some 2,700 horse, 4,300 foot, and 66 artillerymen. As before, some units were dispatched from other ports.[219] Ten days later, the fleet arrived in Germany, and Charles Gustavus landed at Wolgast. In early October, he rode into Prague with his 8,000 men.[220] Until then, Charles Gustavus had little opportunity to realise his position as commander-in-chief. Essentially, he had functioned as the commander of the reinforcements only.

The Siege of Prague

Meanwhile, a Swedish corps under Hans Christoph von Königsmarck had invaded Bohemia. Five days after the battle of Zusmarshausen, Wrangel dispatched Königsmarck to raid the Emperor's hereditary lands. What Wrangel had in mind was a two-pronged operation, so he also ordered Wittenberg to invade Bohemia from Silesia.[221]

Königsmarck left the Swedish main field army immediately, with only 1,500 horse: his own dragoon regiment and life company of horse and the four

218 Björn Asker, *Karl X Gustav* (Lund: Historiska Media, 2010), pp.88–9.
219 Mankell, *Uppgifter* 2, p.292; *Från Femern och Jankow*, pp.294–5. The unit list provided in the latter contains some errors but also includes more details on real numbers, since the available manpower did not always correspond to plans.
220 *Från Femern och Jankow*, pp.57–60, 295; Tingsten, *De tre sista åren*, p.62.
221 *Från Femern och Jankow*, p.307.

Ernst Odowalsky.

Rudolf von Colloredo-Waldsee. (Attributed to Frans Luyckx; Skokloster Castle)

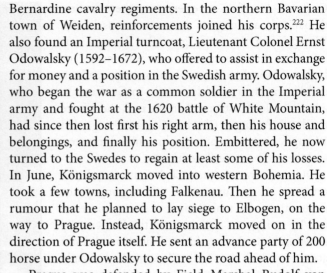

Bernardine cavalry regiments. In the northern Bavarian town of Weiden, reinforcements joined his corps.[222] He also found an Imperial turncoat, Lieutenant Colonel Ernst Odowalsky (1592–1672), who offered to assist in exchange for money and a position in the Swedish army. Odowalsky, who began the war as a common soldier in the Imperial army and fought at the 1620 battle of White Mountain, had since then lost first his right arm, then his house and belongings, and finally his position. Embittered, he now turned to the Swedes to regain at least some of his losses. In June, Königsmarck moved into western Bohemia. He took a few towns, including Falkenau. Then he spread a rumour that he planned to lay siege to Elbogen, on the way to Prague. Instead, Königsmarck moved on in the direction of Prague itself. He sent an advance party of 200 horse under Odowalsky to secure the road ahead of him.

Prague was defended by Field Marshal Rudolf von Colloredo-Waldsee (1585–1657), who had previously distinguished himself in the Mantua war and at the battle of Lützen. Although he had only 1,000 soldiers, they were reinforced by perhaps 10,000 to 12,000 burgher militia.[223] However, their combat readiness was low, there were no defensive patrols, and the general belief among the defenders was that Prague was safe. After all, Swedish armies had passed through before, under commanders as formidable as Banér and Torstensson, but none had brought a sufficiently strong army to lay siege to the large city. Königsmarck's small corps would surely not make the attempt. Moreover, Colloredo-Waldsee thought that Königsmarck's corps was on its way to another target, either Elbogen or perhaps Melnik, where he could join forces with Wittenberg, who was on his way from Silesia.

But it was not a siege that Königsmarck had in mind when he closed in on Prague with 2,000 horse and 1,000 foot. The infantry, all of them musketeers, had been mounted on artillery and baggage horses so that they could keep up with the cavalry. All baggage and artillery were left behind, guarded by 200 dragoons. Moving rapidly, the corps only halted a few hours from Prague. There the men rested until about 8:00 p.m. Then, under cover of darkness, they approached the sleeping city.[224]

Odowalsky had prepared lists of all the palaces around Prague Castle and their owners. The palaces were

---

222 *Ibid.*, p.307; Tingsten, *De tre sista åren*, p.59.
223 *Från Femern och Jankow*, p.309.
224 On the siege of Prague, see *Från Femern och Jankow*, pp.307–323; Hedberg, *Kungl. Artilleriet*, pp.261–2. For a more recent work, see Lars Ericson, "Prag 1648", Lars Ericson et al., *Svenska slagfält* (np: Wahlström & Widstrand, 2003), pp.181–8.

all located on the west side of the River Moldau, which was known as the *Kleinseite* ("small side"). Königsmarck intended to take all of them in a surprise attack, so that the rich booty inside could be secured. Königsmarck issued an order that all who were found bearing arms should be killed, and anybody who appeared in a window should be shot. During the night, the strike force moved against its targets, which also included the western base of the stone bridge across the River Moldau (modern-day Charles Bridge), so as to prevent reinforcements from the city on the east side of the river. Odowalsky led the vanguard, 100 musketeers armed with snaphance or possibly wheellock muskets that could be carried cocked and ready to fire, even if held concealed under one's clothes, and which did not give a tell-tale light and smell.

The attack began before dawn, around 2:30 a.m. It was the 26 July 1648, the very same day Charles Gustavus's fleet arrived in Germany.

The daring operation was an astounding success. Königsmarck's men rapidly gained control of the entire *Kleinseite*. Colloredo-Waldsee was almost caught in the assault. He had to flee through his garden and vineyard to climb over the city wall before he found a boat that took him across the river. For two days, the soldiers looted Prague Castle and the palaces, which were full of valuables, famous objects of art, and books, including the personal collection of the late Emperor Rudolf II. The haul was immense. Some contemporary accounts estimated its value to some seven million Reichsthalers. This was the richest booty ever acquired by any Swedish army. But from a military perspective, the intruders also got hold of all artillery in Prague, between 60 and 70 cannons with plenty of munitions. Königsmarck soon had his men open fire on the city on the other side of the river with the captured artillery.

Colloredo-Waldsee was unable to prevent Prague Castle from falling to the Swedes. However, it could have been worse for the Imperials. At the time when Königsmarck and Odowalsky made their initial plans in Weiden, Emperor Ferdinand III stayed in Prague Castle. The raid can also be seen in this light, as yet another attempt to strike at the very head of enemy resistance, in the manner first attempted by Banér. But the Emperor had already moved on when the Swedes arrived. Besides, the city of Prague itself, on the eastern side of the River Moldau, held out. Significant Imperial reinforcements, seven regiments of horse under Field Marshal Hans Christopher von Buchheim, arrived already on the day after Königsmarck's assault, raising the number of Imperial regulars to some 4,000 to 5,000.[225] Nonetheless, Colloredo-Waldsee's continuous and bold defence of the city of Prague halted the Swedish invasion of Bohemia and saved the ancestral Habsburg lands in Austria. Thus, Colloredo-Waldsee saved the Empire twice: first by delaying the Swedish attack at Lützen, which may have been the decisive factor in Gustavus Adolphus losing his life in the battle, and second by halting Königsmarck's offensive into the very heart of the Empire.

Still, four days after Königsmarck's assault, Wittenberg brought further Swedish reinforcements from Silesia: some 3,500 men, 16 cannons, and

---

225 *Från Femern och Jankow*, p.319.

two mortars.[226] Within days, he continued south towards Tabor, which he stormed in late August. Tabor was another refuge for the wealthy, for which reason the conquest resulted in a rich booty. However, the operation against Tabor, beyond Prague and further to the south, was carried out because of orders from Wrangel and was primarily a means to increase pressure on Piccolomini. Having taken Tabor, Wittenberg returned to Prague. However, in September he set out again, this time with an all-mounted corps (possibly 4,000 horse and eight cannons) towards Budweis which was located even further south than Tabor. By the Swedish accounts, this was a continuation of the policy to apply pressure on Piccolomini. The plan succeeded, and Imperial units were diverted to Budweis. However, the Imperial command in Austria believed that Wittenberg would continue all the way to Linz, to disrupt the Imperial supply lines, encourage revolts among the Austrian peasants, and possibly even attempt the capture of the Emperor, who was in Linz.[227]

Meanwhile, Königsmarck was in the unusual position of laying siege to one of the largest cities of the Empire with a force that was significantly smaller than that of the defenders, perhaps only half their number. In fact, Colloredo-Waldsee had felt sufficiently strong to dispatch Buchheim with some cavalry to the south after Wittenberg, to prevent him from threatening southern Bohemia (a plan that did not end well; in late September Buchheim was surprised, defeated, and captured by Wittenberg).

But the discrepancy in numbers between besiegers and besieged would soon change. In early October, Charles Gustavus brought reinforcements, an additional 6,000 men (3,000 horse and 3,000 foot) and plenty of artillery (2 twenty-four-pounders, six 12-pounders, eight 3-pounders, eight petards, and 1,000 hand grenades). The infantry included the Life Guard under Magnus Gabriel De la Gardie and several national units, including a battalion from the Södermanland Regiment under its colonel, the Estonian noble Johann von Vietinghoff (1580–1685), and squadrons from the Småland, Västgöta, and Karelian Cavalry Regiments.[228] In comparison, the Imperial regulars in Prague by then had been reduced to 1,200–1,300 horse and 1,400 foot.[229]

The Swedish army built a new bridge across the Moldau so that they could attack the city from the east. On 13 October, the Swedes made the first attempt to storm Prague. However, the burgher militia, stiffened by Colloredo-Waldsee's few remaining soldiers, university students, and even monks, held on tenaciously, pushing back the Swedes. A second assault on 25 October was pushed back, too.

Total Swedish casualties at Prague from July to October were relatively few, only some 500 to 700 men (including one officer, a lieutenant, and seven soldiers who fell during the initial assault on the west side). The defenders lost 130 dead during the initial assault, and, during the subsequent fighting,

---

226 *Ibid.*, p.317.
227 *Ibid.*, pp.321–2.
228 *Ibid.*, p.325; citing a letter from Charles Gustavus to Wittenberg, 20 August 1648 (O.S.).
229 *Ibid.*, p.326; citing archive documents in Prague.

The Swedish siege of Prague, 1648. (*Theatrum Europaeum*)

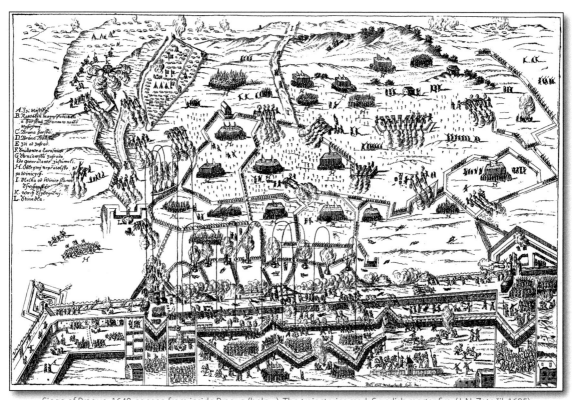

Siege of Prague, 1648, as seen from inside Prague (below). The trajectories mark Swedish mortar fire. (J. N. Zatočil, 1685)

219 dead and 475 wounded according to Bohemian records, which might be incomplete.[230]

A number of Swedish soldiers who later would achieve prominence fought in the siege of Prague. One of them was Claes Uggla (1614–1676), who later would make a name for himself as an admiral. The army officer at Prague in time became one of the most experienced Swedish senior naval officers.

The fighting in Prague continued until rumours of the peace agreement in Westphalia reached the city in early November. By then, Charles Gustavus had left Königsmarck and Wittenberg in command at Prague; however, when he on the following day learnt of the peace agreement, he immediately hurried back to Prague to end the fighting. An armistice was agreed. With confirmation of the news a few days later, hostilities finally ceased.

The Peace of Westphalia

The loss of Bavaria at Zusmarshausen in May, the ongoing siege of Prague from July onwards, and a further loss at Lens on the French front (where the Prince of Condé defeated Archduke Leopold William who then commanded the Spanish Army of Flanders) in August 1648 finally broke Emperor Ferdinand III's will to fight. The Emperor agreed to sign a peace treaty.

By then, peace negotiations had been ongoing for considerable time. The Swedish delegation was headed by Johan Oxenstierna, the son of Chancellor Axel Oxenstierna, who was assisted by Johan Adler Salvius.

Johan Oxenstierna.

The Peace of Westphalia confirmed Sweden's new status as a great power. In northern Germany, Sweden gained control over the Oder, Weser, and Elbe estuaries. On the southern Baltic Sea shore, the territorial gains encompassed the important port of Wismar, with the districts of Poel and Neukloster, and the entire western Pomerania (*Vorpommern*) with the island of Rügen and the port of Stralsund. Sweden also acquired the westernmost part of eastern Pomerania (*Hinterpommern*) with the towns of Stettin, Gartz, and, on the eastern bank of the Oder, Damm and Gollnow. In addition, Sweden received the islands of Usedom and Wollin. On the North Sea, Sweden secured the bishoprics (now transformed into secular duchies) of Bremen and Verden (except the town of Bremen itself), with the port of Stade, and the district of Wildeshausen. Through these acquisitions, Sweden became an Estate of the Empire, with the right to admission to the Imperial Diet (*Reichstag*). Sweden also accepted a restitution of five million Reichsthalers (1.8 million in cash, 1.2 million in assignations within one year, and two million in assignations within two years).By the

---

230 *Från Femern och Jankow*, p.337; Ericson, "Prag 1648", pp.181, 187; Ericson Wolke, Larsson; and Villstrand, *Trettioåriga kriget*, p.180.

time of the peace agreement, Sweden had also acquired its first colony, New Sweden in North America, and was in the process of establishing a colony in West Africa.

The Swedish assault on and siege of Prague was one of those events which, in hindsight, appear deeply symbolic of the conflict as a whole. From the Swedish perspective, it is suggestive that the sudden raid, the last of the war, resulted in the richest booty ever taken by a Swedish army. After all, the Thirty Years' War was characterised by the systematic looting of everything from supplies to everyday goods to valuables needed to pay for the war effort. In Prague, the booty consisted not only, or mainly, of supplies and money. The vast collection of art treasures and books which the Habsburgs had amassed over the centuries, throughout the empire and beyond, and often as war booty, was now transferred to Sweden, where much of it remains in private and public collections to this day.

Johan Adler Salvius.

Besides, from the perspective of the inhabitants of Prague, it is telling that those burghers and Bohemian nobles who in 1618 had risen in revolt on behalf of the Protestant faith, 30 years later fought yet harder, and ultimately more successfully, on behalf of the Empire and its Catholic Emperor. A man in their midst was Jaroslav von Martinitz (Czech: Jaroslav Bořitaz Martinic; 1582–1649). On 23 May 1618, Martinitz was one of those Catholic council members who barely survived being thrown out of a window in Prague Castle in the incident subsequently known as the Defenestration of Prague, which marked the outbreak of the Bohemian Revolt and the Thirty Years' War. Later, the Emperor rewarded Martinitz with an appointment as governor of Bohemia. However, when Swedish soldiers before dawn on 26 July 1648 broke into his palace, they badly manhandled Martinitz who, moreover, suffered a rapier wound in the hip. Thus, Martinitz became the victim not only of the first act of aggression during the Thirty Years' War, but also of the final act of organised warfare. Although badly wounded, he survived the final act, too.

Demobilisation

After the war, Sweden had to demobilise most of its military forces in Germany. The Imperial army, under Piccolomini, and the Bavarian one would have to demobilise, too.[231] Only the French army, still at war with Spain, faced no such needs. Everybody at the peace negotiations knew that demobilisation would be no easy task for either party, and that it would be expensive and time-consuming. The Crown had incurred many debts during

---

231 On demobilisation, see Antje Oschmann, *Der Nürnberger Exekutionstag 1649–1650: Das Ende des Dreißigjährigen Krieges in Deutschland* (Münster: Aschendorff, 1991). For details on the final pay to those soldiers who were paid off, see *Ibid.*, pp.650–1, 656–7. The senior commanders received significant monetary compensation, too. *Ibid*, pp.658–9.

the war, and even with the restitution agreed upon, there was no way to settle all debts. The Crown did not only owe money to merchants who had paid for supplying the war effort but had also incurred considerable debt to those generals, colonels, and other types of military entrepreneurs who had supplied men and fought on the German battlefields. Eventually, the Crown found no other means to pay them than to transfer land ownership, in Germany and the conquered province of Halland but also in Sweden and Finland. These lands became alienated noble lands, free of taxation. As a short-term solution, this was beneficial to the Crown. However, in due time the alienation of land would cause significant stress to the Crown's finances.

Besides, somebody also had to pay off the common soldiers. Most Swedish soldiers were Germans who knew no other trade than soldiering. Some were Protestant exiles from Bohemia and Austria, who had no home to which they could return. A few were Bernardines, who no longer had any hope of a separate military identity, nor of lands of their own, which had been Bernard of Saxe-Weimar's original motivation.

Besides, Charles Gustavus, the new commander-in-chief, was ambitious and warlike, and not eager for peace. Nonetheless, he accepted the considerable task of demobilising the army in Germany. His principal counterpart was Piccolomini, who had the same duty with regard to the Imperial forces. It was not only hard work, and the two became friends. Besides, in early 1649, Charles Gustavus during a visit to Kassel met Emilie (1626–1693), the oldest daughter of Landgravine Amalie Elisabeth of Hesse-Kassel. Emilie had inherited the beauty and intellect of her mother, and she was recently married to Henri Charles de La Trémoille (1620–1672), Prince of Taranto. Nonetheless, Charles Gustavus and Emilie became good friends and continued to exchange letters for some time. Still, demobilisation took up most of Charles Gustavus's time. By September 1649, Charles Gustavus, Wrangel, and Piccolomini were able to celebrate that they had agreed on a demobilisation plan. Charles Gustavus entertained the group at a Peace Banquet in Nuremberg, during which the delighted Wrangel fired off his pistol at the ceiling, stating that since it was now peace, he had no further use for ammunition.

Meanwhile, Charles Gustavus showed that he was up to the task of handling the huge Swedish army in Germany. Without him, it is unlikely that the agreed-upon demobilisation process would have taken place as well as it did. He dismissed supernumerary officers (some of whom did not exist; a common occurrence in the enlisted units). He reorganised incomplete companies into new ones (thereby reducing their number to 403, from more than twice as many before reduction[232]), thus reconciling the actual and nominal strength of the army. Those regiments which he suspected of disloyalty or mutinous tendencies were broken up, with the men scattered in different districts. Those mutinies which actually occurred, at Überlingen, Neumarkt, Langenargen, Mainau, Eger, and Schweinfurt, were suppressed. Some of the unrest took place because the soldiers in these garrisons, having

---

232 Tingsten, *De tresistaåren*, p.87.

Carl Gustav Wrangel, 1652.
After the war, 38 years old,
and painted by a skilled artist,
Wrangel presents an almost
regal posture in this equestrian
portrait. (David Klöcker
Ehrenstrahl)

put down roots there, refused to be redeployed to Pomerania, or God forbid, distant Sweden. Most of the men who were ordered to march to Pomerania for continued service deserted along the way. Of those enlisted units which Charles Gustavus planned to retain, it was only the Life Guard which could be maintained at establishment strength. By 1650, when most of the demobilisation had taken place, Sweden retained only 4,100 enlisted soldiers in Germany. This included Wrangel's Regiment, the Old Blue, which was the last of the old regiments enlisted under Gustavus Adolphus. It retained the name Blue Regiment until 1652, when the regiment formally was dissolved.[233] Although the mutual demobilisation process in its essentials progressed smoothly, a number of contended bases remained until quite late. The last Swedish garrison to leave the non-Swedish territories in Germany was the one at Vechta in Westphalia, which departed only in May 1654. Until then, Vechta was retained as a guarantee for unpaid debts.[234]

233 Lars Ericson, *Krig och krigsmakt under svensk stormaktstid* (Lund: Historiska Media, 2004), p.125.
234 Asker, *Karl X Gustav*, p.98.

2

Raising the Swedish Army

The systems and organisations already put in place to raise the Swedish army during the reign of Gustavus Adolphus (and described in the previous volume) remained and continued to function for the duration of the war.

Nonetheless, minor changes were introduced to fine-tune the means of raising troops. In 1635 the conscription rate of 1 in 10 for both crown and noble peasants, first introduced in 1627, was abandoned. It was replaced by a conscription rate of 1 in 15 for crown peasants and 1 in 30 for noble peasants. However, the quotas were again increased already in 1636, to 1 in 10 and 1 in 20, respectively. Since the quotas favoured peasants who worked for nobles, an increasing number of rural men soon turned to the nobility for employment, thus reducing their risk of conscription. Over time, the Crown accordingly did not receive as many conscripts as in the past.[1]

While the quotas primarily favoured the nobility, who lost fewer workmen to conscription, in 1642 the system for raising conscripts was amended in a manner which found greater popular acceptance. Henceforth, groups of farms were responsible for supporting a soldier who served for life. Where formerly the quota had been calculated by head (*bondetal*), henceforth it was calculated by farmstead (*gårdatal*). Although the number of troops to be conscripted was unchanged, the new system allowed more flexibility. Besides, the farmstead organisation, unlike the previous organisation into groups of 10 men, was permanent. The system thus became more stable.[2] For Crown peasants, the farmstead organisation consisted of 10 farms, while for noble peasants, it comprised 20 farms. Better-off peasants could hire a substitute in advance.

Nonetheless, conscription was again on the rise in the 1640s. In Finland, for instance, conscription took place every year from 1640 to 1648, with the sole exception of 1646. The annual intake was from 3,700 to 5,200 new soldiers.[3]

A key problem with fresh conscripts was that they were unused to the diseases that thrived in the German towns and in the field army. This

---

1   Petri, *Kungl. Första livgrenadjärregementets historia* 2, pp.245–6.
2   Tom Gullberg and Mikko Huhtamies, *På vakt i öster* 3 (np: Schildts, 2004), p.199.
3   Ericson Wolke, Larsson; and Villstrand, *Trettioåriga kriget*, p.266.

shortcoming did not necessarily apply to the officers, who were often veterans. Many officers, including in the national regiments, were Scots or Germans who had spent years on campaign. Not so the recent conscripts. Each batch of conscripts needed a period of acclimatisation in one of the Baltic shore garrisons in Germany, before the men had a reasonable chance to survive campaign conditions. However, the reality of acclimatisation was grim; it entailed a large share of the fresh conscripts dying within less than a year. There was little that contemporary medicine could do to ameliorate the situation. From the Crown's perspective, a significant share of fresh conscripts would rapidly die, "like flies" in the words of Gustavus Adolphus, regardless of how and where they were deployed. In fairness, the death rate of rural people moving into Swedish towns was high, too, for the same reason. Rural farming communities were generally more isolated, so country people had less resistance to disease than townsmen. Yet, while acclimatising in the shore garrisons, the fresh conscripts would, while they lasted, serve to uphold Swedish rule there. If needed, the survivors could later be sent as reinforcements to the field army. It was a harsh calculation but one caused by necessity and the realities of its time.

War conditions naturally affected the budgetary plans laid in Stockholm. The demands of the ongoing war together with political ambitions among leading individuals tended to drive army size beyond what the state could afford. The rank and file needed to secure regular income and sustenance. When pay was not forthcoming, mutinies and pay strikes were common.

This was particularly noticeable among enlisted troops. While not necessarily disloyal, it was understood that they served in exchange for pay. Most had no other source of providing for themselves or their families. When the army was not paid reasonably regularly, it would mutiny. An army mutiny was essentially a labour strike, which might last until the men received some satisfaction. We have seen how in 1635, the German colonels of the Swedish army in Germany held Axel Oxenstierna as a de facto hostage in their camp near Magdeburg for some time because of the arrears of pay owed them. He had to promise that if they had not been paid when a peace agreement was signed, they could come to Sweden to collect the money owed.

The mutinies were exceptional situations in the Swedish army. However, the lack of resources and often money to pay the enlisted troops resulted in frequent breakdowns in discipline, command, and control that were less serious than a mutiny but still affected operations. Senior commanders such as Banér freely admitted as much in his reports to Oxenstierna (to explain his need for cash, for sure). For instance, in November 1636 Banér wrote that "Quartermaster Ramm has stayed behind in Mecklenburg without my previous knowledge."[4] And then in March 1638, about the troops, "I could do no more than promise [to pay] them again and again in Her Majesty's name with the most plausible excuses I could think of." In the same letter, Banér added that the infantrymen habitually threw away their weapons while on the march and exchanged their equipment for food.[5] In May 1638, he

4 Banér to Oxenstierna, 19 November 1636 (O.S.), *AOSB* 2:6, pp.339–53, on p.349.
5 Banér to Oxenstierna, 18 March 1638 (O.S.), *AOSB*2:6, pp.525–32, on pp.529, 530.

reported that there no longer was any discipline in the army.[6] The situation did not improve over time. In April 1641, Banér again noted, this time on the strength of his units: "There would be no serious gaps in their numbers if only the stragglers, plunderers, and robbers, whose irresponsibility there is no means of checking, would return to the ranks."[7]

Sweden's Military Strength

Although Sweden had substantial military forces in Germany, the Swedish Crown also needed to maintain garrisons and field units in the Swedish–Finnish heartland and in the overseas possessions of Estonia, Livonia, and Ingria. Before the 1635 Truce of Stuhmsdorf, the Polish-Lithuanian Commonwealth remained a serious threat, against which significant numbers of men had to be held in readiness both in the heartland and overseas, including in Prussia. A latent threat from the Commonwealth remained even thereafter, since Ladislaus IV of Poland still claimed the Swedish Crown. As a result, Oxenstierna was careful not deploy too many men in Germany, at least not when it seemed unnecessary in relation to the existing enlisted units and certainly not before the Truce of Stuhmsdorf. Most of the national troops were retained in Sweden, Finland, and in the Swedish possessions to the east of the Baltic Sea.

So, how many armed men could Sweden field when all resources were taken into account? To calculate Sweden's total military forces, the bulk of Sweden's national troops, those outside Germany, must be included. As noted, the field armies in Germany primarily consisted of men enlisted on the Continent.

In 1644, when Sweden was engaged in ongoing operations in both Germany and Denmark and had mobilised for war on both fronts, the Crown still expected to raise the total number of national troops to some 54,000 soldiers and 6,000 sailors. Of these, 26,000 men would be deployed in Sweden: 17,800 men in field units (4,600 horse, 500 dragoons, and 12,700 foot), and another 8,200 in garrisons. A total of 11,200 men were to be deployed in Estonia, Livonia, and Ingria or were already there (4,800 in field units and 6,400 in garrisons). In addition, a total of 13,700 men (1,500 horse and 12,200 foot) were planned for deployment in Germany or were already there, where they would serve together with the enlisted units that had been raised in Germany (roughly 30,000 men, of which about half served in garrisons[8]). Finally, from 3,300 to 3,700 soldiers would be embarked on warships, to support the at least 6,000 sailors who served as sailing crews. Although we do not know whether all the planned units were formed, the records show that the manpower existed, and that there even was a small

---

6   Banér to Oxenstierna, 7 May 1638 (O.S.), *AOSB* 2:6, pp.536–41, on p.538.
7   Banér to Oxenstierna, 22 March 1641 (O.S.), *AOSB* 2:6, pp.838–42, on p.840.
8   For further discussion on the number of Swedish soldiers, see Mankell, *Uppgifter* 1, pp.232–3.

surplus of available men.[9] This means that all told, Sweden by then had some 90,000 men under arms. Furthermore, this was sustainable and no desperate measure taken in extreme need. We have seen that the war with Denmark was something that the Swedish regency government went into voluntarily, and in full knowledge of what it would entail. The mobilisation was thoroughly planned and was in no way regarded as a national emergency.

In the end, the numbers actually deployed for the war with Denmark and Norway were somewhat smaller than envisaged. We have seen that Horn's field army which moved into Scania consisted of 10,600 men while Henrik Fleming's corps which invaded Jämtland consisted of no more than 1,400.

It is thus clear that Oxenstierna and his associates even when engaged in foreign campaigns were careful always to maintain a substantial force of reliable soldiers in readiness to defend Sweden's core territories.

This pattern of force management came to prevail for the rest of the war. In 1645, the field armies in Germany and Jutland consisted of some 28,500 men. Of these, Torstensson's main field army accounted for some 15,600 men in total (8,130 cavalry, 400 dragoons, and 6,135 foot, plus officers). Königsmarck's army consisted of a total of 8,500 men (3,750 cavalry, 330 dragoons, and 3,950 foot, plus officers), while Helmuth Wrangel, in Jutland, had some 4,700 men in total (2,820 cavalry, 650 dragoons, and 880 foot, plus officers). At the same time, there were some 16,250 men in garrisons. In total, the Swedish forces in Germany then accounted for some 45,000 men.[10]

After the war with Denmark, Sweden demobilised some national troops. However, the number of Swedish national troops in Germany rose to yet higher levels. In 1647, when the total number of national troops, including the estimated number of fresh conscripts, had been reduced from 54,000 to 48,759 men (11,410 horse and 37,349 foot), the number that were or would be deployed in Germany was raised to some 18,200.[11]

In early 1648, the total Swedish military forces in Germany consisted of some 63,000 men. Of these, some 37,500 men served in the field army, while 25,500 men served in garrisons. Of the total, about 17,700 were national troops while the rest were enlisted on the Continent.[12] About a third served as cavalry, and two thirds as infantry. For obvious reasons, garrisons consisted of infantry and the occasional dragoons. National troops constituted a quarter of the field army and a third of the Swedish garrison troops in Germany (Table 8).

---

9   Mankell, *Uppgifter* 1, p.185; Mankell, *Uppgifter* 2, pp.275–8; citing data from 1644. Not all figures add up, so either there were printing errors, Mankell miscalculated, or the original documents contain minor errors.

10   Mankell, *Uppgifter* 1, p.200; Mankell, *Uppgifter* 2, pp.278–82. Again, his reprinted documents seem to include some printing errors, and in addition, the number of officers has to be estimated.

11   Mankell, *Uppgifter* 1, p.209; Mankell, *Uppgifter* 2, pp.287–91.

12   Mankell, *Uppgifter* 1, p.222; Mankell, *Uppgifter* 2, pp.293–7.

Table 8. Swedish military forces in Germany, early 1648. (Source: Mankell *Uppgifter* 2, pp.293–7)

Type	Field Armies	Garrisons
Cavalry		
National	3,058	–
Enlisted	17,678	–
Dragoons	2,085	–
Dragoons	–	560
Infantry		
National	6,070	–
Enlisted	8,620	–
National	–	8,616
Enlisted	–	16,264
Total	**37,511**	**25,440**
Cavalry	20,736	
Dragoons	2,645	
Infantry	39,570	
Total	**62,951**	
National	17,744	
Enlisted	45,206	
Total	**62,951**	

It follows that when the Thirty Years' War ended, Sweden's total military might have exceeded 110,000 men, deployed at home and abroad. It needs to be emphasised that regardless of Oxenstierna's hopes to the contrary, Sweden could not pay for such numbers based on the extraction of land resources in the theatres of operations. Nor did the erratically paid out foreign subsidies cover more than a minor share of the expenses. The war did not feed itself. As a result, the burden of war fell on the Swedish taxpaying population. Nonetheless, for the purpose of peace negotiations and the division of spoils, it was the Swedish military presence in Germany that counted, so the number of soldiers was maintained.

In 1648, the Swedish military forces in Germany consisted of no less than 85 regiments of horse, of a total of 438 companies, and 60 regiments of foot, of a total of 477 companies. In total, Sweden controlled 915 companies distributed among field armies and 119 garrisons throughout Germany.[13]

In comparison, France had, on German soil, only 14 regiments of horse, of a total of 126 companies, and 11 regiments of foot, of a total of 306 companies, that is, a grand total of 432 companies. Hesse had five regiments of horse, of a total of 58 companies, and 13 regiments of foot, of a total of 166 companies, that is, a grand total of 224 companies.

---

13   *Amore pacis: Geographische Carten von gantz Teuttschlandt* (1648), prepared on behalf of the Swedish supreme commander in Germany. For a modern study based on more data but with similar conclusions, see Antje Oschmann, *Der Nürnberger Exekutionstag 1649–1650: Das Ende des Dreißigjährigen Krieges in Deutschland* (Münster: Aschendorff, 1991), pp.550–67.

Although we only know the number of companies, not their individual strength, it is clear that on German soil, Oxenstierna controlled more than twice as many soldiers as Mazarin, indeed more men than France and Hesse together.[14] It is easy to assume France to be the controlling power in the war, since France had a large population, was wealthy, and paid subsidies to its allies. However, when France joined the war in 1635, the country had few experienced soldiers and professional commanders. In comparison, the Spanish and Imperial armies had years of combat experience. France had simply been at peace for too long. While there had been Huguenot rebellions and minor wars in Italy and Lorraine, such actions could not compare to the professionally conducted operations then ongoing in Germany. Moreover, France had to fight on several fronts at the same time, dividing its strength between Spain, Italy, and the Netherlands. It could not focus as strongly on Germany as well. As a result, France needed Sweden as much as Sweden needed France. With regard to manpower, in 1648 it was the Swedish, not the French, army which was the dominant force in Germany. Moreover, Sweden retained significant military forces in its Scandinavian heartland and Baltic possessions.

Besides, the contribution of the Hessian army to the anti-Habsburg alliance should be noted. At the time of the Peace of Westphalia, Amalie Elisabeth, the Regent of Hesse-Kassel, was the third most powerful ruler within the alliance, after Oxenstierna and Mazarin. She was also the only ruler of a German state which, like Sweden, received a compensation payment for its part in the war.

---

14 The French army in Germany has been estimated to have consisted of 21,000 men, while the Hessian army similarly has been estimated as some 11,000. *Från Femern och Jankow*, p.383.

3

Army Organisation

Central Organisation

Gustavus Adolphus and Oxenstierna had begun the process of establishing properly authorised government departments, including a department of war, to which the King would delegate his authority already in the late 1610s. However, the process had been slow, and it was only on 15 June 1630, immediately before his departure to Germany, that Gustavus Adolphus established a formal department for military affairs. Known as the War Council or War Court (Swedish: *Krigsrådet, Krigsrätten*), the department was led by the Grand Marshal of the Realm (*Riksmarsk*), Jacob De la Gardie, and at first primarily functioned as a supreme military court.

The introduction of a fully developed system of administration was not completed until the formal adoption of the Instrument of Government of 1634, which effectively became Sweden's first constitution. The Instrument of Government formalised the position of the great officers of state, that is, the five leading members of the Swedish Council of the Realm (who also constituted the regency government before the Queen came of age). These were, in order of precedence, the Lord High Justiciar (*Riksdrots*), the Grand Marshal of the Realm (*Riksmarsk*), the Grand Admiral of the Realm (*Riksamiral*), the Lord High Chancellor (*Rikskansler*), and the Lord High Treasurer (*Riksskattmästare*). With the constitution of 1634, each of these five officers became the head of a distinct department of government, each known as a *collegium*. The second of these was the Department of War (*Krigscollegium*), responsible for the administration of the army.[1]

The Provincial Regiments

In early 1633, Oxenstierna sent the regency government a proposal on a form or instrument of Government, that is, the organisation of the Swedish government as a whole, which he had previously discussed with the late

---

1   The others were the Supreme Court, Admiralty, Chancery, and Exchequer.

King. Earlier drafts had existed since the 1620s, so while some details may have been new, the idea was not. For the army, the proposal entailed a return to the old peacetime territorial regiment organisation, from which field regiments of foot would be raised. He also proposed a return to the old organisation of six territorial regiments in Sweden and three in Finland.[2] However, soon Oxenstierna's opinion on the matter changed, and in late 1633, he proposed a radically different organisation. Oxenstierna now proposed an organisation of 12 regiments of foot in Sweden and six in Finland. He proposed that these regiments each would consist of 1,600 men, divided into eight companies with a strength of 200 men. From this organisation, a field organisation consisting of companies with a strength of 150 men would be raised.[3] However, Oxenstierna went further. He also suggested that the concept of peacetime organisation should be abolished, and the 18 regiments of foot even in peacetime would be organised into companies of 150 men. Then the entire army would be ready at once, without any time-consuming reorganisation, when war broke out. In effect, this entailed a reduction in the number of men. On the other hand, Oxenstierna also proposed the use of 10 enlisted regiments and a few additional enlisted companies, in total consisting of 12,300 men. The enlisted units would be based in Estonia, Livonia, and Prussia.[4] Following some discussion in the regency government, in 1634 an organisation of 20 infantry regiments was adopted as part of the Instrument of Government of 1634.[5]

The Instrument of Government of 1634 directed that the army should consist of 20 infantry regiments (13 in Sweden and seven in Finland) and eight cavalry regiments (five in Sweden and three in Finland).[6] As before, each cavalry regiment should have an establishment strength of 1,000 horses, divided into eight companies each of 125 horses. Two cavalry companies constituted a cavalry squadron, from which follows that a squadron had a nominal strength of 250 horses. Likewise, each infantry regiment should consist of 1,200 men, divided into eight infantry companies each of 150 men. Four infantry companies constituted a battalion, from which follows that a battalion had a nominal strength of 600 men.[7]

The regiments were noted in the order of seniority in Table 9.

2   Petri, *Kungl. Första livgrenadjärregementets historia* 2, pp.192–3; G. B. C:son Barkman, *Gustaf II Adolfs regementsorganisation vid det inhemska infanteriet: En studie över organisationens tillkomst och huvuddragen av dess utveckling mot bakgrunden av kontinental organisation* (Stockholm: Meddelanden från Generalstabens krigshistoriska avdelning, 1931), p.195.

3   Petri, *Kungl. Första livgrenadjärregementets historia* 2, p.193; Barkman, *Gustaf II Adolfs regementsorganisation*, p.197.

4   Petri, *Kungl. Första livgrenadjärregementets historia* 2, p.194; Barkman, *Gustaf II Adolfs regementsorganisation*, p.198.

5   § 31, Instrument of Government (1634). See also Barkman, *Gustaf II Adolfs regementsorganisation*, p.200.

6   § 31, Instrument of Government (1634).

7   Petri, *Kungl. Första livgrenadjärregementets historia* 2, p.195.

Table 9. The provincial regiments, 1634. (Source: Instrument of Government, 1634)

Regiment	Geographical area	Later Known As
Cavalry		
The Retinue of Nobles (*Adelsfanan*)	Sweden and Finland	The Retinue of Nobles in Sweden and Finland
Uppland, Västmanland, Närke, and Värmland Cavalry Regiment (*Upplands, Västmanlands, Närke och Värmlands ryttare*)	Central Sweden	Life Regiment of Horse
Västgöta and Dal Cavalry Regiment (*Västgöta och Dals ryttare*)	Västergötland and Dal, Sweden	Västgöta Cavalry Regiment
Finland Cavalry Regiment (*Finlands ryttare*)	Åbo County and Satakunta, Finland	Åbo and Björneborg Cavalry Regiment
Småland and Öland Cavalry Regiment (*Smålands och Ölands ryttare*)	Småland and Öland, Sweden	Småland Cavalry Regiment
Tavastland and Nyland Cavalry Regiment (*Tavastelands och Nylands ryttare*)	Tavastland and Nyland, Finland	Nyland and Tavastehus Cavalry Regiment
Östergötland and Södermanland Cavalry Regiment (*Östergötlands och Södermanlands ryttare*)	Östergötland and Södermanland, Sweden	Östgöta Cavalry Regiment
Karelian Cavalry Regiment (*Karelska ryttare*)	Viborg och Nyslott Counties, Finland	Viborg and Nyslott (Karelian) Cavalry Regiment
Infantry		
Uppland Regiment (*Upplands regemente*)	Uppland, Sweden	Uppland Regiment
Västgöta Regiment (*Västgöta regemente*)	Skaraborg County, Sweden	Skaraborg Regiment
Finnish Regiment (*Finska regementet*)	Åbo County, Finland	Åbo Regiment
Södermanland Regiment (*Södermanlands regemente*)	Södermanland, Sweden	Södermanland Regiment
Småland Regiment (*Smålands regemente*)	Kronoberg and Jönköping Counties, Sweden[8]	Kronoberg Regiment Jönköping Regiment
Second Finnish Regiment (*Andra finska regementet*)	Satakunta, Finland	Björneborg Regiment
Dalecarlia Regiment (*Dalregementet*)	Dalecarlia and Bergslagen, Sweden	Dalecarlia Regiment
Östgöta Regiment (*Östgöta regemente*)	Östergötland, Sweden	Östgöta Regiment
Tavastian Regiment (*Tavaste regemente*)	Tavastland, Finland	Tavastehus Regiment
Hälsinge Regiment (*Hälsinge regemente*)	Hälsingland and Ångermanland, Sweden	Hälsinge Regiment
Second Västgöta Regiment (*Andra västgöta regemente*)	Dal, Sweden	Västgöta-Dal Regiment

---

8   The Småland Regiment already consisted of two field regiments, one from Kronoberg and one from Jönköping, and for practical reasons they retained their separate existence.

Regiment	Geographical area	Later Known As
Third Västgöta Regiment (*Tredje västgöta regemente*)	Elfsborg County, Sweden	Elfsborg Regiment
First Karelian Regiment (*Första karelska regementet*)	Viborg County (Karelia), Finland	Viborg Regiment
Second Karelian Regiment (*Andra karelska regementet*)	Savolax, Finland	Savolax Regiment
Västmanland Regiment (*Västmanlands regemente*)	Västmanland, Sweden	Västmanland Regiment
Norrland Regiment (*Norrlands regemente*)	Norrbotten and Västerbotten, Sweden	Västerbotten Regiment
Second Småland Regiment (*Andra Smålands regemente*)	Kalmar County and Öland, Sweden	Kalmar Regiment
Nyland Regiment (*Nylands regemente*)	Nyland, Finland	Nyland Regiment
Värmland Regiment (*Värmlands regemente*)	Närke and Värmland, Sweden	Närke-Värmland Regiment
Österbotten Regiment (*Österbottens regemente*)	Österbotten, Finland	Österbotten Regiment

The adopted organisation was regarded as the one suitable for times of peace and, most importantly, within the limits imposed by the country's financial resources. In reality, there were already more standing national regiments than this, in addition to many detached Swedish and Finnish battalions and companies in Germany (for this calculation, the enlisted units were not included since they were not national troops). In 1635, an inventory found as many as 80 surplus companies of Swedish and Finnish infantry, which in effect corresponded to an additional 10 infantry regiments. Because of the ongoing war, they could hardly be disbanded, so they were retained in the overall military structure. As for the organisation at home (eight cavalry and 20 infantry regiments), it was decided that it had to be retained, and in addition three enlisted regiments would be added.[9]

Many of these regiments already existed at the time of the regency government's decision, and they accordingly date their foundation to an earlier year. Certainly, the existing connection to a particular province or county meant that regiments, even then, would have recognised their links to past formations. Still, it might be argued that the regiments did not yet have a permanent existence before this date.

In late 1636, Oxenstierna and the regency government decided to increase the number of infantry regiments from 20 to 23. One new provincial regiment would be formed in Sweden and two in Finland. In Sweden, the Småland Regiment already consisted of two field regiments, one from Kronoberg and one from Jönköping, and for practical reasons both had retained their separate existence. The Småland Regiment was accordingly divided into two, the Kronoberg Regiment and Jönköping Regiment.[10] In Finland, the situation was similar with the Nyland Regiment and the First Karelian Regiment, both

9   Barkman, *Gustaf II Adolfs regementsorganisation*, pp.201–2.
10 Petri, *Kungl. Första livgrenadjärregementets historia* 2, p.218.

of which consisted of units that for practical reasons already had separate identities in the field. Henceforth, the Nyland formations became known as the West Nyland Regiment and East Nyland Regiment, respectively, while the Karelians were divided into the West Viborg Regiment and East Viborg Regiment, respectively.[11]

The reorganisation of the army took place under wartime conditions. Since many regiments already included detached companies serving overseas, it was not easy to reconcile the theoretical organisation with reality. While the regimental reorganisation was carried out, the number of companies, their strength, and allocation into battalions often diverged far from the norms established in Stockholm. In late 1643, for instance, the eight cavalry regiments had mostly conformed to the new organisation. The exception was the Åbo and Björneborg Cavalry Regiment which consisted of not eight but 12 companies, of which eight were in Germany. However, the regiment's total manpower roughly corresponded to regulations, which meant that the eight companies in Germany were seriously understrength. As for the infantry, almost all regiments still had supernumerary detached companies spread throughout Germany in either garrisons or field army. Strictly speaking, it was only the Hälsinge Regiment which conformed to the approved organisation, with four companies at home, four companies in Germany, and roughly the correct number of men.[12]

One cannot discuss the wartime regiment without also mentioning its civilian camp followers. Each regiment was accompanied by private merchants, sutlers, who sold food supplies and other goods to the soldiers. Although civilians and acting in a private capacity, they were frequently listed in the regimental muster rolls since they performed a vital function.[13] Yet, the sutlers were only one kind of civilian camp followers. Since all had to be accommodated in camp, other civilians beside sutlers were also, at times, listed in the rolls. When the Old Blue Regiment marched into Nördlingen in 1634, it consisted of 980 common soldiers plus officers, 14 cannons, and 40 munition wagons. However, the supply train also included wives, children, baggage-servants, sutlers, and as many as 350 widows. Judging from the requested supplies that the town had to provide, the regiment consisted of more than 3,000 "mouths" that needed to be fed, in addition to 350 horses and donkeys. The number of camp followers would accordingly seem to have been twice the number of soldiers.[14]

Perhaps this number was unusually high, because the Old Blue was an old and well-established regiment. Yet, all regiments included large numbers of camp followers. When Lieutenant Colonel Normand's regiment of foot, which formed part of the units under Bernard of Saxe-Weimar, in 1634 was quartered in Dinkelsbühl, it consisted of 853 soldiers and 98 officers divided

11 Helge E. Wigren, *Kungliga Nylands Regemente 1626–1809* (Jyväskylä: Nylands Brigad, 2006), p.41.

12 Mankell, *Uppgifter* 2, pp.273–4, which details the number of units and men at home and abroad in late 1643.

13 *Kungl. Svea Livgardes Historia* 3:2, pp.560–2.

14 Richard Brzezinski, *The Army of Gustavus Adolphus* 2: *Cavalry* (London: Osprey, Men-at-Arms 262, 1993), p.47.

Swedish supply train, second battle of Breitenfeld, 1642. While some people have made camp, others are still moving, and those nearest the front seem in a funk to escape. (Drawn by fortification officer Conrad Maesberg (later ennobled as Mardefelt); Military Archives, Stockholm; Photo: Medströms, detail)

into nine companies. However, with them travelled 722 civilians, including 336 women, 108 children, 76 youngsters, 103 servants, 62 baggage-servants, and 11 sutlers with families.[15]

The Cavalry Company

Cavalry company organisation and establishment strength stayed the same as established by Gustavus Adolphus, that is, 125 horses.[16] The cavalry, unlike the infantry, counted its strength in horses, not men. However, it is difficult to assess the real strength of the cavalry companies. For instance, if we refer to a Swedish archive document from 1634 which lists the regiments and

---

15 Peter Engerisser, *Von Kronach nach Nördlingen: Der Dreißigjährige Krieg in Franken, Schwaben und der Oberpfalz 1631–1635* (Weißenstadt: Verlag Heinz Späthling, 2004), p.513.

16 It has been suggested that in autumn 1639, the cavalry company establishment strength was raised from 125 to 150 horses. As a result, the company's manpower would have increased from 112 to 138 men, and henceforth, a cavalry regiment would consist of 1,200 horses, as compared to 1,000 previously. As an example to illustrate this, Stålhandske's regiment in early March 1639 included 971 horses in eight companies (an average of 121 horses per company), to which would be added 200 horses, that is, 25 per company (which would produce an average of 146 horses). Jägerhorn, *Hårdast bland de hårda*, pp.61, 162, 165. While such plans indeed were made for this particular regiment, this was the result of practical considerations relating to the raising of men and horses, not the introduction of a new cavalry company organisation. Other examples illustrate the retention of the existing organisation, for example, Olof Silverlood's company of the Västgöta Cavalry Regiment which in 1648 counted 110 cavalrymen and a staff unit of 18. Rumenius, *Wästgöta Ryttare*, p.17.

respective strength of all the Swedish armies in Germany, it is obvious that it relies not on knowledge of real numbers but on averages. Each cavalry company is counted as having a strength of 60 men. This is clearly an estimate, since no company had an establishment strength which corresponded to this figure. Moreover, the figure of 60 men has been assessed as too high, and it has been proposed that the real number should be reduced by a third, which would produce a company strength of only 40 men.[17]

As before, the cavalry fought in squadrons, each on paper consisting of two companies. Montecuccoli gives the average strength of a Swedish squadron as 200 to 300 men, with the men formed up in three ranks.[18]

The Infantry Company

The infantry company's establishment strength, a nominal 150 men, remained unchanged, too, and the men continued to be formed up in six ranks. However, the company's internal organisation changed. Manuals to the Swedish model of warfare issued immediately after the reign of Gustavus Adolphus still focused on the corporalship as the lowest unit, with two corporalships constituting what might be called a platoon and three platoons per company. However, from this time the manuals describe a simplified organisational structure. First, the pike corporalships were reorganised to conform to the musketeer corporalships. Henceforth, all corporalships, whether of pikemen or musketeers, consisted of 24 men (that is, four files). This meant that the number of pikemen in a corporalship was higher than in the past. Second, henceforth the company was divided into two corporalships of pikemen (48 men) flanked on each side by two corporalships of musketeers (48 men), that is, a total of 144 men plus 12 officers, for a grand total of 156 men. The 12 officers were the same as in the previous organisational structure, that is, a captain, lieutenant, ensign, two sergeants, an armourer, *furier*, company standard bearer, muster-roll scribe, and three drummers.[19] As a result, the new type of company consisted of 48 pikemen and 96 musketeers, in contrast with the past organisation of 54 pikemen and 72 musketeers. The increase in the number of shot at the expense of the pike was striking. The proportion of pike had fallen to approximately one third of the foot.

It must be remembered that this was the establishment strength only. In the field, this number of men was seldom achieved.

The aforementioned Swedish archive document from 1634 which lists the regiments and respective strength of all the Swedish armies in Germany

---

17 Mankell, *Uppgifter* 1, pp.134–5; Mankell, *Uppgifter* 2, pp.194–7.
18 Thomas M. Barker, *The Military Intellectual and Battle: Raimondo Montecuccoli and the Thirty Years War* (Albany, New York: State University of New York Press, 1975), p.91; translating Montecuccoli's *Sulle battaglie* which he wrote while in Swedish captivity.
19 Lorentz von Troupitzen, *Kriegs Kunst: Nach Königlicher Schwedischer Maniereine Compagny zurichten, in Regiment, Zug- und Schlacht-Ordnung zubringen, zum Ernst anzuführen, zugebrauchen, und in essewürcklich, zuunterhalten* (Frankfurt-am-Main: Matthaeus Merian, 1633), pp.10–25 with plates; Wendelin Schildknecht, *Harmonia in fortalitiis construendis, defendendis & oppugnandis* 3 (Stettin: Johann Valentin Rheten, 1652), pp.160–63.

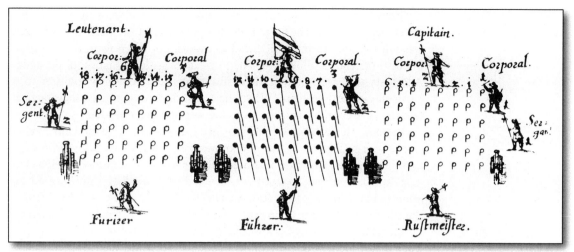

Swedish infantry company deployed in line, as described and illustrated by Lorentz von Troupitzen. (Troupitzen, *Kriegs Kunst*, 1633)

counts each infantry company as having a strength of 100 men. However, this is clearly an estimate only, and again it has been proposed that the real number should be reduced by a third.[20]

The Infantry Battalion and Brigade

The infantry battalion essentially remained unchanged, that is, four companies still constituted one battalion. As before, the pikemen formed up in the centre, which Montecuccoli referred to as a "pike battalion" of 192 men flanked by "sleeves" of more numerous musketeers.[21] However, with companies frequently far below establishment strength, battalions, too, varied widely in strength.

The brigade system introduced by Gustavus Adolphus was abolished within two years of the battle of Lützen. Turner noted that the brigade formation remained in use "for one year after the Kings death; but after that time, I saw it wear out when Defensive Arms first, and then Pikes came to be neglected, and by some vilipended".[22]

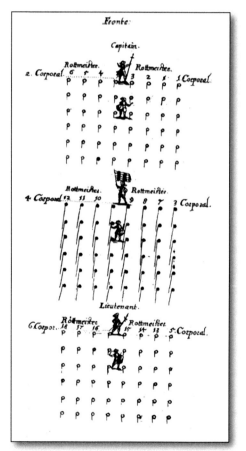

Swedish infantry company deployed in column, again described and illustrated by Lorentz von Troupitzen. (Troupitzen, *Kriegs Kunst*, 1633)

20 Mankell, *Uppgifter* 1, pp.134–5; Mankell, *Uppgifter* 2, pp.194–7.
21 Barker, *Military Intellectual and Battle*, p.90; translating Montecuccoli's *Sulle battaglie*.
22 Sir James Turner, *Pallas Armata: Military Essayes of the Ancient Grecian, Roman, and Modern Art of War, Written in the Years 1670 and 1671* (London: Richard Chiswell, 1683), p.229. Turner is not the most reliable witness on affairs in Germany, and here he seems to be more concerned over the decline of armour and pikes, a concern he also expressed elsewhere. However, Turner does state clearly that it was the brigade

Turner's observation was correct, even though his conclusion on the reason why was not. The brigade deployment used at Breitenfeld and Lützen was not the final form of the Swedish model, nor did it form the zenith of Swedish tactical development. The intricate brigade formation of Gustavus Adolphus was essentially a defensive formation. It was a solution to a particular tactical problem. When the opposing forces changed their tactical doctrine, the complex brigade structure was no longer needed.

Besides, Gustavus Adolphus's brigade formation depended on having troops well-trained in its use. We know, from illustrations by eyewitnesses, that the brigade formation was used at the battle of Oldendorf in 1633. The next, and last, major engagement in which the Swedish army formed up infantry in the brigade formation was the battle of Nördlingen in 1634. There the Swedes went on the offensive, not defensive, and the terrain was ill suited for intricate formations. As a result, Sweden lost the battle, but Sweden also lost a major share of the infantry trained in the brigade formation.

Henceforth, the well-trained soldiers on which the brigade system depended were not always available. Moreover, with current Swedish tactical doctrine increasingly emphasising the offensive, for which simpler deployment models sufficed, it was natural to abandon Gustavus Adolphus's brigade formation. The brigade was accordingly modified into something simpler that also could be used by less well-trained soldiers.

The man behind the simplified brigade formation was almost certainly Johan Banér. At least the change took place under his watch. Although Banér no doubt saw a need for change, he also had to adapt to the altered circumstances. Henceforth, two battalions would form one brigade. The forward battalion, which previously had constituted the centre of the brigade, was abolished.[23] Besides, Banér frequently found it necessary to combine depleted companies from several regiments into a single weak battalion. At the 1636 battle of Wittstock, for instance, Banér deployed his men into what was referred to as brigades, each with a strength of from about 400 to 1,000 men, but which in reality was no more than an ad hoc formation that each consisted of, at most, two weak battalions.

The complex brigade formation was from this time onwards neither needed nor desired. The tactical unit of infantry henceforth became the battalion.

However, this change was not always observable in the written sources. Since weak battalions, sometimes consisting of companies from several regiments, continued to be deployed together in what still was referred to as brigades, references to brigades in descriptions of the Swedish army remained common for decades after the actual brigade formation of Gustavus Adolphus had been abandoned. Yet, these references, especially in the second half of the century, denoted battalions, not brigades, and were used to distinguish them from the higher formation, the regiment.

---

system which was abandoned, and he was in the Swedish army in Germany at the time. Besides, Turner's statement is supported by subsequent army manuals, such as Troupitzen's *Kriegs Kunst*, which do not describe the brigade formation.

23 Petri, *Kungl. Första livgrenadjärregementets historia* 2, p.227.

Swedish infantry and cavalry formations at the second battle of Breitenfeld, 1642. Carl Gustav Wrangel (marked D) is illustrated in the centre of the map. To the extent that the details can be relied upon as accurate, several depleted infantry companies have been combined into two battalions (by then sometimes still called brigades). Likewise, 12 depleted cavalry companies have been combined into three squadrons. (Drawn by fortification officer Conrad Maesberg (later ennobled as Mardefelt); Military Archives, Stockholm; Photo: Medströms, detail)

Training

As part of the 1634 constitutional reform, regulations were also issued on how the troops of the provincial regiments should be trained in times of peace. Most of the weapons and equipment of the regiments should be stored in central depots in the Crown's fortresses in castles. When an entire regiment was gathered, for a muster or other reason, weapons should be issued and exercises in field formations should be held. Furthermore, weapons for one corporalship per company should be retained and stored in a suitably located church. The soldiers should be exercised every Sunday, in conjunction with church services.[24] These occasions should not be interpreted as military field manoeuvres with combined units under realistic conditions, in the sense that developed later in the century.[25] At most, one regiment at a time exercised in formation. The emphasis seems to have been on maintaining and moving in formation, as well as weapons handling.

Enlisted Units

The use of enlisted units continued, but due to the nature of the war, some changes took place. Most noteworthy were perhaps the separate destinies of

---

24 *Ibid.*, pp.214–15. In 1650 or 1652, the Department of War suggested to double this amount, that is, to maintain muskets and pikes for a total of four corporalships instead of one. However, this increase was never implemented, and King Charles Gustavus soon after his coronation in 1654 had to issue an order to do so. *Ibid.*, p.298.

25 Fredholm von Essen, *Charles XI's War*, pp.21–2.

Partisan used by the Drabant or Life Guard company, mid seventeenth century. The type corresponds closely to the model in 1646 issued to Queen Christina's Drabant Guard, with a black silk tassel and a black pole. Total length 2.4 m and head length 37.7 cm. (Skokloster Castle)

the colour regiments. In 1635, the survivors of the Yellow Regiment and Green Regiment went into French service together with Bernard of Saxe-Weimar.

Meanwhile, the Old Blue and White Regiments remained in Swedish service, the Old Blue until 1652, when the regiment formally was dissolved, and the White at least until January–February 1643 when it participated in Torstensson's siege of Freiberg.[26]

In July 1644, Oxenstierna suggested that the enlisted Household Regiment (*Hovregementet*) should be re-established. This was the regiment which, because of the preponderance of German- and English-speaking officers, was better known, in German, as the *Leibregiment* and, in English, as the Life Regiment. It was also frequently referred to as the Life Guard. Men were enlisted, and in January 1645, Queen Christina appointed the young Magnus Gabriel De la Gardie colonel of the regiment. De la Gardie belonged to the group of Christina's personal friends at court, but as noted, he was also the son of the Grand Marshal of the Realm, Jacob De la Gardie, and could be expected to know what he was doing. The regiment would have five battalions of four companies each.[27]

There had been a Life Guard even in the interim period. The Life Guard company which brought the King's corpse to Stockholm had remained in existence as Christina's Life Guard. Although under Christina's youth, the Life Guard primarily had a ceremonial function, it remained as a core for the new Life Guard regiment established when the young Queen came of age. Units from the new regiment took part in the war against Denmark and Norway.

The Artillery and Fortification

Since the artillery still was regarded as a semi-civilian institution, it did not fall under the purview of the War Council when it was established in 1630, and its personnel was accordingly not listed as military personnel

---

26 Tingsten, *Fältmarskalkarna*, p.224.
27 Barkman, Lundkvist, and Tersmeden, *Kungl. Svea Livgardes Historia* 3:2, pp.132–3. The Life Guard organisation, with no less than 20 companies, each consisting of 148 men including officers, differed from that of other regiments.

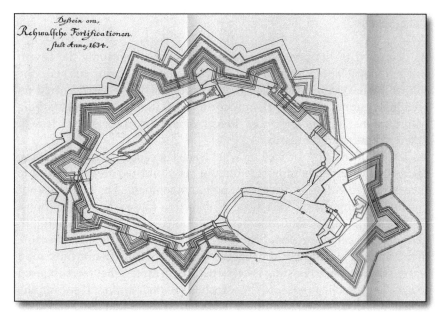

Fortifications of Reval, 1634.
(Ludvig W:son Munthe, after
contemporary original)

(even though they by then functioned as such and served under military law). Instead artillery personnel were listed as employees of the Royal Court. This situation did not change until 1633, when the artillery personnel were moved into the list of military personnel. While Oxenstierna suggested the establishment of a dedicated Artillery Regiment as part of the work leading up to the Instrument of Government of 1634, it took until 1636 before the foundation for an artillery regiment in Sweden was set up. Moreover, it took until 1638 before the artillery organisation was reported as subordinated the Department of War.[28]

The Fortification Corps and the position of qartermaster-general, with the rank of colonel, among the duties of which also was military intelligence, remained part of the artillery until 1641. At that time, some of these officers were transferred into a new, independent staff unit, known by the same name or simply as the Fortification (Swedish: *Fortifikationen*). Its first head became the quartermaster-general, Olof Hansson Örnehufvud (1600–1644; born as Olof Hansson Swart).[29] The Fortification Corps remained formally subordinated the national chief of artillery (*rikstygmästare*) until 1645, after which it gradually, in the period up to 1653, became fully independent under the new quartermaster-general, Johan Andersson Lenaeus (*c*.1610–1674; soon ennobled as Wärnschöld).[30] Mapmaking became the responsibility of the Fortification Corps already in 1635, with the appointment of Örnehufvud as quartermaster-general and head of the Fortification.[31]

---

28   Hedberg, *Kungl. Artilleriet*, pp.50–52, 303.

29   Ludvig W:son Munthe, *Kongl. Fortifikationens historia 2: Fortifikationsstaten under Örnehufwudh och Wärnschiöldh, 1641–1674* (Stockholm: Norstedt & söner, 1906), pp.1–2.

30   *Ibid.*, pp.124–5; Hedberg, *Kungl. Artilleriet*, p.145.

31   Ludvig W:son Munthe, *Kongl. Fortifikationens historia 1: Svenska fortifikationsväsendet från nyare tidens början till inrättandet af en särskild fortifikationsstat år 1641* (Stockholm: Norstedt & söner, 1902), p.521.

Logistics

As described in the previous volume, logistics was not only the key to waging war, it also formed the daily background to army life. For the soldier, battles were exceptional events in a lifestyle that was centred on seemingly eternal marches back and forth across the country, the gathering of provisions and supplies, and longer or shorter stays in quarters of different kinds and standards.

The Swedish army focused on what has been called offensive logistics: the deliberate invasion of hostile but not yet plundered areas which were then exploited either by direct occupation accompanied by billeting and/ or looting or by the indirect form of extortion known as contributions, in cash and goods (food, clothes, munitions, and transportation), in exchange for being left alone. The system of raising contributions became increasingly sophisticated during the war, since army commands soon learnt how to tap into existing fiscal structures to divert what was supposed to have been public funds into the war chests of their armies. However, the system was detrimental to military efficiency in so far that it depended on the detachment of garrisons that held ground and ensured the continued flow of contributions. These garrisons were then unavailable for field operations.

Before Sweden had a properly functioning armaments industry, weapons and equipment had typically been imported from the Dutch Republic or, the source of the supplies, Germany, where indeed most were manufactured. Such goods still needed to be acquired. Already during the time of Gustavus Adolphus, the territory in Germany under Swedish control had been divided into supply regions. The southern ones were lost after the battle of Nördlingen, but the first bridgehead in the north remained of central importance for the communication lines between the Swedish heartland and the field army in southern Germany. Besides, certain supply depots remained in the south as well. Several supply depots included manufacturing facilities, in which cannons, ammunition, mines, and gunpowder were manufactured. Obsolete or captured bronze cannons were recast so as to conform to the Swedish calibre system. The great rivers provided communication routes between supply regions and the field army. A very important manufacturing and supply depot was Erfurt, located in Thuringia. Erfurt had been a centre for Swedish supply activities almost since the arrival of Gustavus Adolphus and remained in Swedish hands until the end of the war. In 1642, Leipzig became yet another important depot. In 1647, a new combined manufacturing and supply deport was established further to the south, in Schweinfurt. Located on the River Main, it was within easy reach by road from the depot in Erfurt. In Westphalia, Minden and Stade functioned as depots, and Stade was, like Wismar, Stralsund, and Stettin on the Baltic Sea coast, also an important receiving port for supplies from the Swedish heartland.[32]

---

32 For details on manufacturing and supply depots for the provision of artillery and munitions, see *Från Femern och Jankow*, pp.296–7.

By 1648, Swedish bases were located throughout Germany. The Swedish army had a total of 119 garrisons. These included five in Alsace (including Benfeld), seven in Swabia (among them Überlingen, Donauwörth, and Nördlingen), seven in Franconia (including Schweinfurt and Windsheim), 14 in Bohemia (most importantly, Leitmeritz and the west side of Prague), five in Moravia (including Olmütz and Neustadt), 10 in Silesia (chief of them Glogau), 10 in Saxony and Thuringia (including Leipzig and Erfurt), four in Brandenburg (including Landsberg), 12 in Westphalia (among them Minden, Nienburg, and Vechta), five in the Upper Palatinate (including Neumarkt and Weiden), seven in Bremen (chief of them Stade), eight in Mecklenburg (most importantly, Wismar), and unsurprisingly, 25 in Pomerania (including Stettin, Stralsund, Greifswald, and Demmin). See Appendix 1 for further details.

In comparison, the French army only had bases in southwestern Germany, with the major share in Alsace (Alsace: 21, Swabia: four, Württemberg: four, Baden: two, Mainz: four, Lower Palatinate: eight, Upper Rhine: six, Electoral Rhine: two, in total 51). This is unsurprising, since the French armies invariably had orders to remain near the Rhine and the source of the Danube – a constant source of argument between the Swedish and French commanders, since the former wanted their French allies to join them in the operations against the Habsburg heartlands. Meanwhile, the Hessian army primarily had bases in the northwest, with a large share in Hesse itself (Hesse: 10, Fulda: two, Westphalia: eight, Cologne: three, Jülich: three, Palatinate: five, and Ostfriesland; 10, in total 41).

The garrisons varied greatly in strength. In 1648, the garrison in Prague consisted of 1,500 men, the one in Leipzig counted 1,200, while the smallest was Schwine Schantz (Schwine bastion) at Schwinemünde, which only consisted of 20 men.[33]

When Gustavus Adolphus invaded Germany, the Swedish army already had extensive knowledge of northern Germany, and sufficient knowledge of conditions elsewhere on the Continent to make strategic decisions. In 1628, if not before, Gustavus Adolphus had instructed his mapmakers and commanders to obtain all available foreign maps and plans of border towns and fortifications, and this order was strictly adhered to by his fortification officers and quartermasters-general. Even so, the army had not, by then, actually carried out combat operations in the new theatre of operations, which meant that for tactical and logistical decisions, the commanders had to consult local maps and knowledgeable persons. Gustavus Adolphus once famously wrote that "here all our maps end", which was followed by a request to Johan Banér to send his most experienced fortification officer and mapmaker, Olof Hansson Swart (ennobled in 1635 as Örnehufvud), to the King's headquarters, if Banér could spare him.[34]

This soon changed. Within a few years, the Swedish armies had sufficient knowledge of the road network to be able, first, to divide into several columns

---

33 Mankell, *Uppgifter*2, pp.295, 297.
34 Gustavus Adolphus to Johan Banér, Jerichow, 2 July 1631 (O.S.); cited in *Slaget vid Jankow*, pp.138–9.

which marched along parallel roads so as to increase speed and maximise the opportunities to find supplies and shelter, and second, to use less well-known but still functioning roads so as to hide movements to enemy eyes.[35] To some extent, the practice of using less frequented and parallel roads was the result of the increasing difficulties in finding supplies in already plundered areas. However, it is obvious from the rapid marches of commanders such as Banér and Torstensson that speed was a primary reason for the choice of secondary and parallel roads, and that their adversaries frequently underestimated the ability of Swedish armies to move rapidly.

With a knowledge of the road system came the opportunity to develop the post office system further. A Swedish postal service had, as part of the war effort, already been established in Germany, and in 1636, the turn came to Sweden, Finland, and the Baltic possessions, too. Certain individuals along the main roads, henceforth known as "post peasants" (*postbönder*), accepted the responsibility to forward letters in exchange for tax exemption. At the same time, dedicated post officers were established in the towns, which coordinated the network of "post peasants". Communication lines to the Continent remained a priority. As a result, postal service from Stockholm to Helsingør would take around five days. From there, a letter could reach Hamburg in about three days. From Hamburg, it took five days to deliver mail to Cologne or Leipzig, six days to Frankfurt-am-Main, nine days to Prague, 10 days to Nuremberg, and 12 days to Vienna. The technically shorter distance from Stockholm to Gothenburg would more likely take seven days, since roads were inferior. Services to the north were far worse, with around 10 days from Stockholm to Umeå in northern Sweden and up to 24 days to Uleåborg in northern Finland. Besides, postal services were frequently delayed for several days while a sufficient number of letters was collected to make it worthwhile to send them onwards.

Following the postal service reform of 1636, efficiency increased further.[36] However, the times mentioned here should not be interpreted as in any way guaranteed. A letter from Stockholm to the army in Germany might easily take four to six weeks, and in extreme cases, including the letter with orders to Torstensson to invade Denmark, the time required was four months.

Since a successful military campaign depended on good communications, military post offices in the areas of operations were established, too. Couriers were then employed to move the letters and dispatches from post to post. For instance, during the 1645 Swedish campaign in Bohemia alone, the army established 14 post offices in various Bohemian town.[37] From 1646 the post between Sweden and the Continent was handled by mounted postmen.[38]

---

35 Försvarsstabens krigshistoriska avdelning, *Vägar och vägkunskap i Mellaneuropa under trettioåriga krigets sista skede* (Stockholm: Generalstabens Litografiska Anstalt, 1948), p.72.

36 Alf Åberg, *När Skåne blev svenskt: Två krig, två freder, snapphanar och försvenskning* (n.p.: SMB, 2013), p.155.

37 Ericson Wolke, Larsson; and Villstrand, *Trettioåriga kriget*, p.263.

38 Åberg, *När Skåne blev svenskt*, p.155

4

Weapons and Equipment

By the 1630s, the Swedish armaments industry had developed a sufficient capacity to supply the army's needs. However, for practical reasons of logistics, much of the war materials for the Swedish military forces on the Continent was manufactured to Swedish orders in the workshops of Germany.[1] Most weapons and equipment within the Swedish army were of the same types as before the death of Gustavus Adolphus. Nonetheless, minor changes took place as the war progressed.

Officers

As before, officers provided their own arms and armour. Field Marshal Gustav Horn wore helmet and armour in battle, at least at Nördlingen where Montecuccoli saw him.[2] In battle, each officer would be armed with two wheellock pistols and a rapier. Infantry officers usually added a partisan, or in case of officers of pike units, perhaps a half-pike five cubits (2.97 m) in length.[3]

Late in the war, flintlock pistols appeared among some officers. So was, for instance, a pair of flintlock pistols made in Paris in the 1640s for Queen Christina. These were not only used for display; Christina was well-trained and notably skilled in shooting, fencing, and horseback riding. Flintlock pistols were also used on campaign by Charles Gustavus, who later would succeed Christina as King Charles X Gustavus.[4]

Johan Banér on horseback. Most paintings of generals in full cuirassier armour no longer represented their appearance on the battlefield. However, some still wore armour, and in light of Banér's dislike of French fashion, he may have been one of them.

TANDEM BONA CAUSA TRIUMPHAT.

---

1   *Från Femern och Jankow*, p.69.
2   Barker, *Military Intellectual and Battle*, p.158; translating Montecuccoli's *Sulle battaglie*.
3   Josef Alm, *Blanka vapen och skyddsvapen från och med 1500-talet till våra dagar* (Stockholm: Rediviva, 1975), p.143.
4   Josef Alm, *Eldhandvapen 1: Från deras tidigaste förekomst till slaglåsets allmänna införande* (Stockholm: Rediviva, 1976), pp.209, 220.

Swedish artillery under-officer, siege of Prague, 1648. (*Theatrum Europaeum*, detail)

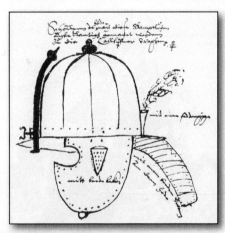

Pattern drawing of cavalry helmet, Leufsta, 1630s. According to the written notes, the helmet should have a brim three fingers broad, broad cheeks, a nasal bar, a feather-pipe, and a broad tail. The pattern is probably inspired by a kettle-hat-like type of helmet common in the Polish-Lithuanian Commonwealth.

However, flintlocks did not become general military issue until after the Scanian War.

Under-officers

Unlike officers, under-officers in the Swedish army received their arms from the Crown. An under-officer, too, was armed with rapier and perhaps pistols. Those serving in the infantry would carry partisans, or (at least in the early years) sometimes a half-pike.[5]

Cuirassiers

In the previous volume it was shown how by the 1630s, many cuirassiers replaced the old visored helmet with the lobster-tailed pot helmet, which in German was known as *zischägge* and ultimately was of Inner Asian origin. Although many, perhaps most, were procured on the Continent, some were manufactured in Sweden. A pattern sketch from the Leufsta arms factory, dated to the 1630s, shows the type of lobster-tailed pot helmet that evidently was designed for the Swedish cavalry and manufactured in Sweden. It is close in style to the *zischägge* but has a brim three fingers broad and broad cheeks. In the 1630s and 1640s, there is some evidence that the helmet type was used by both horse and foot.[6]

The change in helmet style was only the beginning. From 1631 onwards, the armour of the cuirassiers was gradually simplified, in effect becoming identical to that of the light horse.[7] Soon, there were no more cuirassiers as such in the Swedish army.

Light Horse

Already before the simplification and eventual disappearance of the cuirassier's armour, the Swedish army had included far more light horse (Swedish: *lättaryttare*; light horsemen) than cuirassiers. They were so named because of their light armour, since no Swedish cavalry operated in a skirmish role on the battlefield.

---

5   Monro, *Monro His Expedition* 2, p.203.
6   Alm, *Blanka vapen*, p.249.
7   Alm, *Eldhandvapen* 1, p.214; Josef Alm, *Arméns eldhandvapen förr och nu* (Stockholm: Kungl. Armémuseum, 1953), p.122.

Each light horseman was expected to wear a helmet and cuirass, consisting of a shot-proof breast- and back-plate. The required armour was not always available, but regulations insisted on this armour throughout the war. Armament would consist of a pair of wheellock pistols and a rapier.

Dragoons

As shown in the previous volume, the number of dragoons increased as the war continued. Dragoons were mounted musketeers who moved on horseback but fought on foot. The proportion of dragoons increased significantly within the horse. In the 1640s, there were already four dragoon regiments in the Swedish army. All dragoons were enlisted.[8]

At first, dragoons received the same muskets as other infantry. Each also carried a rapier. Some may have been equipped with axes as well. There is no information in the arsenal archives that pistols ever were distributed to dragoons during the Thirty Years' War. Swedish dragoons wore helmets but no breastplates. They wore shoes, not riding boots, and no spurs.[9] Having said this, over time dragoons increasingly began to dress and operate like cavalry. From about 1635, the Stockholm armoury began distributing small numbers of snaphance muskets to dragoon units.[10]

Mounted huntsman, firing musket. Better-off dragoons would have dressed in this style. From a hunting rifle made in Saxony, 1639. (Wrangel's armoury, Gripsholm Castle)

Musketeers

The Swedish army retained the Dutch-style 10-bore matchlock musket (drilled for a ball weighing one tenth of a pound, corresponding to a nominal calibre of 19.7 mm), which had been introduced by Gustavus Adolphus. The 10-bore musket's large calibre gave it greater range and, more importantly, a somewhat increased penetrative power than other muskets.

Yet, due to the shortages in slow-match that plagued Sweden throughout the Thirty Years' War, soldiers on garrison duty were repeatedly ordered to use muskets with snaphance locks, not matchlocks. In 1635, large numbers of snaphance muskets were dispatched overseas to the fortresses of Riga, Narva, Ivangorod, and Kexholm (Käkisalmi). In 1644, the garrison of Elfsborg Castle was ordered to use snaphance muskets instead of matchlocks. These were some of the most important Swedish fortresses. Indeed, the existing

8   Theodor Jakobsson, *Lantmilitär beväpning och beklädnad under äldre Vasatiden och Gustav II Adolfs tid* (Stockholm: Generalstaben, 1938), p.121.
9   Henning Hamilton, *Afhandling om krigsmaktens och krigskonstens tillstånd i Sverige, under Konung Gustaf II Adolfs regering* (Stockholm: Kongl. Vitterhets Historie och Antiquitets Academiens handlingar 17, 1846), p.209; Alm, *Arméns eldhandvapen*, pp.114–15; Jakobsson, *Lantmilitär beväpning och beklädnad*, p.121.
10 Brzezinski, *Army of Gustavus Adolphus* 2, p.16.

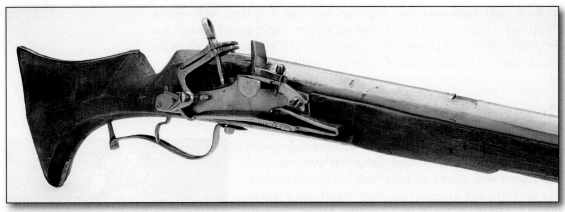

Snaphance musket. (Skokloster Castle)

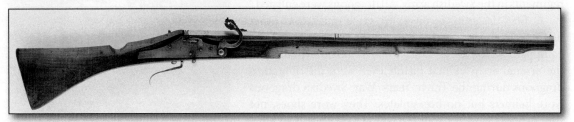

Matchlock musket, seventeenth century. Total length 125.5 cm, barrel length 86.4 cm, weight 3.91 kg, and calibre 19 mm. Sufficiently short and lightweight to be used without a fork rest, this type of musket was far more common in the army than the snaphance musket. However, most muskets were longer still, with a total length of some 155 cm. (Royal Armoury, Stockholm)

supplies of snaphance muskets continued to be distributed to fortresses for many years to come, well after the end of the Thirty Years' War.[11]

As was mentioned in the previous volume, the navy, too, used muskets with snaphance locks, since they were less likely than the matchlock muskets to cause fires aboard. Snaphance muskets were also distributed among levied peasants for territorial defence. For these reasons, snaphance muskets for military use, which by then probably meant 10-bore, remained in production until very late, although in smaller numbers than the matchlock muskets. For instance, the Swedish gun factory in Söderhamn from September 1635 to September 1636 delivered 4,393 matchlock muskets and 369 snaphance muskets to the Crown. In 1638, the Stockholm arsenal received 10,026 new matchlock muskets and 141 new snaphance muskets.[12]

Gustavus Adolphus had worked to standardise the muskets and pistols produced for the army, but despite these efforts, at the time of his death standardisation had not yet been achieved. At some point in the late 1630s, the Crown accordingly decided to standardise all muskets and pistols produced in the Swedish factories as to length, calibre, and style. Patterns were drawn up; however, they were not followed very closely by the factories. In December 1640, an inspector was appointed to oversee that the pattern was followed, but this had but little effect.[13] As a result, it was in January 1646

---

11 Alm, *Arméns eldhandvapen*, pp.111–12.
12 Alm, *Eldhandvapen* 1, pp.168, 192.
13 Alm, *Arméns eldhandvapen*, p.97.

decided to deliver patterns to all factories, with which they would have to comply. Henceforth, each matchlock musket was supposed to have a total weight of 4.675 kg. A snaphance musket was to have a total weight of 5.1 kg.

The newly produced weapons were test-fired, and although barrels usually were fine, some factories then added inferior locks – a practice that the Crown henceforth would not accept. The problems with inferior quality were serious, however, and there were several reports over the years, perhaps with a spike in the mid 1640s, that soldiers were so badly wounded by misfire accidents and burst gun barrels that they lost both hands and limbs. A major cause of accidents was probably the variable characteristics of the black powder, the manufacture of which still left much to desire.[14]

The safety problems were perhaps one reason why these muskets still were mostly used with a fork rest. Another was the recoil, which was significant. In the early seventeenth century, the situation was already difficult. Already the influential military theorist Johann Jacobi von Wallhausen had in 1615 advised the musketeer, when firing, to rest the musket on the right side of his chest, not the shoulder, since the recoil was so hard that after six or eight shots, he would no longer be able to use his arm if he rested the weapon on the shoulder.[15] The fork rest presumably helped by taking some of this force, which otherwise might physically harm the soldier, something which is attested to even in late seventeenth-century documents.[16] Yet, the fork rest was frequently discarded. It was, for instance, not used during sieges.

Most Swedish infantry muskets were still sturdily built with simple iron fittings. However, by the end of the war, brass fittings might be used for selected units. Notably, on the occasion of Queen Christina's coronation in 1650, her guard carried muskets with brass fittings and stocks painted black, in the German manner, so as to produce the yellow and black colours of the House of Vasa.[17]

Swedish common soldiers, siege of Prague, 1648. When manning trenches and engaged in other siegeworks, musketeers would discard their fork rests, had they not already done so. (*Theatrum Europaeum*, detail)

Pikemen

Those infantrymen who did not carry muskets were armed with pikes. These had a regulation length of nine cubits (5.35 m). By tradition, a pikeman was valued higher than a musketeer. However, the task of carrying a pike and the associated armour had long been unpopular with the men. Already Monro complained that soldiers often would "cut off the lengths of their

14 Alm, *Eldhandvapen 1*, pp.171–2, pp.183–4; Alm, *Arméns eldhandvapen*, p.98.
15 Engerisser, *Von Kronach nach Nördlingen*, p.553; citing Johann Jacobi von Wallhausen, *Kriegskunst zu Fuß* (1615 edition), p.38.
16 Jakobsson, *Lantmilitär beväpning och beklädnad*, p.98 n.1.
17 Alm, *Arméns eldhandvapen*, p.98.

Pikes, as often is seene upon marches" when they were tired of carrying their weapons.[18]

As we have seen, the share of pikemen fell in the Swedish army. The trend had begun in the Swedish military forces in Germany already under Gustavus Adolphus, and it continued after his death.

Infantry Armour

During the 1630s, the soldiers began to discard armour. The cavalry henceforth wore only breast- and back-plates, and sometimes only the former. As noted, even the cuirassiers abandoned their heavy armour. Most infantry stopped wearing armour altogether. This included even the pikemen, who had most reason to retain armour.

Rapiers

Each soldier carried a rapier as a sidearm. Unlike the early "Swedish-style" rapier used previously, with its characteristic S-shaped quillons, rapiers within the Swedish army from the 1630s onwards increasingly often lacked quillons altogether. Instead, the hilt had a guard to protect the hand.

A typical rapier of this style, believed to be a cavalryman's rapier from the 1640s, has a blade length of 80.5 cm and a width of 4.0 cm. The hilt is of blackened iron. Very similar Swedish rapiers, although dated to the mid seventeenth century (and tentatively identified as being of model year 1653 for common soldiers), have a blade length of around 80 cm and a width of 4.5–4.8 cm. The weight is from around 1.6 to 1.8 kg.[19]

For natural reasons, officers carried similar but more ornamented rapiers. The rapier worn by Carl Gustav Wrangel, from the 1640s, is of a type common in the Dutch Republic. It has a total length of 100.8 cm, a blade length of 85.0 cm, and a width of 3.15 cm. The rapier has a small shell guard to protect the hand. Wrangel is known to have carried the rapier in 1652, since it is illustrated in the equestrian portrait of him reproduced elsewhere in this volume. However, by then he had probably used it for several years.

A highly embellished example of the same type is Lennart Torstensson's rapier from *c.* 1645. Similar in style to Wrangel's rapier, it has a total length of 107.8 cm, a blade length of 92.5 cm, and a width of 2.6 cm. While it would function as a weapon, it did not provide much protection to the hand.

A similar rapier was also carried by Charles Gustavus when he served as cavalry captain in 1642. The rapier has a total length of 103.2 cm, a blade length of 86.4 cm, and a width of 2.7 cm. It has a thumb ring and two side-rings, the outer one larger than the inner but both fitted with a pierced shell guard.

---

18 Monro, *Monro His Expedition* 2, p.191.
19 Josef Alm, "Flottans handvapen", *Sjöhistorisk Årsbok 1953–54* (Stockholm: Föreningen Sveriges Sjöfartsmuseum i Stockholm, 1954), pp.67–147, on pp.78–9; Heribert Seitz, *Svärdet och värjan som armévapen* (Stockholm: Kungl. Armémuseum, 1955) p.137.

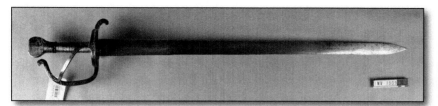

Swedish cavalry rapier, 1640s. (Army Museum, Stockholm; formerly of the private collection of the late Harry Orre)

Swedish rapier, mid 17th century, identified as model year 1653. (Army Museum, Stockholm)

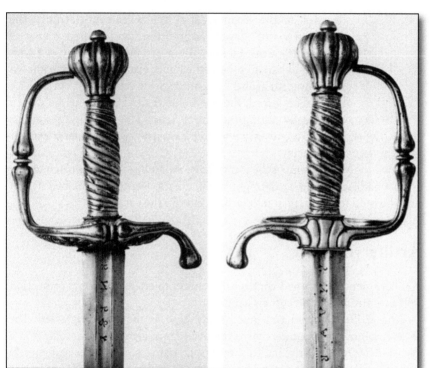

Carl Gustav Wrangel's rapier. Made in Germany in the 1640s, this is also the rapier depicted in the 1652 portrait of Wrangel by Ehrenstrahl. Total length 100.8 cm, blade length 85.0 cm, and width of 3.15 cm. (Skokloster Castle)

Rapier carried by the future King Charles X Gustavus when he served as cavalry captain, 1642. (Royal Armoury, Stockholm)

Lennart Torstensson's rapier, c. 1645. Manufactured in Germany, the hilt is probably English. (Skokloster Castle)

Rapier carried by the future King Charles X Gustavus when he served as cavalry captain, 1642. The two side-rings, the outer one larger than the inner but both fitted with a pierced shell guard, make this an early type of the so-called Walloon sword which subsequently developed into the standard-issue rapier of the Swedish army. (Royal Armoury, Stockholm)

Schwedendegen, manufactured in Germany, *c.* 1650. The double hilt bars distinguish this type from Swedish army-issue rapiers. (Royal Armoury, Stockholm)

Such a rapier, with an open hilt that usually came with a thumb ring and two large side-rings, one or commonly both fitted with a frequently pierced shell guard, in time became generally referred to as a "Walloon sword" (French: *épée wallonne*), due to its origin in the Dutch Republic. However, there is no evidence that the name was in use already during the Thirty Years' War, and it probably derives from the late seventeenth century. It is commonly believed that the French name derives from 1672, but by then, the type had been in general service throughout northern Europe for at least three decades. In the second half of the seventeenth century, the "Walloon sword" developed into the standard-issue rapier of the Swedish army. Incidentally, a variant of this type, but with double hilt bars to protect the hand, eventually became known as a "Swedish sword" (German: *Schwedendegen*), but as with the Wallon sword, there is no evidence that the name was in use already during the Thirty Years' War. Besides, despite its name, the type subsequently known as a *Schwedendegen* was never regular issue in the Swedish army.

It was only by the end of the war that the rapier began to be worn hanging from a baldric slung over the right shoulder. The waistbelt remained in use, and it would indeed return into fashion later in the century.

Artillerymen

Artillerymen were armed with muskets and rapiers for personal protection and as a means to protect their cannons.[20]

The artillery system continued to develop as the war progressed. The few remaining 48-pounders were removed from army service, following a decision by Queen Christina. This was unsurprising, since the decision merely was the culmination of a trend begun already during the reign of her father. The older 6-pounders, too, were removed. The highly successful regimental artillery was retained, but it, too, saw continued developments. By the end of the war, the original regimental three-pounders were gradually replaced with a new type of 3-pounder, with a longer barrel (2.5 to 2.9 m long). This increased lethality further at longer distances. Torstensson compensated the greater weight of the new type of regimental artillery with the introduction of more horses to provide mobility. Twelve-pounders remained in widespread service and can be said to have formed the backbone of the artillery system within the field armies, even though they almost always were fewer in numbers than the regimental three-pounders.[21]

20 Hedberg, *Kungl. Artilleriet*, p.80.
21 *Ibid.*, p.70.

Engineers and Sappers

It was shown in the previous volume that engineers and sappers at first formed part of the artillery. As a result, the artillery units included a variety of tools, building and bridging materials, pontoon bridges, and similar equipment. After the reign of Gustavus Adolphus, however, engineering equipment was gradually moved from the artillery to the supply train.[22]

Even so, engineers and sappers remained under the control of the quartermaster-generals. When the army was on the march, and there was reason to expect local peasants to have built timber obstacles, that is, abatis, or barricades of felled trees (a traditional feature of northern warfare), then the quartermaster-general would ensure that men armed with suitable tools to clear the obstacles marched in the vanguard. As an example, when Horn marched into Scania in early 1644, the quartermaster-general, the aforementioned Olof Hansson Örnehufvud, made sure to assign the initial marching order as follows: 50 horse, followed by 100 commanded musketeers and four regimental cannons, which in turn was followed by 500 pioneers equipped with the appropriate tools.[23]

Swedish siege artillery at Wasserburg-am-Inn, Bavaria, 15 June 1648. (*Theatrum Europaeum*)

In addition, engineers and sappers played a vital role in the fortification of camps. Around the camp, they customarily built a dense system of outlying redoubts and artillery batteries. Field fortifications were constructed from earth, rock, and wood from the surrounding area and to some extent depended on what was locally available. Wicker baskets filled with earth and stones were used as gabions when the soil-cover was insufficient for trenches and ramparts. The Swedish army was known for its fortification skills, and many of their standard practices were much later adopted by the French fortification expert Sébastien Le Prestre de Vauban (1633–1707), to whose name they were linked for future generations. Unlike the Imperial army, which had excellent engineers, too, but relied on more dogmatic systems of geometric fortification planning, the Swedes adapted their fortifications to the landscape. This is obvious from contemporary prints but has also been confirmed by archaeological excavations. Yet, good as the static defences were, they did not constitute the entire set of defences. The Swedish army relied on its engineers, but standard procedure was to complement the static defences with dynamic ones in the form of regular cavalry patrols.[24]

22 *Ibid.*, p.80.
23 Munthe, *Kongl. Fortifikationens historia* 2, p.49; which copies the complete order of march in a document dated 11 February 1644 (O.S.).
24 Václav Matoušek, et al., *Třebel 1647: A Battlefield of the Thirty Years' War from the Perspective of History, Archeology, Art-history, Geoinformatics, and Ethnology* (Prague: Krigl, 2017), pp.95–6, 154, 156–7, 159–62.

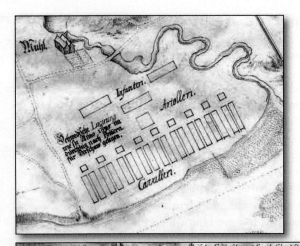

Swedish camp at Dirschau, Prussia, 1634. The camp faces the River Vistula, which enables easy lines of communication, and is flanked by a stream, on which is located a mill. The infantry, artillery, and cavalry units each have their predetermined locations. (Map made by Polish–Lithuanian Commonwealth military cartographer Friedrich Getkant)

Battle of Töpel (modern-day Teplá), Bohemia, 9 September 1647. Left: The town of Töpel inside the Imperial camp. Right: The Swedish camp, adapted to the landscape. (*Theatrum Europaeum*)

Operations around Triebel, Bohemia, 19 August 1647. Left: The Swedish camp. Right: The Imperial camp. The Swedish engineers have surrounded the camp with an outer perimeter of remote redoubts and artillery batteries (marked E). At the same time, dynamic defences in the form of regular cavalry patrols (marked F) provide additional security. (*Theatrum Europaeum*)

Grenadiers

Grenadiers were specialist infantrymen armed with a musket and several grenades each. Over time, the use of explosive grenades grew within the artillery, and it is unsurprising that their use by the infantry increased, too. Grenades intended to be thrown by hand were originally developed for siege work, since grenades enabled the attackers to clear a breach of defenders before exploiting it. At the siege of Swedish-held Regensburg in 1634, the Swedish commandant Major General Lars Kagg set up units armed with grenades. However, these units were temporary and were not retained after the siege.[25]

Timber mantlet used as cover for a Swedish sniper at the siege of Prague, 1648, together with hand grenades (below) and incendiary wreaths (above). The incendiary wreath (Swedish: *beckkrans*) was a wreath of incendiary materials such as straw, tow, or oakum soaked in pitch or tar, no less than 40 cm in diameter and at times wrapped around an iron frame for stability and enclosed in sailcloth. Particularly common in naval warfare, the device was also used during sieges. The incendiary wreath could be used offensively, to ignite an enemy structure, or for battle-field illumination. In 1585, Rudolf van Deventer recommended that an incendiary wreath be filled with eight pounds of purified saltpetre, eight pounds of 'good gunpowder', two pounds of sulphur, and an 'equal amount' of resin, after which the wreath should be moistened with oil and turpentine. Several incendiary wreaths remain in Swedish museums. (J. N. Zatočil, 1685)

---

25 Alm, *Eldhandvapen* 1, 250; Jakobsson, *Lantmilitär beväpning och beklädnad*, p.138. On the siege, see Peter Engerisser, "Eine bisher unbekannte Ansicht der Belagerung Regensburgs im Jahr 1634", *Verhandlungen des Historischen Vereins für Oberpfalz und Regensburg* p.148 (Regensburg: Verlag des Historischen Vereins für Oberpfalz und Regensburg, 2008). Available online at <www.engerisser.de/Belagerung_Regensburgs1634.pdf>.

Naval Personnel

There still was little difference between the army and navy when it came to service conditions, and many infantrymen served as shipborne infantry.

Naval personal weapons included rapiers, of the same type as was used by the infantry, or sabre-like cutlasses that also existed in small numbers. The navy often received army surplus rapiers. In addition, the navy employed a variety of spears, half-pikes, and pikes. Naval regulations for pikes were identical to army regulations. Half-pikes were to be five cubits in length, again the same as in the army. From at least 1635, the navy also utilised a small number of partisans, used by under-officers. In addition, sailors employed axes, both as tools and weapons. As for firearms, the navy employed muskets, blunderbusses, and pistols. Most were matchlocks, although the navy knew that they formed a fire hazard and accordingly preferred snaphance locks. Pistols intended for the navy, so-called boarding pistols (Swedish: *änterpistoler*), usually had snaphance locks and were occasionally carried several at a time, hanging from bandoliers.[26] Finally, the navy employed hand grenades and a large variety of incendiaries.[27]

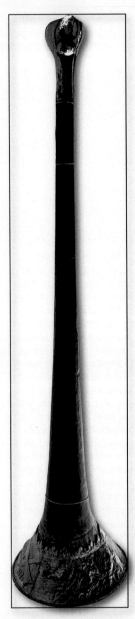

Speaking-trumpet (megaphone), more than 1 m long and according to tradition used by Carl Gustav Wrangel at the battle off Fehmarn, 1644. (Skokloster Castle)

26 Alm, "Flottanshandvapen", pp.72, 76–83, 85–7.
27 *Ibid.*, p.91. See also Michael Fredholm von Essen, "On the Trail of Rocketry: The Enigma of Scandinavian Naval Pyrotechnics in the Sixteenth to Eighteenth Century", *Arquebusier* 30:6 (2008), pp.24–39.

5

Uniforms, Dress, and Appearance

Changes in Military Fashion

Fashion continued to change, and the latter half of the Thirty Years' War was no exception. In the previous volume, it was shown that Spanish fashion prevailed in Sweden and the Swedish army into the 1620s. However, by this time Dutch fashion grew increasingly influential, not only in industrial goods ranging from muskets to rapiers and warships but also in personal dress. Army clothing was affected, too, and henceforth, many officers began to dress in the Dutch manner. Yet, in the Swedish army a different style of clothes had already become apparent during the war in the Polish-Lithuanian Commonwealth. Gustavus Adolphus himself had, at times, appeared in Polish dress, consisting of a red, Oriental-style caftan decorated with white braid and velvet cuffs. The Oriental caftan likely also contributed to the popularity of the casack as military dress. Yet, and of more lasting importance, the caftan became the immediate forerunner of the French coat, which together with the long vest in the second half of the century achieved an enduring position in Western male dress. Henceforth, French fashion gained an increasingly influential position. Younger officers such as Carl Gustav Wrangel readily adopted these styles, while older and more irritable ones such as Banér disliked the new fads.

Cavalry officers at the siege of Brünn, 1645. The officer on the left wears a French coat of the latest fashion.

Around 1635, the breeches again grew longer and narrower, reaching down slightly more than in the past, and they were no longer tied below the knees but remained open, following French fashion.

The old Spanish collar or ruff had been stiffened with starch, which essentially prevented men of standing from allowing their hair to grow long. Even when the starched collar was abandoned, many had continued to wear short hair, including Gustavus Adolphus. However, already in the 1620s long hair grew more common. The trend was facilitated by the introduction of

Swedish officer at the siege of Prague, 1648. Armed with a partisan, he wears a high-crowned hat, casack, wide breeches open at the bottom, and boots.
(*Theatrum Europaeum*)

Lennart Torstensson with cravat, painted by David Beck, probably during the period 1647–1651 when Beck was active in Sweden.

Lennart Torstensson with cravat, dated 1648 and painted by an unknown artist.

the cravat in or around 1636.[1] Over time, the cravat replaced the old collar altogether. The cravat was a neckband, the forerunner of the modern tailored necktie and bow tie, which originated, as the name implies, from a style worn by Croat cavalry. It is known from two portraits that Lennart Torstensson wore the cravat, which by then must have reflected recent fashion. One of them, dated 1648, was painted by an unknown artist, apparently soon after Torstensson's return to Sweden. The other, painted by David Beck, is very similar. Beck was only active in Sweden during the period 1647–1651, which would suggest a date of around the same time.

Hats grew taller until about 1640, with a pointed crown, but remained very wide-brimmed. Modern re-enactment has shown that for musketeers, a wide brim might protect the soldier's eyes from the flames that flared up from the priming pan when firing the musket. Around 1640, fashion changed, and the crown again grew flat for a few years. From this time, the brim decreased in size, too. Plumes also became less common. Occasionally, the plume was replaced with a ribbon or a single, long feather, but most officers discarded the plume altogether. For the infantry, hats remained wide brimmed.

From around 1640, boots became tighter and were usually no longer worn with the upper part folded down. The shape of shoes grew longer and, no longer pointed, were henceforth cut diagonally in front. Often the right and left shoes could then be used interchangeably, since they were cut identically.

An officer frequently wore an embroidered or silk sash across the breast or tied around the waist, the colour of which sometimes indicated the army in which he served. During the reign of Gustavus Adolphus, there was not yet any standardised sash colour in the Swedish army. After the death of Gustavus Adolphus, however, Swedish officers increasingly often wore blue sashes edged in gold. The fashion grew so common that it was once believed that after the death of Gustavus Adolphus, blue sashes, usually with yellow borders, became standard within the Swedish army. However, in western Europe almost all high-quality sashes, regardless of colour, had gold fringes, so blue and gold is unlikely to have functioned as an identifying field sign.[2]

This conclusion is also supported by the actual field signs known to have been used. At Wittstock in 1636, the Swedish soldiers wore green cloth bands around their arms as a field sign. From the late 1630s, Swedish soldiers increasingly often used twisted bands of straw worn on the hat and/or left arm as field signs. They were used at the storm of Leipzig in 1637, the capture

---

1   R. Broby-Johansen, *Kropp och kläder: Klädedräktens konsthistoria* (Stockholm: Rabén & Sjögren, 2nd edn 1985), p.149.
2   Brzezinski, *Army of Gustavus Adolphus* 2, p.21.

Beige-grey felt hat, mid 17th century. Marked as 'pattern for Queen Christina's infantry' and clearly intended for general issue. Brim: diameter 530 mm, circumference 1630 mm, and width 180–185 mm. Crown: height 167 mm and diameter 250 mm. The outer edge of the brim is protected by a sewn band of wool and linen. One of very few surviving infantry hats of the period. (Army Museum, Stockholm)

Musketeer of unknown nationality, mid 17th century. Representative of those who served in the Swedish army, this sketch was later used as a model for battle paintings of the war. The breeches are wide, but not open at the bottom. (Johan Philip Lemke)

of Bautzen in 1639, and in the second battle of Breitenfeld in 1642. Blue scarves only appeared at the very end of the Thirty Years' War. It was only at Jankow in 1645 that Swedes used "blue signs in the standards", which likely were strips of blue cloth tied at the finials, in the manner of cravats.[3] At Königsmarck's surprise raid into Prague in 1648, the Swedish troops put oak leaves into their hat bands as a field sign.

Uniforms

The first significant addition to the uniforms of the Swedish army after the King's death came in early 1633, when plans were made to bring home the corpse under dignified circumstances. This entailed memorial services and a parade in July in which the Life Guard company and a few companies from the Östergötland and Uppland Regiments were given special mourning uniforms. These consisted of black jackets, breeches, and hats. The companies which received mourning uniforms accompanied the King's corpse to Sweden, so the uniforms were not used

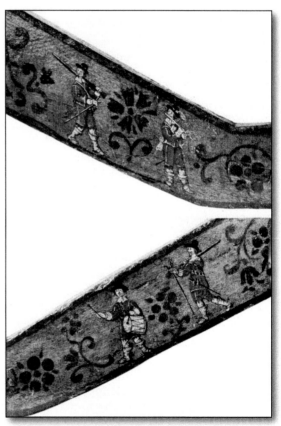

Drummer, piper, and musketeers. The men wear red jackets and breeches with yellow lining, yellowish boots, and black hats. The breeches appear to be open at the bottom, suggesting a date in the 1640s. (Paintings on a contemporary artillery carriage model, Army Museum, Stockholm)

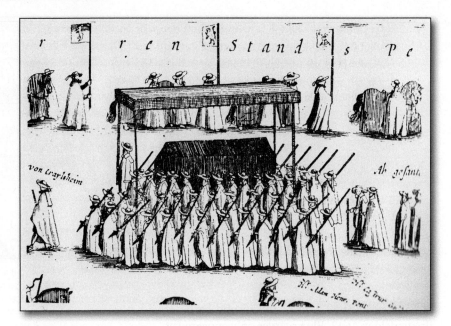

The Drabant or Life Guard company around Gustavus Adolphus's coffin, Wolgast, 26 July 1633. The men, wearing long coats, hold their partisans with the head downwards as a sign of respect for the late King.

on campaign. Moreover, the survivors of the Östergötland Regiment were demobilised upon the regiment's return to Sweden.[4]

Black clothes, incidentally, were in late 1635 also distributed to at least one enlisted unit, although as a means of saving cloth, not in commemoration of the late Gustavus Adolphus. At this time, Arvid Svensson's enlisted dragoon company was given old black cloth for uniforms and stockings from the mourning draperies that had covered walls and ceilings in the widowed Queen's apartments since her husband's death.[5]

Supply problems persisted throughout the war. As late as in 1645, there were complaints that new conscripts from Sweden still arrived in Germany dressed in their original peasant clothes. Moreover, the soldiers already there at the time frequently lacked acceptable dress. There still remained problems with the procurement of winter clothes. This problem persisted in Germany but also in Sweden, where the garrisons of the border forts usually lacked proper clothing. Often, the commanders had to procure simple, undyed woollen cloth just to provide some cover for the men.[6]

Artillerymen generally dressed similarly to the infantry. Most appear to have worn grey clothes, and this eventually became common practice for artillerymen in the Swedish army.

Since the Life Guard company, following its departure to Stockholm with the King's corpse, primarily had ceremonial duties, this was also reflected in their uniforms and weapons. First, they received the aforementioned mourning uniforms of black cloth. In 1635, they instead returned to the Vasa colours of yellow and black. Uniforms henceforth were yellow with black

---

4   Petri, *Kungl. Första livgrenadjärregementets historia* 2, pp.189–90.
5   Brzezinski, *Army of Gustavus Adolphus* 2, p.16.
6   Erik Bellander, *Dräkt och uniform: Den svenska arméns beklädnad från 1500-talets början fram till våra dagar* (Stockholm: P. A. Norstedt & Söner, 1973), pp.114–15.

trim and black hats. Pikemen wore cloaks, musketeers casacks. Both types were yellow, like the rest of the uniform. The difference may have been that casacks had sleeves. Arms and armour were made more decorative, too. In 1645, it was decided that unlike in the field armies, the Life Guard when on court duty would wear shining breastplates and helmets. At first, the armourers experimented with removing the black from regular breastplates, but it was found to be too time-consuming. It was cheaper to order new sets, which never had been blackened. The new ones were instead polished. Weapons for court duty were embellished, too, some of them gilded. Even halberds were briefly reintroduced for some soldiers of noble status.[7]

---

7   Barkman, Lundkvist, and Tersmeden, *Kungl. Svea Livgardes Historia* 3:2, pp.491–2, 495, 514–15.

6

Tactics and Strategy

Tactical Doctrine

The Swedish model as established by Gustavus Adolphus was a combined arms model, in which the key arm, the infantry, acted in unison with the cavalry and field artillery. Gustavus Adolphus aimed for a combination of hitting-power, mobility, and defensive strength. Hitting-power was achieved through firepower (musketeers and regimental artillery) in combination with shock (charging pikemen and cavalry). Mobility was assured by the army's superior organisation and training. The army's defensive strength was the result of the combination of hitting-power and mobility, since it allowed the army to close with the enemy rapidly and thus avoid excessive losses from the opponent's firepower.

Cavalry Tactics

Gustavus Adolphus had attempted to increase the cavalry's firepower by attaching platoons with musketeers to the cavalry units. This was a new solution to the problem of combining firepower, mobility, and defensive capability.

The serious flaw in the joint cavalry–musketeer formation was that the infantry musketeers could not move as fast as the cavalry. Gustavus Adolphus did not solve the question of how to combine shock and firepower in a cavalry context. He provided a better solution than what was generally available, but he did not reach what he probably had hoped to achieve. As a result, after the death of Gustavus Adolphus, Bernard of Saxe-Weimar changed the tactical doctrine introduced by the Swedish king. He retained many aspects of the Swedish model, including its aggressive aspects, but ordered his cavalry to charge at the gallop, independent of infantry support.[1] We have seen how Bernard later went into French service, where he recommended the adapted

---

1 Ebbe Gyllenstierna, "Karl Gustav Wrangel och Henri Turenne: Svensk och fransk krigföring under trettioåriga krigets sista skede", *Meddelande* 36 (Stockholm: Armémuseum, 1976), pp.39–51, on p.47.

tactical doctrine to Henri de La Tour d'Auvergne, Viscount of Turenne, who then served under him. Turenne referred to this type of cavalry charge as in the Swedish manner (*à la suèdoise*) and advocated the doctrine in France.[2]

Meanwhile, the share of cavalry within the army grew, and cavalry became the offensive arms within the army. As a result, in the mid seventeenth century the cavalry regained its former position as the premier arms. Yet, in full-scale battles, the cavalry horses constituted a limiting factor. Most could not carry on for more than four or five hours, before they needed rest.

Besides, as noted, the importance of both cavalry and dragoons grew in relationship to the increasing scarcity of supplies. Only horse had the required mobility to cover sufficient distances to find the increasingly scarce supplies that remained available.

Infantry Tactics

Swedish infantry tactics changed little after the death of Gustavus Adolphus. The Swedish model continued to emphasise the offensive. Pikemen and musketeers remained arrayed in no more than six lines, with the pikemen in the centre. The musketeers were trained to fire in volleys (salvoes), several ranks at a time. Following a volley, the pikemen would charge the enemy.

Yet, the share of pikemen in the army fell, and organisation was simplified, for practical reasons but also to accommodate soldiers who were less well trained and disciplined in comparison to previous Swedish armies. Over time, this resulted in an increased focus on infantry firepower, which came to reduce the previous emphasis on the shock provided by charging pikemen. The infantry then became a defensive arm, and it was up to the cavalry to charge the enemy. Over time, the infantry began to be seen primarily as a stable base around which the cavalry could operate in set battles. Nonetheless, infantry was needed to lay siege to towns and fortresses, and to man them afterwards.

Later in the century, Swedish tactical doctrine for the infantry would again emphasise the offensive, and to an even greater extent than under Gustavus Adolphus. At the time, offensive tactics would be reintroduced by officers who had served in the Thirty Years' War.[3]

Artillery Tactics

The Swedish system of field artillery, and in particular regimental artillery, continued to develop throughout the war.

---

2   Turenne later recommended the doctrine to a young Swedish officer, Nils Bielke, who together with the experienced Rutger von Ascheberg in 1676 reintroduced it in the Swedish army, with considerable success (and, incidentally, called it a charge in the French manner, *à la française*). Fredholm von Essen, *Charles XI's War*, p.18.

3   *Ibid.*, p.128.

Swedish artillery tactics reached its peak performance in the seventeenth century under the artillery expert Torstensson. Under his guidance, the field artillery was characterised by mobility and independence, which was fully developed in the 1645 battle of Jankow, where the efficient use of artillery seems to have been a decisive factor in the Swedish victory. At Jankow, the Swedish artillery was constantly in play, moving from location to location and deploying in various formations. When terrain allowed, the artillery would even deploy in double ranks ("in multiple ranks behind each other", *in mehreren Reihen hinter einander*, in the words of Montecuccoli who was there), the rear rank firing above the lower rank deployed in front.[4] Presumably the regimental cannons formed the lower rank, while the heavy artillery was deployed at some distance behind and above them. During sieges, such as the 1648 siege of Prague, the artillery even deployed in three ranks, each above the other.[5]

The regimental cannons retained their importance in the Swedish army. We have seen how by the end of the war, the original regimental 3-pounders were gradually replaced with new 3-pounders with longer barrels, which increased lethality at longer distances, and how Torstensson compensated the greater weight with the introduction of more horses to provide mobility. However, Torstensson also improved the heavy artillery further. By reducing the weight of the gun carriages and adding more draught horses to the teams, he significantly increased the mobility of even heavier cannons. For instance, 24-pounders were moved by transporting the cannon barrels and carriages separately, each drawn by more than 20 horses, and then joining them together on the chosen site.

Unfortunately for the army, few Swedish commanders later in the century displayed Torstensson's aptitude for using artillery. As their tactics increasingly focused on aggressive charges, not even the Swedish regimental artillery could maintain sufficient speed to keep up. Further developments in artillery tactics had to wait until the second half of the Great Northern War (1700–1721).

Strategy and Grand Strategy

Although the Swedish war aims, unsurprisingly, transformed over time, Oxenstierna wanted three key objectives before he would accept a peace. In the Latin terminology then employed in diplomatic discourse, he wanted, first, *satisfactio coronae*, that is, recompensation for the Swedish Crown for the war effort in the form of German ports and territories on the Baltic coast. Swedish bases there would protect Sweden's core territories from any invasion launched from the same ports. Oxenstierna also wanted *assecuratio pacis*, that is, security guarantees that would protect the peace from the threat of Habsburg domination of the Empire. Swedish territories in northern Germany went some way to assuage this threat, while admission to

4   Montecuccoli, *Ausgewählte Schriften* 2, p.580.
5   Hedberg, *Kungl. Artilleriet*, p.262.

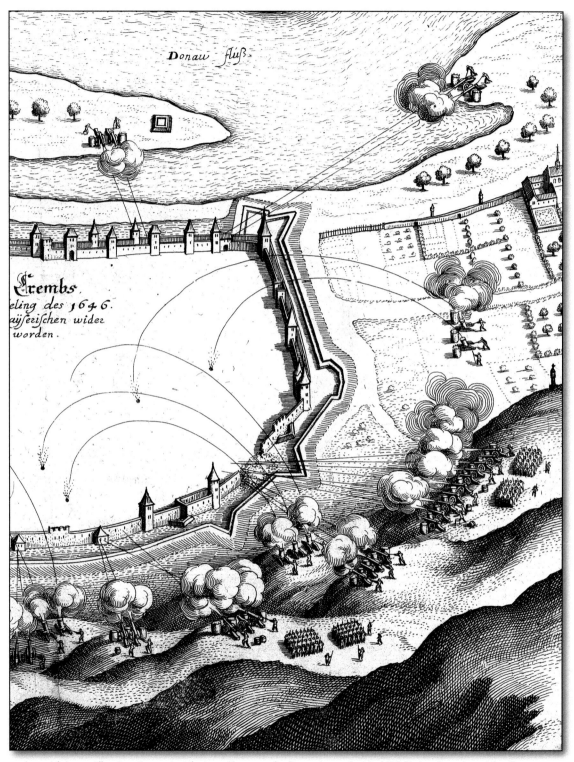

Imperial siege artillery in action against the town Krems-an-der-Donau, Lower Austria, 1646. During sieges Imperial artillery, too, deployed in multiple ranks when the terrain permitted.

the Imperial Diet (*Reichstag*) was another. A third was the creation of some kind of association of Protestant German states under Swedish leadership. Finally, Sweden needed *satisfactio militum*, that is, monetary restitution of its expenses and in particular for the foreseen expenses of demobilising the numerous enlisted soldiers.[6] These were the war objectives. If needed, either, or both, of the first two objectives could be dropped, but not the monetary restitution. Without it, there was no way the Swedish Crown could cover its heavy debts to the generals, colonels, and others who had provided enlisted units, nor could the soldiers be paid off.

Although the Swedish strategy temporarily found itself somewhat lost after the death of Gustavus Adolphus, many of his core beliefs and strategic priorities continued to guide Oxenstierna and the Swedish commanders. Offensive war remained the cornerstone of Swedish strategy. It was cheaper to fight on foreign territory, since most of the costs could then be defrayed by passing the burden onto the shoulders of the enemy and his population, according to the argument that *bellum se ipsum alet* ("war feeds itself"). The continued focus on offensive operations was the result of Sweden's persistent lack of resources, which strongly encouraged rapid, decisive action over prolonged campaigns, for which there usually was neither men, supplies, nor money. Swedish commanders continued to seek battle when they considered themselves at an advantage, yet did not rush to battle when there was no dire need. A main objective remained to protect the lines of communication. Almost as important was the objective to impair the opponent's ability to wage war by gaining control of or, that failing, ravaging his supplies and base areas.

It is often claimed that Gustavus Adolphus's successors lacked his strategic vision. This is not necessarily correct. However, one key advantage of the Protestant alliance certainly died with the Swedish King: Gustavus Adolphus had been able, through his personal and royal charisma, enhanced by judicious propaganda and already current superstition about a Lion from the North, to keep the Protestant alliance together. Oxenstierna, for all his ability, did not enjoy this advantage. Neither did his field marshals, who were competent, sometimes even brilliant, but nonetheless were no more than regular military men in a war already teeming with soldiers of noble birth. Kingship had a quality of its own when it comes to raise support, and it was no longer available. It will never be known whether Gustavus Adolphus could have fought the war to an early and successful conclusion, had he survived Lützen (probably not), but it was already then obvious that there was nobody else on the Protestant side, general or statesman, who could. There was simply not enough unity on what the Protestant alliance was meant to achieve. Return Germany to the situation ante bellum? Replace the Emperor? Push back the Catholic faith?

We have seen that a key tenet of Oxenstierna's strategic thought was that the war in Germany should be fought primarily with enlisted German soldiers, and that Sweden should act within a coalition of Protestant powers.

6   Antje Oschmann, *Der Nürnberger Exekutionstag 1649–1650: Das Ende des Dreißigjährigen Krieges in Deutschland* (Münster: Aschendorff, 1991), p.39.

Moreover, the operations should be paid for by others, France and the Netherlands if possible but when subsidies were unavailable, then by the German princes and territories. For sure, Sweden should be the leader of the coalition, but actual military operations should preferably be carried out by Germans. The strategy explains why after the death of Gustavus Adolphus, Oxenstierna was eager to include so many German princes in the Swedish army, reward them with high rank, and give them important commands.

As noted, not all Swedish generals agreed with this strategy. Banér, in particular, was opposed, which, incidentally, might explain why he left command for a while in 1633. Banér argued that the German princes were not necessarily loyal to the Swedish cause, and that the newly raised German units lacked the training and discipline of the existing Swedish army. Instead of involving German princes, Banér suggested the formation of two strong, wholly Swedish field armies, respectively commanded by Horn and himself. These two armies would then go on the offensive against the Habsburg heartland, until the Emperor agreed to peace. Meanwhile, the allied Germans could safeguard lines of communications and other easy tasks.[7]

Oxenstierna did not agree, and unlike Banér, he was too cautious to leave the Swedish core territories undefended against potential attacks from Denmark or the Polish-Lithuanian Commonwealth. Instead, Oxenstierna ordered the preservation of Swedish national units, which henceforth mostly were retained in garrisons along the Baltic shore. Oxenstierna was also concerned over the risk that Imperial troops might reconquer some of the Protestant territories in Germany which had joined the Swedish cause. Besides, logistical constraints militated against the concentration of forces to only a couple of locations.

Yet, the audacity of Banér's plan may not have derived from mere arrogance. Banér had probably realised another significant determinant of the German war. Although Continental military entrepreneurs eventually had offered their services to the Swedish Crown, few had done so before the 1631 victory at Breitenfeld. Besides, many of the newly raised enlisted units were fresh and unseasoned. It was the training and fighting experience of the Swedish army that had made it successful, not the number of men. After years of fighting in Livonia and Prussia, the Swedish army consisted of seasoned regiments, veteran soldiers, and skilled officers. The men provided by the German princes were simply no good, in Banér's assessment, nor could money buy an experienced army. This had been shown beyond any doubt at Breitenfeld in 1631, in which Horn had coolly turned the tide with his well-trained veterans while John George's freshly raised Saxons fled. Expressed in modern terms, seventeenth-century warfare depended more on fighting experience and training than on market forces and the ability to raise fresh regiments.

Would Banér's daring strategy have worked? The Empire was weakened after the battle of Lützen, but so was the main Swedish field army. A decisive campaign as proposed by Banér, if all went well, might conceivably have

---

7   Banér to Oxenstierna, 20 November 1632 (O.S.), *AOSB* 2:6, pp.81–3.

compelled the Emperor to agree to peace. However, what then? Would such a peace agreement have resulted in any permanent gains or, indeed, a stable outcome? Banér's suggested strategy was essentially a gamble. Sweden might have won the war spectacularly, but a major defeat of either of the two proposed Swedish armies would almost certainly have resulted in, if not a disaster, then at least a stalemate. At that point the superior resources of the Empire and the lack of stable alliances in the rear could have cost Sweden the gains already achieved. Oxenstierna was too cautious to hazard everything on the gut feeling of a fighting man, however experienced, so he did not take up Banér's proposal. Instead, he reserved decisions of strategy for himself.

While grand strategy accordingly was left in the hands of Oxenstierna, his generals continued to follow the strategies used so far, especially those that seemed to work well.

Following the battle of Nördlingen in 1634, Swedish field armies seldom exceeded 15,000 men. On the other hand, the ratio of cavalry in the field armies grew to as much as half or even two thirds of the total army. Cavalry had logistical demands that exceeded those of the infantry, since, first, horses had to be supplied, and, second, the horses, too, needed equipment and fodder. At least the cavalry enjoyed a greater mobility and range in its own foraging capability. The regular cavalry was coming into its own and would soon assume the leading role in the northern armies.

One major reason for the growth in cavalry within the Swedish army was the repeated grand raids into the Habsburg dynastic heartlands of Bohemia and Lower Austria from 1639 onwards. The raids combined two objectives, both of which demanded strong cavalry forces. First, they were attempts to provoke the Emperor into either giving battle on his own territory, or else see it devastated. Second, they were intended to follow the doctrine of Gustavus Adolphus to fight Sweden's war on enemy territory, where supplies, plunder, and contributions could be gathered in sufficient quantities to pay for the war. With this in mind, Banér's, Torstensson's, Wrangel's, Königsmarck's, and in extension Charles Gustavus's, recurrent invasions of Bohemia make perfect sense. The same can be said of Banér's devastation of Saxony in 1636, Torstensson's ravaging of Saxony in early 1645, and Wrangel's and Turenne's devastation of Bavaria in 1646 and again in 1648. These were not senseless, and pointless, raids of individual generals, nor were they primarily carried out for their commanders to acquire loot which could be sent back to their estates in Sweden (which should not be interpreted as a lack of interest on their behalf in acquiring wealth). The grand raids were the logical outcome of a deliberate strategy to win the war by applying pressure on the Emperor in the ongoing peace negotiations, but they were also, equally importantly, a means to retain and feed the army. The Swedish government and army in Germany were not against peace negotiations, but peace should be negotiated from a position of strength, and with due consideration of Sweden's territorial and financial needs. Peace was a war objective but it was not the cause for which Sweden was fighting.

Besides, the ultimate aim of these campaigns was not to locate the enemy field army with the intention to defeat it decisively in a pitched battle. Like the strategy of Gustavus Adolphus before them, the Swedish generals knew that battles were risky, and that a major loss might wipe out all the territorial and political gains already achieved. If they had not learnt this already from Gustavus Adolphus, they certainly learnt it from the defeat at Nördlingen, which resulted in the immediate loss of most Swedish influence in southern Germany. Another defeat of this magnitude, in particular during the ongoing peace negotiations in Westphalia, could have resulted in the collapse of Swedish power on the Continent. It certainly would have placed the Swedish diplomats in a much weaker position vis-à-vis their negotiating partners. The notion of achieving a gainful peace through a decisive victory on the battlefield and the destruction of an enemy army was not yet part of Swedish strategic thought, and it can be argued that such notions, which emerged later, had little relationship to reality. Torstensson, who was not shy to lead his army into battle and habitually planned his actions better than most, summarised the then Swedish view on the risks of offering battle:

> There is nothing more hazardous than to chance a battle. You may lose it through a thousand unforeseen accidents, even when you have carefully taken all measures and steps available to the most flawless military expertise.[8]

Torstensson's contribution to Swedish tactical and strategic thought cannot be overstated. Years later, having become King of Sweden, the warlike Charles Gustavus concluded that "for everything which I know [of military affairs], I should give thanks to Torstensson".[9]

8   Englund, *Ofredsår*, p.384.
9   *Slaget vid Jankow*, p.8.

7

The Navy

Background and Warship Strength

When the modern Danish and Swedish navies emerged in the early sixteenth century, both developed swiftly because of the struggle between the two countries over hegemony in the Baltic region. The Nordic Seven Years' War (1563–1570) between Sweden on the one side and Denmark and its possession Norway, Lübeck (the informal capital of the Hanse), and the united Kingdom of Poland and Grand Duchy of Lithuania on the other was the first modern war at sea in Europe between fleets of sailing ships armed with cannon. During the war, the Danish and Swedish navies grew to be the then largest sailing fleets in Europe, both becoming equal in size to the English around 1565 and each surpassing the English in numbers by 1570.[1]

The rivalry between Sweden and Denmark over hegemony in the Baltic continued throughout the seventeenth century. Denmark still controlled both sides of the Danish Straits, through which all maritime trade into and out of the Baltic had to pass. In 1611, Denmark used its then possessions in present southern Sweden as bases for military attacks against the Swedish port of Kalmar in the east, on the Baltic Sea, and the newly established port of Gothenburg in the west (in existence although formally founded only in 1621), facing the North Sea. One of several reasons for the war was the reduction in customs duties, the Sound tolls, paid to the Danish Crown when part of the maritime trade to Sweden was diverted from the Danish Straits to Gothenburg. During the war, Danish fleets blockaded, mostly successfully, both Gothenburg and Kalmar. By 1613, Sweden had to accept harsh terms to end the war.

Before the 1620s, there was no real separation of Sweden's armed forces into an army and a navy. The King's officers served both on land and at sea, as did the King himself. Army infantry and gunners were often called out for shipboard service. Gustavus Adolphus's Articles of War of 1621, although

---

1 On the early modern Danish and Swedish navies, see Jan Glete, "Naval Power and Control of the Sea in the Baltic in the Sixteenth Century", John B. Hattendorf and Richard W. Unger (eds), *War at Sea in the Middle Ages and Renaissance* (Woodbridge, Suffolk: Boydell Press, 2003), pp.217–32, on pp.221–5, 227–8, 230, 232.

written for the army, provided rules on discipline and military legislation which were enforced for those serving on ships, too. Although a concept for a naval version of the Articles was prepared in 1628, it was not really implemented until 1644 when special legislation for the navy was finally adopted. However, Sweden had a modern navy, and during the latter half of the Thirty Years' War, the navy can be said gradually to have become a separate service.

This was to a considerable extent the work of Admiral Claes Fleming (1592–1644). Gustavus Adolphus had no later than 1620 appointed Fleming to the position as the navy's second in command. Fleming was then a young but experienced officer who already in 1613 had served on the Muscovite frontier in Jacob De la Gardie's Life Company. Two years later, he participated in the siege of Pskov. Soon Fleming also showed his skills as a naval commander. In time, he came to overhaul the navy establishment, improving it considerably. As mentioned, under Gustavus Adolphus the process of establishing distinct departments of government, each known as a *collegium*, was already underway. A naval department, later called the Department of the Admiralty (*Amiralitets collegium*), was established around 1618. With the Swedish constitution introduced in 1634, a third of the distinct departments of government became the Admiralty (*Amiralitetet*), responsible for the administration of the navy. It was headed by the Grand Admiral of the Realm (*Riksamiral*).[2]

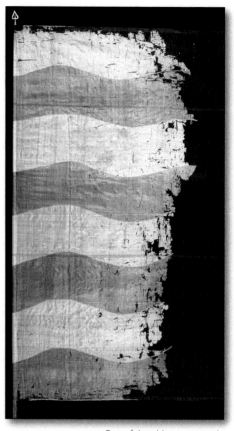

One of the oldest preserved Swedish flags probably made in 1620. It was used as one of six infantry company colours on board the Swedish warships that carried Maria Eleonora, the bride of Gustavus Adolphus, to Sweden. Accordingly used as a Swedish flag on a naval warship, it was not yet the Swedish triple-tailed naval flag which was introduced a few years later. However, blue and yellow flags of this type were used by Swedish warships since at least 1585 and were flown during the siege of Riga in 1621. (Army Museum, Stockholm)

Previously, the construction of warships had been contracted with yards all over Sweden, including in Lake Mälaren, although under the supervision of the Crown. While this meant that local labour and taxes paid in kind could be utilised, construction was slow and the decentralisation probably made it difficult to learn from technical progress that took place elsewhere. From 1618, naval shipbuilding was instead centralised, although still handled by private entrepreneurs. Fleming consolidated the building of new warship into two naval shipyards, the navy yard in Stockholm, under the command of the admiral in charge of the dockyards, often referred to as the port admiral (*holmamiral*), and a private yard in the town of Västervik. Occasional warships were also built in Gothenburg. The consolidation of warship construction was good for quality control. However, private entrepreneurs continued to play a key role. This concerned all fields of naval procurement, from shipbuilding to cannon production, the import of canvas for sails, and even the regular maintenance of ships and gear. Indeed, up to and including 1628 the Admiralty transferred the entire burden of administration to private contractors by leasing out the naval shipyards in long-term contracts. These entrepreneurs, many of whom came from the Dutch Republic, would build

---

2   Einar Wendt, *Amiralitetskollegiets historia* I: 1634–1695 (Stockholm: Lindberg, 1950), p.34.

warships but also smaller vessels, such as pinnaces (smaller full-rigged ships of a type that later would develop into the frigate), galiots (small ships with nearly flat bottoms which enabled navigation in shallow waters and more commonly were used as merchantmen), and galleys (oared vessels with two or three square-rigged masts), the latter for the inshore navy. Most Swedish warships carried a single full deck of cannons. However, during the 1620s, Gustavus Adolphus ordered more ships, including larger vessels with two full gun decks and armed with heavier guns than the ubiquitous 12-pounder, which was the most common naval cannon.

Sweden already had a substantial navy. Being a country of far-flung settlements connected by waterways but few good roads, Sweden had always relied on ships for maintaining supply and communication links. The first modern navy had been established in the 1520s by Gustavus I Vasa, the grandfather of Gustavus Adolphus. Since then, the navy had grown in size and strength. It continued to do so throughout the wars fought by Gustavus Adolphus, although some attrition and battle losses naturally took place (Table 10). It was only in 1646, after the defeat of Denmark, that the Crown again allowed the navy to decrease in size, and then it did so because it had to: four warships were sold to France and several others were handed over to private businessmen whom the Crown owed money.

The Swedish flagship *Vasa*, an example of the new, larger type of warship ordered by Gustavus Adolphus in the 1620s. The *Vasa* was built in 1628 but sank on her maiden voyage. Salvaged after three centuries, she is now on display in the Vasa Museum, Stockholm. This model shows what she looked like when newly built. (Vasa Museum, Stockholm; photo: author)

The *Vasa*'s stern, as it looked when newly built. (Photo: author)

The original stern, in its present condition. When new, the woodcarvings were painted in bright colours. (Vasa Museum, Stockholm; Photo: Medströms)

Table 10. Number of warships in the Swedish navy. (Source: Glete, *Navies and Nations*, p.607)

Number of warships divided in size groups (metric tons)				
Year	100–500	501–1,000	1,001–1,500	1,500+	Total
1615	25	5	–	–	30
1620	26	7	1	–	34
1625	24	13	2	–	39
1630	17	12	2	–	31
1635	28	20	3	2	53
1640	18	19	3	2	42
1645	26	28	2	2	58
1650	13	26	2	1	42

Smaller ships were used, too, most notably pinnaces, galiots, and fireships, the latter of which belonged to no particular type.

The Crown could also make use of armed merchantmen, so as to increase fleet size further. These were usually flutes of the Dutch type, which was the most common type of cargo-carrier in the region. In 1629, the Crown chartered the "Ship Company" (Swedish: *Skeppskompaniet*), which was an association of Sweden's port towns which agreed to purchase or hire 16

Swedish warships collect tolls at Pillau, *c.* 1626. The painting also depicts the henceforth standard Swedish triple-tailed naval flag which was introduced in the 1620s. (Photo: Medströms)

armed merchantmen for the Crown's transportation needs. The ships were hired directly by the navy as needed, and many were used for the invasion of Germany in 1630. Later, the Ship Company engaged in trade with western Europe (but this was not a success, and the company was dissolved in 1636). From 1645, the Crown instead introduced a new customs policy which favoured Swedish-built and Swedish-owned armed merchantmen suitable for navy service. A far more successful policy than the previous one, this scheme provided more ships than the navy could hire, and the system successfully remained in operation for decades after the end of the Thirty Years' War. In fact, while the merchantmen which took advantage of the policy flew Swedish flags and were crewed by Swedish sailors, the owners were frequently Dutch, for whom the investment in customs-free auxiliary ships was a most profitable proposition.[3]

Yet, most of the navy's sailors were raised from the coastal population in the traditional manner. As a result, most were coastal fishermen rather than blue-water sailors, and their skills were no longer sufficient to man modern warships. Sweden still relied on the tradition of raising men from the coasts to man its navy, despite the inability of this obsolete system to supply experienced blue-water sailors.

Sweden had a geographical problem as well. The chief naval base and naval shipyard, Stockholm, was well-protected within an extensive archipelago, but with the prevailing winds, it was difficult to move the fleet out to sea. Moreover, Stockholm's harbour was blocked by ice until well into April each year. Finally, Stockholm was located far from the main theatre of operations, which caused communication and logistical problems, both with regard to supplies and when repairs were needed.

In comparison, Denmark had a geographical advantage. Denmark's chief naval base, Copenhagen, was located on a main shipping lane, enjoyed the use of an almost continuously ice-free harbour, and moreover was located

---

3   Jan Glete, *The Swedish Fiscal-Military State and Its Navy, 1521–1721* (Stockholm University working paper, nd), pp.24–5.

in the southern Baltic, which was the main theatre of operations in any war between Denmark and Sweden. Besides, Copenhagen usually enjoyed a westerly wind, which made it easy for the Danish fleet to leave port.

For these reasons, Danish naval crews were generally more experienced than Swedish ones. Their sailing season was longer, which meant that they had more time to get accustomed to their ships and tasks. Moreover, many of the Danish sailors, and an even larger share of those from Norway, had previously served on Dutch merchantmen or warships. Besides, the Danish navy also employed many experienced foreign sailors, hired in Amsterdam and Hamburg. This, too, made their crews more skilled. The contrast with most Swedish sailors who, at best, had a background as inshore fishermen is striking.

A key task for the navy was to secure the sea lines of communication. Both men and supplies were regularly transported to and from Germany, and the navy had to protect the transports. Troops and equipment were regularly shipped from a variety of Swedish ports to Stralsund, Rostock, Wismar, and Lübeck. Special embarkation facilities for horses including distinctive bridges were constructed in Dalarö port, near Älvsnabben in the southern Stockholm archipelago, at Elfsborg Castle in Sweden, and Helsingfors in Finland.

The normal sailing season was from May through October. However, the needs of war tended to prolong the sailing season. During the time of military operations in the Commonwealth, the navy had to extend the sailing season until operations took place throughout the winter as well. As a result, the navy became familiar with prolonged operations, even though such only took place when wartime conditions demanded it.

The Inshore Navy

Sweden also had an inshore navy, consisting of shallow-draught vessels, primarily square-rigged galleys and rowing boats of a type known as *lodja*, with a sprinkling of flat-bottomed river transports of a type known as *struts* (or *struss*). The name *lodja* was of Slavic origin, but it is unclear if it was only the name or also the type of river vessel which was adopted in the early seventeenth century. Either way, the *lodja* was an open rowing boat which also might carry a mast or two. It was sufficiently large to take soldiers and the occasional 5- and 3-pounder cannon. In 1607, the Swedish Crown ordered the construction of 60 vessels of the *lodja* type, each with 12 pairs of oars and able to carry 160 men and supplies for two months. In addition, the weight should not impede the crew from dragging the vessel a considerable distance overland, for instance from one river to another in the style of the old Viking longship. Smaller vessels of the type were built, too, with a crew of only 40 men and six to eight pairs of oars.[4]

4   Svensson, *Svenska flottanshistoria* 1, pp.76–7.

Swedish fleet at the siege of Riga, 1621. This contemporary drawing depicts all types of ships then in the Swedish navy, including warships, pinnaces, galleys, and the smaller vessels of the *lodja* and *struts* type. (Georg Schwengel)

A small sailing vessel of the *struts* type. The spritsail is mistakenly depicted above, not below, the bowsprit. (Crest of the Strusshielm family, House of Nobility, Stockholm)

Pinnace, in the port of Wismar. Although this is the Commonwealth ship *King David*, Swedish pinnaces were identical. The crew has taken down the main yard and are bending (tying) on the mainsail.

The *struts* was a flat-bottomed single-masted boat which was commonly used for moving goods on rivers. Unlike the *lodja*, it was decked. It was very similar to the Dutch boyer (*boeier*), a small coaster, and there is some evidence that in Sweden the two terms were used interchangeably, for instance the boyer *Oxen*, built in Stettin in 1641, which in 1656 was referred to as a *gaffelstruts*.[5]

Although primarily used inshore and on the major rivers, we have seen how an inshore fleet of 66 vessels under Henrik Hansson were dispatched to Ystad in Scania. The original plan was for the inshore fleet to support the naval landing in Denmark. When this proved impossible, Hansson was ordered to support Horn's siege of Malmö in 1644. However, the inshore vessels were too small and poorly armed to stand a chance against Danish warships, so they proved unable to blockade Malmö.

The inshore navy existed because the Swedish navy also had to maintain an amphibious capability, for which it since about 1540 used galleys. The Swedish-built galleys were a new innovation, which previously had not been used in Scandinavia. In those days, they were somewhat smaller than the typical Mediterranean galley, but later in the century larger galleys were built as well. By 1590, Sweden had the fourth largest galley fleet in Europe, after Spain, the Ottoman Empire, and Venice. Their use could be defensive or offensive. It was not only the Baltic Sea that had to be secured; Sweden also had to control estuaries and important rivers. In 1625, for instance, 24 galleys were used in an attack along the river Dvina on Commonwealth positions deep within Livonia. In 1626, 24 galleys were used during the Swedish landing in Prussia. However, following these operations, the construction of galleys was halted. In 1632, the navy still had more than 20 galleys. However, soon after they were phased out.[6] Perhaps the perceived need for amphibious operations diminished after the establishment of naval bases on the north German shore. This was not the end of the use of galleys for inshore operations, however. In the Great Northern War of 1700–1721, they made a comeback, and later in the century, the inshore navy was formally transferred from the navy to the army.

During the Thirty Years' War, the use of riverine sailing vessels increased instead. Riverine transport played a vital role in the movement of supplies, artillery, and sometimes men from the northern base areas to the southern theatres of operations. Some vessels were armed with cannons.

Inshore squadrons were established also in major lakes. During Gustavus Adolphus's campaigns in Muscovy, he maintained an inland squadron on Lake Ladoga, and later, on Lake Peipus. When Carl Gustav Wrangel in 1647 began to style himself Admiral of Lake Constance, he controlled 13 vessels on the lake, armed with cannons in the prow.

---

5   Lars Bruzelius, Maritime History Virtual Archives (<www.bruzelius.info/Nautica/Shipbuilding/Types/struss.html>); citing AK reg. 14 March 1656.

6   Jan Glete, "Vasatidens galärflottor", Hans Norman (ed.), *Skärgårdsflottan: Uppbyggnad, militär användning och förankring i det svenska samhället 1700–1824* (Lund: Historiska Media, 2000), pp.37–49.

Manpower

In 1622, the total number of sailors was just above 2,000.[7] This number increased until by 1629, the total number of sailors in service was some 3,200.[8] At the time of Gustavus Adolphus's death in 1632, the total number of sailors was 3,255. In addition, 2,730 soldiers were detached for shipboard duty.[9] Since the navy continued to grow, more men were needed.

From 1629, most sailors were raised in the towns, which contracted to supply a certain number of sailors. However, in 1634 the sailor's holding (*båtsmanshåll*) system was restored, with all coastal regions in Sweden and Finland eligible. According to this system, a peasant would enter into a contract with the Crown to provide revenues for a sailor. In return, the peasant benefited from tax exemption and freedom from conscription. He could choose either to serve himself during the formal six-month sailing season, during which his wife and children took care of the farm, or he could pay another person to serve. Although possibly intended as a temporary measure for the duration of the war, the system became permanent and was indeed extended further.[10] In 1634, the Admiralty envisaged sailors from what was referred to as regiments. This term was only used for administrative purposes, since the men were divided as needed into ships' crews. In 1635, the navy introduced the "perpetual sailor's holding" (*ständigt båtsmanshåll*), in similarity to the "perpetual soldier's holding" (*ständigt knektehåll*) used in some provinces to provide revenues for soldiers. The perpetual sailor's holdings provided a permanent force of some 3,000 men. When the war with Denmark broke out, this was not enough. In times of war, the Crown could raise additional, temporary troops. This was decided by the Crown on a case by case basis and granted by parliament. Although this means generally was taken to raise temporary army soldiers, it was in 1644 decided, with the parliament's approval, that the towns and peasants would have to find additional temporary sailors during such years when the navy was fully mobilised. The system was appropriately referred to as a "redoubling" (Swedish: *fördubbling*). When the navy in 1645 had reached its largest size during the war, its manpower consisted of 6,152 officers and sailors and 3,256 soldiers.[11]

Unlike the army, the navy remained fundamentally native Swedish in composition. A key reason for this was the reliance on conscription and sailor's holdings. However, the practical need of having everybody aboard the ship communicating in the same language may have been a factor, too.

The best sailors were those recruited from merchant ships. They already knew the tasks that had to be carried out. In addition, they were more

7 Ericson, *Krig och krigsmakt*, pp.112, 121.
8 Urban Skenbäck, *Sjöfolk och knektar på Wasa* (Stockholm: Sjöhistoriska museet, Wasastudier 11, 1983), p.81.
9 G. Hafström, "Flottans återupprättande under Gustaf Adolfs regering", *Tidskrift i Sjöväsendet*, Jubileumshäfte Gustaf II Adolf 1632–1932, pp.27–45, on p.42.
10 Skenbäck, *Sjöfolk*, pp.75–6, 80.
11 Mankell, *Uppgifter* 2, p.283.

resistant to the many diseases that commonly decimated naval crews, since they already had encountered, and survived, some of them. However, Sweden was far from the international centres of maritime commerce, and it was more difficult for the Swedish naval officers to find experienced crews than it was for their Danish counterparts, who had access to exactly this kind of men.

In times of war, each warship was commonly manned by a number of soldiers corresponding to one third of the naval crew. The largest warships were expected to carry some 163 soldiers each, while smaller warships had from 33 to 77 soldiers each, depending on size.[12] The number of soldiers varied according to mission and availability. At the battle off Fehmarn, the ratio of sailors and soldiers was approximately 3:2 on the Swedish warships, while on the ships of the auxiliary fleet, which had been provided with Swedish soldiers, too, the corresponding ratio was approximately 2:1.[13]

A warship usually had only two or, at most, three commissioned officers: the captain and one or two lieutenants. They might, or not, have previous naval experience. The senior non-commissioned officer was the ship's master (överskeppare), who was a professional mariner. Unlike the officers, he would stay with the ship throughout the winter, since he was in charge of maintenance and preparations for the next sailing season. On a small ship, the ship's master would be in sole command, since no officer would serve on board. The ship's master was assisted by a master's mate (underskeppare). Another important non-commissioned post was that of boatswain (högbåtsman), who led the ordinary sailors and also was responsible for damage control when in battle. Then there would be a pilot (styrman, a title from the 1620s onwards separated into three degrees of seniority) who was familiar with the winds and currents of the area of operations and was responsible for navigation. A pilot had to supply his own navigational instruments. The ordinary sailing crew was divided into two watches, each of which included a leading sailor (skeppman) to assist the officer, usually a lieutenant, in command of the watch. A watch was subdivided into two quarters, each directed by a quartermaster (kvartermästare). The sailing crew took turns on duty, with each watch spending four hours on duty at a time. The crew also included specialists of various kinds, including the cook, a carpenter (timmerman) or sometimes several, and a drummer or trumpeter for signalling. The master gunner (from the 1620s onwards known as konstapel) would command the gunners (bysseskyttar) who directed the soldiers who were assigned to handle the shipboard artillery. A large ship would have a chaplain. Before 1657, only a large ship would have a barber-surgeon.[14]

---

12 *Ibid.*, pp.277–8; citing data from 1644.
13 *Slaget vid Femern*, p.66.
14 Fred Hocker, *Vasa: A Swedish Warship* (Stockholm: Medströms, 2015), pp.102–5.

Swedish sailor, 1628. Clothes based on archaeological finds from the Vasa. (Vasa Museum, Stockholm; photo: author)

Swedish pilot, as depicted in the first Swedish naval instruction manual from 1644, written by Johan Månsson. Common sailors would not have been as well-dressed as this pilot.

Ship's crew from a contemporary votive ship, Kållered Church, Västergötland. From left to right: drummer, captain (armed with a broad longsword), pilot in jacket and breeches, trumpeter (instrument missing), two crewmen. Most wear long coats to protect against the cold.

Swedish sailors at the battle off Fehmarn, 1644. (Skokloster Castle)

Tactics

Naval battles in the Baltic Sea had been decided by the use of cannon instead of boarding and hand-to-hand combat since the Nordic Seven Years' War of 1563–1570. However, in the early years of the reign of Gustavus Adolphus, Swedish naval tactics still emphasised boarding, which indeed often was regarded as the preferred means of attacking the enemy. Gustavus Adolphus wanted to break free from this, increasingly obsolete model, and his orders in the 1620s to build larger warships with more and better shipboard artillery was a step in this direction.

However, this change in tactical doctrine took time, not least because of the difficulties in finding and retaining experienced sailing crews. Boarding accordingly remained a preferred method of winning a sea battle throughout the Thirty Years' War and beyond.

Before battle took place, the admiral would give instructions to his captains, including on which signals to be used and the assignment of each captain. However, during actual battle each captain essentially acted on his own. He would select an enemy ship of similar size to his own and then attack it. It was only from 1644 onwards, during the war with Denmark, that Swedish fleets began to coordinate their movements to any higher degree.

Every battle began with a period of manoeuvring, during which the respective fleets attempted to gain the favourable position. Early seventeenth-century sailing rigs allowed only a limited ability to sail to windward. This meant that the fleet to windward had the advantage of the other, since it could choose whether to initiate or decline battle.

Ships commonly reduced sail before engaging, since this made the ship easier to handle and also improved visibility. This was important, since the cannons were aimed by moving the ship, not the cannons. For most of the Thirty Years' War, the cannons of Swedish warships were not provided with wedges under the breech to adjust elevation and range. Instead, there would be a simple bar across the back of the gun carriage which was set for point-blank elevation. Naturally, only the artillery on one side of the vessel could concentrate fire on one particular target. Even so, due to the construction of seventeenth-century ships, it was impossible to bring all guns on one side to bear on a single target. It was only the guns in the middle of the ship which could be so concentrated. For obvious reasons, the stern and bow guns could only fire in their respective directions. However, because of the curving shape of the ship, even those guns on the side which were positioned near the stern and bow of the ship might not be able to bear on an enemy directly to the side.

In addition to round shot, which was the most common type of shot, the Swedish navy also employed chain shot, which was designed to damage the rigging and tear holes in sails, both of which reduced the enemy ship's ability to manoeuvre. Other, less common but still employed types of shot included spike shot and scissor shot, which were believed, probably in error, to cause more damage in close quarters. Ships did not carry large supplies of ammunition. The Swedish navy generally allocated 30 shots per cannon to its warships, with the appropriate volume of gunpowder. This was only raised to 50 shots per cannon in 1658.

Ship's cannon. (Vasa Museum, Stockholm; photo: author)

Chain shot and scissor shot. (Vasa Museum, Stockholm; photo: author)

When firing against the enemy crew exposed on the upper deck, grapeshot cartridges (multiple balls of musket or larger size in a cartridge) or case-shot (smaller balls or scrap metal in a canister) would be used, in similarity to the regimental artillery in land battles. However, the area effect of a round shot hit should not be underestimated. Although a round shot might not penetrate the thick oak sides of a proper warship, its energy was still transferred to the ship's structure, causing sharp splinters of wood to break loose. This would create a cone-shaped cloud of wooden splinters inside the hull. Each splinter had the capacity to maim one or more crewmen, and since conditions were cramped, the danger of being hit by splinters was considerable when under enemy fire. If the round shot penetrated, it would bounce through the hull, causing additional damage wherever it passed.

Finally, there was musket fire. Musketeers would be stationed in the tops at the mastheads, on the upper deck, or in the quarter galleries to fire at enemy crewmen. This was the task of the soldiers who formed part of the crew of most warships, except for those who had been assigned as gunners.

Once the ship came alongside the enemy, the soldiers would board. The final struggle would be fought hand to hand, just like on land, with muskets, axes, boarding pikes, and cutlasses or rapiers. Because of the expense of building and outfitting a warship, it was usually deemed preferable to capture an enemy ship instead of sinking it.

A tactics of last resort was to blow up one's own ship, so as to prevent its capture by the enemy. Although this was not formally regulated, except possibly in local instructions, the practice seems to have been commonplace. Charges would be prepared in advance. A ship would only be blown when there was no hope of recovery, and in the heat of battle, it does not seem to have been difficult to find men willing to fire the fuse. At the battle off Oliwa near Danzig in 1627, two Swedish warships (*Solen* and *Tigern*) were lost. Both commanders ordered their ships blown. However, only the *Solen* succeeded. On the *Tigern*, the crewman carrying the match was killed before he could reach the fuse, so the ship was captured instead.[15] Perhaps inspired by this incident, Vice Admiral Henrik Fleming in 1628 issued the following order:

> If it happens, God forbid, that a ship is so hard beset by enemy ships that all senior officers are shot dead and no help is available, then some honest Swede and faithful man should soon set fire to the gunpowder magazine and thus, like a man, take revenge for the death of his officer and fellow brethren.[16]

---

15 Incidentally, the *Tigern* was recaptured when Swedish troops took the port town of Wismar from Imperial forces in 1632.

16 Fleming to the Fleet off Danzig, 10 September 1628 (O.S.); cited in Katarina Villner, *Under däck: Mary Rose – Vasa – Kronan* (Stockholm: Medströms, 2012), p.155.

Subversion and Disease

Beyond open battle, the navy was exposed to other, more clandestine dangers. While Wrangel's fleet spent the winter 1644–1645 in Wismar, his men exposed a conspiracy to blow up a couple of the ships. A Pomeranian named Hans Grefft was found to have in his possession two portable fire-bombs. Each consisted of a travelling trunk, fully loaded with straw, pitch, sulphur, and gunpowder. To each trunk had also been added a clockwork timer which enabled the operator to place the bomb, set the timer with a delay up to 12 hours, and make his escape in good time before detonation. The navy took a dim view of the conspiracy, so Grefft was tortured and eventually executed under gruesome conditions.[17]

Yet, an even higher risk was posed by disease. In addition to the numerous diseases which afflicted the army garrisons, shipboard conditions posed further danger, for instance from scurvy, caused by a lack of vitamin C.

The navy was aware of the dangers of scurvy, and of how to prevent it. This is evident from correspondence between Vice Admiral Henrik Fleming and the Admiralty in 1628. Fleming informed the Admiralty and Oxenstierna that he had managed to purchase some 200 lemons from a Dutchman in order to prevent scurvy. Unfortunately, the Dutchman did not have any more, so further supplies were urgently needed.[18]

There was an awareness of the need for personal hygiene, even though this might have been difficult to live up to while on shipboard duty. Swedish and Finnish culture had a tradition of regular bathing, and the navy yard had a bath house, with two men employed to operate it.

There was also an expectation that crews would know how to swim. That many Scandinavians could swim was explicitly and repeatedly mentioned already in the well-known *Historia de Gentibus Septentrionalibus*, a monumental work by Olaus Magnus on the Nordic countries, which was first published in Rome in 1555. There are also records from the seventeenth century which suggest that many knew how to swim. While navy records are not explicit on this point, they take for granted that people who were not trapped underwater would have a good chance of surviving until they were rescued, which would suggest at least some swimming skills.[19]

There were few facilities for medical treatment of the wounded beyond the limited care provided by those few barber-surgeons who served on large ships. Medical treatment was free, unless the wound had been caused while brawling, in which case the wounded sailor had to pay the barber-surgeon for the treatment. From 1628 onwards, certain ships were designated as hospital ships, to which the ill and disabled could be moved while the campaign was still ongoing. At the same time, it was decided that at least the soldiers on shipboard duty would be rotated back to land after every two months spent at sea. For obvious reasons, these measures could not always be implemented in times of war. During extended naval operations, such as the 1628 blockade

---

17 Englund, *Ofredsår*, p.372.
18 Fleming's report to Oxenstierna, 27 July 1628 (O.S.); cited in Villner, *Under däck*, p.187.
19 Hocker, *Vasa*, p.129.

of Danzig, more than a third of the crews might end up dead or too ill to serve. Particularly serious was the loss to illness of the few specialists aboard, such as pilots, master gunners, and carpenters.

There was an understanding that the Crown should provide aid to the widows and children of fallen and crippled sailors. From at least 1624, but probably earlier, the navy set aside funds to provide financial aid in such cases. In 1642, the Admiralty established a fund for the same purpose. It was decided that some of the money for the fund would be taken from fines collected for misdemeanours, while the remaining share would be collected as a percentage of the wages of all who served in the navy. To this would be added charitable contributions. In addition, a limited number of old or semi-crippled sailors might find employment in the naval yards, where they worked tending the bath house or with similar light duties.

8

The Military Presence in Sweden's Overseas Colonies

New Sweden

In the reign of Gustavus Adolphus, Sweden constantly needed more revenues. Oxenstierna soon realised that foreign trade and the establishment of colonies abroad constituted one means of raising state revenue. In 1626, both Oxenstierna and Gustavus Adolphus invested in the first such venture of its kind, the "Swedish South Seas Company" (Swedish: *Svenska Södersjökompaniet*), which received a government monopoly to trade with Asia, Africa, and the Americas. However, the project failed to take off. Moreover, we have seen how the Crown in 1629 established the Ship Company to provide armed merchantmen for the Crown's transportation needs. In 1631, the two companies merged.

In 1637, Sweden made plans to import tobacco and furs from North America, preferably from a colony of its own. For this purpose, the South Seas Company was restructured as the "New Sweden Company" (Latin: *Nova Suecia*; Swedish: *Nya Sverige*), which reflected the name chosen for the intended colony. Most of the capital was put up by Oxenstierna and Admiral Claes Fleming, who simultaneously was the head of the Board of Commerce. Oxenstierna regarded the enterprise as yet another commercial venture which, with a little bit of luck, might bring revenues to the Crown. As commander of the first expedition, the company board chose Peter Minuit (1594–1638), a Dutchman who previously had been governor of the Dutch colony of New Netherland, with its capital New Amsterdam (modern-day New York), and knew local conditions. Although a commercial venture, the expedition was military in character and subject to military law. A former lieutenant colonel, Måns Nilsson Kling (1600–1657), was appointed lieutenant to Minuit and put in command of the 23 soldiers who accompanied the expedition. Kling had worked his way up from the ranks in the Jönköping Regiment. All soldiers were paid by the company, not the Crown, but as noted, the Crown stood firmly behind the venture. Ships were provided by the navy or taken from those that had belonged to the Ship Company.

In late 1637, the two warships *Calmare Nyckel* and *Fågel Grip* departed from Gothenburg. In April 1638, they sailed up the Delaware River, a major river on the Atlantic coast of North America. Having landed, Minuit purchased land from the local Lenape Indians, and then established Fort Christina in what presently is Wilmington, Delaware, in the United States. This became the first centre of the colony, which was named New Sweden. Orders from Stockholm were very clear on one point: the colonists should maintain friendly relations with the Indians, both the Lenape, an Algonquian people, and the neighbouring Susquehannock, an Iroquois people. Following the death of Minuit at sea, Kling became acting governor. In the following years, additional Swedish colonists were brought to North America. Some were former soldiers who had been convicted for desertion or other offences, but a few volunteers of peasant stock, both Swedes and Finns, followed them, including a Swede, Peter Gunnarsson Rambo (previously Ramberg), who became the founder of a large family, and a Finn, Martti Marttinen or Mårten Mårtensson, whose great-grandson John Morton in 1776 was one of the signatories of the American Declaration of Independence. The colony grew, but its inhabitants did not establish villages. Instead, those who broke new land for the purposes of farming lived in isolated homesteads in the forest, in the same type of log houses that they already were accustomed to in Sweden and Finland, thus introducing this kind of architecture to North America. As for the original soldiers, some remained in the colony, while others returned to Sweden, when new soldiers arrived to relieve them. As before, the sea voyages were carried out by warships. Whereas most ship officers were Dutchmen who had signed on in return for a monthly salary, the sailors were typically Swedish navy conscripts. Many of the latter accompanied the Atlantic voyage with great reluctance, and quite a few deserted during the customary stopover in the Dutch Republic.

In February 1643, a new governor arrived in New Sweden. This was Johan Printz, the officer from the Västgöta Cavalry Regiment who had to surrender Chemnitz in 1640. New Sweden had failed to produce revenues, so in 1642 Oxenstierna and Fleming reorganised the company with fresh capital. In addition, a large share of the colony's expenses would henceforth be borne by the Crown. The governor and some other officials, including the colony's chaplain, would receive government salaries, and the Admiralty would cover the costs of the warships, officers, and crews. But Oxenstierna and Fleming also needed a capable new governor, and the resourceful Printz fit the bill. In addition, the governor needed noble rank, so that he could negotiate on an equal level with the Dutch and English governors in North America. Despite his previous dismissal from the army, Printz was accordingly ennobled in conjunction with his appointment as governor. Printz brought additional military reinforcements, which raised the military might of New Sweden to Printz himself, four lieutenants, two constables, a master of the watch, a trumpeter, a drummer, a provost, and 24 men.

Under Governor Johan Printz, the colony grew rapidly. Printz had the same orders as previous governors, that is, to

Johan Printz.

maintain peaceful relations with the local Indians. Relations were mostly good, although over the years, a handful of colonists were killed in incidents involving Indians. Yet, Printz got on well with the Indian chiefs, who due to his bulk called him "Big Belly". However, a new problem had arisen, not with the Indians but with the neighbouring Dutch and English colonies. With them, too, Printz was ordered to maintain good relations, but if the other Europeans persisted in claiming the Swedish territories, he should oppose violence with violence. For this reason, additional defences were built. First, in October 1643, Printz had a fort built which was called New Elfsborg (Swedish: *Nya Elfsborg*), in which was deployed eight 3-pounders and a mortar. The fort, which dominated the river, was garrisoned by 13 soldiers under Printz's second in command, a former lieutenant from the Åbo and Björneborg Cavalry Regiment named Sven Skute. In case of hostilities, we can assume that Printz intended to bring additional men to crew the cannons. Second, at about the same time, Printz had a fort named New Gothenburg (Swedish: *Nya Göteborg*) built on a small island close to what eventually became Philadelphia, Pennsylvania. New Gothenburg was manned by 12 men and 12 cannons. Again, we can presume that Printz intended to bring reinforcements in case of real hostilities. On the other side, he did not have that many soldiers to begin with, so a real war would need the calling out of levies from the isolated Swedish homesteads. Printz reported home that military supplies were needed, including gunpowder, shot, cannonballs, and a hundred cuirasses "on account of the arrows of the savages". He also requested a clerk who knew Latin; the Dutch and English neighbours persisted in sending him formal letters in Latin, and Printz, the former student of theology, complained that after 27 years in the army, his hands were more used to handling muskets and pistols than Tacitus and Cicero.

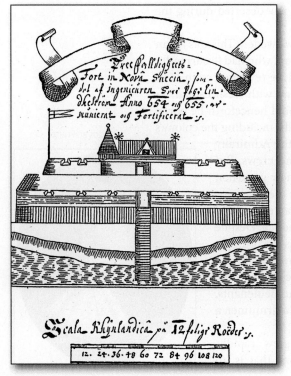

The Swedish Fort Trefaldighet ('Fort Trinity'), New Sweden. This was the former Dutch Fort Casimir, which Sweden seized in 1654, following the outbreak of hostilities between the Dutch and Swedish colonies in North America. Note the Swedish naval flag. (Per Lindeström)

Yet other, smaller fortifications were built as well. Whether by chance or design, the Swedes in North America followed the same combined military and mercantile strategy previously practised in the Baltic Sea. There, the Swedes had aimed to take control over the important rivers at their point of departure into the sea so as to control, and tax, trade passing through. In the same way, the Swedes in North America built their forts along the Delaware River so as to cut off the Dutch from direct trade with the Indians. By 1647, the Swedes controlled trade along the Delaware.

However, this policy eventually backfired. From 1648 onwards, the Swedish Crown paid little attention to New Sweden. Admiral Fleming had fallen in battle in 1644, and Oxenstierna was busy wrapping up the war in Germany. Relations with the neighbouring English and Dutch colonies were always somewhat tense, and henceforth they deteriorated rapidly. Serious rivalry between the Swedish and Dutch colonies broke out in 1648. This was a conflict which, ultimately, New Sweden could not expect to win. First, the Dutch enjoyed a considerable superiority in numbers. Second, the neglect from Stockholm resulted in shortages in necessary goods. The difficulties brought dissent to the colony, and in 1653, Printz, who understood how things were going, tendered his resignation as governor and returned to Sweden. In 1654, with the arrival of a new but less experienced Swedish governor, Johan Risingh (1617–1672), serious hostilities at once broke out between Swedes and Dutch. Although Captain Sven Skute, who had remained in New Sweden, with 21 men captured the Dutch Fort Casimir, established on territory that the Swedes deemed was part of New Sweden, the conquest was a temporary success. The Dutch governor of New Netherland, Peter Stuyvesant (1611/1612–1672), already had more men, cannons, and ships. Moreover, upon Stuyvesant's request, a Dutch warship with 36 cannons and 200 soldiers was sent from the Dutch Republic. To this was added additional ships, a French privateer, and yet more soldiers, in total some 600 to 700 men. In 1655, the Dutch expedition moved into the Swedish colony. In face of this overwhelming force, the Swedish forts, none of which had a garrison larger than some 30 men, surrendered, one after the other. Both the Lenape and Susquehannock provided some support to the Swedes during the campaign, but this could not change the outcome. The campaign was over in little more than two weeks. New Netherland absorbed all lands that had been New Sweden. However, most of the settlers remained, and they continued to maintain a distinct Swedish and Finnish character for more than a century. In this, at least, the colony was a success.

Conditions in America occasionally caused unusual military problems. Not because of the geography and terrain, which were not very different from conditions in northern Scandinavia except that the climate was better, but with unknown wildlife. In 1654, a newly arrived Swedish soldier one night suddenly raised the alarm when on guard duty at Fort Christina. When asked why, he responded: "Don't you see that the forest is full of musketeers with burning slow match?" What he had seen, for the first time, was American fireflies.[1]

In the same year, Governor Risingh sent a report to Stockholm. In it, he noted that he needed additional gunpowder and shot. He already had ordinary muskets (almost certainly matchlock muskets), but he wanted some new French muskets and leather pouches in which to

Dutch siege of Fort Christina, New Sweden, 1655. The town of Christina has already been captured, and the Dutch lines traverse the town's regular street pattern. (Per Lindeström)

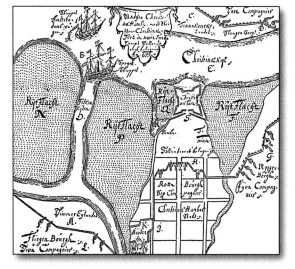

---

1   Per Lindeström, *Per Lindeströms resa till Nya Sverige 1653–1656* (Stockholm: Wahlström & Widstrand, 1923), pp.116–17. Lindeström was a fortification officer who in 1653 accompanied newly appointed Governor Johan Risingh to New Sweden and later wrote a book about the colony.

keep paper cartridges. At the time, French muskets meant flintlock muskets, which were not yet in common Swedish military use. During the subsequent Dutch invasion, the Swedes were armed with matchlock muskets, rapiers, and what was referred to as pikes, which likely were partisans or half-pikes.

The Swedish Gold Coast

New Sweden was not the only colony established at the time. There was also the Swedish Gold Coast (Swedish: *Svenska Guldkusten*), located in West Africa. However, the Gold Coast colony was an endeavour quite different in character from New Sweden. For one thing, it was primarily a mercantile venture, with traders and soldiers but no settlers looking for land to farm. This was also reflected in how the colony came into existence, not as a state initiative but as a private business proposal from the Swedish–Dutch industrialist Louis De Geer.

With the end of the Thirty Years' War in 1648, De Geer's charter on exporting Swedish copper ended. To diversify his business activities, De Geer had already, at his own expense, arranged a few voyages to West Africa in 1646–1647 to test the market. At first, African slaves were moved from Guinea on the Gold Coast to the Portuguese island of São Tomé where they were traded for sugar, which then was sold with good profit in Amsterdam. This soon developed into a triangular trade: European manufactured goods were exported to West Africa, where the resulting revenues purchased slaves which were moved to São Tomé or, even more lucratively, the West Indies, where the revenues from the slave trade bought sugar and other colonial products which were then transported to Europe where they sold at high prices. Having tested the market, De Geer tried to convince the Swedish Crown to invest in the venture. Although Oxenstierna and the Council of the Realm showed little enthusiasm, Queen Christina approved of the plan, and in 1648, De Geer and the Crown entered into a mutual agreement. Two ships were dispatched to West Africa, from Stade in the recently conquered Bremen-Verden. The voyage proved a huge commercial success.

In 1649, Louis De Geer accordingly established the 'Swedish Africa Company' (Swedish: *Svenska Afrikanska Kompaniet*), which received a royal monopoly on trade south of the Canary Islands. He immediately began to plan for an expedition to Africa. As leader of the expedition, De Geer appointed Hendrik Carloff, an adventurer who claimed, possibly correctly, to have been born in Finland and who since 1637 had worked for the Dutch West India Company in Dutch Brazil and West Africa. Carloff's early life remains unknown, but his name suggests that his family possibly derived from one of the Muscovites who in the previous century had gone into Swedish service. Be that as it may, the Swedish expedition under Carloff in 1650 founded the colony named the Swedish Gold Coast on the Gulf of Guinea in modern-day Ghana. This was a territory dominated by the Akan kingdoms. One of these was the kingdom of Efutu, and the colony was centred on Oguaa, its most important town and port. The kingdom of Efutu was ruled by King Bredeva, who agreed to sell the necessary lands for a number of trading posts to the

Swedish Africa Company. In response, Queen Christina sent a letter to the King so as to seal the friendship of their two kingdoms. Soon the company began to build forts to protect its trading posts, which were scattered around Cabo Corso (modern-day Cape Coast). The chief fort, a timber construction, was eventually named Carolusborg, after King Charles Gustavus who by then had assumed the throne.

Europeans were not yet as militarily and technologically superior over the native kingdoms as they would become a century or two later. They were also very few in numbers. For this reason, the Swedish Gold Coast for military purposes relied on the raising of local soldiers. Strictly speaking, the soldiers were unfree, since the company negotiated an agreement with the King of Efutu, which enabled them to purchase Efutu soldiers as needed. However, the unfree soldiers should not be confused with the slaves that the Akan kingdoms sold for manual labour overseas. While the soldiers in a legal sense were not freemen, they were well treated and willing to fight, when needed. This need arose rapidly in the Swedish Gold Coast. The Dutch competitors of the Swedish company wanted the Swedes gone, and they soon sent armed ships to prevent the Swedes from unloading and loading goods except at night. The Dutch also raided the Swedish trading station in Anomabu, which was located on the territory of the neighbouring kingdom of Fante. In response, the Swedes and their Efutu soldiers moved into Accra, where the Dutch maintained an important trading post, in order to make the Dutch representative there think twice about their actions. The Swedes and their Efutu soldiers also boarded and took a Dutch merchant ship which had stopped in Oguaa without permission. It contained a valuable cargo, including 700 kg of ivory. For a while, it seemed that the Swedish Africa Company and its Efutu allies were doing well.

However, eventually Carloff fell out with the company board in Stockholm. In 1656, he was replaced as governor. As a result, Carloff, enraged, turned to Denmark, which by then already had plans to establish its own colony in West Africa. Carloff accordingly led a Danish expedition to the Gold Coast in late 1657. With the help of other locally recruited soldiers, he in 1658 raided and destroyed the Swedish trading posts, one after the other. In the final showdown, Carloff and his men also received the support of the Dutch Africa Company, which had its own soldiers in the region. Together, they attacked, seized, and plundered Carolusborg, which was claimed for Denmark.

When Carloff returned to Denmark, laden with booty, Denmark had just suffered several defeats in a war with Sweden and had agreed to hand over large territories. The Swedish Crown accordingly demanded the return of the Gold Coast colony and the handover of Carloff and his plunder. However, tipped off by the Danes, Carloff rapidly fled to the Dutch Republic, where he had powerful friends, with as much loot as he could bring aboard a smaller ship. Subsequently, Carloff made a successful career as a slaver on behalf of the Dutch and French, until the Dutch made him Governor of Tobago between 1676 and 1677. Meanwhile in the Gold Coast in 1659, Carloff's second in command, upon hearing the news of Sweden's victory over Denmark, rapidly sold the entire Gold Coast colony to the Dutch for a bargain price.

He then went into hiding in Angola with the money which he had been paid. Essentially the entire Swedish Gold Coast had been embezzled.

However, this was not the end of the story. The King of Efutu was dissatisfied with the developments. He wanted the Swedes back. As a result, in 1660 after only a few months the King sent his field commander Acroissen Tay with several hundred men to retake Carolusborg.[2] The Efutu soldiers overwhelmed the Dutch, and later in the same year the colony was returned into Swedish hands. As for the Danes, the King of Efutu granted them another location for a fort and trading post.

Unhappy about these developments, in spring 1662 the Dutch again attacked the Swedish colony. The new Swedish governor, Tönnies Voss, managed to defend Carolusborg for a year. By then, neither Sweden nor the Swedish Africa Company had the resources to send assistance. In spring 1663, the Dutch finally stormed Carolusborg. They then seized the whole Swedish Gold Coast. The Dutch eventually paid damages for the conquest, which marked the formal end to the Swedish Africa Company.

---

2   The Efutu field commander was known to the Swedes as Johan Claesson, which perhaps provided the inspiration for the Swedish author Janne Lundström in the 1970s to write a series of cartoons and novels about a Swedish boy named Johan Klasson Tay, or Johan Vilde ("John Savage"), who fled from the slave trade and went native in the Gold Coast.

9

The Legacy of the Swedish Military State

The impact abroad of Swedish military tactics was described in the previous volume, including how the Swedish model of warfare was copied by most west and north European militaries. Sweden's ally Muscovy based its entire set of new formation regiments on the Swedish pattern, while the Swedish model laid the foundation for subsequent improvements in British infantry and French cavalry tactics. The Swedish regimental artillery was copied by many, including France, the Empire, and Muscovy. But influences went far beyond mere tactics.

In early 1638, Field Marshal Alexander Leslie temporarily returned to Scotland. By then, he had been in Swedish service for 30 years. Now, however, tensions between Scotland and England were mounting. A state of civil war was imminent. Returning to Sweden later in the year, Leslie requested a release from service. At the same time, he requested artillery for the Scottish cause. Oxenstierna and the regency government did not wish to lose the able field marshal, but they also felt that due to his long and loyal service, they could not refuse his request to return home. For the same reason, they also agreed to supply Leslie with the requested armaments. However, to avoid being seen as condoning war against England, the regency government argued that the weapons would be provided under the pretext of reward for loyal service. Eventually, it was decided to provide the weapons – 2,000 muskets and artillery supplies – to private merchants who in turn would forward them to Scotland. Even so, the regency government decided that the supplies would be handed over free of tax, so for those in the know, there was no doubt that it was the Swedish Crown which supplied the armaments. The regency government also supported other Scottish requests for military supplies, including in 1640 that of Colonel John Cochrane, another veteran of the Swedish army. Swedish ships were dispatched to deliver the supplies.[1]

---

1   Alexia Grosjean, "General Alexander Leslie, the Scottish Covenanters and the *Riksråd* Debates, 1638–1640", Allan I. Macinnes, Thomas Riis, and Frederik Pedersen (eds), *Ships, Guns and Bibles in the North Sea and the Baltic States, c.1350–c.1700* (East Linton, East Lothian: Tuckwell Press, 2000), pp.115–38, on pp.116–18, 122–3.

The work of Scottish officers such as Leslie and Cochrane in Swedish service was fundamental to the success of the Scottish Covenanting movement. From 1637 to 1640, at least 302 Scottish officers in Swedish service returned to Scotland. The peak years of departure were 1638 and 1639. Most were ensigns and lieutenants (60 of each). The second largest category consisted of captains (in total 48 men). In addition, there were six majors, 18 lieutenant colonels and colonels, three major generals, and one field marshal (Leslie).[2] At the time of their return home, these men included some of the most experienced officers in the Swedish army. The influx of men with recent military experience and knowledge of the new technology and tactics implemented in the Swedish army had a substantial impact on the Scottish military effort. Indeed, it has been shown that the Scottish military at this point established a number of practices which were copied from the Swedish military system, including the establishment of military districts, national conscription, and up-to-date command and control.[3] Another veteran of Swedish service, Colonel Robert Monro, had already in 1637 published his military memoirs which included a manual to the Swedish military system. In 1644, he republished this text under a new name which emphasised that what he regarded as the "Scotch Military Discipline" derived from Sweden.[4]

That Monro and the other Scots by then regarded Sweden as a model was unsurprising. During the time of the Thirty Years' War, the Swedish Crown had established the capability to send, at short notice, a combat-ready and professional national army to the Continent, with the full support of a strong navy. Since the army was national in origin, it could be raised rapidly, without waiting for negotiations with military entrepreneurs. Moreover, it became possible to maintain an army fully trained in current organisation and tactical doctrine, something which military entrepreneurs never could guarantee. Furthermore, because of the frequent wars the army was usually experienced, with a significant share of veterans, which was an additional boon.

However, the capability to raise and dispatch such an army meant that the Crown had to be able to finance both army and navy from domestic sources. The Crown accordingly developed the administrative ability to mobilise the necessary resources in the form of trained men, horses, armaments, provisions, and ships. While both Gustavus Adolphus and Oxenstierna preferred to fight their wars overseas, where war at least to some extent might feed itself, this observation overlooks the obvious: Sweden first needed the military and naval superiority to take the war overseas – where it then could feed itself. Without a professional army and navy already in existence, the option to take the war abroad was simply unavailable.

---

2   *Ibid.*, pp.124–5. On these individuals, see also Steve Murdoch and Alexia Grosjean, *The Scotland, Scandinavia and Northern European Biographical Database* (SSNE) (<https://www.st-andrews.ac.uk/history/ssne/>). Scots continued to serve in Swedish armies in the 1640s and beyond. Murdoch and Grosjean, *Alexander Leslie*, pp.145–9, 151–4, 167–8.

3   Grosjean, "General Alexander Leslie", p.126, with references.

4   Robert Monro, *The Scotch Military Discipline Learned from the Valiant Swede, and Collected for the Use of All Worthy Commanders Favouring the Laudable Profession of Armes* (London: William Ley, 1644).

To build these capabilities was no easy undertaking. Few European states, even among those far wealthier and populous than Sweden, were able to maintain large permanent armies and navies before 1650. On a per capita level, it was only the Dutch Republic which surpassed Sweden in the ability to sustain permanent military forces.[5] Sweden, hitherto more known for state poverty than abundant resources, could not rival the financial might of the Dutch. Nonetheless, the required capabilities were achieved, and it tells something about the ability of Gustavus Adolphus, Oxenstierna, and their associates that they succeeded in their chosen task. In the previous volume we have seen how, following the Danish invasions during the Kalmar War of 1611–1613, Gustavus Adolphus and Oxenstierna applied a three-pronged model to Sweden: the Crown would provide security throughout the realm through a modern army; this secure environment would enable modernisation, which they interpreted as the introduction of a functioning administration and modern industry; and the private and Crown-supported economic initiatives inherent in modernisation would enable the economic reform necessary to pay for the costs of building security. The three concepts – security, modernisation, and economic reform – were interlinked. Gustavus Adolphus and Oxenstierna understood that to succeed, they could not have one without the others.

Sweden developed rapidly during the Thirty Years' War. Gustavus Adolphus and his field marshals and admirals developed the army and navy until both surpassed most rivals. Judged by the eagerness with which other European militaries copied Swedish tactics and armaments, the Swedish army might indeed, for a while, have been the most modern of its kind. Meanwhile, Oxenstierna and his associates built a functioning administration and modern industry, which in turn enabled a thorough economic reform. Sweden ended the Thirty Years' War with a large, modern army, an efficient machinery of state, and significant economic resources (although state finances still lagged behind). None of this had been available at the outset.

The modernisation of the army produced yet another, possibly unforeseen effect: the professionalisation of senior officers and promotion based on talent, not birth. The prolonged war effort caused a need for increasing numbers of skilled officers. The old noble families did not have the manpower to supply this demand, yet noble status remained a requirement for the highest ranks. As a result, the number of non-noble officers grew significantly, and many were subsequently ennobled, in particular when they reached the rank of captain or higher (lieutenants and lower officers were generally not ennobled), so that they could be promoted further. In 1641, for instance, the Tavastland and Nyland Cavalry Regiment had a total of 87 officers, of whom less than eight percent were nobles. In 1648, the nobles constituted 17 percent. All were of Finnish origin, and the majority can be assumed to have been ennobled in service. In addition, of the remaining non-noble officers in

---

5   Jan Glete, "The Swedish Fiscal-Military State in Transition and Decline, 1650–1815", *Mobilizing Money and Resources for War during the Early Modern period*, XIV International Economic History Congress, Helsinki, 21–25 August 2006, pp.4, 9.

1648, as many as 60 percent had entered service as common cavalrymen and achieved their promotion due to ability.[6]

Talented officials were needed in administration, finance, and trade, as well. Again, the old noble families lacked the necessary manpower. This led to a growing share of recently ennobled men who had the ability to run the complex machinery of state developed by Oxenstierna. Likewise, Sweden needed industrialists, and the truly successful entrepreneurs were almost invariably ennobled. By 1650, roughly half of all nobles were recently ennobled. The process continued, and by the end of the century, 80 percent of the nobility derived from men recently ennobled. The nobility had developed into what best perhaps can be described as a meritocratic aristocracy.[7]

For these reasons, the character of the nobility changed rapidly during the war. While the new nobles, without doubt, added to the collective expertise, it should not be assumed that all initiatives lay with them. The old nobility, too, evolved. The process had begun already before Gustavus Adolphus but accelerated from his reign onwards. The nobility transformed from what in the previous century had been a group of illiterate, medieval-style strongmen into members of a pan-European nobility, which sent its sons to study at the great universities on the Continent. But the transformation did not stop there. By the end of the Thirty Years' War, the nobility was rapidly developing into what can only be called entrepreneurs and industrialists. Many of them constituted the real driving force behind economic reform, trade, manufacturing, and commerce, surpassing the burghers in innovation. Moreover, as a group they grew increasingly tolerant in their views. As an example, and against the views of the clergy, the nobility advocated increased religious tolerance. Possible more the outcome of utilitarianism than any real desire to promote freedom of thought, the nobility nonetheless regarded religious tolerance as a necessity to attract foreign capital into the country and promote free trade.[8] Since commoners who hoped for promotion emulated the nobles in behaviour and attitudes, the overall result was a genuine increase in tolerance and rational thought. The immediate effect should not be overstated, but a change had occurred. For instance, when from 1668 the fear of witchcraft suddenly led to persecution of alleged witches in Sweden, it was provincial officials and parish priests who typically succumbed to the popular delusions and had the alleged witches hunted down and sentenced to death. In contrast, the nobility, bishops, and senior military officers generally proved less eager to hand out death sentences and were far more sceptical of the claims of witchcraft.[9]

---

6   Jägerhorn, *Hårdast bland de hårda*, p.163.
7   Peter Englund, *Det hotade huset: Adliga föreställningar om samhället under stormaktstiden* (Stockholm: Atlantis, 1989), pp.153, 182, with references.
8   *Ibid.*, pp.145–6.
9   Ericson, *Krig och krigsmakt*, pp.219–52, on pp.224–6. Why their reactions were so different remains an intriguing question; perhaps the emerging middle class felt more threatened by perceived deviant behaviour, or perhaps the growing interest among senior officers in rational thought and science, which in time would transform society into the Age of Reason, simply made the latter less gullible. Michael Fredholm von Essen, "Religious Beliefs in the Early Modern Swedish Army", *Arquebusier* 34: 1 (2014), pp.2–11.

By the end of the Thirty Years' War, Sweden had transformed from a backward, late feudal kingdom into a modern state, in which talent and rational thought not only was valued but also formed a means of personal and societal advancement. Through its military prowess, Sweden had achieved regional great power status and acquired a small maritime empire. On the Continent, Sweden from 1648 onwards constituted one of the guarantors of the Peace of Westphalia, which has been described as the beginning of the modern international system, based upon peaceful coexistence among sovereign states. Less obvious, but in the long term possibly more important, was that the military achievement also had developed Sweden itself, laying a ground for future progress. There had been a human cost for this, from disease, famine, and battlefield loss, but without Gustavus Adolphus, Oxenstierna, and the reformed military, it is by no means certain that Sweden and its former territories in northern Europe would have grown into the prosperous region that it eventually became. Sweden's position of guarantor of the Peace of Westphalia, and in extension, its position of great power continued until the 1815 Congress of Vienna, which concluded the Napoleonic wars. The Congress also marked the end of Sweden's military engagements abroad, at least until the peacekeeping operations of the twentieth century.

Appendix I

Swedish garrisons in Germany, 1648

Based on *Amore pacis: Geographische Carten von gantz Teuttschlandt* (1648), prepared on behalf of the Swedish supreme commander in Germany and in the Swedish National Archives, Stockholm. For a modern study of the garrisons and their evacuation, see Antje Oschmann, *Der Nürnberger Exekutionstag 1649–1650: Das Ende des Dreißigjährigen Krieges in Deutschland* (Münster: Aschendorff, 1991), pp.499–549.

Alsace
Benfelt
Oberkirch
Reinau Redoubt
Oberehenheim
Dambach

Swabia
Überlingen
Mainau Island
Langenargen Castle
Donauwörth
Rain Redoubt
Nördlingen
Dinkelspiel

Franconia
Schweinfurt
Windsheim
Wertheim Castle
Neuhaus Castle
Mergenthal Castle
Pappenheim Castle
Horneck Castle

Bohemia
Prague Kleinseite and Castle
Leitmeritz
Tetchen Castle
Tabor
Brandeis Castle
Brixen Castle
Friedland Castle
Greiffenstein Castle
Cosselitz Castle
Burgerlitter Castle
Carlstein Castle
Bischofteinitz Castle
Konopischt Castle
Eger

Moravia
Olmütz
Neustadt
Eulenburg Castle
Fülneck Castle
Sternberg Castle

Silesia
Jägerndorf
Drachenberg Castle
Ohlau
Jaur
Lischewitz
Hirschberg
Glogau
Schloss Zetsche
Porcheim Castle
Brochenheim Castle

Saxony and Thuringia
Leipzig Town and Castle
Erfurt
Cyriaksburg Castle
Mansfelt Castle
Hoff Castle
Halberstadt
Aschersleben
Osterwick
Hornburg Castle
Querfurt Castle

Brandenburg
Driesen Redoubt
Gardeleben
Wolfsburg Castle
Landberg

Westphalia
Minden
Bückeburg Castle
Hoya Castle
Nienburg
Lemgow
Vechta
Fürstenau Castle and Town
Drechenverden Castle and Town
Bistel Castle
Wittlage Castle
Auburg Castle
Pyrmont Castle

Upper Palatinate
Weiden
Neumarkt
Sultzberg Castle

Falckenberg Castle
Waldeck Castle

Bremen
Stade
Buxtehude
Brehmervörde Castle
Ratenburg Castle
Otterberg Castle
Langenwedel Castle
Thedinghausen Castle

Mecklenburg
Wismar
Bützow
Wahlfisch Redoubt
Pöhl Castle
Warnemünde Redoubt
Dömitz Castle
Plau Castle
Bleckede Castle

Pomerania
Stettin
Zollschanz ('Customs Redoubt')
Löckenitz Castle
Damm
Greiffenhagen Redoubt
Wollin
Colberg
Schiefelbein Castle
Stralsund
Dänholm Redoubt
Neuefähr Redoubt
Damgarten Redoubt
Tribsee Redoubt
Greifswald
Wicker Redoubt
Wolgast Castle
Penemünde Redoubt
Swine Redoubt
Benow Redoubt
Anklam
Demmin
Überkmünde town and Castle
Loitz town and Castle
Klempenow Castle
Kabel Redoubt

Appendix II

The German Children's Rhyme about Oxenstierna

In the introduction, the German children's rhyme about Oxenstierna was translated as follows:

> *Pray, child, pray!*
> *Tomorrow comes the Swede,*
> *Tomorrow comes the Oxenstierna,*
> *He will soon teach you to pray.*
> *Pray, child, pray!*

The German original can be found in Herbert Langer, *Trettioårigakriget* (np: Natur och Kultur. 2nd edn 1989; first published 1978 as *Hortus Bellicus*), p.243, which presents the rhyme as follows:

> *Bet, Kinnl bet!*
> *oitza kinnt da Schwed,*
> *oitza kinnt da Oxensterna,*
> *wiard ma Kinnl betn lerna.*
> *Bet, Kinnl, bet!*

For the rhyme in somewhat old but standard German, see Reginbald Möhner, *Ein Tourist in Oesterreich während der Schwedenzeit: Aus den Papieren des Pater Reginbald Möhner, Benedictiners von St. Ulrich in Augsburg* (Linz: F. I. Ebenhöch, 1874; edited by Albin Czerny), 12, which presents the rhyme as follows:

> *Beth Kind, Beth,*
> *Morgen kommt der Schwed,*
> *Morgen kommt der Ochsenstern,*
> *Der wird dir schon bethen lern.*

It can be assumed that there were other dialectal variants as well. All versions of the rhyme share the deeply held fear of the Swedish, Protestant soldier, who might turn up any moment to disrupt and devastate community life, just like he did in Saxony, Bavaria, Bohemia, and Moravia.

Colour Plate Commentaries

Front and Rear Cover

C-1. Field Marshal Johan Banér at Chemnitz, 1639

Although most paintings of generals in full cuirassier armour no longer represented their true appearance on the battlefield, some still wore armour. In light of Johan Banér's dislike of French fashion, he may have been one of them. Based on contemporary drawings of Banér in action, he wears a wide-brimmed felt hat instead of a helmet. Banér carries a rapier of the type which grew increasingly common within the Swedish army from the 1630s onwards. Unlike the early 'Swedish-style' rapier previously used within the army, the new type lacked quillons. Instead, the hilt had a guard to protect the hand. As befits his position, Banér also carries a field marshal's command baton.

When mounted on horseback, the upper part of the high riding boots was kept up so as to protect the leg. This is the manner in which Banér wears his boots here. On foot, he would instead have folded down the boots, so that the boot shaft hung loosely around the lower legs. Inside the boots, he wears the customary long linen stockings decorated with embroidery or lace at the top so that it could be seen when the boot was folded down. Such a stocking was known as *strövling*. Banér also wears a wide, laced linen collar of the type subsequently known as a van Dyke collar. The blue sash had existed for some time, and from roughly this time onwards, it became a characteristic accessory of Swedish army officers.

C-2. Cavalryman, Västgöta Cavalry Regiment, at Chemnitz, 1639

In the Swedish army, each horseman should wear helmet and cuirass, consisting of a shot-proof breastplate and backplate. This cavalryman wears the standard, blackened regulation cuirass. In addition, he wears a helmet of the type manufactured in the 1630s in the arms factory at Leufsta, Sweden. This helmet, of which a pattern description but no actual samples remain, was to have a brim three fingers broad, broad cheeks, a nasal bar, a feather-pipe, and a broad tail. A cavalryman should be armed with a pair of wheellock pistols and a rapier. This trooper still wears the early 'Swedish-style' cavalry rapier, which remained in service until about 1640. He also has not yet adopted the latest fashion in breeches. From around 1635, breeches again grew longer and narrower, reaching down slightly more than in the past, and they were no longer tied below the knees but remained open, following French fashion. Not so this cavalryman's breeches, which remain in the old style which in any case was more suited for horseback riding. His only concession to modern fashion is the cravat, which was introduced in or around 1636.

Plate 1. The Swedish army at Wittstock, 1636

1-1. Resting pikeman, after the battle

This plate is based on a contemporary painting by an eyewitness of Swedish soldiers resting after the battle of Wittstock. This pikeman has adopted the new fashion of no longer tying the breeches below the knees, instead allowing them to remain open. He still wears most of the blackened regulation armour (helmet and cuirass consisting of both breastplate and backplate), but he has discarded the tassets that were meant to protect the upper thighs. As we have seen (in *Lion from the North*, Vol. 1), many pikeman discarded even the cuirass during the war. In 1635, Axel Oxenstierna requested the government in Stockholm not to send any more cuirasses. He explained that 'there is no need to send here any cuirass or helmets for either horse or foot, since they are little used, and mostly discarded because of the long marches that are here carried out'.

1-2. Resting musketeer, after the battle

This musketeer, too, is in need of rest after the fighting. With the battle over, he has either removed or run out of slow-match (match-cord) for his matchlock musket. The Swedish army estimated the daily consumption of slow-match as 2.7 m per musketeer. He wears a leather bandolier slung over the left shoulder holding a powder horn and 12 or more wooden flasks for gunpowder (each with enough powder for a single shot). As a sidearm, he carries the customary early 'Swedish-style' rapier. Like the pikeman, he carries his few personal belongings in a haversack, which he also employs as a cushion.

Plate 2. The Swedish army at Breitenfeld, 1642

2-1. Swedish musketeer

This soldier has arrived as part of recent reinforcements from Sweden, so he is dressed in clothes of simple, undyed woollen cloth, locally procured where he was conscripted. While the style of dress, as well as his equipment, is identical to those issued in Germany, the grey colour of the cloth has a very drab look. However, with the severe losses to disease among newly arrived conscripts, this is probably the least of his problems. He is armed with the standard-issue military 10-bore musket (a calibre which eventually was standardised as 20 mm), manufactured in Sweden but in Dutch style, which he uses with a fork rest. However, instead of the usual 12 or more wooden flasks for gunpowder, this musketeer belongs to the minority who carried pre-made paper cartridges, each containing a measured charge of gunpowder, in a cartridge box. As a sidearm, he carries the customary early Swedish-style rapier. By this time, the style was regarded as unfashionable, and many officers would have acquired more up-to-date rapiers. However, new conscripts would certainly be armed from existing stocks.

2-2. Well-to-do dragoon

Dragoons were mounted musketeers. Issued with matchlock muskets, they moved on horseback but fought on foot. Swedish dragoons wore supposed to wear helmets but no breastplates. Likewise, they were expected to wear shoes, not riding boots, and no spurs. However, being enlisted soldiers, dragoons who had the means frequently upgraded their dress and equipment. In fact, most dragoons were selected among those infantrymen who owned a horse, so already from the outset they were generally better off than most infantry. As a result, dragoons increasingly often dressed and fought like cavalrymen, since the latter service was regarded as yet more prestigious than that of dragoons. This particular dragoon has acquired a long coat to protect himself against bad weather and riding boots with spurs of the type used by the cavalry. If he ever was issued with a helmet, he has traded it for a wide-brimmed felt hat with a long plume hanging from the rear, like a fox tail (à la renard).

Plate 3. The Swedish army at Jankow, 1645

3-1. Cavalry officer

This cavalry officer, based on a contemporary painting of the 1645 siege of Brünn, displays a very stylish French coat. He also wears a wide-brimmed felt hat with not one but two extravagant plumes hanging from the rear, like a fox tail (à la renard). At this time, plumes were becoming less common. While some officers replaced the plume with a ribbon or a single, long feather, most discarded the plume altogether. Not so this dashing cavalry officer, who no doubt aims to follow the latest in French fashion. He has discarded all armour, even the shot-proof breastplate and backplate. Unusually for an officer at this time, he still carries an early but very serviceable Swedish-style rapier, so we can assume that he knows his business, despite the French manners so much disliked by some members of the older generation, including the late Field Marshal Banér.

3-2. Infantry officer

By this time, virtually all infantry officers, and many common soldiers, had adopted the French fashion of no longer tying their breeches below the knees. This infantry officer, based on a contemporary painting of the 1645 siege of Brünn, wears a casack as his main garment. This was a very popular dress among soldiers. The tall hat with a flat crown and small brim is typical of the period, too. Future Swedish king Charles Gustavus wore one in a well-known portrait from the same time. This infantry officer has decorated his hat with a ribbon instead of a plume. Armed with a partisan and rapier, the officer might also bring a pair of wheellock pistols into battle. Like all officers, he has provided his own weapons.

Plate 4. The Swedish army at the siege of Prague, 1648

4-1. Infantry officer

Although dressed in an ordinary coat, there is no doubt that he is an officer because of the cut and materials of his garments. His breeches follow the French style, and although serving in the infantry, he wears boots, not shoes, as a personal choice. The tall hat with flat crown follows current fashion, too. This veteran officer has spent several years at war, and he still carries his early but serviceable Swedish-style rapier. There is no longer any other aspect of his armament or clothing that shows that he was born in Sweden, not Germany. By this time, German was the language of command in many units, and we can assume that this officer speaks it well, and that he probably is more proficient in writing German than Swedish. The reconstruction is based on a contemporary print depicting the siege of Prague.

4-2. Musketeer

Like most musketeers, this soldier wears shoes and stockings instead of boots. Instead of the regular wide-brimmed felt hat worn by probably most soldiers, he has acquired a Montero. This is a cap with a spherical crown and pull-down flaps to protect ears and neck in cold weather. When not pulled down, the flaps constituted the upper peak, as depicted here. Increasingly popular among soldiers, the Montero may originally have been intended as a hunter's cap. The Montero was never regulation-issue in the Swedish army, but it was common on the Continent. Like many musketeers, he has abandoned the use of a fork rest. Both contemporary illustrations and texts frequently note Swedish musketeers without fork rests, and during a siege, the fork rest was probably regarded as of limited use.

Plate 5. The Swedish artillery at the siege of Prague, 1648

5-1. Artilleryman

In the early years of the war, the artillery was still regarded as a semi-civilian institution, even though artillerymen served under military law. This situation did not change until 1633, when the artillery personnel were moved into the list of military personnel. Like Lennart Torstensson, their leader and key proponent, all artillerymen had some level of scientific training. However, such specialist training was not necessarily provided to those infantrymen who were detached to assist with the heavy lifting and transportation of artillery pieces. Nonetheless, artillerymen generally dressed similarly to the infantry, and this specialist is no exception. Most artillerymen appear to have worn grey clothes, and this eventually became common practice for artillerymen in the Swedish army.

5-2. Artillery under-officer

In the same way that artillerymen dressed like infantry, this artillery under-officer is barely distinguishable in appearance from any infantry under-officer. Like the artillerymen who served in his command, the under-officer was a specialist, too. Without capable under-officers of this kind, the artillery could not have reached the mobility and independence which became the hallmark of Swedish artillery tactics under Torstensson. In many engagements, the Swedish artillery was constantly in play, moving from location to location.

Plate 6. Swedish levies on the Norwegian border, 1644

6-1. Levied irregular in winter clothes
The Swedish Crown customarily levied troops among the peasants. This was done through a quota that the peasants had to fill. Levied troops would not be trained, and they had to pay for their own weapons and supplies. On the other hand, they were only required to serve at home, even though the Crown from time to time might call for volunteers who accepted to fight outside their own province. Some such levies were even used for offensive warfare, such as Daniel Buscovius's levied Dalecarlian volunteers who in exchange for a year's tax exemption agreed to take part in a winter expedition to conquer the Norwegian settlements of Särna, Idre, and Hede. Mostly, however, levied troops manned defensive bastions along the external borders, in effect functioning as a kind of border guard. The levied peasants would serve for a time, then be replaced by other levies from the same area. The Crown directed that former soldiers should be selected as leaders of the levies. This well-to-do irregular is one of Buscovius's men. Although only armed with a hunting spear, some might have carried muskets as well. Because of the winter cold, he wears clothes of wool and fur, including woollen mittens and a scarf. Well-insulated shoes of the Lapp style were much desired for operations during winter conditions, not only in northern Scandinavia but within the army as well. Skis had been used in previous wars and came in a variety of types, some long and narrow, and others, including this pair, short and broad. As a general rule, the longer skis were more common the further to the north one travelled.

6-2. Levied irregular in summer clothes
This levied soldier is dressed in the characteristic dress of a seventeenth-century Dalecarlian, including an almost Phrygian-style felt cap and long trousers, which were worn tied under the knees. There is reason to believe that by the time of the Thirty Years' War both these garment styles, which ultimately may have derived from the Pontic region, had been used in Sweden, basically unchanged, for more than a millennium. The man carries a matchlock musket with the necessary gear and a utility knife. Since he also has to provide his own supplies, he keeps it in a haversack slung across the shoulder. The reconstruction is based on a drawing by the Florentine diplomat Lorenzo Magalotti, who visited Sweden in 1674 and wrote a comprehensive treatise of the country and its people.

Plate 7. The Swedish army in New Sweden

7-1. Musketeer, New Sweden

This soldier is armed regulation-style, like any Swedish musketeer, with a matchlock musket and a rapier. As for dress, he wears an ordinary wide-brimmed felt hat, shirt, jacket, and breeches. He does not carry a fork rest, since there would have been little use for it in North America. His one unexpected item of dress is the Indian-style deerskin moccasins which he wears instead of the usual shoes. The Swedish fortification officer Per Lindeström compared the Indian deerskin moccasin to the shoes worn by Lapps in northern Scandinavia, which we know were popular in winter in the Swedish army. Moccasins were likely popular among the Swedish settlers in North America, too. Although the Swedish colonists aimed to dress in the same style as in the old country, there were shortages in New Sweden and with most of the population living in isolated farmsteads, many are likely to have adopted Indian-style footwear for daily use, if for no better reason than as a means to save their 'proper' shoes, which would be reserved for visits to the church and other formal occasions.

7-2. Navy sailor

Most Swedish navy sailors were conscripts, even though the Crown also enlisted some professionals, in particular from the Dutch Republic, for blue-water operations, such as the voyages to North America and West Africa. The Crown provided navy sailors with clothing. As a result, they ended up dressed in much the same way as sailors of merchant ships. This sailor wears a jacket and breeches of a style based on archaeological finds from the warship *Wasa*, which sunk in 1628. To this might be added a long coat (not illustrated), when weather conditions were poor. He also wears leather gloves and a *karpus*, a round woollen cap with flaps that could be turned down to protect the eyes, ears, and neck. Although this kind of headgear, too, was found on the warship *Wasa*, this particular headgear is based on a painting of the battle off Fehmarn in 1644. Similar ones are also depicted as worn by the crew from a votive ship from about the same time in Kållered Church, Västergötland. In winter, the *karpus* might be fur lined.

Plate 8. The Swedish army on the Gold Coast

8-1. Navy under-officer

This well-to-do navy under-officer wears fundamentally the same dress as the navy sailor, although the cut and materials of his garments are noticeably better. The reconstruction is based on a Swedish pilot, as depicted in the first Swedish naval instruction manual from 1644, written by Johan Månsson. The under-officer carries a rapier, which he would only bring on formal occasions or when expecting to take part in an immediate boarding action. In other situations, the rapier would be in the way for his work.

8-2. African officer, Swedish Gold Coast

Since there were no regular Swedish troops on the Swedish Gold Coast, the colony for military purposes relied on the raising of local Efutu soldiers. These soldiers were purchased from the King of Efutu as needed. While these men were not freemen, in a legal sense, they were well treated and willing to fight for their masters. They are perhaps best compared to the slave soldiers then used in various parts of the Islamic world, of the type known under names such as *ghulam*, *mamluk*, and so on, who also were unfree but not used for manual labour. This soldier, based on a painting by Albert Eckhout from 1641, currently in the National Museum, Copenhagen, is armed in the customary manner, with spear and several javelins. His main weapon, however, is an Akan sword of the type which soon would develop into the Asante state sword *afena*, later associated with kings and chiefs. The *afena* sword is curved, broad at the point but gradually tapering towards a hilt of wood, consisting of two spheres at either end of a cylindrical grip. In the sword carried by this officer, both the two hilt spheres and the scabbard are covered in ray skin (*etwum*). The scabbard is also embellished by a large red shell, affixed just below the hilt. The shape of the sword is believed to have been influenced by the scimitars carried by Arab traders, who for centuries had visited the Akan states as part of the slave trade with the Muslim world. When this officer entered into Swedish service, he also received a shirt of trade cotton cloth. Trade cloth from overseas was an important commodity in the slave trade. Woven in India and shipped to Europe, trade cloth was re-exported by slave traders to West Africa and the West Indies. Such cottons were usually plain, dyed, or loom-patterned with stripes and checks. This particular garment is of the perhaps most common type, white cotton patterned with indigo stripes.

Plate 9. General Johan Banér's Life Regiment of Horse (Riksarkivet, Stockholm. Author's photos)

General Johan Banér's Life Regiment of Horse began as Banér's life company of horse raised immediately after landing in Germany in 1630. In 1632, the company was expanded into a life regiment. The cypher GAKVS reads *Gustavus Adolphus König von Schweden* ('Gustavus Adolphus King of Sweden). The cornet with a white field belongs to Banér's Life Company. Eventually, the use of white colour for the colonel's life company became commonplace in the Swedish army, but at this time, only some regiments had adopted the custom. Among them were both Banér's Life Regiment of Horse (depicted here) and Banér's Regiment of Foot (depicted in Plates 13–14, *Lion from the North*, Vol. 1). Note the fringes and tassels, which were typical additions to cavalry cornets.

We know the appearance of many Swedish flags from the period because they were depicted in a book by Reginbaldus Möhner, a monk in Augsburg who in the period from 1632 to 1635 painted a large number of flags and standards from both Swedish units and their opponents. The illustrations here are photographs of copies, deposited in the Swedish Military Archives, of the originals painted by Möhner. The copies, probably made in the early 1930s in connection with the research carried out for the General Staff work *Sveriges Krig*, were according to a handwritten note made by a Major E. Nordenfalk. This would likely be Major Erland Nordenfalk, who later was director of the Löfstad Castle Museum. However, it remains possible that the copies instead were made by Major Ejnar Nordfeldt of the General Staff's Department of Military History, who was engaged in the Thirty Years' War research project and made many of the maps and sketches published by the project. Since all participants in the project have passed away, it was not possible to reach a certain conclusion on the illustrator's identity.

Plate 10. Duke Bernard of Saxe-Weimar's Life Regiment of Horse (Riksarkivet, Stockholm. Author's photos)

After the battle of Breitenfeld in 1631, Duke Bernard of Saxe-Weimar's Life Regiment of Horse assumed the name of the King's Life Regiment of Horse (a title until then held by the cavalry regiment of Johann Philip von Ortenburg who died in June 1631). Bernard's regiment fought under this name at Lützen, after which the regiment finally became known as Duke Bernard of Saxe-Weimar's Life Regiment of Horse. Henceforth, it followed Bernard's army. Notably, one of the regiment's cornets included the text *Gustavus Adolphus, Rex Suecorum* ('Gustavus Adolphus, King of the Swedes').

Plate 11. Major General Patrick Ruthven's Cavalry Regiment (Riksarkivet, Stockholm. Author's photos)

Möhner depicted Major General Patrick Ruthven's Cavalry Regiment in or soon after 1632. This was probably a regiment which Ruthven enlisted in Germany in early 1632. At the same time, he also enlisted a regiment of foot (depicted in Plate 30, *Lion from the North*, Vol. 1). The cornets illustrated here are somewhat reminiscent of the colours of the regiment of foot, which supports the hypothesis that the regiments were enlisted at the same time.

Plate 12. Duke William of Saxe-Weimar's Life Regiment of Horse (Riksarkivet, Stockholm. Author's photos)

Duke William of Saxe-Weimar's Life Regiment of Horse was yet another of the Weimar regiments which went into Swedish service. The cypher HWZS reads *Herzog Wilhelm zu Sachsen* ('Duke William of Saxe'). The regiment had 12 companies.

Plate 13. Duke Hans Ernst of Saxe-Weimar's Life Regiment of Horse (13.1); Captain Gottfried Holtzmüller's Dragoon Company (13.2); Colonel Wolf Ebert Horneck's Regiment of Foot (13.3) (Riksarkivet, Stockholm. Author's photos)

All Weimar brothers who went into Swedish service brought a life regiment of horse, and Hans Ernst, the youngest of the three Weimar brothers, was no exception. Duke Hans Ernst of Saxe-Weimar's Life Regiment of Horse consisted of eight companies.
Captain Gottfried Holtzmüller was commissioned to raise a dragoon company of 150 men in August 1631. In 1633, his unit served in Horn's army. In 1632, Colonel Wolf Ebert Horneck (d. 1638) commanded three infantry companies in Speyer, a political centre of the Rhineland Palatinate, where he served as the Swedish commandant. He later enlisted more men until his unit reached regimental strength. The plate depicts the 8th company of Horneck's Regiment of Foot.

Plate 14. Colonel Nicolaus Dietrich Sperreuter's Cavalry Regiment (Riksarkivet, Stockholm. Author's photos)

Colonel Nicolaus Dietrich Sperreuter's Cavalry Regiment was raised in Pomerania in 1630. In 1635, then Major General Sperreuter briefly assumed control of the Swedish Weser army. Soon afterwards, he resigned from the Swedish army. Some of his regiments remained in Swedish service, however, and it seems likely that this cavalry regiment did, too. Most company cornets of Sperreuter's regiment were very simple in design, consisting of only one base colour.

Plate 15. Colonel Robert Munro of Foulis's Cavalry Regiment (Riksarkivet, Stockholm. Author's photos)

Colonel Robert Munro of Foulis commanded two regiments in Swedish service, one of horse and one of foot. These are the known cornets of Robert Munro of Foulis's Cavalry Regiment. The regiment remained in Swedish service after the death of its colonel in 1633.

Plate 16. Colonel Robert Munro of Foulis's Cavalry Regiment (continued) (Riksarkivet, Stockholm. Author's photos)

The remaining cornets of Colonel Robert Munro of Foulis's Cavalry Regiment.

Plate 17. Colonel Jürgen Ernst von Wedel's Cavalry Regiment (Riksarkivet, Stockholm. Author's photos)

Originally raised in 1631 by Colonel Reinhold von Goltz, the regiment consisted of eight companies of horse. However, Goltz died in April 1631, and the regiment became Colonel Jürgen Ernst von Wedel's Cavalry Regiment. In 1634–1635, the regiment fought in the army commanded by Banér. Möhner made drawings of all eight company cornets of the regiment.

Plate 18. Colonel Jürgen Ernst von Wedel's Cavalry Regiment (continued) (Riksarkivet, Stockholm. Author's photos)

The remaining cornets of Colonel Jürgen Ernst von Wedel's Cavalry Regiment.

Plate 19. Johann Bernhard von Öhm's Cavalry Regiment (Riksarkivet, Stockholm. Author's photos)

Raised for the war in Prussia in 1626, Johann Bernhard von Öhm's Cavalry Regiment was one of Gustavus Adolphus's oldest enlisted cavalry regiments. This, incidentally, explains the wear and tear of its older cornets. The less worn cornets probably represent companies raised in the summer of 1631. The white cornet is the colonel's life company. The regiment's colonel, Johann Bernhard von Öhm (also spelled Ehm; 1587–1657), fought in numerous engagements during the Thirty Years' War, from the battle of Fleurus in 1622 until the end of hostilities in 1648. Öhm served under Gustavus Adolphus in Prussia from 1626 onwards and at Alte Feste and Lützen in 1632.

Plate 20. Colonel Georg aus dem Winckel's Old Blue Regiment of Foot, c. 1633-1635 (20.1); Colonel Georg aus dem Winckel's Dragoon Company, 1635 (20.2) (Riksarkivet, Stockholm. Author's photos)

From 1634 onwards, the Blue Regiment of Foot, then often known as the 'Old Blue Regiment' (*Alt-Blau Regiment*), functioned as the senior regiment of the army in Germany and the Life Regiment of Foot of, in turn, Field Marshals Banér, Torstensson, Wrangel, and Charles Gustavus. The regiment also received new colours, one of which was depicted by Möhner sometime in the period 1633–1635, when the regiment was under the command of Colonel Georg aus dem Winckel (1596–1639), who had led the Blue Regiment since 1630. Although only one colour of the new type was depicted, it gives some idea of what the new series of colours looked like. (For the old colours of the Blue Regiment, see Plates 9–10, *Lion from the North*, Vol. 1).

In 1635, Möhner also made a drawing of Colonel Georg aus dem Winckel's Dragoon Company. Since Winckel was colonel of the Old Blue Regiment of

Foot, it is conceivable that he converted one company from this regiment into a dragoon company.

Plate 21. Colonel Thomas Sigmund von Schlammersdorff's 'New' Regiment of Foot (Riksarkivet, Stockholm. Author's photos)

The Schlammersdorff family provided several officers and regiments to the Swedish army. One of them was Colonel Thomas Sigmund von Schlammersdorff(d. 1637?), the cousin of Major General Balthasar Jacob von Schlammersdorff (d. 1635) who also was in Swedish service. In 1620, Thomas Sigmund von Schlammersdorff was in Bavarian service as a lieutenant colonel. Schlammersdorff went into Swedish service as a colonel in 1630, after which he for a while raised troops on behalf of others. In 1631, Schlammersdorff raised a regiment of foot of his own. However, it surrendered at Neuburg-an-der-Donau in Bavaria in 1633 and lost its colours (the colours of both this regiment and that of his cousin Major General Balthasar Jacob von Schlammersdorff are illustrated in Plates 19–20 and 23–24, *Lion from the North*, Vol. 1). Schlammersdorff then raised a new regiment, this one, which was fortunate in avoiding the battle of Nördlingen in 1634 only because Field Marshal Gustav Horn, to whose army the regiment was attached, in July had left it to garrison Augsburg together with the eight Finnish companies of Caspar Ermes's Savolax Regiment. Schlammersdorff's new regiment soon had to surrender Augsburg, but it was allowed to depart for Ulm. Schlammersdorff eventually fell into Imperial captivity with the fall of Wolgast in December 1637. He died in captivity soon afterwards. Möhner's drawings depict the colours of all companies of the regiment.

Plate 22. Colonel Thomas Sigmund von Schlammersdorff's 'New' Regiment of Foot (continued) (Riksarkivet, Stockholm. Author's photos)

The remaining colours of Colonel Thomas Sigmund von Schlammersdorff's 'New' Regiment of Foot.

Plate 23. Colonel John Forbes's Regiment of Foot (Riksarkivet, Stockholm. Author's photos)

Möhner copied the colours of all companies of Colonel John Forbes's Regiment of Foot. The colours carry references to Gustavus Adolphus (including the cypher GASR, which reads *Gustavus Adolphus Sueciae Rex*, 'Gustavus Adolphus, Sweden's King') as well as various Protestant texts. One colour is marked 1632, another 1633, which shows that the colours were issued on separate occasions. There were several individuals named John Forbes in the Swedish army. This regiment is presumably the John Forbes's

Regiment which participated in the battle of Wittstock in 1636. Möhner identified the companies as those of Captains Schlott, Alexander Forbes, and Melchior Bart. The white colours were carried by Forbes's life company.

Plate 24. Colonel John Forbes's Regiment of Foot (continued) (Riksarkivet, Stockholm. Author's photos)

The remaining colours of Colonel John Forbes's Regiment of Foot. Möhner identified the companies as those of Captains Ulrich Ulff and Christian Schmidt, Major Ruth, and Captain Konrad Öchstlich.

Plate 25. Colonel Johann Michael Rau's Regiment of Foot (Riksarkivet, Stockholm. Author's photos)

At the time of the battle of Nördlingen in 1634, several of the Duchy of Württemberg's regiments were in Swedish service. Colonel Johann Michael Rau's Regiment of Foot was the most important of the Württemberg units, and its colours display obvious links to Württemberg. Rau, appointed colonel in 1632, was at the time of his appointment the senior officer from Württemberg. However, he was removed from this position already in 1633.

Plate 26. Colonel Johann Schneidewind's Regiment of Foot (Riksarkivet, Stockholm. Author's photos)

Johann Schneidewind took part in the battle of Breitenfeld in 1631. He also participated in the battle at Rain-am-Lech ('Crossing of the Lech') in 1632. Soon afterwards, Möhner copied the colours of all companies within Schneidewind's Regiment of Foot, which formed part of the army of Christian, Count Palatine of Birkenfeld-Bischweiler. Schneidewind's Regiment carried colours of the Swedish type. Like some Swedish units, Schneidewind's life company carried a colour with a white base and the text *Gustavus Rex Sueciae* ('Gustavus King of Sweden'). Schneidewind's Regiment fought at Nördlingen in 1634, where Schneidewind fell into Imperial captivity. Following his release, Schneidewind rejoined the Swedish army. By 1638, Schneidewind, promoted to Major General, was reportedly in the process of enlisting ten regiments to be paid for with English funds. This was at least the information which George of Brunswick-Lüneburgthen provided in a letter to Gallas. The enlistment effort did not prevent Schneidewind from beating off an Imperial raid later in the year.

Plate 27. Colonel Johann Schneidewind's Regiment of Foot (continued) (Riksarkivet, Stockholm. Author's photos)

The remaining colours of Colonel Johann Schneidewind's Regiment of Foot.

Plate 28. Colonel Philipp von Liebenstein's Regiment of Foot (Riksarkivet, Stockholm. Author's photos)

In 1631, Philipp von Liebenstein (1593–1637) enlisted a regiment of foot at Erfurt in the service of Duke William of Saxe-Weimar. In early 1632, he joined the Swedish army. Following the battle of Nördlingen in 1634, Philipp von Liebenstein's Regiment of Foot served under Bernard of Saxe-Weimar. Möhner copied the colours of all companies within the regiment. The colour with a white base was the colour of Liebenstein's life company.

Plate 29. Colonel Philipp von Liebenstein's Regiment of Foot (continued) (Riksarkivet, Stockholm. Author's photos)

The remaining colours of Colonel Philipp von Liebenstein's Regiment of Foot.

Plate 30. Formerly Catholic cavalry and dragoon units (Riksarkivet, Stockholm. Author's photos)

The victories of Gustavus Adolphus in the early 1630s persuaded many Catholic units to change sides. A number of formerly Catholic units remained in the Swedish army after his death. Möhner copied their flags as well. This plate depicts three cavalry cornets, judging from their common base colour and motifs possibly from the same unit, and a swallow-tailed dragoon guidon.
We do not know how long these units retained their original flags after switching sides, especially if they carried conspicuously Catholic motifs. Often new colours were issued, but time and resources for this were not always available. Besides, it hardly mattered. Occasionally, even newly raised regiments received captured trophy colours, if there was no time to manufacture new ones. For this reason, it is likely that several of these flags remained in Swedish service.

Plate 31. Formerly Catholic infantry units (Riksarkivet, Stockholm. Author's photos)

Yet more flags of formerly Catholic units, this time the colours of infantry units.

Plate 32. The Imperial Circles

For military and taxation purposes, the Empire was divided into regional groupings of states known as Imperial Circles. During the war, each was commonly regarded as a separate theatre of operations. The Peace of

Westphalia in 1648, which concluded the Thirty Years' War, forced some changes to the system, which otherwise was retained. The most important change was that the Burgundian Circle was divided into the Spanish Netherlands and the Dutch Republic, taking into the account that the Peace of Münster between the Dutch Republic and Spain earlier in the year had concluded the Eighty Years' War.

Further Reading

As mentioned in the previous volume, the English reader is well supplied when it comes to sources on the Swedish army in the Thirty Years' War, due to the wealth of contemporary information in books such as *The Swedish Intelligencer*, *The Swedish Discipline*, the *True Relation* of Sydnam Poyntz (despite its many inaccuracies), and Colonel Robert Monro's regimental history *Monro, His Expedition with the Worthy Scots Regiment*. There is also Sir James Turner's *Pallas Armata*, which although published many years later, includes glimpses of the Swedish army in action in Germany. In other European languages, there is *Le soldat svedois*, a contemporary history of the war compiled by Friedrich Spanheim the Elder. Spanheim's book was published in French, Italian, and German. In German, we also have Bogislaff Philip von Chemnitz's *Königlichen Schwedischen in teutschland geführten Kriegs*, which was the official Swedish history of the war, and the multi-volume *Theatrum Europaeum*, a chronicle of events in Europe in the period 1618–1718 by the publisher Merian in Frankfurt-am-Main, which provides numerous details and illustrations. For those who want an Imperial perspective, there is Galliazo Gualdo Priorato's *History of the Late Warres and Other State Affaires of the Best Part of Christendom*. Priorato writes as an historian but he served as a soldier in the war, and his *History* was translated into English already in 1648. There are also many other contemporary sources to the events of the war, quite a few of which contain details of military interest. One of the most interesting is the field diary by the German enlisted soldier Peter Hagendorf, who from 1625 to 1649 described his daily activities in a notebook. The highest rank that Hagendorf ever attained, briefly, was that of captain, so his diary shows the war from the perspective of the under-officer. The diary has been published at least in German and Swedish. In German, there are also two military manuals which describe the Swedish model of war: Lorentz von Troupitzen's *Kriegs Kunst* and Wendelin Schildknecht's *Harmonia in fortalitiis construendis, defendendis & oppugnandis*, both of which describe the Swedish military model, including how it developed after the death of Gustavus Adolphus.

Having said this, sources such as *The Swedish Intelligencer*, *Le soldatsvedois*, and *Theatrum Europaeum* are compilations of newsletters and propaganda, for which reason they cannot always be taken at face value. Even Monro, who was an officer in the Swedish army, and Chemnitz, who was the official Swedish historian, used such materials to describe events of which they had no personal knowledge. Their information must accordingly be assessed with care when used as sources. As for the prints of battles in the *Theatrum Europaeum*, due to artistic license they were regarded as unreliable sources even by contemporaries.

A key source to the history of the Swedish army during the Thirty Years' War is the multi-volume work *Rikskansleren Axel Oxenstiernas skrifter och brefvexling* (AOSB), which includes Oxenstierna's letters and state papers. It was published in the period 1888–2018 and currently also exists in the form of a database maintained by the Swedish National Archives. The printed volumes appeared in two series: a first series which contains Axel Oxenstierna's own letters and state papers and a second series which contains letters addressed to him by others, among them numerous reports from his generals.

Unsurprisingly, the Swedish army is the subject of a number of reference works only published in the Swedish language. Key modern reference works include the various volumes on the war published by the Swedish General Staff and its successor, the Defence Staff. They contain many valuable archive documents relating to the Swedish army and are reliable in its use of official records including orders of battle, casualty lists, and logistical inventories. The General Staff at first planned to continue its multi-volume work on the wars under Gustavus Adolphus until the end of the Thirty Years' War. However, the Second World War intervened, and most of its researchers received other duties relating to the war effort. After the war, neither funding nor interest remained for a continuation. Society as a whole, including academe, was weary of warfare in Germany, and the military found the events of modern military history more stimulating as topics of study than those of the past. Nonetheless, the Defence Staff published several additional volumes, primarily of an anniversary character. These include volumes on *Slaget vid Femern 1644* (without the customary academic references), *Slaget vid Jankow 1645*, and, finally, *Från Femern och Jankow till Westfaliska freden*, which covers the final years of the war.

Unfortunately, the Defence Staff's military historians never published the history of the period between 1632 and 1644. As a result, the most recent *detailed* histories of this period of the Thirty Years' War in the Swedish language were published in the 1930s by Lars Tingsten (1857–1937), a retired general and former minister of war. Tingsten was a well-known military historian and his works are fundamentally sound. However, he intended them as popular histories, so unlike the General Staff works, they contain essentially no references and do not reprint archive documents. Besides, some bias, in particular in favour of Banér, is perceptible in Tingsten's works. There is, accordingly, a real need for continued research into archive documents for the years between 1632 and 1644. More can, no doubt, be learnt by re-examining the events from this (with the exception of Nördlingen) underresearched period. Yet, for the lack of anything better, Tingsten's works are essential sources to the Swedish army in the Thirty Years' War.

Tingsten, as well as most later military historians, based most of his quantitative data on the two-volume work *Uppgifter rörande svenska krigs magtens styrka* by the mid nineteenth-century Swedish soldier, military historian, and politician Julius Mankell (1828–1897). Mankell worked from archive documents, primarily in the National Archives, copied by hand the figures on unit strengths, garrisons, and so on from these documents, which he then entered into his manuscript, although generally without indicating exactly which document he had used. Then, before the work was concluded, Mankell took a break from his research, joined the Polish 1863 uprising against Russian rule, and ended up in an Austrian prison. Moreover, having returned to his post in the Swedish army after the suppression of the Polish uprising, Mankell was unavailable when his two-volume work was printed. For these reasons, he readily admitted that the printed books contain numerous errors. This sometimes makes the information in Mankell's work difficult to verify; yet, for those who are unable to access the original archive documents, it is the best there is on the subject. The National Archives still hold major parts of the field archives of Carl Gustav Wrangel and Charles Gustavus, but not those of Lennart Torstensson, which seems to have been lost, and only little from Johan Banér.

There is also the multi-volume *Kungl. Svea Livgardes Historia*, by Bertil C:son Barkman and others, which describes the history of the Swedish Royal Life Guard. Although this work covers a far longer period of time and, since it focuses on the Life Guard, does not cover every incident of the war, it updates and often provides a better reading of the sources than the General Staff works. Publication started in 1937 and was not concluded until 1983. Some additional information is provided by other regimental histories, of which the multi-volume *Kungl. Artilleriet*, by Jonas Hedberg and others, which describes the history of the Royal Artillery, is the most useful. Publication began in 1975 and apparently reached its conclusion in 2011. The history of Swedish fortification is retold in the multi-volume *Kongl. Fortifikationens Historia*, by Ludvig W:son Munthe and others, which was published between 1902 and 1970.

While the focus of the present volume and its predecessor on Gustavus Adolphus's army is the Swedish army and not the general history of the Thirty Years' War, the reader who may wish to delve deeper into the events of the war, beyond those of the Swedish army, is well-served by several recent sourcebooks. These include *The Thirty Years War: A Documentary History* by Tryntje Helfferich (Indianapolis, Indiana: Hackett Publishing Company, 2009); *The Thirty Years War: A Sourcebook* by Peter H. Wilson (Basingstoke, Hampshire: Palgrave Macmillan, 2010); and *Experiencing the Thirty Years War: A Brief History with Documents* by Hans Medick and Benjamin Marschke (Boston: Bedford/St. Martins, 2013). For a discussion on the contemporary sources, see, for instance, Geoff Mortimer's *Eyewitness Accounts of the Thirty Years War, 1618–1648* (Basingstoke, Hampshire: Palgrave, 2002).

Since most studies on the Swedish army of the Thirty Years' War are published in other languages than English, the following bibliography is limited to the works most frequently referenced in notes and most useful for continued research. Other works are only mentioned in the notes.

Bibliography

Contemporary Sources and Compilations

Amore pacis: Geographische Carten von gantz Teuttschlandt (1648). Broadsheet with a map prepared on behalf of the Swedish supreme commander in Germany on the orders of Quartermaster-General Cornelis van den Büsch, with details on Swedish garrisons. Swedish Military Archives (KrA), National Archives, Stockholm (KrA, Hist. Plan. 1648: 24 fol., *Amore Pacis*).

Anon., *Le soldat svedois ov Histoire de ce qui s'est passé en Àllemagne depuis l'entrée du Roy de Suede en l'année 1630 jusques apres sa mort.* np, 1633. Compiled by Friedrich Spanheim the Elder and published in several editions and locations. The version used here is from the Bavarian State Library.

Anon., *The Swedish Discipline, Religious, Civile, and Military* 1–3 (London: Nathaniel Butter and Nicholas Bourne, 1632. Edited by William Watts. Reprinted in facsimile by Pallas Armata, Tonbridge, Kent, 1998)

Anon., *The Swedish Intelligencer* 1–4. London: Nathaniel Butter and Nicolas Bourne, 1632–1633. Compiled by William Watts (reprinted in facsimile by Pallas Armata, Tonbridge, Kent, 1995)

Chemnitz, Bogislaff Philip von, *Königlichen Schwedischen in Teutschlandgeführten Kriegs.* 2 vols (Stettin: Georg Rethe, 1648, Stockholm: Johannis Janssonius, 1653)

Hagendorf, Peter, *Ein Söldnerleben im Dreißigjährigen Krieg: Eine Quelle zur Sozialgeschichte* (Berlin: Akademie Verlag, 1993). Edited by Jan Peters.

Hagendorf, Peter. *Sedan stack vi staden i brand: En legoknekts dagbok från trettioåriga kriget* (Stockholm: Ordfront & Armémuseum, 2006. Edited by Jan Peters. Swedish translation of the above)

Hallendorff, Carl (ed.), *Sverges Traktater med främmande magter jemte andra hit hörande handlingar* 5:2 (1632–1645) (Stockholm: P. A. Norstedt & Söner, 1909)

Mankell, Julius, *Uppgifter rörande svenska krigsmagtens styrka, sammansättning och fördelning sedan slutet af femtonhundratalet, jemte öfversigt af svenska krigshistoriens vigtigaste händelser under samma tid* (Stockholm: C. M. Thimgren, 1865)

Merian, Matthaeus, *Theatrum Europaeum*, 21 vols (Frankfurt-am-Main: Matthaeus Merian,1633–1738). Available from various web sites, including those of Universitätsbibliothek Augsburg (<www.bibliothek.uni-augsburg.de>) and Wolfenbütteler Digitalen Bibliothek (<http://diglib.hab.de>).

Monro, Robert, *Monro, His Expedition with the Worthy Scots Regiment (Called Mac-Keyes Regiment)* (London: William Jones, 1637. Reprinted in facsimile by Pallas Armata, Tonbridge, Kent, 1994)

Montecuccoli, Raimondo, *Ausgewählte Schriften des Raimund Fürsten Montecuccoli* 1–4 (Vienna: Kriegs-Archiv/W. Braumüller, 1899–1901). Edited by Alois Veltzé.

Oxenstierna, Axel. *Rikskansleren Axel Oxenstiernas skrifter och brefvexling.* Multiple volumes and database (Stockholm: P. A. Norstedt & Söner/Swedish National Archives (RA), 1888–2018)

Poyntz, Sydnam, *A True Relation of These German Warres From Mansfield's Going Out of England Which Was in the Yeare (1624) untill This Last Yeare 1636 Whereof My Self Was an Eywitnesse of Most I Have Here Related as Followeth, by mee Sydnam Poyntz* (Concluded 1637, first published 1908 by the Camden Society, edited by A. T. S. Goodrick. Reprinted in facsimile by Pallas Armata, Tonbridge, Kent, 1992)

Priorato, Galliazo Gualdo, *An History of the Late Warres and Other State Affaires of the Best Part of Christendom, Beginning with the King of Swethlands Entrance into Germany, and Continuing to the Yeare 1640* (London: John Hardesty, Thomas Huntington, and Thomas Jackson, 1648. Reprinted in facsimile by Pallas Armata, Tonbridge, Kent, 1996)

Schildknecht, Wendelin, *Harmonia in fortalitiis construendis, defendendis & oppugnandis* (Stettin: Johann Valentin Rheten, 1652)

Troupitzen, Lorentz von, *Kriegs Kunst: Nach Königlicher Schwedischer Maniereine Compagny zurichten, in Regiment, Zug- und Schlacht-Ordnung zubringen, zum Ernst anzuführen, zugebrauchen, und in essewürcklich, zuunterhalten* (Frankfurt-am-Main: Matthaeus Merian, 1633)

Turenne, *Histoire du vicomte de Turenne, Maréchal général des armées du Roi 3: Contenant les Mémoires du M. de Turenne* (Paris: Jombert, 1773)

Turner, Sir James, *Pallas Armata: Military Essayes of the Ancient Grecian, Roman, and Modern Art of War, Written in the Years 1670 and 1671* (London: Richard Chiswell, 1683)

Turner, Sir James, *Memoirs of His Own Life and Times* (Edinburgh, 1829)

Wallenstein, Albrecht von, *Albrechts von Wallenstein, des Herzogs von Friedland und Mecklenburg, ungedruckte, eigenhändige vertrauliche Briefe und amtliche Schreiben aus den Jahren 1627 bis 1634* (Berlin: G. Reimer, 1828–1829). Edited by Friedrich Förster.

Wallenstein, Albrecht von, *Waldsteins Correspondenz: Eine Nachleseaus dem K. K. Kriegsarchive in Wien*. 2 vols (Vienna: Karl Gerold, 1865–1866). Edited by Beda Dudik.

Wallhausen, Johann Jacobi von, *Kriegskunst zu Fuß* (Leeuwarden: Claude Fontaine, 1630. First published 1615)

Wallhausen, Johann Jacobi von, *Kriegskunst zu Pferdt* (Frankfurt-am-Main: Johann Theodor de Bry, 1616)

Wallhausen, Johann Jacobi von, *Defensio patriae oder Landrettung* (Frankfurt-am-Main: Daniel Aubrij, David Aubrij, and Clement Schleichen, 1621)

Later Studies

Åberg, Alf, "Gustaf II Adolf och hans skotska krigare", *Livrustkammaren – Journal of the Royal Armoury* 16: 1 (1982): pp.1–21

Åberg, Alf, *The People of New Sweden: Our Colony on the Delaware River, 1638–1655* (Stockholm: Natur och Kultur, 1988).

Alm, Josef, *Blanka vapen och skyddsvapen från och med 1500-talet till våra dagar* (Stockholm: Rediviva, 1975. First published 1932)

Alm, Josef. *Eldhandvapen 1: Från deras tidigaste förekomst till slaglåsets allmänna införande* (Stockholm: Rediviva, 1976. First published 1934)

Alm, Josef, *Arméns eldhandvapen förr och nu*. Stockholm: Kungl. Armémuseum, 1953.

Alm, Josef, "Flottans handvapen", *Sjöhistorisk Årsbok 1953–54* (Stockholm: Föreningen Sveriges Sjöfartsmuseum i Stockholm, 1954: pp.67–147)

Asker, Björn, *Karl X Gustav* (Lund: Historiska Media, 2010)

Barker, Thomas M., *The Military Intellectual and Battle: Raimondo Montecuccoli and the Thirty Years War* (Albany, New York: State University of New York Press, 1975)

Barkman, G. Bertil C:son. *Gustaf II Adolfs regementsorganisation vid det inhemska infanteriet: En studie över organisationens tillkomst och huvuddragen av dess utveckling mot bakgrunden av kontinental organisation* (Stockholm: Meddelanden från Generalstabens krigshistoriska avdelning, 1931)

Barkman, G. Bertil C:son, *Kungl. Svea Livgardes Historia, 2: 1560–1611* (Stockholm: Stiftelsen för Svea Livgardes Historia, 1939)

Barkman, G. Bertil C:son; Sven Lundkvist; and Lars Tersmeden, *Kungl. Svea Livgardes Historia* 3:2: *1632 (1611)–1660* (Stockholm: Stiftelsen för Svea Livgardes Historia, 1966)

Bellander, Erik, *Dräkt och uniform: Den svenska arméns beklädnad från 1500-talets början fram till våra dagar* (Stockholm: Kungl. Armémuseum/P.A. Norstedt & Söner, 1973)

Blackmore, David J., *'Destructive and Formidable': British Infantry Firepower, 1642–1765*. Nottingham Trent University, dissertation, 2012.

Brzezinski, Richard, *The Army of Gustavus Adolphus 1: Infantry*. London: Osprey, Men-at-Arms 235, 1991.

Brzezinski, Richard. *The Army of Gustavus Adolphus 2: Cavalry* (London: Osprey, Men-at-Arms 262, 1993)

Droste, Heiko, "Johan Adler Salvius i Hamburg: Ett nätverksbygge i 1600-talets Hamburg", Kerstin Abukhanfusa (ed.). *Mare nostrum: Om Westfaliska freden och Östersjön som ett svenskt maktcentrum* (Stockholm: Riksarkivet, 1999: pp.243–55)

Engerisser, Peter, *Von Kronach nach Nördlingen. Der Dreißigjährige Krieg in Franken, Schwaben und der Oberpfalz 1631–1635*.(Weißenstadt: Verlag Heinz Späthling, 2004)

Engerisser, Peter; and Pavel Hrnčiřík, *Nördlingen 1634: Die Schlacht bei Nördlingen – Wendepunkt des Dreißigjährigen Krieges* (Weißenstadt: Verlag Heinz Späthling, 2009)

Englund, Peter, *Ofredsår* (Stockholm: Atlantis, 1993)

Ericson, Lars, "Fortifikationens ritare", *Att illustrera stormakten: Den svenska Fortifikationens bilder 1654–1719* (Lund: Historiska Media, 2001: pp.23–27)

Ericson, Lars, *Krig och krigsmakt under svensk stormaktstid* (Lund: Historiska Media, 2004)

Ericson, Lars, and Fred Sandstedt, *Fanornas folk: Den svenska arméns soldater under 1600-talets första hälft* (Stockholm: Armémuseum, 1982)

Ericson, Lars; Martin Hårdstedt; PerIko: Ingvar Sjöblom; and Gunnar Åselius, *Svenska slagfält* (np: Wahlström & Widstrand, 2003)

Ericson Wolke, Lars; Göran Larsson; and Nils Erik Villstrand, *Trettioåriga kriget: Europa i brand 1618–1648* (Lund: Historiska Media, 2006)

Ericson Wolke, Lars; and Martin Hårdstedt, *Svenska sjöslag* (np: Medströms, 2009)

Försvarsstabens krigshistoriska avdelning, *Slaget vid Femern 1644 13/10 1944: Minnesskrift* (Gothenburg: Sjöhistoriska samfundet, 1944)

Försvarsstabens krigshistoriska avdelning, *Slaget vid Jankow 1645 24/2 1945: Minnesskrift* (Stockholm: Försvarsstabens krigshistoriska avdelning, 1945)

Försvarsstabens krigshistoriska avdelning, *Från Femern och Jankow till Westfaliska freden: Minnesskrift* (Stockholm: Generalstabens Litografiska Anstalt, 1948)

Försvarsstabens krigshistoriska avdelning, *Vägar och vägkunskap i Mellaneuropa under trettioåriga krigets sista skede* (Stockholm: Generalstabens Litografiska Anstalt, 1948)

Fredholm von Essen, Michael, *Charles XI's War: The Scanian War between Sweden and Denmark, 1675–1679* (Warwick: Helion, 2019).

Fredholm von Essen, Michael, *The Lion from the North: The Swedish Army during the Thirty Years' War, 1618–1632*, vol. 1 (Warwick: Helion, 2020)

Frost, Robert I., *The Northern Wars: War, State and Society in Northeastern Europe, 1558–1721* (Harlow, Essex: Longman, 2000)

Gäfvert, Björn. "Kartor och krig: Svensk militär kartering under Trettioåriga kriget", *Krig och fred i källorna* (Riksarkivet: Årsbok för Riksarkivet och Landsarkiven, 1998: pp.88–100)

Gäfvert, Björn, "Att känna territoriet: Svensk kartering under Trettioåriga krigets dagar", Kerstin Abukhanfusa (ed.), *Mare nostrum: Om Westfaliska freden och Östersjön som ett svenskt maktcentrum* (Stockholm: Riksarkivet, 1999: pp.74–92)

Generalstaben, *Sverigeskrig 1611–1632* (Stockholm: Generalstaben, 1936–1939)

Glete, Jan, *Navies and Nations: Warships, Navies and State Building in Europe and America, 1500–1860*. 2 vols (Stockholm: Almqvist & Wiksell International, *Acta Universitatis stockholmiensis* (Stockholm Studies in History) 48:1, 1993)

Grosjean, Alexia, *An Unofficial Alliance, Scotland and Sweden 1569–1654* (Leiden: Brill, 2003)

Gullberg, Tom; and Mikko Huhtamies, *På vakt i öster*, vol. 3 (np: Schildts, 2004)

Gyllenstierna, Ebbe, "Karl Gustav Wrangel och Henri Turenne: Svensk och fransk krigföring under trettioåriga krigets sista skede", *Meddelande 36* (Stockholm: Armémuseum, 1976: pp.39–51)

Hamilton, Edward; and Anders Sandström, *Sjöstrid på Wasas tid: Taktik, artilleri och handeldvapen* (Stockholm: Sjöhistoriska museet, Wasastudier 9, 1982)

Hamilton, Henning, *Afhandling om krigsmaktens och krigskonstens tillstånd i Sverige, under Konung Gustaf II Adolfs regering* (Stockholm: Kongl. Vitterhets Historie och Antiquitets Academiens handlingar 17, 1846)

Hazelius, Kim, *De kallades snapphanar: Friskyttar, rövare & bondeuppbåd* (Bjärnum: Bokpro, 2006)

Hedberg, Jonas (ed.), *Kungl. Artilleriet: Yngre vasatiden* (Stockholm: Militärhistoriska Förlaget, 1985)

Hocker, Fred., *Vasa: A Swedish Warship*. Stockholm: Medströms, 2015)

Jägerhorn, Sebastian, *Hårdast bland de hårda: En kavalleriofficer i fält* (Stockholm: Medströms, 2018)

Jakobsson, Theodor, *Lantmilitär beväpning och beklädnad under äldre Vasatiden och Gustav II Adolfs tid*. Published both separately and as Suppl. Vol. 2 in Generalstaben, *Sverigeskrig 1611–1632* (Stockholm: Generalstaben, 1938)

Langer, Herbert, *Trettioåriga kriget* (np: Natur och Kultur, 2nd edn 1989. First published 1978 as *Hortus Bellicus: Der Dreißigjährige Krieg*)

Lindqvist, Herman, *Våra kolonier: De vi hade och de som aldrig blev av* (Stockholm: Albert Bonnier, 2015)

Łopatecki, Karol; and Wojciech Walczak, *Mapyiplany Rzeczypospolitej XVII w. znajdującesię w archiwach w Sztokholmie / Maps and Plans of the Polish Commonwealth of the 17th C. in Archives in Stockholm* 1. Warsaw: Ministerstwo Kulturyi Dziedzictwa Narodowego, 2011)

Marks, Adam, *England, the English and the Thirty Years' War (1618–1648)* (University of St. Andrews, dissertation, 2012)

Matoušek, Václav, et al., *Třebel 1647: A Battlefield of the Thirty Years' War from the Perspective of History, Archeology, Art-history, Geoinformatics, and Ethnology* (Prague: Krigl, 2017)

Munthe, Ludvig W:son, *Kongl. Fortifikationens historia 1: Svenska fortifikationsväsendet från nyare tidens början till inrättandet af en särskild fortifikationsstat år 1641* (Stockholm: Norstedt & söner, 1902)

Munthe, Ludvig W:son, *Kongl. Fortifikationens historia 2: Fortifikationsstaten under Örnehufwudh och Wärnschiöldh, 1641–1674* (Stockholm: Norstedt & söner, 1906)

Murdoch, Steve, 'The Northern Flight: Irish Soldiers in Seventeenth-century Scandinavia'. Thomas O'Connor and Mary Ann Lyons (eds), *The Ulster Earls and Baroque Europe: Refashioning Irish Identities, 1600–1800* (Dublin: Four Courts Press, 2010: pp.88–109)

Murdoch, Steve; and Alexia Grosjean, *Alexander Leslie and the Scottish Generals of the Thirty Years' War, 1618–1648* (Abingdon: Routledge, 2016)

Murdoch, Steven; Kathrin Zickermann; and Adam Marks, "The Battle of Wittstock 1636: Conflicting Reports on a Swedish Victory in Germany", *Journal of the Scottish Society for Northern Studies* 43 (2012): pp.71–109.

Nováky, György, *Handelskompanier och kompanihandel: Svenska Afrikakompaniet 1649–1663* (Uppsala University, dissertation, 1990)

Oschmann, Antje, *Der Nürnberger Exekutionstag 1649–1650: Das Ende des Dreißigjährigen Krieges in Deutschland* (Münster: Aschendorff, 1991)

Parker, Geoffrey, *The Thirty Years' War* (np: Barnes & Noble, 1993. First published by Routledge, 1987)

Petri, Gustaf; with Erik Westman, *Kungl. Första livgrenadjärregementets historia 2: Östgöta regemente till fot 1619–1679*. Stockholm: P. A. Norstedt & Söner, 1928.

Picouet, Pierre, *The Armies of Philip IV of Spain, 1621–1665: The Fight for European Supremacy* (Warwick: Helion, 2019)

Pleiss, Detlev, *Bodenständige Bevölkerung und fremdes Kriegsvolk: Finnen in deutschen Quartieren 1630–1650* (Turku: Åbo Akademi, 2017)

Roberts, Michael, *Sweden as a Great Power 1611–1697: Government; Society; Foreign Policy* (London: Edward Arnold, 1968)

Roberts, Michael, "Oxenstierna in Germany, 1633–1636", *Scandia* 48:1 (1982): pp.61–105.

Rumenius, John, *Wästgöta Ryttare i 30:åriga kriget: 1000 frivilliga bönder drar ut i kriget 1630* (Stockholm: Nyblom, 1987)

Rystad, Göran (ed.), *Historia kring Trettioåriga kriget* (Stockholm: Wahlström & Widstrand, 1963)

Seitz, Heribert, *Svärdet och värjan som armévapen* (Stockholm: Kungl. Armémuseum, 1955)

Skenbäck, Urban, *Sjöfolk och knektar på Wasa* (Stockholm: Sjöhistoriska museet, Wasastudier 11, 1983)

Steckzén, Birger, *Karl Gustaf Wrangels fälttåg 1646–1647 till och med fördraget i Ulm* (Uppsala: Almqvist & Wiksell, dissertation, 1920)

Steckzén, Birger, "Arriärgardesstriden vid Zusmarshausen 7 maj 1648", *Historisk Tidskrift* 41 (1921): pp.135–48.

Steckzén, Birger, "Striden om Jämtland 1644–1645", Gustaf Näsström (ed.). *Jämtländska studier: Festskrift till Eric Festin XII.X.MCMXXVIII (Fornvårdaren)* (Östersund: Heimbygda, 1928: pp.263–93)

Steckzén, Birger, *Johan Banér* (Stockholm: Hugo Geber, 1939)

Svensson, S. Artur (ed.), *Svenska flottans historia 1* (Malmö: Allhem, 1942)

Tingsten, Lars, *Huvuddragen av Sveriges politik och krigföring i Tyskland efter Gustav II Adolfs död till och med sommaren 1635* (Stockholm: Militärlitteraturföreningens förlag 157, 1930)

Tingsten, Lars, *Fältmarskalkarna Johan Banér och Lennart Torstensson såsom härförare* (Stockholm: Militärlitteraturföreningens förlag 164, 1932)

Tingsten, Lars, *De tre sista åren av det trettioåriga kriget jämte den västfaliska freden* (Stockholm: Militärlitteraturföreningens förlag 171, 1934)

Villner, Katarina, *Under däck: Mary Rose – Vasa – Kronan* (Stockholm: Medströms, 2012)

Wendt, Einar, *Amiralitetskollegiets historia* I: 1634–1695 (Stockholm: Lindberg, 1950)

Wetterberg, Gunnar, *Kanslern: Axel Oxenstierna i sin tid*, 2 vols (Stockholm: Atlantis, 2002)

Biographical Databases

Murdoch, Steve; and Alexia Grosjean, *The Scotland, Scandinavia and Northern European Biographical Database* (SSNE). Website <https://www.st-andrews.ac.uk/history/ssne/>

Riksarkivet (Swedish National Archives), *Svenskt biografiskt lexikon* (SBL). Website <https://sok.riksarkivet.se/SBL/>

Warlich, Bernd, *Der Dreißigjährige Krieg in Selbstzeugnissen, Chroniken und Berichten*. Website <https://www.30jaehrigerkrieg.de/>